Group Benefits

Huebner School Series   *Gary K. Stone, Editor*

Fundamentals of Financial Planning
Robert M. Crowe and Charles E. Hughes (eds.)

Readings in Income Taxation
James F. Ivers III (ed.)

Group Benefits: Basic Concepts and Alternatives
Burton T. Beam, Jr.

Retirement Planning for a Business and Business Owner
Kenn Beam Tacchino

Retirement Planning for Individuals
K.B. Tacchino, W.J. Ruckstuhl, E.E. Graves, and R.J. Doyle, Jr.

Readings in Wealth Accumulation Planning
James F. Ivers III and Eric T. Johnson (eds.)

Readings in Estate Planning I
Ted Kurlowicz (ed.)

Readings in Estate Planning II
Ted Kurlowicz (ed.)

Planning for Business Owners and Professionals
Ted Kurlowicz, James F. Ivers III, and John J. McFadden

Financial Planning Applications
W.J. Ruckstuhl, J.B. Kelvin, D.M. Cordell, and D.A. Littell

Retirement Planning Handbook
David A. Littell and M. Donald Wright (eds.)

Tax Planning for Business Operations
Jeffrey B. Kelvin

The primary purpose of this series is to provide timely reading materials tailored to the educational needs of those professionals pursuing the Chartered Life Underwriter and Chartered Financial Consultant designation programs offered by the Solomon S. Huebner School of The American College. These publications should also be of interest to other persons seeking further knowledge in the broad area of financial services.

Huebner School Series

Group Benefits: Basic Concepts and Alternatives
Fifth Edition

Burton T. Beam, Jr.

The American College/*Bryn Mawr, Pennsylvania*

This publication is designed to provide accurate and authoritative information about the subject covered. The American College is not engaged in rendering legal, accounting, or other professional service. If legal or other expert advice is required, the services of an appropriate professional should be sought.

Library of Congress Catalog Card Number 92-75706
ISBN 0-943590-45-0

Printed in the United States of America

To my mother

About the Author

Burton T. Beam, Jr., CPCU, CLU, ChFC, is director of continuing education and associate professor of insurance at The American College. Mr. Beam did his undergraduate work at the University of Oregon and holds graduate degrees from that institution and the University of Pennsylvania. Prior to joining·The American College, Mr. Beam was on the faculties of the University of Florida and the University of Connecticut. He has written extensively in the area of group insurance and has had articles published in several professional journals, including *Benefits Quarterly,* the *Journal of the American Society of CLU & ChFC,* and *The Practical Lawyer.* He is also coauthor of *Employee Benefits,* a textbook used at many colleges and universities. Mr. Beam is an assistant editor of the *Journal of the American Society of CLU & ChFC* and serves on the editorial board of *Benefits Quarterly.* He serves on the examination task force of the IAFP Registry of Financial Planning Practitioners and is a member of the American Risk and Insurance Association and the Academy of Financial Services.

Contents

Preface   *xi*

1   *Introduction to Group Benefits*   *1*

2   *Basic Concepts of Group Insurance*   *7*

3   *The Governmental Environment*   *17*
     for Group Insurance

4   *Group Life Insurance:*   *43*
     Term Coverage

5   *Group Life Insurance:*   *72*
     Postretirement Coverage

6   *Group Disability Income Insurance*   *95*

7   *Group Medical Expense Insurance:*   *117*
     Providers and Basic Coverages

8   *Group Medical Expense Insurance:*   *156*
     Major Medical, Contract Provisions,
     and Taxation

9   *Additional Group Insurance Benefits*   *196*

10   *Employee Benefit Marketing*   *219*

11   *Group Insurance Pricing*   *232*

12   *Alternative Funding Methods*   *256*

13   *Other Group Benefits*   *269*

14   *Group Benefit Plan Design*   *290*

15   *Cafeteria Plans*   *305*

                                  Appendix   *322*

                                      Index   *327*

Preface

The first edition of this book in 1982 was prompted by the absence of a single group insurance textbook in the marketplace that totally met the needs of students in the CLU and ChFC programs. In preparing the first edition, several criteria were used. First, it had to be as up-to-date as possible. Second, it had to discuss the products and services for groups of all sizes, from multiple-employer welfare arrangements for the small groups to alternative-funding methods (including self-insurance) for the large groups. Third, it had to be oriented to the broad constituencies served by the CLU and ChFC programs rather than to just agents, home-office employees, or corporate-benefit specialists. Finally, it had to explain the decisions involved in designing an employee benefit plan and not merely describe the products available. These criteria are still being followed in the fifth edition.

The field of group benefits continues to change rapidly. Nowhere have the changes occurred any faster than in the area of medical expense coverage. Employers, still concerned with rising costs, are continuing to turn to self-funding and managed care. Even traditional indemnity plans are adding more elements of managed care with the inclusion of managed maternity programs, the requirement of preapproval of specialists, and the use of carve-out programs for the treatment of mental illness and substance abuse. Employers are reacting to the new accounting rules of the Financial Accounting Standards Board, frequently with reductions in benefits for retirees. Some employers are also broadening the eligibility for benefits to include domestic partners other than spouses. Employers also face considerable uncertainty about the effects of the Americans with Disabilities Act on medical expense plans and other benefit programs.

Changes are also taking place in other areas of employee benefits. Group universal life insurance continues to increase in popularity as products are redesigned to provide broader coverage and more liberal eligibility rules for benefits. Group term carve-out plans to provide life insurance protection to key employees are also gaining wider acceptance. To encourage the use of mass transportation, Congress has rewritten the rules that apply to benefits for free parking and commuting expenses.

These changes are all included in the current edition of the book. In addition, many other revisions have been made to reflect changing practices in the employee benefit arena. Numerous suggestions for improvement from readers of the previous edition have also been incorporated in the book.

The revision of a book such as this one is not the product of only one person. For their help I particularly wish to thank

- The CLU and ChFC students, instructors, and other readers who have offered numerous suggestions for improvement. No book can be properly revised without feedback from those who use it. I hope readers of this edition will continue to give me this needed feedback.
- Edwin T. Johnson, CLU, and Christopher J. Gavigan of Noble Lowndes/ Johnson; and Arnold M. Katz, CLU, of Brokerage Concepts, Inc., who reviewed significant portions of the fourth edition and made many invaluable suggestions that have been incorporated in this edition.
- The many employees of insurance companies and other benefit specialists who have patiently taken the time to answer my questions and provide me with much valuable information.
- My fellow faculty members at The American College, who are always a valuable source of information as well as excellent reviewers of the material.
- The editorial staff of The American College. The book is much more readable because of the editing of Barbara Keyser and Lynn Hayes.
- The production staff of The American College under the direction of Jane Hassinger. Special thanks should be extended to Evelyn Rice.
- My assistant, Nancy Cornman, for the pleasant and helpful way she performs all the tasks I ask her to do.

The book is better because of the hard work of all these people.

Group Benefits

Introduction to Group Benefits

While few would argue that employee benefits are a major part of the overall compensation for working, even employee benefit specialists disagree over the precise meaning of the term *employee benefits*. However, regardless of the definition used, those in the field agree that the significance of the term has increased in recent years.

The narrowest definition of employee benefits includes only employer-provided benefits for situations involving death, accident, sickness, retirement, or unemployment. Even with this approach there is disagreement over whether the definition should include benefits that are financed by employer contributions but are provided under social insurance programs, such as workers' compensation insurance, unemployment insurance, and social security.[1] On the other hand, the broadest definition of employee benefits includes all benefits and services, other than wages for time worked, that are provided to employees in whole or in part by their employers.

This book will use a broad definition and define employee benefits as including the following five categories:[2]

- legally required payments for government programs. These include employer contributions to such programs as
    social security
    unemployment compensation insurance
    workers' compensation insurance
    nonoccupational disability insurance
- payments for private insurance and retirement plans. These include the cost of establishing such plans, as well as contributions in the form of insurance premiums or payments through alternative funding arrangements. Benefits are provided under these plans for personal loss exposures such as
    old age
    death
    disability
    medical expenses
    dental expenses
    legal expenses
    property and liability losses
- payments for time not worked. These include
    vacations
    holidays
    jury duty
    maternity leave
    National Guard duty

- extra cash payments to employees. These include cash payments other than wages and bonuses based on performance. Benefits in this category include
  - educational assistance
  - moving expenses
  - suggestion awards
  - Christmas bonuses
- cost of services to employees, such as
  - subsidized cafeterias
  - employee discounts
  - wellness programs
  - day care
  - financial planning programs
  - retirement counseling
  - free parking

The first category is usually referred to as social insurance, and the last four categories are commonly called group benefits. This book will focus on the group benefits, with the major exception of retirement plans, which will be left to other authors in this series to discuss in their books on pensions. While all the other topics will be covered, the major emphasis in this book will be on the remaining topics in the second category, which when lumped together are referred to as *welfare benefits* (the legal term) or *group insurance* (the term better understood by laymen).

THE GROWTH AND SIGNIFICANCE OF GROUP BENEFITS

In a 1990 study of 1,000 companies the United States Chamber of Commerce found that the average payment for employee benefits was equal to 38.4 percent of payroll.[3] Of this figure 8.8 percent of payroll went for the employer's share of legally required social insurance payments, 5.5 percent for payments to private pension plans, and 9.9 percent for medical and medically related benefits. The remaining 14.2 percent was for all other types of benefits, with paid vacations being the single most costly item. The study showed substantial variations among business firms, with overall percentages ranging from less than 20 percent to more than 65 percent. Large variations were also shown by industry, with the primary and fabricated metal, machinery, transportation, and rubber industries having the highest percentages and the textile and apparel industries having the lowest. Benefit payments generally increased for firms within specific industries as the number of employees increased, and the percentages tended to be highest in the East North Central states and lowest in the Southeast.

The Chamber of Commerce study also estimated that employee benefits for all employees within the United States amounted to slightly over $1 trillion in 1990 and that this figure was equal to 37.9 percent of payroll. The reason for the discrepancy between the estimated percentage (37.9) and what was found in the survey mentioned above (38.4) is that the survey was weighted in favor of larger firms. The Chamber of Commerce estimated that the 37.9 percent figure had grown from 3 percent in 1929, 21.5 percent in 1965, 30 percent in 1975, and 35.5 percent in 1986. While the percentages for all categories of employee benefits have increased in recent years, the most rapid increases have occurred in legally required payments (because of increased social security taxes) and payments for private insurance (because of increasing costs for medical expense benefits).

FACTORS INFLUENCING THE GROWTH OF GROUP BENEFITS

No single factor can be identified as the reason for the substantial growth in group benefits. Rather, this growth has resulted from a combination of elements, many of which are applicable to employee benefits in general. Frequently mentioned factors include (1) industrialization, (2) the influence of organized labor, (3) wage controls, (4) cost advantages, (5) inflation, and (6) legislation.

Industrialization

During the 19th century the United States made the transition from an agrarian economy to one characterized by increasing industrialization and urbanization. The economic consequences of death, sickness, accidents, and old age became more significant as individuals began to depend more on monetary wages than on self-reliance and family ties to meet their basic needs. As a result some employers began to provide retirement, death, and medical benefits to their employees. While benevolence may have influenced the decision to provide such benefits, the principal reason was probably the realization by employers that it was in their own best interest to do so. Not only did such benefits improve morale and productivity, they also reduced employee turnover and the expenses associated with it.

While some of the earlier benefits were paid directly by employers, the development of group insurance enabled these benefits to be funded by systematic payments to an insurance company. As group insurance became more common, employers were faced with adopting new or better plans to remain competitive in attracting and keeping employees. This competitiveness in employee benefits continues to exist.

Organized Labor

Since a Supreme Court ruling in 1949, there has been no question about the right of labor unions to legally negotiate for employee benefits. Although union pressures prior to that time had frequently resulted in the establishment or broadening of employee benefit plans, this ruling strengthened the influence of labor unions.

Labor unions have also affected benefits for nonunion employees. Some employers provide generous benefit plans in an effort to discourage their employees from unionizing. In addition, employers with both union and non-union employees often provide the same benefits for the nonunion employees as those stipulated in the union contracts.

Wage Controls

Employee benefit plans grew substantially during World War II and the Korean War. Although wages were frozen, no restrictions were imposed on employee benefits, thus making them an important factor in attracting and retaining employees in labor markets with little unemployment. When wage controls were instituted in the early 1970s, no unusual growth took place in employee benefit plans because the duration of the controls was relatively short and the unemployment rate was higher than in previous years.

Cost Advantages

Because of the economies associated with group underwriting and administration, benefits can usually be obtained at a lower cost through group insurance than through separate policies purchased by individual employees. Similar savings can be realized by directly providing employees with certain services, such as financial planning, day-care centers, and subsidized meals. The Internal Revenue Code also provides favorable tax treatment to employer contributions for certain types of group benefits. The employer may deduct most group insurance contributions as usual business expenses, and employees will often have no taxable income as a result of employer contributions in their behalf. In addition, benefits from certain types of group insurance plans and payments or services from any other types of group benefit programs may be received tax free by employees, even if provided by employer contributions. The extent of the favorable tax treatment applicable to group benefits will be discussed in detail in later chapters. Nevertheless, it should be noted here that the types of group benefits with the most favorable tax treatment also tend to be the most prevalent. (See the Appendix for a summary of the federal income tax treatment of group benefits.)

Inflation

The inflation rate in recent years has also affected group benefits. When benefit levels are related to employees' wages, the level and cost of these benefits will increase as wages increase; when benefit levels are stated as fixed amounts, inflation results in employee pressure for increases. For most employers the cost of group benefits has been increasing at a rate faster than wages, primarily because of the skyrocketing increase in the cost of providing medical expense benefits.

Legislation

Most states have traditionally limited the types of groups that are eligible for group insurance coverage as well as the types, and in some cases the amounts, of coverage that could be written. In recent years the majority of these states have liberalized their laws and allowed more group insurance products to be available to an increasing variety of groups.

The federal government and many states have passed legislation mandating that certain benefits be included in group insurance contracts or that existing benefits be broadened. Examples include legislation requiring benefits for maternity, alcoholism, and drug abuse. These added benefits have also increased the cost of providing group insurance coverage.

Other benefits, such as family leave, must now be provided by many employers.

THE FUTURE

The consensus among employee benefit specialists is that in the absence of adverse economic conditions group benefits will continue to evolve and grow. While there is anything but unanimous agreement about what the specifics of these changes will be, there is reasonable agreement about general trends in the near future:

- Firms with fewer than 50 employees, and especially those with fewer than 10, will continue to be a major market for new benefit plans—particularly group insurance. Over the last few years many insurance companies have developed products for this market, so that many of the economies of scale previously available only to large employers can now be obtained by small firms as well.
- The cost of providing medical expense benefits will continue to rise faster than the general rate of inflation. These escalating costs will be met by employer and government efforts to contain them.
- The federal government will continue to require employers to provide both active and retired employees with certain types or levels of benefits. In effect, employers will be providing many benefits that were previously thought to be the responsibility of individuals and the government.
- More and more employees will have benefits provided under cafeteria plans and will be able to substantially design their own benefit programs.
- Changing demographics will lead to growth in certain benefits, such as day-care centers for working couples and retirement planning and long-term care for the aging population.
- The efforts to contain medical costs and the general increasing awareness of good health make the outlook promising for wellness and employee-assistance programs.

THE IMPORTANCE OF BENEFIT PLANNING

The significant growth in employee benefits has called for increasingly complex decisions. Whether these decisions are by employers providing benefits, unions negotiating for benefits, or employees selecting benefit options, the need for proper benefit planning is crucial. One difficulty in writing a textbook of this nature is determining where to discuss the many issues and decisions that must be faced if proper planning is to take place. A conscious decision to delay a thorough discussion of benefit planning until later chapters was made so that the reader could better understand the issues, products, tax laws, and funding methods that have an impact on planning. While the final chapter of the book is devoted entirely to planning and is the only place certain issues are discussed, other planning issues are handled where appropriate throughout the book.

However, a brief treatment of the benefit-planning process is appropriate here to make readers aware that benefit planning is much more than a description of the many types of plans and provisions that are the subject of much of this book.

The Benefit-Planning Process

Employee benefit planning is a dynamic process that must continually be reviewed and modified if an overall benefit plan is to meet the changing needs of a changing environment. The first step in this process is to determine the employer's objectives. Is the benefit package to be in line with the competition? Or is it to be viewed as a leader, better enabling the firm to attract employees?

Once the employer's objectives are determined, a plan should be designed to meet these objectives. In this process it is necessary to analyze the costs of the plan, both from a short-term and a long-term standpoint. If the costs are excessive and the plan has been designed in the most cost-effective manner, the employer's objectives will need revision. A major determinant of a benefit plan's cost is the method of funding. Should it be insured, funded from current revenues, or funded by some combination of the two approaches? Employers are increasingly using alternatives to traditional funding arrangements in an effort to reduce costs.

The third step in the process is to implement the plan. This may be as simple as adding an additional vacation day or as complex as taking competitive proposals for a pension plan from insurance companies, trust departments of banks, and other providers of services.

A crucial step in the employee benefit planning process is to communicate the plan properly to participating employees. Without good communication it is often difficult for an employer's objectives to be realized effectively. Communication has become more than merely describing benefits; it also involves letting employees know the value of the benefits.

Finally, employers should monitor the performance of the plan and make any necessary changes. As new benefits or funding arrangements appear on the scene, should they be considered? Has the character of the work force changed so that a different benefit package would better meet the needs of employees?

Throughout this book the issues and decisions that are part of this process will be discussed.

NOTES

1. The Social Security Administration uses a narrow definition in its studies of employee benefit plans. Its definition includes only benefits not underwritten or paid directly by the federal, state, or local governments.
2. These categories are based on those listed in Robert M. McCaffery, *Managing the Employee Benefits Program*, American Management Association, 1972. They are also similar to those used by the United States Chamber of Commerce in its broad definition of employee benefits.
3. United States Chamber of Commerce, *Employee Benefits*, 1991. This study is updated annually.

2

Basic Concepts of Group Insurance

This first chapter on group insurance is devoted to an introduction of its basic characteristics, with particular emphasis on underwriting. The chapter also briefly discusses the reasons for the increasing use of alternatives to the traditional fully insured group insurance contract. The chapter concludes with a few significant statistics about the major categories of group insurance.

GROUP INSURANCE CHARACTERISTICS

Group insurance is characterized by a group contract, experience rating of larger groups, and group underwriting. Perhaps the best way to define group insurance is to compare its characteristics with those of individual insurance, which is underwritten on an individual basis.

The Group Contract

In contrast to most individual insurance contracts the group insurance contract provides coverage to a number of persons under a single contract issued to someone other than the persons insured. The contract, referred to as a *master contract*, provides benefits to a group of individuals who have a specific relationship to the policyowner. Group contracts usually cover individuals who are full-time employees, and the policyowner is either their employer or a trust established to provide benefits for the employees. Although the employees are not actual parties to the master contract, they can legally enforce their rights. Consequently employees are often referred to as third-party beneficiaries of the insurance contract.

Employees covered under the contract receive *certificates of insurance* as evidence of their coverage. A certificate is merely a description of the coverage provided and is not part of the master contract. In general, a certificate of insurance is not even considered to be a contract and usually contains a disclaimer to that effect. However, some courts have held the contrary to be true when the provisions of the certificate or even the explanatory booklet of a group insurance plan varies materially from the master contract.

In individual insurance the coverage of the insured normally begins with the inception of the insurance contract and ceases with its termination. However, in group insurance individual members of the group may become eligible for coverage long after the inception of the group contract, or they may lose their eligibility status long before the contract terminates.

Experience Rating

A second distinguishing characteristic of group insurance is the use of experience rating. If a group is sufficiently large, the actual experience of that particular group will be a factor in determining the premium the policyowner will be charged. It should be noted that the experience of an insurance company will also be reflected in the dividends and future premiums associated with individual insurance. However, such experience will be determined on a class basis and will apply to all insureds in that class. This is also true for group insurance contracts when the group's membership is small. The use of experience rating will be discussed in chapter 11.

Group Underwriting

The applicant for individual insurance must generally show evidence of insurability. For group insurance, on the other hand, individual members of the group are usually not required to show any evidence of insurability when initially eligible for coverage. This is not to say that there is no underwriting, but rather that underwriting is focused on the characteristics of the group instead of on the insurability of individual members of the group. As with individual insurance, the underwriter must appraise the risk, decide on the conditions of the group's acceptability, and establish a rating basis.

The purpose of group insurance underwriting is twofold: (1) to minimize the problem of *adverse selection* (meaning that those who are likely to have claims are also those who are most likely to seek insurance) and (2) to minimize the administrative costs associated with group insurance. Because of group underwriting coverage can be provided through group insurance at a lower cost than through individual insurance.

Underwriting considerations peculiar to specific types of group insurance will be discussed in later chapters. However, there are certain general underwriting considerations applicable to all or most types of group insurance that affect the contractual provisions contained in group insurance contracts as well as insurance company practices pertaining to group insurance. These general underwriting considerations include the

- reason for the group's existence
- stability of the group
- persistency of the group
- method of determining benefits
- provisions for determining eligibility
- source and method of premium payments
- administrative aspects of the group insurance plan
- prior experience of the plan
- size of the group
- composition of the group
- industry represented by the group
- geographic location of the group

Reason for Existence

Probably the most fundamental group underwriting principle is that a group must have been formed for some purpose other than to obtain insurance for its members. Such a rule protects the group insurance company against the adverse selection that would likely exist if poor risks were to form a group just to obtain insurance. Groups based on an employer-employee relationship present little difficulty with respect to this rule.

Stability

Ideally an underwriter would like to see a reasonable but steady flow of persons through a group. A higher-than-average turnover rate will result in increased administrative costs for the insurance company as well as for the employer. If turnover exists among recently hired employees, the resulting costs can be minimized by requiring employees to wait a certain period of time before becoming eligible for coverage. However, such a *probationary period* does leave newly hired employees without protection if their previous group insurance coverage has terminated.

A lower-than-average turnover rate often results in an increasing average age for the members of a group. To the extent that a plan's premium is a function of the mortality (death rates) and the morbidity (sickness and disability rates) of the group, such an increase in average age will result in an increasing premium rate for that group insurance plan. This high rate may cause the better risks to drop out of a plan, if they are required to contribute to its cost, and may ultimately force the employer to terminate the plan because of its increasing cost.

Persistency

An underwriter is concerned with the length of time a group insurance contract will remain on the insurance company's books. Initial acquisition expenses, often including higher first-year commissions, frequently cause an insurance company to lose money during the first year the group insurance contract is in force. Only through the renewal of the contract for a period of time, often 3 or 4 years, can these acquisition expenses be recovered. For this reason firms with a history of frequently changing insurance companies or those with financial difficulty are often avoided.

Determination of Benefits

In most types of group insurance the underwriter will require that benefit levels for individual members of the group be determined in some manner that precludes individual selection by either the employees or the employer. If employees could choose their own benefit levels, there would be a tendency for the poorer risks to select greater amounts of coverage than the better risks would select. Similarly adverse selection could also exist if the employer could choose a separate benefit level for each individual member of the group. As a result this underwriting rule has led to benefit levels that are either identical for all employees or determined by a benefit formula that bases benefit levels on some specific criterion, such as salary or position.

Benefits based on salary or position may still lead to adverse selection because disproportionately larger benefits will be provided to the owner or top executives, who may have been involved in determining the benefit formula. Consequently most insurance companies have rules for determining the maximum benefit that may be provided for any individual employee without evidence of insurability. Additional amounts of coverage either will not be provided or will be subject to individual evidence of insurability.

The general level of benefits for all employees is also of interest to the underwriter. For example, benefit levels that are too high may encourage overutilization and malingering, while benefit levels that are unusually low may lead to low participation if a plan is voluntary.

Determination of Eligibility

The underwriter is also concerned with the eligibility provisions that will be contained in a group insurance plan. As mentioned, many group insurance plans contain probationary periods that must be satisfied before an employee is eligible for coverage. In addition to minimizing administrative costs, a probationary period will also discourage persons with known medical conditions from seeking employment primarily because of a firm's group insurance benefits. This latter problem is also addressed by the requirement that an employee be actively at work before coverage commences or by limiting coverage for preexisting conditions, particularly with major medical coverage.

Most group insurance plans normally limit eligibility to full-time employees since the coverage of part-time employees may not be desirable from an underwriting standpoint. In addition to having a high turnover rate, part-time employees are more likely to seek employment primarily to obtain the group insurance benefits that are available. Similar problems exist with seasonal and temporary employees, and consequently eligibility is often restricted to permanent employees.

Premium Payments

Group insurance plans may be contributory or noncontributory. Members of *contributory plans* pay a portion, or possibly all, of the cost of their own coverage. When the entire portion is paid by employees, these plans are often referred to as fully contributory or employee-pay-all plans. Under *noncontributory plans* the policyowner pays the entire cost. Since all eligible employees are usually covered, this is desirable from an underwriting standpoint because adverse selection is minimized. In fact, most insurance companies and the laws of many states require 100 percent participation of eligible employees under noncontributory plans. In addition, the absence of employee solicitation, payroll deductions, and underwriting of late entrants into the plan results in administrative savings to both the policyowner and the insurance company.

Most state laws prohibit an employer from requiring an employee to participate in a contributory plan. The insurance company is therefore faced with the possibility of adverse selection since those who elect coverage will tend to be the poorer risks. From a practical standpoint 100 percent participation in a contributory plan would be unrealistic since for many reasons some employees neither desire nor need the coverage provided under the plan. However, insurance companies will require that a minimum percentage of the eligible members of a group elect to participate before the contract will be issued. The common requirement is 75 percent, although a lower percentage is often acceptable for large groups and a higher percentage may be required for small groups. It should be noted that a 75 percent minimum requirement is also often a statutory requirement for group life insurance and sometimes for group health insurance.

A key issue in contributory plans is how to treat employees who did not elect to participate when first eligible but who later desire coverage, or who dropped coverage and want it reinstated. Unfortunately this desire for coverage may arise when these employees or their dependents have medical conditions that will lead to claims once coverage is provided. To control this adverse selection, insurance companies commonly require individual evidence of insurability by these employees or their dependents before coverage will be made available. However, there is one exception. Some plans have periodic open enrollment periods during which the evidence-of-insurability requirement is lessened or waived for a short period of time.

Insurance companies frequently require that the employer pay a portion of the premium under a group insurance plan. This is also a statutory requirement for group life insurance in most states and occasionally for group health insurance. Many group insurance plans set an average contribution rate for all employees, which in turn leads to the subsidizing of some employees by other employees, particularly in those types of insurance where the frequency of claims increases with age. Without a requirement for employer contributions younger employees might actually find coverage at a lower cost in the individual market, thereby leaving the group with only the older risks. Even when group insurance already has a cost advantage over individual insurance, its attractiveness to employees is enhanced by employer contributions. With constantly increasing health-care costs employer contributions help cushion rate increases to employees and thus minimize participation problems as contributions are raised. In addition, underwriters feel that the absence of employer contributions may lead to a lack of employer interest in the plan and consequently poor cooperation with the insurance company and poor plan administration.

Administration

To minimize the expenses associated with group insurance, the underwriter will often require that certain administrative functions be carried out by the employer. These commonly include communicating the plan to the employees, handling enrollment procedures, collecting employee contributions on a payroll-deduction basis, and keeping certain types of records. In addition, employers are often involved in the claims process. Underwriters are concerned not only with the employer's ability to carry out these functions but also with the employer's willingness to cooperate with the insurance company.

Prior Experience

For most insurance companies a large portion of newly written group insurance consists of business that was previously written by other insurance companies. Therefore it is important for the underwriter to ascertain the reason for the transfer. If the transferred business is a result of dissatisfaction with the service provided by the prior insurance company, the underwriter must determine whether his or her insurance company can provide the type and level of service desired. Since an employer is most likely to shop for new coverage when faced with a rate increase, the underwriter must evaluate whether the rate increase was due to excessive claims experience. Often, particularly with larger groups, poor claims experience in the past is an indication that there might be poor experience in the future. Occasionally, however, the prior experience may be due to circumstances that will not continue in the future, such as a catastrophe or large medical bills for an employee who had died, totally recovered, or terminated employment.

Excessive past claims experience may not result in coverage denial for a new applicant, but it will probably result in a higher rate. As an alternative changes in the benefit or eligibility provisions of the plan might eliminate a previous source of adverse claims experience.

The underwriter must determine the new insurance company's responsibility for existing claims. Some states prohibit a new insurance company from denying (by using a preexisting-conditions clause) the continuing claims of persons that were covered under a prior group insurance plan if these claims would otherwise be covered under the new contract. The rationale for this "no-loss no-gain" legislation is that claims should be paid neither more liberally nor less liberally than if no transfer had taken place. Even in states that have no such regulation, an employer may still wish to provide employees with continuing protection. In either case the underwriter must evaluate these continuing claims as well as any liability of the previous insurance company for their payment.

Finally the underwriter must be reasonably certain that the employer will not present a persistency problem by changing insurance companies again in the near future.

Size

The size of a group is a significant factor in the underwriting process. With large groups there is usually prior group insurance experience that can be used as a factor in determining the premium, and considerable flexibility also exists with respect to both rating and plan design. In addition, adjustments for adverse claims experience can be made at future renewal dates under the experience-rating process.

The situation is different for small groups. In many cases coverage is being written for the first time. Administrative expenses tend to be high in relation to the premium. There is also an increased possibility that the owner or major stockholder might be interested in coverage primarily because he or she or a family member has a medical problem that will result in large immediate claims. As a result contractual provisions and the benefits available tend to be quite standardized in order to control administrative costs. Furthermore, because past experience for small groups is not necessarily a realistic indicator of future experience, most insurance companies use pooled rates under which a uniform rate is applied to all groups that have a specific coverage. Since poor claims experience for a particular group is not charged to that group at renewal, more restrictive underwriting practices relating to adverse selection are used. These include less liberal contractual provisions and in some cases individual underwriting for group members.

Composition

The age, sex, and income of employees in a group will affect the experience of the group. As employees age, the mortality rate increases. Excluding maternity claims, both the frequency and the duration of medical and disability claims also increase with age.

At all ages the death rate is lower for females than for males. However, the opposite is true for medical expenses and disability claims. Even if maternity claims are disregarded, women as a group tend to be hospitalized and disabled more frequently and to obtain medical and surgical treatment more often than men, except at extremely advanced ages.

Employees at high income levels tend to incur higher-than-average medical and dental expenses. This is partly because practitioners sometimes base charges on a patient's ability to pay. (Since most individuals now have health insurance, this practice is less common than in the past.) In addition, higher-income persons are more likely to seek specialized care or care in more affluent areas, where the charges of practitioners are generally higher. On the other hand, low-income employees can also pose problems. Turnover rates tend to be higher, and there is often difficulty in getting and retaining proper levels of participation in contributory plans.

Adjustments can be made for all these factors when determining the proper rate to charge the policyowner. The major problem arises in contributory insurance plans. To the extent that higher costs for a group with a less-than-average mix of employees are passed on to these employees, a lower participation rate may result.

Industry

The nature of the industry represented by a group is also a significant factor in the underwriting process. In addition to different occupational hazards among industries, employees in some industries have higher-than-average health insurance claims that cannot be directly attributed to their jobs. Therefore insurance companies commonly make adjustments in their life and health insurance rates based on the occupations of the employees covered as well as on the industries in which they work.

In addition to occupational hazards the underwriter must weigh other factors as well. Certain industries are characterized by a lack of stability and persistency and thus may be considered undesirable risks. The underwriter must also be concerned with the impact that changes in the economy will have on a particular industry.

Geographic Location

The size of medical claims varies considerably among geographic regions and must be considered in determining a group insurance rate. For example, medical expenses tend to be higher in the Northeast than in the South and higher in large urban areas than in rural areas.

A group with employees geographically scattered will also pose more administrative problems and probably result in greater administrative expense than a group at a single location. In addition, the underwriter must determine whether the insurance company has the proper facilities to service policyowners at their locations.

ALTERNATIVE FUNDING METHODS FOR GROUP INSURANCE

As the cost of providing insurance benefits to employees has risen, employers have increasingly turned from fully insured plans to alternative funding methods to minimize this cost. In some cases these alternative methods consist of variations in group insurance contracts, such as premium-payment delays and reserve-reduction arrangements. At the opposite end of the spectrum are totally self-funded (self-insured) plans, in which no insurance is purchased and benefits are paid from either current revenue or a trust to which periodic payments have been made. Between these two extremes are programs such as minimum-premium plans, stop-loss arrangements, and big-deductible plans that combine various aspects of traditionally insured plans with those of self-funding. Even when self-funding is used, employers often contract with an insurance company or other organization for administrative services.

These alternative funding methods will be discussed in detail in chapter 12. At this point, however, it should be noted that the use of alternative funding methods does not eliminate the need for making decisions regarding such factors as eligibility, benefit levels, and claims handling. In most cases provisions for these factors will be similar, if not identical, to the provisions found in the types of group insurance contracts that will be discussed throughout this book.

THE SIGNIFICANCE OF GROUP INSURANCE

In chapter 1 overall employee benefit statistics were presented to emphasize the magnitude of group benefits. Specific statistics (as of 1990) can also be given for the major categories of group insurance.[1]

Group Life Insurance

- Coverage amounting to $3.8 trillion is in force under approximately 700,000 master contracts and 140 million certificates of insurance. This amount represents a doubling of the amount of insurance in force since 1990.
- Over 99 percent of the coverage in force is term insurance.
- Employer-employee groups account for approximately 90 percent of coverage in force.

- Group insurance amounts to almost 40 percent of total life insurance coverage, up from 20 percent in 1950.
- The amount of coverage under the average-size group life insurance certificate covering persons in employer-employee groups is approximately $25,000, compared to about $35,000 under the average-size ordinary life insurance policy in force.
- Over 700,000 beneficiaries each year receive a total of over $10 billion in benefits.

Group Disability Income Insurance

- About 60 percent of persons in the work force have some type of short-term protection provided through group arrangements. Slightly more than half of these persons have some or all of their coverage under group insurance contracts, while the remainder have coverage solely under formal plans using total self-funding.
- The number of persons with short-term group protection has remained relatively stable during the last decade, but an increasing portion of the coverage is provided by self-funded plans.
- Approximately one-fourth of persons in the work force have some form of long-term protection through group insurance arrangements.
- Group coverage accounts for approximately 80 percent of disability income protection. During the last decade the number of persons covered under group arrangements grew at a faster rate than the number of persons covered under individual insurance contracts.

Group Medical Expense Insurance

- Since 1970 premiums for medical expense coverage have risen from approximately $20 billion to over $200 billion. In 1970 this amount represented less than 3 percent of disposable personal income; in 1990 it represented about 6 percent. Almost 90 percent of these premiums represent the cost of coverage under group insurance arrangements, as opposed to individual insurance.
- In recent years the percentage of persons with medical expense protection under group arrangements with insurance companies, Blue Cross and Blue Shield, and independent plans (including health maintenance organizations and preferred provider organizations) has increased, while the percentage of persons having individual coverage has decreased. During the last 10 years the number of persons with coverage from group contracts of insurance companies has remained stable at about 100 million. The number covered by Blue Cross and Blue Shield has decreased somewhat to about 75 million, while the number covered by HMOs, PPOs, and self-funded plans has more than doubled to 70 million. Note that some persons have coverage from more than one type of provider, and the total number of persons represented by these statistics is about 180 million.
- During the last 10 years the percentage of the civilian population under age 65 having some form of hospital and surgical benefits from nongov-

ernmental sources has remained relatively stable at about 80 percent. However, the percentage of those with major medical benefits rose from less than 60 percent to over 70 percent, while the percentage of persons with dental coverage grew from less than 20 percent to over 60 percent.

NOTE

1. Sources: American Council of Life Insurance, *Life Insurance Fact Book*; and Health Insurance Institute of America, *Source Book of Health Insurance Data*. Both sources are updated annually.

3

The Governmental Environment for Group Insurance

The character of group insurance has been greatly influenced by the numerous laws and regulations that have been imposed by both the state and federal governments. The major impact of state regulation has been felt through the insurance laws governing insurance companies and the products they sell. Traditionally these laws have affected only those benefit plans funded with insurance contracts. However, as a growing number of employers are turning toward self-funding of benefits, there has been an increasing interest on the part of state regulatory officials to extend these laws to plans using alternative funding methods. The federal laws affecting group insurance, on the other hand, have generally been directed toward any benefit plans that are established by employers for their employees, regardless of the funding method used.

STATE REGULATION

Even though the United States Supreme Court has declared insurance to be commerce and thus subject to federal regulation when conducted on an interstate basis, Congress gave the states substantial regulatory authority by the passage of the McCarran-Ferguson Act (Public Law 15) in 1945. The act exempts insurance from certain federal regulations to the extent that individual states actually regulate insurance. In addition, it provides that most other federal laws are not applicable to insurance unless they are specifically directed at the business of insurance.

As a result of the McCarran-Ferguson Act a substantial body of laws and regulations has been enacted in every state. While no two states have identical laws and regulations, there have been attempts to encourage uniformity among the states. The most significant influence in this regard has been the National Association of Insurance Commissioners (NAIC), which is composed of state regulatory officials. Since the NAIC has as one of its goals the promotion of uniformity in legislation and administrative rules affecting insurance, it has developed numerous model laws. Although states are not bound to adopt these model laws, many have been enacted by a large number of states.

Some of the more significant state laws and regulations affecting group insurance include those pertaining to the types of groups eligible for coverage, benefit limitations, contractual provisions, and taxation. Moreover, since many employers have employees in several states, the extent of the regulatory jurisdiction of each state is a question of some concern.

Eligible Groups

Most states do not allow group insurance contracts to be written unless a minimum number of persons are insured under the contract. This requirement, which may vary by type of coverage and type of group, is most common in group life insurance, where the minimum number required for plans established by individual employers is generally 10 persons. A few states have either a lower minimum or no such requirement. A higher minimum, often 100 persons, may be imposed on other plans, such as those established by trusts, labor unions, or creditors. Only about half the states impose any minimum number requirement on group health insurance contracts. Where one exists, it is usually either 5 or 10 persons.

The majority of states also have insurance laws concerning the types of groups for which insurance companies may write group insurance. Most of these laws specify that a group insurance contract cannot be delivered to a policyowner in the state unless the group meets certain statutory eligibility requirements for its type of group. In some states these eligibility requirements even vary by type of coverage. While the categories of eligible groups may vary, at least five types of groups are acceptable in virtually all states: individual employer groups, negotiated trusteeships, trade associations, creditor-debtor groups, and labor union groups. Other types of groups, including multiple-employer trusts, are also acceptable in some states. Some states have no insurance laws regarding the types or sizes of groups for which insurance companies may write group insurance. Rather, eligibility is determined by the underwriting standards of insurance companies.

Individual Employer Groups

The most common type of eligible group is the individual employer group in which the employer may be a corporation, a partnership, or a sole proprietorship. Many state laws are very specific about what constitutes an employee for group insurance purposes. In addition to those usually considered to be employees of a firm, coverage can generally be written for retired employees and employees of subsidiary and affiliated firms. Furthermore, individual proprietors or partners are usually eligible for coverage as long as they are actively engaged in and devote a substantial part of their time to the conduct of the organization. Similarly directors of a corporation may also be eligible for coverage if they are also employees of the corporation.

Negotiated Trusteeships (Taft-Hartley Trusts)

Negotiated trusteeships are formed as a result of collective bargaining over benefits between a union and the employers of the union members. Generally the union employees are in the same industry or a related one. For the most part these industries, such as trucking or construction, are characterized by frequent movement of union members among employers. The Taft-Hartley Act prohibits employers from paying funds directly to a labor union for the purpose of providing group insurance coverage to members. Payments must be made to a trust fund established for the purpose of providing benefits to employees. The trustees of the fund must be made up of equal numbers of representatives from the employers and the union. The trustees can elect either to self-fund benefits or to purchase insurance contracts with themselves as the policyowners. Since eligible employees include only members of the collective-bargaining unit, benefits for nonunion employees must be provided in some other manner.

Negotiated trusteeships differ from other types of groups in the way benefits are financed and the way eligibility for benefits is determined. Employers often make contributions based on the number of hours worked by the employees covered under the collective-bargaining agreement, regardless of whether these employees are eligible for benefits. Eligibility for benefits during a given period is usually based only on some minimum number of hours worked during a previous period. For example, a union member might receive coverage during a calendar quarter (even while unemployed) if he or she worked at least 300 hours in the previous calendar quarter. This situation, where the employees for whom contributions are made may differ from those who are eligible for benefits, presents a unique problem for the underwriter. Rates must be adequate to build up the contingency reserves necessary to pay benefits in periods of heavy layoffs, during which a large portion of contributions cease but eligibility for benefits continues.

While negotiated trusteeships normally provide benefits for the employees of several employers, they can also be established for the employees of a single employer. However, situations involving collective bargaining with a single employer will usually result in the employer's being required to provide benefits for the employees under a group insurance contract purchased by the employer. Although benefits and eligibility are specified in the bargaining agreement, the employer is the policyowner and the group is an individual employer group rather than a negotiated trusteeship. This approach also enables the employer to provide benefits for nonunion employees under the same contract.

Trade Associations

For eligibility purposes a trade association is an association of employers that has been formed for reasons other than obtaining insurance. In most cases these employers are in the same industry or type of business. In many such associations there is frequently a large number of employers who do not have the minimum number of employees necessary to qualify for an individual employer group insurance contract. While in some states the master contract is issued directly to the trade association, in most states it is necessary that a trust be established. Through payment of premiums to the association or the trust, individual employers may provide coverage for their employees.

Both adverse selection and administrative costs tend to be greater in trade association groups than in many other types of groups. Therefore most underwriters and state laws require that a minimum percentage of the employers belonging to the association, such as 50 percent, participate in the plan and that a minimum number of employees, possibly as high as 500, be covered. In addition, individual underwriting or strict provisions regarding preexisting conditions may be used, and employer contributions are usually required. To ensure adequate enrollment the underwriter must determine whether the association has the resources as well as the desire to promote the plan enthusiastically and to administer it properly.

Creditor-Debtor Groups

Creditor-debtor relationships give rise to groups that are eligible for group term life insurance and group disability income insurance. While the types of creditors and debtors may vary, coverage is normally made available for organizations such as banks, finance companies, and retailers with respect to time-payment purchases, personal loans, or charge accounts. A unique feature of group credit insurance is that the creditor must be the beneficiary of the coverage in addition to being the policyowner even though the debtors are the insured. In group credit life insurance any payments to the creditor must be used to cancel the insured portion of the debt; in group credit disability income insurance any payments must be used to relieve the debtor of making periodic payments during the insured period of disability. Premiums for group creditor insurance may be shared by the creditor and the debtor or may be totally paid by either party.

The following traditional restrictions imposed by eligibility statutes also reflect insurance company underwriting practices:

- maximum amount of coverage. Many states limit the maximum amount of coverage that may be written on a single debtor. In addition, since the amount of coverage can never exceed the amount of the indebtedness, coverage decreases as the debt is paid.
- maximum loan duration. It is common for states to limit the loan duration under contributory plans to maximum periods, such as 5 or 10 years. There is usually no maximum loan duration if the cost of the coverage is paid by the creditor.
- minimum participation percentage. Many states require that all eligible debtors be insured when the creditor pays the entire premium and that at least 75 percent of eligible debtors be insured under contributory plans.
- minimum number of entrants into the plan. In many cases this number is 100 for each policy year.

Because of the abuses associated with such factors as coercion, excessive premium rates, and lack of disclosure, many states have additional regulations pertaining to group credit insurance. Common provisions include

- proper disclosure to the debtor, including a description of the coverage and the charge for the coverage
- an option for the debtor to provide coverage through existing insurance or the purchase of a policy from another source
- a requirement that the charge by a creditor to a debtor for coverage may not exceed the premium charged by the insurance company
- a refund of any unearned premium paid by the debtor if the indebtedness is paid prior to its scheduled maturity
- limitations on the maximum rates that may be charged by insurance companies

While this book will concentrate on the use of group insurance as an employee benefit, it should be noted that group creditor insurance, particularly creditor life insurance, is a significant and growing form of group insurance.

According to the American Council of Life Insurance, $250 billion of credit life insurance was in force at the end of 1990, under approximately 70 million individual policies or certificates of group insurance. Detailed statistics are not available, but it is estimated that between 80 and 90 percent of this amount is group insurance. While the amount of credit life insurance has increased within the past decade, the majority of the growth has been in the average size of the policy or certificate of insurance rather than in the number of policies or certificates of insurance.

Labor Union Groups

Labor unions may establish group insurance plans to provide benefits for their members, with the master contract issued to the union. In addition to the prohibition by the Taft-Hartley Act of employer payments to labor unions for insurance premiums, state laws generally prohibit plans in which union members pay the entire cost from their own pockets. Consequently the premiums come solely from union funds or partially from union funds and partially from members' contributions. Labor union groups account for a relatively small amount of group insurance, most of which is life insurance.

Multiple-Employer Welfare Arrangements

The final type of eligible group designed to provide benefits for employees is the multiple-employer welfare arrangement (MEWA). MEWAs are a common but often controversial method of marketing group benefits to employers who have a small number of employees. MEWAs are legal entities (1) sponsored by an insurance company, an independent administrator, or some other person or organization and (2) organized for the purpose of providing group benefits to the employees of more than one employer. Each MEWA must have an administrator who is either an insurance company or a professional administrator. MEWAs may be organized as trusts, in which case there must be a trustee that may be an individual but is usually a corporate trustee, such as a commercial bank.

MEWAs are generally established to provide group benefits to employers within a specific industry, such as construction, agriculture, or banking. However, employers are not required to belong to an association. MEWAs may provide either a single type of insurance (such as life insurance) or a wide range of coverages (for example, life, medical expense, and disability income insurance). In some cases alternative forms of the same coverage are available (such as comprehensive health insurance or basic health insurance).

An employer desiring to obtain insurance coverage for its employees from a MEWA must subscribe and become a member of the MEWA. The employer is issued a joinder agreement, which spells out the relationship between the MEWA and the employer and specifies the coverages to which the employer has subscribed. It should be noted that it is not necessary for an employer to subscribe to all coverages offered by a MEWA.

A MEWA may either provide benefits on a self-funded basis or fund benefits with a contract purchased from an insurance company. In the latter case the MEWA, rather than the subscribing employers, is the master insurance contract holder. In either case the employees of subscribing employers are provided with benefit descriptions (certificates of insurance in insured MEWAs) in a manner similar to the usual group insurance arrangement.

In addition to alternative methods of funding benefits, MEWAs can also be categorized according to how they are administered, that is, whether by an insurance company or by a third-party administrator. It is generally agreed that there are three types of MEWAs. Unfortunately the terminology used to describe the three types is not uniform and is often misleading. In this text the following terminology and definitions will be used:

- fully insured multiple-employer trust (MET). Benefits are insured and the MET is administered by an insurance company. (Prior to 1982 all MEWAs were referred to as METs. At that time ERISA was amended to clarify the regulation of such arrangements. The act used the term *multiple-employer welfare arrangement* rather than the term *multiple-employer trust*. Over time, MEWA has become the accepted overall terminology, but most insurance companies continue to use the term *MET* to describe fully insured MEWAs as a way to distinguish them from the more controversial self-funded MEWAs.)
- insured third-party-administered MEWA. Benefits are insured and the MEWA is administered by a third party.
- self-funded MEWA. Benefits are self-funded and the MEWA is administered by a third party.

Fully Insured METs. Fully insured METs are established and administered by insurance companies, with a commercial bank usually acting as trustee. Coverage under such METs is normally marketed by the sales force of the insurer involved and may be made available to other licensed producers. It should be noted that a trust purchases coverage from the insurance company, and what is being marketed to employers is the availability of insurance through participation in the trust, not an insurance contract from the insurance company.

Fully insured METs were developed to provide group insurance to small employer groups. A single insurance company may have one MET or several, with each designed for a different industry (such as construction or manufacturing). Through the use of METs insurance companies have attempted to provide group insurance at a cost lower than the cost of a direct sale to the employer or to individual employees. Regulatory restrictions regarding minimum group size are overcome since the employees of many small employers are insured under a single group contract issued to the trust. Costs are also minimized because each type of coverage offered by the trust tends to be standardized for all employers using the trust.

In addition, underwriting standards have been developed to minimize the problems of adverse selection and the higher administrative costs associated with providing coverage to small groups of employees. While these standards vary among companies, some common examples include the following:

- more stringent participation requirements, such as 100 percent, for employers with fewer than five employees
- a requirement that life insurance coverage be purchased. This tends to be a profitable and stable form of coverage for insurance companies. In

some cases the more life insurance coverage that is purchased, the more comprehensive the medical expense benefits that are made available.
- limitations on the period of time for which rates are guaranteed, rarely more than 6 months
- probationary periods for new employees, often 2 or 3 months
- restrictive provisions for preexisting conditions
- limitations on the amounts of life insurance coverage available on a simplified or guaranteed-issue basis (for example, $10,000 for four or fewer employees; $20,000 for five or more). Additional coverage may be available but individual evidence of insurability will be required.
- limitations on the amount of long-term disability insurance coverage that will be issued, such as 50 percent or 60 percent of income, subject to a $1,000 monthly maximum
- ineligible groups. Most METs have a lengthy list of ineligible groups, including those characterized by poor loss experience or high turnover rates.

Since it has generally been accepted under insurance regulatory law that an insurance contract is subject to regulation by the state in which the contract was delivered, many insurers have established METs where they consider the regulatory climate to be favorable. This has allowed an insurance company, in effect, to offer a nationally standardized contract to small employers (through subscribing to the trust) rather than different contracts to comply with the regulatory requirements in each subscriber's state. However some states require METs to make their coverage conform to applicable state law when an employer from that state becomes a subscriber.

During the 1980s the importance of METs (and insured, third-party-administered MEWAs) decreased somewhat. Some insurers, primarily because of difficulties in providing medical expense coverage to small employers, left the group insurance business. HMOs increasingly and successfully sought business from smaller employers. In addition, many employers—particularly those with 25 to 100 employees—are more likely to use self-funding. However, in many parts of the country METs remain a major source of group insurance coverage for small employers.

Insured Third-Party-Administered MEWAs. Insured third-party-administered MEWAs are similar to fully insured METs in that benefits are provided through an insurance contract issued to a trust. However, these MEWAs are administered by some person or organization other than an insurance company.

The impetus for the establishment of an insured third-party-administered MEWA may come from either the insurance company or the administrator. An insurance company desiring to enter the MEWA field may feel it lacks the expertise or resources to administer MEWAs properly at a competitive cost. Consequently a number of insurance companies have sought out third-party administrators to provide many of the necessary administrative functions. The third-party administrators under such arrangements are normally organizations either specializing in the administration of various types of insurance programs or specializing solely in the management of MEWAs. In addition to general administrative duties the third-party administrator (subject to the insurance company's rules) may be involved in any or all of the following functions associated with MEWAs: underwriting, claims administration, benefit design, or marketing.

Third-party administrators desiring to enter the MEWA field or hoping to increase their share of MEWA business might seek out insurance companies to provide the insurance coverages for the MEWAs they wish to establish. Some of these administrators specialize in the administration of insurance programs; others are insurance agents or brokers who desire a product over which they can have marketing control.

Unfortunately the experience of insured third-party-administered MEWAs was not always satisfactory. There were several instances of mismanagement that caused some of these MEWAs to cease operations. In some cases eagerness to enter the field resulted in inadequate rates or lax underwriting; in other situations administrators were more interested in management fees and sales commissions than in making a profit for the insurance company. While such occurrences have tarnished the image of insured third-party-administered MEWAs in the past, it should be noted that many operated successfully and were managed by capable administrators. Two factors have minimized these difficulties in recent years. First, insurance companies, aware of past experiences, are cautious as they enter the field, giving particular regard to the selection of their administrators. Second, some states have passed legislation aimed at regulating administrators of MEWAs and other insurance arrangements.

Self-funded MEWAs. Self-funded MEWAs are normally established and marketed by the persons or organizations who will administer them. The MEWA does not purchase an insurance contract, except possibly for stop-loss coverage; instead benefits are self-funded with premiums paid by subscribing employers. While many self-funded MEWAs have operated successfully and have been well administered, others have gone bankrupt and left participants with unpaid claims. (Under an insured MEWA the insurer would be responsible for paying claims even if the MEWA failed.) Again administrators often did not charge enough to establish proper reserves for future benefits, or they were more concerned with generating management fees and sales commissions than in properly managing the MEWA. In some cases outright fraud was involved.

In 1982 Congress enacted legislation that provides for state regulation of self-funded MEWAs. For several years state insurance departments had tried to obtain the power to shut down mismanaged MEWAs, but the administrators of these plans argued that they were exempted from state regulation by ERISA. The legislation made clear that insured MEWAs were subject to state regulation. Self-funded MEWAs can apply for ERISA certification, but even if it is granted, the MEWA will still be subject to state rules governing reserves and contributions. In addition, while ERISA certification is pending, a MEWA will have to meet all state insurance regulations, or else the state can force it to cease operations. State regulation also applies if a MEWA either fails to apply for certification or is denied certification.

Initially the overall effect of the 1982 legislation was to greatly reduce the number of self-funded MEWAs. However, two major factors caused an increase in their numbers. First, many insurers abandoned the small group market or became increasingly strict in their underwriting. As a result self-funded MEWAs became the only alternative for some employers. Second, MEWAs frequently wrote coverage at a cost significantly below the cost of alternative coverage, often because of inadequate actuarial calculations regarding the size of future claims and the need for establishing adequate reserves.

Unfortunately the resurgence of self-funded MEWAs was accompanied by many bankruptcies and unpaid claims. The General Accounting Office estimates that between 1988 and 1991 almost 200 self-funded MEWAs failed and left nearly 400,000 employees with $132 million of unpaid claims. There seems to be little doubt that many states have been unsuccessful in adequately regulating MEWAs. Even when appropriate laws exist, many MEWAs simply ignore them. The insurance department finds out about a MEWA only when a complaint is received, and by then the MEWA may be in serious financial difficulty or out of business.

At the time of this writing there is legislation in Congress that would impose an element of federal regulation on self-funded MEWAs. They would be required to register with the Labor Department and send copies of the registration to all states where they offered or provided benefits. The federal government could also force a MEWA to cease operations immediately if it was not operating in accordance with state law.

Other Groups

Numerous other types of groups may be eligible for group insurance under the regulations of many states. These include alumni associations, professional associations, veterans' groups, savings account depositors, and credit card holders. Insurance company underwriting practices and state regulation may impose more stringent requirements on these types of groups than on those involving an employer-employee relationship. Individual evidence of insurability is frequently required for other than small amounts of coverage. In addition, a larger minimum size is generally imposed upon the group.

Contractual Provisions

Through its insurance laws every state provides for the regulation of contractual provisions. In many instances certain contractual provisions must be included in group insurance policies. These mandatory provisions may be altered only if they result in more favorable treatment of the policyowner. Such provisions tend to be most uniform from state to state in the area of group life insurance, primarily because of the widespread adoption of the NAIC model bill pertaining to group life insurance standard provisions. As a result of state regulation, coupled with industry practices, the provisions of most group life and health insurance policies are relatively uniform from company to company. An insurance company's policy forms can usually be used in all states. However, riders may be necessary to bring certain provisions into compliance with the regulations of some states.

Traditionally the regulation of contractual provisions has focused on provisions pertaining to such factors as the grace period, conversion, and incontestability rather than on those pertaining to the types or levels of benefits. These latter provisions have been a matter between the policyowner and the insurance company. However, in recent years this has changed in many states. In some states certain benefits, such as well-baby care and treatment for alcoholism or drug abuse, must be included in any group insurance contract; in other states they must be offered to group policyowners but are optional. Still other state laws and regulations specify minimum levels for certain benefits if those benefits are included.

It is interesting to note that with few exceptions the regulation of contractual provisions affects only those employee benefit plans funded with insurance contracts because provisions of ERISA seem to exempt employee benefit plans from most types of state regulation. However, there are exceptions to this exemption, including insurance regulation and therefore the provisions in insurance contracts. As a result of this ERISA exemption states have few laws and regulations applying to the provisions of uninsured benefit plans. However, ERISA does not exempt uninsured plans from state regulation in such areas as age and sex discrimination, and laws pertaining to these areas commonly apply to all benefit plans. A few states are also trying to mandate other types of benefits for uninsured plans, and ultimately the issue will probably have to be settled by Congress or the Supreme Court.

Benefit Limitations

Statutory limitations may be imposed on the level of benefits that can be provided under group insurance contracts issued to certain types of eligible groups. With the exception of group life insurance these limitations rarely apply in situations involving an employer-employee relationship. In the past most states limited the amount of group life insurance that could be provided by an employer to an employee, but only Texas still has such a restriction. However, several states limit the amount of coverage that can be provided under contracts issued to groups other than individual employer groups. In addition, some states limit the amount of life insurance coverage that may be provided for dependents.

Taxation

Every state levies a premium tax on foreign (out-of-state) insurance companies licensed to do business in their state, and most states tax the premiums of insurance companies domiciled in their state. These taxes, which are applicable to premiums written within a state, average about 2 percent.

The imposition of the premium tax has placed insurance companies at a competitive disadvantage with alternative methods of providing benefits. Premiums paid to health maintenance organizations are not subject to the tax, nor are premiums paid to Blue Cross–Blue Shield plans in many states. In addition, the elimination of this tax is one cost saving under self-funded plans. Because the trend toward self-funding of benefits by large corporations has resulted in the loss of substantial premium tax revenue to the states, there have been suggestions that all premiums paid to any type of organization or fund for the purpose of providing insurance benefits to employees be subject to the premium tax.

Where state income taxation exists, the tax implications of group insurance premiums and benefits to both employers and employees are generally similar to those of the federal government. Employers may deduct any premiums paid as business expenses, and employees have certain exemptions from taxation with respect to both premiums paid on their behalf and benefits attributable to employer-paid premiums.

Regulatory Jurisdiction

A group insurance contract will often insure individuals living in more than one state—a situation that raises the question of which state or states have regulatory jurisdiction over the contract. This issue is a crucial one since factors such as minimum enrollment percentages, maximum amounts of life insurance, and required contract provisions vary among the states.

Few problems arise if the insured group qualifies as an eligible group in all the states where insured individuals reside. Individual employer groups, negotiated trusteeships, labor union groups, and creditor-debtor groups fall into this category. Under the *doctrine of comity*, by which states recognize within their own territory the laws of other states, it is generally accepted that the state in which the group insurance contract is delivered to the policyowner has governing jurisdiction. Therefore the contract must conform only to the laws and regulations of this one state, even though certificates of insurance may be delivered in other states. However, a few states have statutes that prohibit insurance issued in other states from covering residents of their state unless the contract conforms with their laws and regulations. While these statutes are effective with respect to insurance companies licensed within the state (that is, admitted companies), their effectiveness with respect to nonadmitted companies is questionable, since states lack regulatory jurisdiction over these companies.

This does not mean that the policyowner may arbitrarily seek out a situs (place of delivery) that is most desirable from a regulatory standpoint. Unless the state of delivery has a significant relationship to the insurance transaction, other states may seek to exercise their regulatory authority. Therefore it has become common practice that an acceptable situs must be at least one of the following:

- the state where the policyowner is incorporated (or the trust is created if the policyowner is a trust)
- the state where the policyowner's principal office is located
- the state where the greatest number of insured individuals are employed
- any state where an employer or labor union that is a party to a trust is located

While a policyowner may have a choice of situs if these locations differ, most insurers are reluctant to issue a group contract in any state unless a corporate officer or trustee who can execute acceptance of the contract is located in that state and unless the principal functions related to the administration of the group contract will be performed there.

The issue of regulatory jurisdiction is more complex for those types of groups that are not considered to be eligible groups in all states. Multiple-employer welfare arrangements are a typical example. If a state has no regulation to the contrary and if the insured group would be eligible for group insurance in other states, the situation is the same as previously described. In addition, most other states will accept the doctrine of comity and will not interfere with the regulatory jurisdiction of the state where the contract is delivered. However, some states either prohibit coverage from being issued or require that it conform with the state's laws and regulations other than those pertaining to eligible groups.

FEDERAL REGULATION

Many aspects of federal regulation have affected the establishment and character of group insurance. The most significant aspects are the

- Age Discrimination in Employment Act
- Civil Rights Act
- Employee Retirement Income Security Act
- Americans with Disabilities Act
- Social Security Act
- Health Maintenance Organization Act
- Internal Revenue Code

This chapter will focus on the first four acts listed, since these have had a similar influence on most types of group insurance. Nondiscrimination rules will also be discussed. The Social Security Act will be discussed in chapters 6 and 8, with emphasis on its effect on the integration of group disability income and group medical expense benefits with the benefits provided under the act. The Health Maintenance Organization Act will be described in chapter 7, along with a general discussion of health maintenance organizations. The income tax implications of the Internal Revenue Code, which may vary for different types of group insurance coverage, will be described in those chapters pertaining to each type of coverage.

The Age Discrimination in Employment Act

In 1986 the Age Discrimination in Employment Act was amended to drop the upper-age limitation from the prohibition against age discrimination for most working persons. The act, passed in 1967, applies only to employers with 20 or more employees and originally affected employees between the ages of 40 and 65. A 1978 amendment increased the maximum age to 70, and the latest change completely eliminates the cap. With some exceptions, such as individuals in executive or high policymaking positions, compulsory retirement is no longer allowed. Employee benefits, which traditionally ceased or were severely limited at age 65, have also been affected by the act. In 1979 the Department of Labor, which was responsible for the enforcement of the act, issued an interpretative bulletin requiring benefits to be continued for older workers. However, some reductions in benefits were allowed. The responsibility for enforcement was later transferred to the Equal Employment Opportunity Commission, which continued to use the interpretative bulletin of the Department of Labor. In 1990 Congress explicitly brought employee benefits under the provisions of the Age Discrimination in Employment Act by codifying the provisions in the interpretative bulletin. It should be noted that while the federal act does not prohibit such discrimination in benefits for employees under age 40 or for all employees of firms that employ fewer than 20 persons, some states may prohibit such discrimination under their own laws or regulations.

The act permits a reduction in the level of some benefits for older workers so that the cost of providing benefits for older workers is no greater than the cost of providing them for younger workers. However, the most expensive benefit—medical expense coverage—cannot be reduced. The following discussion is limited to reductions after age 65—probably the most common age for reducing benefits, even though reductions can start at an earlier age if they are justified on a cost basis. It should be emphasized that these restrictions apply only to benefits for active employees. There are no requirements under the act that any benefits be continued for retired workers.

When participation in an employee benefit plan is voluntary, an employer can generally require larger employee contributions instead of reducing benefits for older employees, as long as the proportion of the premiums paid by older employees does not increase with age. Thus if an employer pays 50 percent of the cost of benefits for younger employees, it must pay at least 50 percent of the cost for older employees. If employees pay the entire cost of a benefit, older employees may be required to pay the full cost of their coverage to the extent that this is a condition of participation in the plan. However, this provision is not applicable to medical expense benefits—employees over age 65 cannot be required to pay more for their coverage than is paid by employees under age 65.

In cases where benefits are reduced, two approaches are permitted; a benefit-by-benefit approach or a benefit-package approach. Under the *benefit-by-benefit approach* each employee benefit may be reduced to a lesser amount as long as each reduction can be justified on a cost basis. Under a *benefit-package approach* the overall benefit package may be altered. Some benefits may be eliminated or reduced to a lesser amount than can be justified on a cost basis, as long as other existing benefits are not reduced or the benefit package is increased by adding new benefits for older workers. The only cost restriction is that the cost of the revised benefit package may be no less than if a benefit-by-benefit reduction had been used. The act also places two other restrictions on the benefit-package approach by prohibiting any reduction in medical expense benefits or retirement benefits.

In reducing a benefit an employer must use data that approximately reflect the actual cost of the benefit to the employer over a reasonable period of years. Unfortunately such data either have not been kept by employers or are not statistically valid. Consequently reductions that have taken place have been based on estimates provided by insurance companies and consulting actuaries. This approach appears to have been satisfactory to the Equal Employment Opportunity Commission. The act allows reductions to take place on a yearly basis or to be based on age brackets of up to 5 years. Any cost comparisons must be made with the preceding age bracket. For example, if 5-year age brackets are used, the cost of providing benefits to employees between 65 and 69 must be compared with the cost of providing the same benefits to employees between 60 and 64.

While reductions in group insurance benefits for older employees are permissible, they are not required. Some employers make no reductions for older employees, but most employers reduce life insurance benefits at age 65 and long-term disability benefits at age 60 or 65.

Group Term Life Insurance Benefits

Basing their conclusions on mortality statistics, most insurance companies feel that group term life insurance benefits can be reduced to the following percentages of the amount of coverage provided immediately prior to age 65:

Age	Percentage
65–69	65
70–74	45
75–79	30
over 79	20

Therefore if employees are normally provided with $20,000 of group term life insurance, employees between the ages of 65 and 69 can be provided with only $13,500; employees between the ages of 70 and 74 can be provided with $9,000, and so forth. Similarly if employees normally receive coverage equal to 200 percent of salary, this coverage may be reduced by 35 percent to 130 percent of salary at age 65, with additional reductions at later ages.

Reductions may also be made on an annual basis. If an annual reduction is used, it appears that a reduction of up to 11 percent of the previous year's coverage can be actuarially justified, starting at age 65 and continuing through age 69. Starting at age 70, the percent should be 9 percent.

In a plan with employee contributions the employer may either reduce benefits as described above and charge the employee the same premium as those employees in the previous age bracket, or continue full coverage and require the employee to pay an actuarially increased contribution.

Group Disability Income Benefits

The act allows reductions in insured short-term disability income plans. However, no reductions are allowed in uninsured salary continuation plans. While disability statistics for those aged 65 and older are limited, some insurance companies feel a benefit reduction of approximately 20 percent is appropriate for employees between 65 and 69, with additional decreases of 20 percent of the previous benefit for each consecutive 5-year period. However, the laws of the few states that require short-term disability income benefits to be provided allow neither a reduction in benefits nor an increase in any contribution rate for older employees.

Under the act two methods are allowed for reducing long-term disability income benefits for those employees who become disabled at older ages. Either the level of benefits may be reduced without altering benefit eligibility or duration, or the benefit duration may be reduced without altering the level of benefits. These reductions again must be justified on a cost basis. Unfortunately no rough guidelines can be given since any possible reductions will vary considerably, depending upon the eligibility requirements and the duration of benefits under a long-term disability plan. For example, one insurance company suggests that if a plan previously provided full benefits until age 70, then the duration of the benefits could be reduced to 12 months for disabilities occurring between the ages of 70 and 74 and 6 months for disabilities occurring after age 74.

Group Medical Expense Benefits

Prior to 1983 most employers were considering the availability of medicare in designing their medical expense plans. In many cases this required an employer to provide additional coverage so that employees between the ages of 65 and 69 had medical expense benefits equivalent to those provided for employees under age 65. However, the Age Discrimination in Employment Act now requires employers to offer *all* employees over age 65 (and any employees' spouses who are also over age 65) the same medical coverage they provide for younger employees (and their spouses). The employer's plan is the primary payer of benefits, with medicare assuming the secondary-payer role. However, employees may reject the employer's plan and elect medicare as the primary payer of benefits, but regulations prevent an employer from offering a health plan or option designed to induce such a rejection. This effectively prohibits an employer from offering any type of supplemental plan to employees who have elected medicare as primary. (However, supplemental and carve-out plans can be used for retirees.) Therefore most employees will elect to remain with the employer's plan unless it requires large employee contributions. When medicare is secondary, the employer may pay the part B premium for those employees who are also eligible for medicare, but the employer has no legal responsibility to do so.

Unlike the provisions applying to other types of benefits under the Age Discrimination in Employment Act, the provisions under the act require that equal health care benefits be provided. Consequently benefits cannot be reduced for older employees because of increasing cost to the employer. In addition, older employees cannot be required to contribute more than younger employees.

When the employer's plan is primary, medicare payments will be made for medical expenses that are covered by medicare but not covered by the employer's plan. For purposes of these payments medicare deductibles and coinsurance will generally not apply. However, medicare benefits are limited to what medicare would have paid in the absence of the employer's plan.

The Civil Rights Act

Traditionally pregnancy has been treated differently from other medical conditions under both individual and group insurance policies. However, the 1978 amendment to the Civil Rights Act requires that women affected by pregnancy, childbirth, or related medical conditions be treated the same for employment-related purposes (including receipt of benefits under an employee benefit plan) as other persons who are not so affected but who are similar in their ability to work. The amendment (also referred to as the Pregnancy Discrimination Act) applies only to the benefit plans (both insured and self-funded) of employers who have 15 or more employees. While employers with fewer employees are not subject to the provisions of the amendment, they may be subject to comparable state laws. Similarly since the amendment applies only to employee benefit plans, pregnancy may be treated differently from other medical conditions under insurance policies that are not part of an employee benefit plan.

While the amendment itself is brief, enforcement falls under the jurisdiction of the Equal Employment Opportunity Commission, which has issued a lengthy set of guidelines containing its interpretation of the amendment. The highlights of these guidelines are as follows:

- If an employer provides any type of disability income or sick-leave plan for employees, the employer must provide coverage for pregnancy and its related medical conditions on the same basis as other disabilities. For example, maternity cannot be treated as a named exclusion in a disability income plan. Similarly an employer cannot limit disability income benefits for pregnancies to a shorter period than that applicable to other disabilities.

- If an employer provides medical expense benefits for employees, the employer must provide coverage for the pregnancy-related conditions of female employees (regardless of marital status) on the same basis as for all other medical conditions. For example, an employer cannot limit hospitalization coverage to $1,500 for pregnancy-related conditions while paying up to 80 percent of expenses for other medical conditions nor can the employer have a preexisting condition clause applying to pregnancy unless the clause also applies to other preexisting conditions in the same manner.

- If an employer provides medical expense benefits for dependents, the employer must provide equal coverage for the medical expenses (including those arising from pregnancy-related conditions) of spouses of both male and female employees. The guidelines do allow a lower level of benefits for the pregnancy-related conditions of spouses of male employees than for female employees but only if all benefits for spouses are lower than those for employees. The guidelines also allow an employer to exclude pregnancy-related benefits for female dependents other than spouses as long as such an exclusion applies equally to the nonspouse dependents of both male and female employees.

- Extended medical expense benefits after termination of employment must apply equally to pregnancy-related medical conditions and other medical conditions. Thus if pregnancy commencing during employment is covered until delivery, even if the employee is not disabled, a similar nondisability extension of benefits must apply to all other medical conditions. However, no extension is required under the guidelines as long as all medical conditions are treated in the same manner.

- Medical expense benefits relating to abortions may be excluded from coverage except when the life of the woman is endangered. However, complications from an abortion must be covered. In addition, abortions must be treated like any other medical condition with respect to sick leave and other fringe benefit plans.

The Employee Retirement Income Security Act

The Employee Retirement Income Security Act was enacted to protect the interests of participants in employee benefit plans as well as the interests of participants' beneficiaries. While all sections of the act (sometimes referred to as the Pension Reform Act) generally apply to pension plans, certain sections also apply to employee welfare benefit plans, including most traditional group insurance plans. The most significant of the sections dealing with employee welfare benefit plans are those pertaining to (1) fiduciary responsibility and (2) reporting and disclosure. Since the act and its accompanying regulations are lengthy and extremely complex, only the highlights of ERISA and its effect on employee welfare benefit plans will be discussed below.

Administration of ERISA

While the responsibility for carrying out the provisions of ERISA is shared by the Department of Labor, the Treasury Department, and the Pension Benefit Guaranty Corporation, the Department of Labor bears the main responsibility for those aspects of ERISA affecting group insurance plans. The Department of Labor has been given responsibility for issuing regulations and enforcing the reporting, disclosure, and fiduciary provisions of the act. The Labor-Management Services Administration, a branch of the Department of Labor, is responsible for the field operations of ERISA, and since it has offices in most major cities, it is a source of information regarding ERISA. Many insurance companies have information available for agents and insureds to guide them in complying with the act.

Employee Welfare Benefit Plans

The employee welfare benefit plans to which ERISA applies are defined as including any plan, fund, or program established or maintained by an employer (or an employee organization) for the purpose of providing for its participants or their beneficiaries, through the purchase of insurance or otherwise, any of the following benefits:

- medical, surgical, or hospital care or benefits
- benefits in the event of sickness, accident, disability, death, or unemployment
- vacation benefits
- apprenticeship or other training programs
- day-care centers
- scholarship funds
- prepaid legal services
- any benefit described in section 302(c) of the Labor Management Relations Act of 1947 (such as holiday pay and severance pay)

However, certain types of employee welfare benefit plans are specifically exempt from regulation under ERISA. Among these are

- government plans
- church plans (unless they elect to be covered)
- plans maintained solely to comply with workers' compensation, unemployment compensation, or disability insurance laws

In addition, through regulations issued by the secretary of labor, certain types of plans have been declared not to be employee welfare benefit plans and are thus exempt from the regulations of ERISA. Among these are

- compensation for work performed under other than normal circumstances (including overtime pay and shift, holiday and weekend premiums)
- compensation for absences from work because of sickness, vacation, holidays, military duty, jury duty, or sabbatical leave and training programs to the extent that such compensation is paid out of the general assets of the employer
- group insurance programs under which (1) no contributions are made by the employer; (2) participation is completely voluntary for employees; (3) the sole function served by the employer, without endorsing the program, is to collect premiums through payroll deduction and remit the amount collected to the insurer; and (4) no consideration is paid to the employer in excess of reasonable compensation for administrative services actually performed (most of the mass-marketed plans described in chapter 9 fall into this category).

The Requirement of a Written Instrument

One of the requirements of ERISA is that every employee welfare benefit plan that is subject to the act's regulations be established and maintained pursuant to a written instrument. This instrument must provide for one or more named fiduciaries who have the authority to control and manage the operation and administration of the plan. In the case of an insured plan the fiduciary (or fiduciaries) will have the responsibility for selecting the insurance carrier. In addition, a plan administrator is usually named. The plan administrator, who has the responsibility for complying with the reporting and disclosure requirements under ERISA, may be the employer (that is, the corporation, partnership, or sole proprietorship) but is usually a benefits committee or a specific person, such as the benefits manager or, in the case of a small firm, the owner. If no plan administrator is named, the plan sponsor is considered to be the plan administrator. In the case of an employee welfare benefit plan established or maintained by a single employer (including those situations where coverage is arranged through a multiple-employer welfare arrangement), the employer is considered to be the plan's sponsor. It should be noted that there is no prohibition against the administrator of a plan also being its named fiduciary.

In addition to naming a fiduciary, the plan instrument must

- provide a procedure for establishing and carrying out a funding policy and method consistent with the objectives of the plan
- provide a procedure for amending the plan and for identifying the persons who have the authority to amend the plan
- specify the basis on which payments are made to and from the plan

A common misconception leading to noncompliance with ERISA is that no plan instrument is required if a plan is insured. The method of funding a plan may affect the details contained in the plan instrument, but a plan instrument is required for every employee welfare benefit plan (except those specifically excluded from ERISA regulations), regardless of whether it is insured.

Establishment of a Trust

Unless the assets of an employee welfare benefit plan consist of insurance contracts or are held by an insurance company, ERISA requires that all assets of an employee welfare benefit plan be held in trust by one or more trustees. The trustee (or trustees) may be named in either the trust instrument or in the written plan instrument or may be appointed by the named fiduciary. The trustee has the exclusive authority and discretion to manage and control the assets of the plan except where the trustee is subject to the direction of the named fiduciary or where the authority to manage, acquire, or dispose of plan assets is delegated to one or more investment managers.

Fiduciary Responsibility

ERISA prescribes very detailed standards for fiduciaries and other parties-in-interest of employee welfare benefit plans. In addition to the named fiduciary (or fiduciaries) in a plan instrument a fiduciary is defined as any person who

- exercises discretionary authority or control over plan management or assets
- provides investment advice to a plan for a fee or other compensation
- has discretionary authority or responsibility in the administration of a plan

ERISA requires that a fiduciary discharge his or her duties regarding a plan solely in the interest of the participants and their beneficiaries and that the fiduciary do so

- for the exclusive purpose of (1) providing benefits to participants and their beneficiaries and (2) defraying reasonable expenses of administering the plan
- with the same care, skill, prudence, and diligence under the given circumstances that a prudent person acting in a like capacity and familiar with such matters would use in a similar situation
- by diversifying the investments of the plan to minimize the risk of large losses, unless under the circumstances it is clearly prudent not to do so
- in accordance with the documents and instruments governing the plan insofar as such documents and instruments are consistent with the fiduciary provisions of ERISA

Any fiduciary who breaches any of these duties is personally liable for the full amount of any loss resulting from such actions. Furthermore, a fiduciary will also be personally liable for similar breaches by another fiduciary to the extent that his or her actions contributed to the other fiduciary's breach. A breach of fiduciary responsibilities can also result in civil penalties and, if the breach is willful, in criminal penalties as well.

ERISA also contains a list of prohibited transactions for parties-in-interest to an employee welfare benefit plan. In addition to fiduciaries a party-in-interest is defined as including

- any counsel or employee of the plan
- any person providing services to the plan
- an employer of any covered employees of the plan
- an employee organization, any of whose members are covered under the plan
- any owner, direct or indirect, of 50 percent or more of the firm sponsoring the plan
- any relative of a party-in-interest
- certain other related corporations, employees, officers, directors, partners, and joint venturers

The results of the prohibited-transactions provision are that a party-in-interest may not

- cause the plan to engage in any transaction with a party-in-interest that constitutes a direct or indirect (1) sale, exchange, or leasing of property; (2) lending of money; (3) extension of credit; (4) furnishing of goods, services, or facilities; or (5) transfer of any plan assets to a party-in-interest or use of any plan assets by or for the benefit of a party-in-interest
- acquire or hold more than 10 percent of the plan assets in employer securities or real estate
- deal with the assets of the plan in his or her own interest or for his or her own account
- act in any capacity in any transaction involving the plan on behalf of a party whose interests are adverse to the interests of the plan, its participants, or its beneficiaries
- receive any consideration for his or her own personal account from any party dealing with the plan in connection with a transaction involving plan assets
- be paid for his or her services, if already receiving full-time pay from an employer whose employees are participants in the plan, except for reimbursement of expenses incurred

Several specific exemptions to these prohibited transactions are provided under ERISA. Two of these exemptions include

- any loans made by the plan to parties-in-interest who are participants of the plan, if such loans are available on a nondiscriminatory basis, are made in accordance with plan rules regarding loans, have a reasonable rate of interest, and are adequately secured
- reasonable arrangements made with a party-in-interest for office space or legal, accounting, or other services necessary for the plan

Additional exemptions from prohibited transactions may be granted by the secretary of labor as long as such exemptions are administratively feasible, in the interest of the plan and its participants, and protective of the rights of participants in the plan. One of these exemptions applies to agents and brokers who receive fees and/or commissions from an employee welfare benefit plan. Without this exemption agents and brokers who are also parties-in-interest would be ineligible to receive such compensation. Essentially the exemption applies as long as the agent or broker is not a trustee, administrator, named fiduciary, or fiduciary with specific written discretionary authority over plan assets.

Reporting and Disclosure—General Requirements

ERISA requires that certain information concerning any employee welfare benefit plan be made available by the plan administrator to some or all of the following: (1) plan participants (including beneficiaries of plan participants who are receiving benefits), (2) the Department of Labor, and (3) the Internal Revenue Service. This information must consist of

- a summary plan description
- a summary of material modification
- an annual return/report—Form 5500 (or one of its variations)
- a summary annual report
- any terminal report
- certain underlying documents

ERISA imposes specific monetary penalties for failure to comply with the reporting and disclosure requirements within the prescribed time periods. In addition, civil and criminal action can be taken against any plan administrator who willfully violates any of the requirements or who knowingly falsifies or conceals ERISA disclosure information.

Summary Plan Description. The summary plan description must be automatically provided to each plan participant and the Department of Labor within 120 days after the adoption of an employee welfare benefit plan. Copies must be provided to new participants within 90 days of first becoming eligible to participate, and an updated summary plan description must be provided once every 5 years if a plan has been materially modified, otherwise once every 10 years. (However, employers must notify employees that they may request a summary of any plan changes during the interim.) The summary plan description must contain the following information:

- name of the plan
- name, address, and telephone number of the plan administrator
- name and address of the plan's sponsor
- name and address of the agent for service of legal process
- name and address of any trustee (or trustees)
- employer identification number assigned to the plan sponsor by the IRS and the plan number assigned by the plan sponsor
- type of employee welfare benefit plan (such as medical expense or disability income)

- type of administration (self-administered or administered by another party)
- sources of contribution to the plan and the method by which these contributions are calculated
- identity of funding medium (not applicable to a fully insured plan unless a separate fund is established apart from the insurance contract)
- ending date of plan's fiscal year (this may or may not coincide with the renewal date of any insurance contract used to fund the plan's benefits)
- eligibility requirements
- if the plan is maintained pursuant to a collective-bargaining agreement, a statement that it is so maintained and that copies are available upon request from the plan administrator
- circumstances that may result in disqualification; ineligibility; or denial, loss, forfeiture, or suspension of benefits
- procedure for filing claims and the remedies available under the plan for the redress of denied claims. Participants must be informed that they will be provided with a written notice specifying the reasons for denial of any claim and that they may request in writing a review of any denied claim by the party who processed it. If the claim is again denied, the participant may make a written request for a review by the plan administrator.
- statement of ERISA rights. Plan participants must be informed that they have the right to (1) examine, without charge, at the plan administrator's office and at other specified locations all plan documents and copies of all documents filed by the plan with the Department of Labor; (2) obtain copies of all plan documents and other plan information upon written request from the plan administrator, who may charge the participant a reasonable fee for the request; and (3) receive a summary of the plan's annual financial report.

ERISA does not require that a summary plan description be provided on a specific form, only that certain information be provided. Some employers use a single document; other employers incorporate much of the required information into the employee benefits handbook provided to their employees.

Summary of Material Modification. The summary of material modification must be automatically provided to each plan participant and the Department of Labor within 210 days after the end of a plan year (that is, the plan's fiscal year) in which a material change has been made in the plan. This summary covers the same information contained in the summary plan description and is essentially an annual update of any information that has been changed.

Annual Return/Report (Form 5500). The annual return/report must be filed with the Internal Revenue Service within 210 days after the end of a plan year. This form, which includes financial information about the plan, must be furnished to any plan participant upon written request to the plan administrator. Form 5500-C is used by employers with fewer than 100 employees.

Summary Annual Report. A summary annual report must be automatically provided to each plan participant within 9 months after the end of a plan year. The information provided in this form is a relatively brief summary of some of the information contained in the annual return/report and consists of a list of the plan's assets and liabilities (or a description of the insurance contract used) and a schedule of the plan's receipts and disbursements.

Terminal Report. A terminal report must be filed with the Internal Revenue Service for a plan that has been terminated. The requirements for a terminal report may be satisfied by the filing of the annual return/report for the final plan year. This report must be furnished to plan participants upon request.

Underlying Documents. Underlying documents consist of those under which the plan was established or is operated, such as a trust agreement or a collective-bargaining agreement. The plan administrator must file these documents with the Department of Labor only if so requested. In addition, certain other records must be provided if requested by the Department of Labor. These documents and records must also be made available to plan participants under certain circumstances.

Reporting and Disclosure — Small Groups

Employee welfare benefit plans that cover fewer than 100 participants at the beginning of a plan year are exempt from certain reporting and disclosure requirements if either of the following conditions is met:

- Benefits are paid as needed solely from the general assets of the employer or employee organization maintaining the plan.
- Benefits are provided exclusively through insurance contracts or policies. The employer (or employee organization) must pay premiums directly from its general assets or partly from its general assets and partly from participants' contributions (provided that contributions by participants are forwarded by the employer to the insurance company within 3 months of receipt). Upon entering the plan contributing participants must be informed of the provisions for the allocations of refunds.

If these requirements are met, the plan administration does not have to furnish a summary annual report to participants or furnish an annual report or terminal report upon request. However, the annual report must be available for examination in the plan administrator's office.

Prior to 1989, it was unnecessary to file Form 5500 (the annual return/report). This form must now be filed for plans that provide legal expenses, educational assistance, and cafeteria benefits. When further guidelines are issued by the IRS, Form 5500 will also be required for the following types of plans: group term life, accident and health, and dependent care.

It should be noted, however, that these plans must still furnish a summary plan description and a summary of material modification to plan participants. In addition, they must furnish certain underlying documents at a participant's request.

The Americans with Disabilities Act of 1990

Many employers must now comply with the Americans with Disabilities Act of 1990 (ADA). The law, which deals with employment, public services, public accommodations, and telecommunications, is the most far-reaching legislation ever enacted in this country to make it possible for disabled persons to join the mainstream of everyday life.

It is estimated that almost 45 million Americans are disabled, and nearly $300 billion of government resources are devoted annually to this group. Of the disabled, 15 million are of working age, but only about 30 percent of these are in the work force, compared to 80 percent of the nondisabled.

As with any social legislation the act provides benefits, including a better quality of life for many disabled persons and an estimated annual savings of $57 million in government benefits to the disabled. However, there are also costs, many of which will be borne by employers. Some of these costs will be in the form of increased expenditures for employee benefits.

Title I of ADA is the portion that pertains to employment. It became effective for employers with 25 or more employees on July 26, 1992. Employers with 15 or more employees must comply as of July 26, 1994. The act makes it unlawful to discriminate on the basis of disability against a qualified individual with respect to any term, condition, or privilege of employment, including recruitment, hiring, promotion, termination, layoff, compensation, sick leave or any leave of absence, and fringe benefits.

Congress gave the responsibility for enforcing Title I to the Equal Employment Opportunity Commission (EEOC). The EEOC felt it was responsible for issuing interpretive guidance so that qualified individuals understood their rights and for facilitating and encouraging compliance by employers. A lengthy Technical Assistance Manual prepared by the agency offers this guidance.

Effect on Employment Practices

The ADA defines a *disabled person* as one who has a physical or mental impairment that substantially limits one or more major life activities, such as caring for oneself, performing manual tasks, walking, seeing, hearing, speaking, breathing, and learning. The EEOC specifically mentions the following as being disabilities: epilepsy, cancer, diabetes, arthritis, hearing and vision loss, AIDS, and emotional illness. A person is impaired even if the condition is corrected, as in the case of a person who is hearing-impaired and wears a hearing aid. The ADA does make one exception to the definition of disability: it specifically excludes persons who are currently engaging in the illegal use of drugs. However, anyone who has successfully completed a supervised rehabilitation program or is currently in such a program is subject to the act's protection as long as he or she is not currently engaging in drug use.

The act does not set quotas or require that the disabled be hired. It does, however, provide that a person cannot be discriminated against if he or she is able to perform the essential functions of a job with or without reasonable accommodation. *Reasonable accommodation* includes making existing facilities that employees use readily accessible and usable by individuals with disabilities. Reasonable accommodation may be as simple as rearranging furniture or changing the height of a work space to accommodate a wheelchair. (There are estimates that at least 50 percent of the disabled can be accommodated with expenditures of $50 or less.) Reasonable accommodations do not include changes that would cause undue hardship to an employer. The act is no more specific than defining *undue hardship* as significant difficulty or expense by the employer in light of such factors as the cost of the accommodation, the employer's financial resources, and the impact on other employees.

With one exception reasonable accommodation is for specific individuals for an individual job. It need not be done just because some disabled person may someday apply for work. The exception is that an employer must make facilities for *applying* for a job accessible to the handicapped and provide employment information that is usable by persons who are hearing- or vision-impaired.

Effect on Employee Benefits

Much less attention has been paid to the effect of ADA on employee benefits. Little has been written in the press, and the act and the Technical Assistance Manual are much more vague. At least one writer has referred to this part of the act as a smoking gun that may ultimately result in significantly increased costs for employers. Although intuition might suggest that the disabled would be more likely than other employees to have conditions requiring ongoing medical care, many employers who have made an effort to hire the disabled have not found this to be the case. In fact, some employers feel the disabled make excellent workers and actually save them money. With jobs more difficult to obtain for the disabled, there is the feeling that the disabled are less likely to switch employers (thus minimizing costs to train new employees) and may actually work harder in order to keep the jobs they have. Whether this situation will continue as more severely disabled persons enter the work force and have more opportunities to change jobs is an unanswered question.

The EEOC guidelines stipulate that employees with disabilities be accorded equal access to whatever health insurance coverage the employer provides to other employees. Preexisting-condition clauses are acceptable as long as they apply to all employees and are not a subterfuge to evade the purposes of the act. Similarly it is permissible to limit coverage for certain procedures or treatments to a specific number per year and to put limits on reimbursements for certain procedures or for the types of drugs or procedures covered as long as the limitations are applied equally to individuals with and without disabilities. The guidelines also address the issue of reducing benefits, but with an example that applies to sick-leave days. The guidelines state that the number of sick days can be reduced for all employees, even if the benefit reduction has an impact on employees with disabilities in need of greater sick leave and medical coverage.

Another portion of the act specifically allows the development and administration of benefit plans in accordance with accepted principles of risk assessment. The EEOC guidelines state that the purpose of the act is not to disrupt the current regulatory climate for self-insured employers, the current nature of insurance underwriting, or current industry practices in sales, underwriting, pricing, administration and other services, claims, and similar related activities based on classification of risks as regulated by the states unless these activities are being used as a subterfuge to evade the purpose of the act.

Some benefit consultants feel that employee benefit plans can continue much as they have been. Others feel that employers will not be so lucky. The enforcement of the act will come from two sources—the EEOC and the courts. Even though the EEOC seems to have been fairly reasonable in its initial interpretation of the act, how will guidelines evolve to address the many unanswered questions that still exist? What will the courts decide when a mentally disabled employee sues an employer because mental health benefits are limited under an employer's plan? Will they decide this is a subterfuge to evade the provisions of the act? If they do, can an employer afford the costs necessary to appeal such a decision?

The question today for employers is what should be done now? Probably very little for the time being. As with ERISA and other federal laws, precise rules will evolve over time. Benefit plans should be analyzed to make sure that they do not discriminate against specific disabilities. For example, the few benefit plans that limit benefits for AIDS are probably on shaky ground, since this is a benefit limitation that applies to a very specific disabled group. Employers should also be extremely careful when reducing benefits to be sure that the reduction is not made because benefits are being used primarily by a group that is disabled.

Nondiscrimination Rules

For many years nondiscrimination rules have applied to employee benefit plans that provided retirement benefits. The purpose of these rules is to deny favorable tax treatment to plans that do not provide equitable benefits to a large cross section of employees. In effect, the owners and executives of a business cannot receive tax-favored benefits if a plan is designed primarily for them. Nondiscrimination rules in recent years have slowly been applied to various other types of employee benefit plans, but these rules, each of which is complex, have not been uniform. Congress attempted to eliminate this lack of uniformity by adding Sec. 89 to the Internal Revenue Code as part of the Tax Reform Act of 1986. This code section was extremely far-reaching and complex, and it would have been very costly both for the government to implement and for employers to comply with. As a result Sec. 89 was repealed in 1989, and all the old nondiscrimination rules it replaced were reinstated. These rules are discussed where appropriate throughout this book.

4

Group Life Insurance: Term Coverage

Traditionally most group life insurance plans were designed to provide coverage during an employee's working years, with coverage usually ceasing upon termination of employment for any reason. Today the majority of employees are provided with coverage that will continue, often at a reduced amount, when termination is a result of retirement. Group term insurance is described in this chapter. The methods and contracts used to provide coverage after retirement will be discussed in chapter 5.

The oldest and most common form of group life insurance is group term insurance. Coverage virtually always consists of yearly renewable term insurance that provides death benefits only, with no buildup of cash values. The group insurance marketplace with its widespread use of yearly renewable term contrasts with the individual marketplace, in which until recently such coverage has accounted for only a small percentage of the life insurance in force. This is primarily due to increasing annual premiums, which become prohibitive for many insureds at older ages. In group life insurance plans the overall premium, in addition to other factors, is a function of the age distribution of the group's members. While the premium for any individual employee will increase with age, the flow of younger workers into the plan and the retirement of older workers tend to result in a relatively stable age distribution and thus an average group insurance rate that remains constant or rises only slightly.

The following discussion of group term insurance focuses largely on common contract provisions, other coverages that are often added to the basic contract, and relevant federal tax laws.

CONTRACT PROVISIONS

The provisions contained in group term insurance contracts are more uniform than those found in other types of group insurance. Much of this uniformity is a result of the adoption by most states of the NAIC Group Life Insurance Standard Provisions Model Bill. This bill, coupled with the insurance industry's attempts at uniformity, has resulted in provisions that are virtually identical among insurance companies. While the following contract provisions represent the norm and are consistent with the practices of most insurance companies, some states may require slightly different provisions, and some companies may vary their contract provisions. In addition, negotiations between a policyowner and an insurance company may result in the modification of contract provisions.

Benefit Schedules

The purpose of the benefit schedule is twofold. It classifies the employees who are eligible for coverage and specifies the amount of life insurance that will be provided to the members of each class, thus minimizing adverse selection because the amount of coverage for individual employees is predetermined. A benefit schedule can be as simple as providing a single amount of life insurance for all employees or as complex as providing different amounts of insurance for different classes of employees. For individual employer groups the most common benefit schedules are those in which the amount of life insurance is based on either earnings or position.

Earnings Schedules

Most group term life insurance plans use an earnings schedule under which the amount of life insurance is determined as a multiple (or percentage) of each employee's earnings. For example, the amount of life insurance for each employee may be twice (200 percent of) the employee's annual earnings. Most plans use a multiple between one and two, but higher and lower multiples are occasionally used. The amount of insurance is often rounded to the next higher $1,000 and for underwriting purposes may be subject to a maximum benefit, such as $100,000. For purposes of the benefit schedule an employee's earnings usually consist of base salary only and do not include additional compensation like overtime pay or bonuses.

An alternative to using a flat percentage of earnings is to use an actual schedule of earnings such as the following:

Annual Earnings	Amount of Life Insurance
Less than $10,000	$ 10,000
$10,000 to $19,999	20,000
$20,000 to $29,999	40,000
$30,000 to $39,999	75,000
$40,000 to $49,999	100,000
$50,000 and over	150,000

This type of schedule may be designed so that all employees receive an amount of coverage that is approximately equal to the same multiple of annual earnings or, as in this example, larger multiples with higher earnings. Benefit schedules usually provide for a change in the amount of an employee's coverage when the employee moves into a different classification, even if this does not occur on the policy anniversary date. For example, the schedule above indicates that the amount of coverage for an employee earning $28,000 would increase from $40,000 to $75,000 if the employee received a $4,000 raise. Some schedules, however, specify that adjustments in amounts of coverage will only be made annually or on monthly premium due dates.

Position Schedules

Position schedules are similar to earnings schedules except that, as the example below shows, the amount of life insurance is based on an employee's position within the firm rather than on the employee's annual earnings.

Position	Amount of Life Insurance
President	$200,000
Vice-presidents	100,000
Managers	60,000
Salespersons	40,000
Other employees	20,000

Because individuals in high positions are often involved in designing the benefit schedule, underwriters are concerned that the benefits for these individuals be reasonable in relation to the overall plan benefits. Position schedules may also pose problems in meeting nondiscrimination rules if excessively large amounts of coverage are provided to persons in high positions.

Even though position schedules are often used when annual earnings can be easily determined, they are particularly useful when it is difficult to determine an employee's annual income. This is the situation when income is materially affected by such factors as commissions earned, number of hours worked, or bonuses that are based on either the employee's performance or the firm's profits.

Flat-Benefit Schedules

Under flat-benefit schedules the same amount of life insurance is provided for all employees regardless of salary or position. This type of benefit schedule is commonly used in group insurance plans covering hourly paid employees, particularly when benefits are negotiated with a union. In most cases the amount of life insurance under a flat-benefit schedule is relatively small, such as $5,000 or $10,000. When an employer desires to provide only a minimum amount of life insurance for all employees, a flat-benefit schedule is often used.

Length-of-Service Schedules

In the early days of group life insurance, length-of-service schedules were relatively common and viewed as a method for rewarding longtime employees. However, because of the current view that the primary purpose of group life insurance is to replace income, such schedules are not extensively used. These schedules may also be considered discriminatory if a disproportionate number of the persons with longer service records are also the most highly paid employees. The following is an example of a length-of-service schedule:

Length of Service	Amount of Life Insurance
Less than 2 years	$ 4,000
2 years but less than 5 years	8,000
5 years but less than 10 years	12,000
10 years but less than 15 years	16,000
15 years but less than 20 years	20,000
20 years or more	25,000

Pension Schedules

Under pension schedules the amount of life insurance is a function of an employee's projected pension at retirement. For example, under an employer's plan the amount of life insurance for each employee might be 100 times the monthly pension that will be payable to the employee at normal retirement age. However, the amount of life insurance may be subject to a maximum benefit.

Combination Benefit Schedules

It is not unusual for employers to have benefit schedules that incorporate elements from several of the various types previously discussed. While there are numerous possible combinations, a common benefit schedule of this type provides salaried employees with an amount of insurance that is determined by a multiple of their annual earnings and provides hourly employees with a flat amount of life insurance.

Reduction in Benefits

It is common for a group life insurance plan to provide for a reduction in benefits for active employees who reach a certain age, commonly 65 to 70. Such a reduction, which is due to the high cost of providing benefits for older employees, will be specified in the benefit schedule of a plan. Any reduction in the amount of life insurance for active employees is subject to the provisions of the Age Discrimination in Employment Act that were discussed in chapter 3.

Benefit reductions fall into three categories: (1) a reduction to a flat amount of insurance; (2) a percentage reduction, such as to 65 percent of the amount of insurance that was previously provided; or (3) a gradual reduction over a period of years (for example, a 10 percent reduction in coverage each year until a minimum benefit amount is reached).

Eligibility

Group insurance contracts are very precise in their definition of what constitutes an eligible person for coverage purposes. In general, an employee must be in a covered classification, work full-time, and be actively at work. In addition, any requirements concerning probationary periods, insurability, or premium contributions must be satisfied.

Covered Classification

All group insurance contracts specify that an employee must fall into one of the classifications contained in the benefit schedule. While these classifications may be broad enough to include all employees of the organization, they may also be so limited as to exclude many employees from coverage. In some cases these excluded employees may have coverage through a negotiated trusteeship or under other group insurance contracts provided by the employer; in other cases they may have no coverage because the employer wishes to limit benefits to certain groups of employees. No employee may be in more than one classification, and the responsibility for determining the appropriate classification for each employee falls on the policyowner.

Full-time Employment

Most group insurance contracts limit eligibility to full-time employees. A full-time employee is generally defined as one who works no fewer than the number of hours in the normal work week established by the employer, which must be at least 30 hours. Subject to insurance company underwriting practices, an employer can provide coverage for part-time employees. When this is done, part-time is generally defined as less than full-time but more than some minimum number of hours per week. In addition, part-time employees may be subject to more stringent eligibility requirements. For example, full-time hourly paid employees may be provided with $20,000 of life insurance immediately upon employment, while part-time employees may be provided with only $10,000 of life insurance and may be subject to a probationary period.

Actively-at-Work Provision

Most group insurance contracts contain an actively-at-work provision, whereby an employee is not eligible for coverage if absent from work because of sickness, injury, or other reasons on the otherwise effective date of his or her coverage under the contract. Coverage will commence when the employee returns to work. The actively-at-work provision is often waived for employers with a large number of employees when coverage is transferred from one insurance company to another and the employees involved have been insured under the previous insurance company's contract.

Probationary Periods

Group insurance contracts may contain probationary periods that must be satisfied before an employee is eligible for coverage. When a probationary period exists, it rarely exceeds 6 months, and an employee will be eligible for coverage on either the first day after the probationary period has been satisfied or on the first day of the month following the end of the probationary period.

Insurability

While most group insurance contracts are issued without individual evidence of insurability, in some instances underwriting practices will require evidence of insurability. This commonly occurs when an employee fails to elect coverage under a contributory plan and later wants coverage or when an employee is eligible for a large amount of coverage. In these cases an employee will not be eligible for coverage until the employee has submitted the proper evidence of insurability and the insurance company has determined that the evidence is satisfactory.

Premium Contribution

If a group insurance plan is contributory, an employee will not be eligible for coverage until the policyowner has been provided with the proper authorization for payroll deductions. If this is done before the employee otherwise becomes eligible, coverage will commence on the eligibility date. During the next 31 days, coverage will commence when the policyowner receives the employee's authorization. If the authorization is not received within 31 days, the employee must furnish evidence of insurability at his or her own expense to obtain coverage. Evidence of insurability will also be required if an employee drops coverage under a contributory plan and wishes to regain coverage at a future date.

Beneficiary Designation

With few exceptions an insured person has the right to name the beneficiary under his or her group life insurance coverage. These exceptions include credit life insurance, where the creditor is the beneficiary, and dependent life insurance, where the employee is the beneficiary. In addition, the laws and regulations of some states prohibit naming the employer as beneficiary. Unless a beneficiary designation has been made irrevocable, an employee has the right to change the designated beneficiary at any time. While all insurance contracts require that the insurance company be notified of any beneficiary change in writing, the effective date of the change may vary depending on contract provisions. Some contracts specify that a change will be effective on the date it is received by the insurance company; others make it effective on the date the change was requested by the employee.

Under individual life insurance policies death benefits are paid to an insured person's estate if no beneficiary has been named or if all beneficiaries have died before the insured. Some group term insurance contracts contain an identical provision; others provide that the death benefits will be paid through a *successive beneficiary provision*. Under the latter provision the proceeds will be paid, at the option of the insurance company, to any one or more of the following survivors of the insured person: spouse, children, parents, brothers and sisters, or executor of the employee's estate. In most cases insurance companies will pay the proceeds to the person or persons in the first category that includes eligible survivors.

Two other provisions, each of which is often called a *facility-of-payment provision*, are sometimes found in group term insurance contracts. The first of these provisions provides that a specified amount, generally $500 or less, may be paid to any person who appears to be entitled to such a sum by reason of having incurred funeral or other expenses relating to the last illness or death of the person insured. The other provisions applies to any beneficiary who is a minor or who is physically, mentally, or otherwise incapable of giving a valid release for any payment received. Under this provision the insurance company has the option, until a claim is made by the guardian for the beneficiary, of paying the proceeds to any person or institution that appears to have assumed responsibility for the care, custody, or support of the beneficiary. These payments will be made in installments in the amount specified under any optional method of settlement previously selected by the person insured, or, in the absence of such a selection, in installments not to exceed some specified amount, such as $100 per month.

Settlement Options

With the exception of survivor income benefit insurance plans (discussed later in this chapter), group term insurance contracts covering employees provide that death benefits will be payable in a lump sum unless an optional mode of settlement has been selected. Each employee insured under the contract has the right to select and change any available mode of settlement during his or her lifetime. If no optional mode of settlement is in force at the death of the employee, the beneficiary generally has the right to elect any of the available options. The most common provision in group term insurance contracts is that the available modes of settlement are those customarily offered by the insurance company at the time the selection is made. The available options are not generally specified in the contract, but information about them is usually provided to the group policyowner. In addition, many insurance companies have brochures available for employees that describe either all or the most common options available. Any guarantees associated with these options will be those that are in effect when the option is selected.

In addition to a lump-sum option, most insurance companies offer all the following options and possibly other options as well:

- an interest option. The proceeds are left on deposit with the insurance company and the interest on the proceeds is paid to the beneficiary. The beneficiary can usually withdraw the proceeds at any time. The amount of any periodic installment is a function of the interest rate paid by the insurance company.
- an installment option for a fixed period. The proceeds are paid in equal installments for a specified period of time. The amount of any periodic installment is a function of the time period and the amount of the death proceeds.
- an installment option for a fixed amount. The proceeds are paid in equal installments of a specified amount until the proceeds plus any interest earnings are exhausted.
- a life income option. The proceeds are payable in installments during the lifetime of the beneficiary. A choice of guarantee periods is usually available during which a secondary beneficiary or the beneficiary's estate will continue to receive benefits even if the beneficiary should die. The amount of any periodic installment will be a function of the age and sex

of the beneficiary, the period for which payments are guaranteed, and the amount of the death proceeds.

Premiums

Group insurance contracts stipulate that it is the responsibility of the policyowner to pay all premiums to the insurance company, even if the group insurance plan is contributory. Any required contributions from employees will be incorporated into the employer's group insurance plan, but they are not part of the insurance contract and therefore do not constitute an obligation to the insurance company by the employees. Rather, these contributions represent an obligation to the employer by the employees and are commonly paid by payroll deduction. Subject to certain limitations, any employee contributions are determined by the employer or as a result of labor negotiations. Most states require the employer to pay at least a portion of the premium for group term insurance (but not for other group insurance coverage), and a few states impose limitations on the amounts that may be paid by any employee. The most common restriction limits the contribution of any employee to the greater of 60 cents per month per $1,000 of coverage or 75 percent of the premium rate for that employee. This limitation is adhered to by companies licensed to do business in the state of New York and is often incorporated into their contracts. However, for some hazardous industries a higher contribution than 60 cents per month is permitted.

Premiums are payable in advance to the insurance company or any authorized agent for the time period specified in the contract. In most cases premiums are payable monthly but may be paid less frequently. The rates used to determine the premium for any policyowner are guaranteed for a certain length of time, usually one year. The periodic premium is determined by applying these rates to the amount of life insurance in force. Consequently the premium actually payable will change each month as the total amount of life insurance in force under the group insurance plan varies. A detailed explanation of premium computations is contained in chapter 11.

Group insurance contracts state that any dividends or experience refunds are payable to the policyowner in cash or may be used at the policyowner's option to reduce any premium due. To the extent that these exceed the policyowner's share of the premium, they must be used for the benefit of the employees. This is usually accomplished by reducing employee contributions or by providing increased benefits.

Claims

The provision concerning death claims under group life insurance policies is very simple. It states that the amount of insurance under the contract is payable when the insurance company receives written proof of death. No time period is specified in which a claim must be filed. However, most companies require the completion of a brief form by the policyowner and the beneficiary before a claim is processed.

Assignment

For many years the owners of individual life insurance policies have been able to transfer any or all of their rights under the insurance contract to another party. Such assignments have been commonly used to avoid federal estate tax by removing the proceeds of an insurance contract from the insured's estate at death. Historically assignments have not been permitted under group life insurance contracts, often because of state laws and regulations prohibiting them. In recent years most states have eliminated such prohibitions, and many insurance companies have modified their contracts to permit assignments, or they will waive the prohibition upon request. Essentially an assignment will be valid as long as it is permitted by and conforms with state law and the group insurance contract. It should be noted that insurance companies will generally require any assignment to be in writing and to be filed with the company.

Grace Period

Group life insurance contracts provide for a grace period (almost always 31 days) during which a policyowner may pay any overdue premium without interest. If the premium is not paid, the contract will lapse at the end of the grace period unless the policyowner has notified the insurance company that an earlier termination should take place. Even if the policy is allowed to lapse or is terminated during the grace period, the policyowner is legally liable for the payment of any premium due during the portion of the grace period when the contract was still in force.

Entire Contract

The entire contract clause states that the insurance policy, the policyowner's application that is attached to the policy, and any individual (unattached) applications of any insured persons constitute the entire insurance contract. All statements made in these applications are considered to be representations rather than warranties, and no other statements made by the policyowner or by any insureds can be used by the insurance company as the basis for contesting coverage. When compared with the application for individual life insurance, the policyowner's application that is attached to a group insurance contract may be relatively short. Most of the information needed by the insurance company is often contained in a preliminary application that is not part of the insurance contract. On the delivery of many group insurance contracts the policyowner signs a final "acceptance application," which in effect states that the coverage as applied for has been delivered. Consequently a greater burden is placed on the insurance company to verify the statements made by the policyowner in the preliminary application.

The entire contract clause also stipulates that no agent has any authority to waive or amend any provisions of the insurance contract and that a waiver of or amendment to the contract will be valid only if it is signed by certain specified corporate officers of the insurance company.

Incontestability

Like individual life insurance contracts, group insurance contracts contain an incontestability provision. Except for the nonpayment of premiums the validity of the contract cannot be contested after it has been in force for a specified period, generally either one or two years. During this time the insurance company can contest the contract on the basis of statements by the policyowner in the application attached to the contract that are considered to be material misrepresentations. Statements by any insured person can be used as the basis for denying claims during this period only if such statements relate to the insurability of the individual. In addition, the statements must have been made in a written application signed by the individual, and a copy of the application must have been furnished to either the individual or his or her beneficiary. It should be pointed out that the incontestability clause will not be of concern to most covered persons, since evidence of insurability is not usually required and thus no statements concerning individual insurability will be made.

Misstatement of Age

If the age of any person covered under a group term insurance policy is misstated, the benefit payable will be the amount that is specified under the benefit schedule. However, the premium will be adjusted to reflect the true age of the individual. This is in contrast to individual life insurance contracts, where benefits are adjusted to the amount that the premium paid would have purchased at the true age of the individual. Under a group insurance contract the responsibility for paying any additional premium or the right to receive a refund belongs to the policyowner and not to the individual employee whose age is misstated, even if the plan is contributory. If the misstated age would have affected the employee's contribution, this is a matter to be resolved between the employer and the employee.

Termination

All group insurance contracts stipulate the conditions under which the contract may be terminated by either the insurance company or the policyowner. The circumstances under which the coverage for a particular insured person will terminate are also specified.

A group term insurance contract can be terminated for nonpayment of premium at the end of the grace period. Insurance companies may also terminate coverage for an individual employer group on any premium due date if certain conditions exist and notice of termination has been given to the policyowner at least 31 days in advance. These conditions include the failure to maintain a stated minimum number of participants in the plan and in contributory plans the failure to maintain a stated minimum percentage participation. The policyowner may also terminate the contract at any time by giving the insurance company 31 days' advance written notice. Moreover, the policyowner has the right to request the amendment of the contract at any time by notifying the insurance company.

The coverage for any insured person will terminate automatically (subject to any provisions for a continuation or conversion of coverage) when any of the following circumstances exist:

- The employee terminates employment.
- The employee ceases to be eligible (for example, if the employee no longer satisfies the full-time work requirement or no longer falls into a covered classification).
- The master contract is terminated by the policyowner or the insurance company.
- Any required contribution by the employee has not been made (generally because the employee has notified the policyowner to cease the required payroll deduction).

Temporary Interruption of Employment

Most group term insurance contracts provide that the employer may elect to continue coverage on employees during temporary interruptions of active full-time employment. These may arise from leaves of absence, layoffs, or the inability to work because of illness or injury. The employer must continue paying the premium, and the coverage may be continued only for a relatively short period of time, such as 3 months, unless the time period is extended by mutual agreement between the employer and the insurance company. Also in electing to continue coverage, the policyowner must act in such a way as to preclude individual selection.

Continuation of Coverage for Disabled Employees

Most group term insurance contracts make some provision for the continuation of coverage on employees whose active employment has terminated due to disability. By far the most common provision in use today is the *waiver-of-premium provision*. Under this provision life insurance coverage is continued without the payment of premium as long as the employee is totally disabled, even if the master contract is terminated. However, certain requirements must be met:

- The disability must commence while the employee is insured under the master contract.
- The disability must commence prior to a specified age, commonly age 60.
- The employee must be totally disabled. Total disability is normally defined as the complete inability of the employee to engage in any gainful occupation for which he or she is or becomes qualified by reason of education, training, or experience.
- The employee must file a claim within a prescribed period (normally 12 months) and must submit annual evidence of continuing disability.

If an employee no longer meets the definition of disability and returns to work, the employee may again be insured under the group insurance contract on a premium-paying basis as long as the employee meets the eligibility requirements

Another provision relating to disabled employees is a maturity-value benefit. Under this type of provision the face amount of a totally disabled employee's group life insurance will be paid to the employee in a lump sum or in monthly installments. Like the extended-death-benefit provision, a maturity-value-benefit provision was once widely used but is no longer common.

A small but growing trend is for disabled employees to be continued as eligible employees under a group insurance contract, with the employer paying the periodic cost of their coverage just as if they were active employees. At the termination of the contract the insurance company has no responsibility to continue coverage unless a disabled employee is eligible and elects to convert coverage and pays any required premiums. However, depending on the provisions of the group insurance plan, the employer may have a legal responsibility to continue coverage on disabled employees in some manner.

Conversion

All group term insurance contracts covering employees contain a conversion privilege that gives any employee whose coverage ceases the right to convert to an individual insurance policy. The terms of the conversion privilege vary, depending upon the reason for the termination of coverage under the group contract. The most generous conversion rights are available to those employees who either have terminated employment or no longer fall into one of the eligible classifications still covered by the master contract. These employees have the right to purchase an individual life insurance policy from the insurance company without evidence of insurability, but it is usually one without disability or other supplementary benefits. However, this right is subject to the following conditions:

- The employee must apply for conversion within 31 days after the termination of employment or membership in an eligible classification. During this 31-day period the employee is provided with a death benefit equal to the amount of life insurance that is available under the conversion privilege, even if the employee does not apply for conversion. Disability and supplementary benefits are not extended during this period unless they are also subject to conversion. The premium for the individual policy must accompany the conversion application, and coverage will be effective at the end of the conversion period.
- The individual policy selected by the employee may generally be any form, except term insurance, customarily issued by the insurance company at the age and amount applied for. Some insurance companies also make term insurance coverage available, and a few states require that employees be allowed to purchase term insurance coverage for a limited time (such as one year) after which an employee must convert to a cash value form of coverage.
- The face amount of the individual policy may not exceed the amount of life insurance that terminated under the group insurance contract.
- The premium for the individual policy will be determined using the insurance company's current rate applicable to the type and amount of the individual policy for the attained age of the employee on the date of conversion and for the class of risk to which the employee belongs. While

one year) after which an employee must convert to a cash value form of coverage.

- The face amount of the individual policy may not exceed the amount of life insurance that terminated under the group insurance contract.
- The premium for the individual policy will be determined using the insurance company's current rate applicable to the type and amount of the individual policy for the attained age of the employee on the date of conversion and for the class of risk to which the employee belongs. While no extra premium may be charged for reasons of health, an extra premium may be charged for any other hazards considered in an insurance company's rate structure, such as occupation or avocation.

It is estimated that only one or two percent of the employees eligible actually take advantage of the conversion privilege. Several reasons account for this. Many employees will obtain coverage with new employers; others are discouraged by the high cost of the permanent insurance to which they must convert. Still others, if they are insurable at standard rates, may find coverage at a lower cost with other insurers and be able to purchase supplementary coverage (such as disability benefits) that are not available under conversion policies. In addition, insurance companies have not actively encouraged group conversions because those who convert tend to be the poorer risks. Finally, since some employers are faced with conversion charges as a result of experience rating (see chapter 11), they are also unlikely to encourage conversion.

A more restrictive conversion privilege exists if an employee's coverage is terminated because the master contract is terminated for all employees or is amended to eliminate eligible classifications. Under these circumstances the employee is given a conversion right only if he or she was insured under the contract for a period of time (generally 5 years) immediately preceding the date on which coverage was terminated. In addition, the amount of insurance that can be converted is limited to the lesser of (1) $2,000 or (2) the amount of the employee's life insurance under the contract at the date of termination reduced by any amount of life insurance for which the employee becomes eligible under any group life insurance policy issued or reinstated by the same or another insurance company within 31 days after such termination.

Accelerated and Living Benefits

Over the last several years many insurers have introduced an accelerated payout provision in their individual life insurance products. Under such a provision an insured is entitled to receive a portion of his or her death benefit while still living if one or more of the following events occur: (1) a terminal illness that is expected to result in death within 6 or 12 months; (2) a specified catastrophic illness, such as AIDS, a stroke, or Alzheimer's disease; and (3) the incurring of nursing home and possibly other long-term-care expenses. The categories of triggering events and the specific definitions of each vary among insurers.

Often what becomes popular in the individual marketplace starts to show up in the group insurance marketplace. Such is the case with accelerated benefits, but the number of insurers offering these benefits is still small.

Most group insurers allow accelerated benefits for terminal illnesses only. About half of these insurers use a life expectancy of 6 months or less; the other half use a life expectancy of 12 months or less. In either case the life expectancy must be certified by a doctor.

The amount of the accelerated benefit is expressed as a percentage of the basic life insurance coverage and may range from 25 percent to 100 percent. In addition, most insurers limit the maximum benefit to a specified dollar amount that may vary from $25,000 to $250,000. Any amount not accelerated is paid to the beneficiary upon the insured's death.

There are no limitations on how the accelerated benefit can be used. It might be used to pay medical expenses and nursing home care not covered by other insurance, or it could even be used to prepay funeral expenses.

Most insurers make a charge for an accelerated benefit, most commonly in the form of an additional premium that may be as high as 7 to 8 percent of the basic group life insurance premium. Instead of increasing the premium, a few insurers charge the insured by reducing the accelerated benefit by an amount equal to the interest that could have been earned on the money over the next 6 or 12 months.

ADDED COVERAGES

Group term insurance contracts often provide additional insurance benefits through the use of riders. These benefits are also forms of group term insurance and consist of (1) supplemental life insurance, (2) accidental death and dismemberment insurance, (3) survivor income benefit insurance, and (4) dependent life insurance. These added benefits may be provided for all employees insured under the basic group term contract or may be limited to certain classes of employees. With the exception of dependent life insurance these coverages may also be written as separate contracts.

Supplemental Life Insurance

The majority of group life insurance plans enable all or certain classes of employees to purchase additional amounts of life insurance. Generally the employer will provide a basic amount of life insurance to all eligible employees on a noncontributory basis. This is commonly a flat amount of coverage or a multiple of annual earnings. The supplemental coverage is contributory and may be either incorporated into the basic group life insurance contract or contained in a separate contract. The latter method tends to be more common when the supplemental coverage is available to only a select group of employees. Although the employee may pay the entire cost of the supplemental coverage, either state laws that require employer contributions or insurance company underwriting practices will often result in the employer's paying a portion of the cost.

The amount of supplemental coverage available will be specified in a benefit schedule. Under some plans an employee must purchase the full amount of coverage; under other plans an employee may purchase a portion of the coverage. The following are two examples of benefit schedules for a basic-plus-supplemental life insurance plan:

Type of Coverage	Amount of Life Insurance
Basic insurance	$10,000
Supplemental insurance	20,000

Type of Coverage	Amount of Life Insurance
Basic insurance	1 times salary
Supplemental insurance	1/2, 1, 1 1/2, or 2 times salary, subject to a maximum (including basic insurance) of $100,000

Giving employees the right to choose their benefit amounts leads to adverse selection. As a result, more stringent underwriting requirements are usually associated with supplemental coverage. These often include requiring individual evidence of insurability, except possibly when the additional amount of coverage is modest. In addition, higher rates may be charged for the supplemental insurance than for the basic coverage.

Accidental Death and Dismemberment Insurance

Many group life insurance contracts contain an accidental death and dismemberment provision that gives additional benefits if an employee dies accidentally or suffers certain types of injuries. Traditionally this group coverage was available only as a rider to a group life insurance contract. Now, however, it is common to find these benefits provided through separate group insurance contracts in which coverage is usually contributory on the part of employees. Such contracts are referred to as voluntary accidental death and dismemberment insurance.

Traditional Coverage

Under the traditional form of accidental death and dismemberment insurance an employee eligible for group life insurance coverage (and electing the life insurance coverage if it is contributory) will automatically have the accidental death and dismemberment coverage if it has been added by the employer. Under the typical accidental death and dismemberment rider the insurance company will pay an additional amount of insurance that is equal to the amount of coverage under the basic group life insurance contract (referred to as the principal sum) if an employee dies as a result of accidental bodily injuries while he or she is covered under the policy. It is specified that death must occur within 90 days following the date that injuries are sustained but some courts have ruled this time period to be invalid and have required insurance companies to pay claims when longer periods have been involved. In addition to an accidental death benefit the following benefit schedule is provided for certain specific types of injuries:

Type of Injury	Benefit Amount
Loss of (including loss of use of):	
Both hands or both feet	The principal sum
The sight of both eyes	The principal sum
One hand and sight of one eye	The principal sum
One foot and sight of one eye	The principal sum
One foot and one hand	The principal sum
One hand	One-half the principal sum
One foot	One-half the principal sum
The sight of one eye	One-half the principal sum

In some cases the accidental death and dismemberment rider is written to provide the same benefits for any accident covered under the contract. However, it is not unusual to have a higher level of benefits for accidents that occur while the employee is traveling on business for the employer. These larger travel benefits may apply to death benefits only. They may also be limited to accidents that occur while the employee is occupying (or entering, alighting from, or struck by) a public conveyance and possibly a company-owned or personally owned vehicle. The following is an example of a benefit schedule reflecting some of these variations:

Type of Loss	Benefit Amount
Death while traveling on business when occupying, boarding, alighting from, or struck by any motor vehicle, airplane, or other conveyance, including company-owned or personally owned vehicles	3 times the principal sum
Death at all other times	2 times the principal sum
Dismemberment	Up to the principal sum (as shown in the previous schedule)

Death benefits are paid in accordance with the beneficiary provision of the group life insurance contract, and dismemberment benefits are paid to the employee. Coverage is usually written to cover both occupational and nonoccupational accidents. However, when employees are in hazardous occupations, coverage may apply only to nonoccupational accidents, in which case employees would still have workers' compensation coverage for any occupational accidents.

Coverage is generally not subject to a conversion privilege. When life insurance coverage continues after retirement, accidental death and dismemberment benefits normally cease. Like the life insurance coverage, however, it may be continued during temporary periods of unemployment. In contrast to the group term insurance policy to which it is attached, group accidental death and dismemberment insurance contains some exclusions. These include losses resulting from

- suicide at any time (It is interesting to note that, except for a few multiple-employer trusts, group term insurance does not contain a suicide provision.)
- disease or bodily or mental infirmity, or medical or surgical treatment thereof
- ptomaines or any infection other than one occurring simultaneously with and through an accidental cut or wound
- war
- travel or flight in any type of aircraft as a pilot, student pilot, or officer or member of the crew (There is a trend toward eliminating this exclusion, particularly when coverage is written on large groups.)

Voluntary Coverage

The provisions of voluntary group accidental death and dismemberment insurance are practically identical to those contained in a group life insurance contract with an accidental death and dismemberment insurance rider. However, there are a few differences. Voluntary plans usually require the employee to pay the entire cost of coverage, and they virtually always provide both occupational and nonoccupational coverage. Subject to limitations, the employee may select the amount of coverage desired, with the maximum amount of coverage available tending to be larger than when coverage is provided through a rider. Another difference is the frequent use in voluntary plans of a common accident provision, whereby the amount payable by the insurance company is limited to a stipulated maximum for all employees killed or injured in any single accident. If this exceeds the sum of the benefits otherwise payable for each employee, benefits are prorated.

Survivor Income Benefit Insurance

Survivor income benefit insurance represents an attempt to more closely relate life insurance benefits to the actual needs of each employee's survivors. Instead of paying death benefits in a lump sum to a named beneficiary, benefits are paid in the form of periodic income to specified dependents who survive the employee. No death benefits are paid unless an employee has qualified survivors, and benefit payments will cease when survivors are no longer eligible. Like regular group term insurance, a survivor income benefit insurance plan may be contributory or noncontributory.

Survivor income benefit insurance plans, which have been available since the 1960s, never gained widespread acceptance. Employees without qualified survivors often view such plans as discriminatory since these employees have no life insurance coverage. Consequently survivor income benefit insurance is normally written in conjunction with a group term insurance plan that will provide a basic amount of life insurance for all eligible employees. This basic amount of life insurance will serve as a means of providing for the burial and other last expenses associated with the death of any employee. In addition, there is a feeling among employers that employees are not as appreciative of a benefit expressed as a certain amount of dollars per month as they would be of one expressed as a larger lump-sum amount. Also the final decision about what type of group life insurance coverage to buy is frequently made by an older executive. Such a person may not view survivor income benefit plans with enthusiasm since they generally provide potentially greater benefits to younger workers who tend to have younger survivors.

Eligible survivors under survivor income benefit insurance coverage generally include only the spouse and any dependent children of the employee. The spouse is typically defined as a person who has been lawfully married to the employee for at least 90 days and who is not legally separated from the employee. A spouse's eligibility to receive benefits usually ceases if the spouse remarries or reaches a certain age, such as 65. At this age it is assumed that the spouse will be eligible for benefits under social security. Some plans also make a payment of one or two years' benefits to spouses who remarry. The purpose of this "dowry payment" is to encourage the spouse to report the remarriage.

Dependent children are defined as unmarried dependent children of the employee, including stepchildren and children who have been legally adopted by the employee. Benefits to dependent children will cease upon marriage or the attainment of a certain age, such as 19. Benefits may be paid longer for unmarried children who are in school.

Under some survivor income benefit insurance plans the benefit amount is determined by the number of eligible survivors even though the entire benefit will be paid to the surviving spouse. Only if there is no surviving spouse or if the spouse later dies will the benefits be paid directly to the children. Under other plans separate benefits are made available to the surviving spouse and the dependent children. These benefits may be based on specified dollar amounts or they may be a function of the salary of the deceased employee.

Some survivor income benefit insurance plans pay a monthly benefit (either a flat amount or a percentage of salary) regardless of the number and types of survivors. In some instances a larger benefit is paid for a certain period of time following the employee's death. This transitional benefit will give the survivors a better opportunity to adjust their standard of living to a level consistent with the regular survivor income benefits. Survivor income benefits are generally substantially less than the employee's former income and are viewed as a supplement to any social security benefits for which the survivors will be eligible. In those few instances in which benefits are more generous, they are likely to be reduced by any social security benefits that will be received. The following are two examples of benefit schedules under group life insurance plans that have been supplemented with survivor income benefit insurance:

Benefit	Amount of Benefit
Basic life insurance for each employee	$25,000
Surviving spouse benefit*	10% of the employee's average monthly salary during the year prior to death
Surviving child benefit*	5% of the employee's average monthly salary during the year prior to death for each child
*Subject to a maximum family benefit of $400 per month	

Benefit	Amount of Benefit
Basic life insurance for each employee	$10,000
Transition survivor benefit for 24 months	$1,000 per month
Survivor benefit after the transition period	$ 500 per month

For regulatory purposes most states treat survivor income benefit insurance the same as group term insurance, including the requirement for a conversion provision. The amount eligible for conversion by an employee is the commuted value of the benefit payments that would be received by eligible survivors if the employee died at the time of conversion. This amount is determined by calculating the present value of potential benefits by using the mortality table and the interest rates employed by the insurance company. The present value of these benefits, which is a function of the number and ages of eligible survivors, can be substantial for an employee with young survivors.

Because of the adverse selection accompanying conversion, insurance companies have been concerned about the size of the conversion benefit. Some states allow the conversion amount to be expressed as a multiple of the potential monthly benefit. On the average this results in a lower conversion amount than if the commuted value is used. A few states also allow insurance companies to market their survivor income benefit product as an "annuity with contingencies." One advantage to having the product considered an annuity is that no conversion provision is required.

Dependent Life Insurance

Some group life insurance contracts provide insurance coverage on the lives of employees' dependents. Dependent life insurance has been viewed as a method of providing the employee with resources to meet the funeral and burial expenses associated with the death of a dependent. Consequently the employee is automatically the beneficiary. The employee also elects and pays for this coverage if it is contributory. Coverage for dependents is almost always limited to employees who are themselves covered under the group contract. Thus if an employee's coverage is contributory, the employee must elect coverage for himself or herself in order to be eligible to elect dependent coverage.

For purposes of dependent life insurance coverage, dependents are usually defined as including an employee's spouse who is not legally separated from the employee, and an employee's unmarried dependent children (including stepchildren and adopted children) who are over 14 days of age but under some specified age, commonly 19 or 21. To prevent adverse selection an employee cannot select coverage on individual dependents. Rather, if dependent coverage is selected, all dependents fitting the definition are insured. When dependent coverage is in effect for an employee, any new eligible dependents are automatically insured.

The amount of coverage for each dependent is usually quite modest. Some states limit the maximum amount of life insurance that can be written, and a few states actually prohibit writing any coverage on dependents. In addition, employer contributions used to purchase more than $2,000 of coverage on each dependent will result in income to the employee for purposes of federal taxation. However, amounts in excess of $2,000 may be purchased with employee contributions without adverse tax consequences. In some cases the same amount of coverage will be provided for all dependents; in other cases a larger amount will be provided for the spouse than for the children. It is also not unusual for the amount of coverage on children to be less until the children attain some specified age, such as 6 months. The following are examples of benefit schedules under dependent coverage:

Class	Amount of Insurance
Each dependent	$2,000

Class	Amount of Insurance
Spouse	50% of the employee's insured amount, subject to a maximum of $5,000
Dependent children: at least 14 days old but less than 6 months 6 months or older	$ 500 $1,000

A single premium applies to the dependent coverage for each employee and is independent of the number of dependents. In some cases the premium may vary, depending on the age of the employee (but not the dependents), but more commonly it is the same amount for all employees regardless of age. Dependent coverage usually contains a conversion privilege that applies only to the coverage on the spouse. However, some states require that the conversion privilege apply to the coverage on all dependents. Assignment is almost never permitted, and no waiver of premium is available if a dependent becomes disabled. However, if the basic life insurance contract contains a waiver-of-premium provision applicable to the employee, the employee's disability will sometimes result in a waiver of premium for the dependent coverage. A provision similar to the actively-at-work provision pertaining to employees is often included for dependents. It specifies that dependents will not be covered when otherwise eligible if they are confined in a hospital (except for newborn children, who are covered after 14 days). Coverage will commence when the dependent is discharged from the hospital.

TAXATION

A discussion of group term insurance is incomplete without an explanation of the tax laws affecting its use. While discussions of these laws are often limited to federal income and estate taxation, federal gift taxation and taxation by the states should also be considered.

Federal Taxation

The growth of group term insurance has been greatly influenced by the favorable tax treatment afforded it under federal tax laws. This section will discuss the effects of these tax laws on basic group term insurance and on coverages that may be added to a basic group term insurance contract. A complete explanation of the federal tax laws pertaining to group term insurance and their interpretation by the Internal Revenue Service would be lengthy and is beyond the scope of the book. Consequently this discussion and subsequent discussions of federal tax laws will only highlight these laws. The Appendix contains a summary of the relevant tax laws, as well as references to the Internal Revenue Code for those who wish to investigate the subject further.

Deductibility of Premiums

In general, employer contributions for an employee's group term insurance coverage are fully deductible to the employer as an ordinary and necessary business expense as long as the overall compensation of the employee is reasonable. The reasonableness of compensation (which includes wages, salary, and other fringe benefits) is usually only a potential issue for the owners of small businesses or the stockholder-employees of closely held corporations. Any compensation that is determined by the Internal Revenue Service to be unreasonable may not be deducted by a firm for income tax purposes. In addition, the Internal Revenue Code does not allow a firm to take an income tax deduction for contributions (1) that are made in behalf of sole proprietors or partners under any circumstances or (2) that are made in behalf of stockholders unless they are providing substantive services to the corporation. Finally, no deduction is allowed if the employer is named as beneficiary.

Contributions by any individual employee are considered payments for personal life insurance and are not deductible for income tax purposes by that employee. Thus the amount of any payroll deductions authorized by an employee for group term insurance purposes will be included in the employee's taxable income.

Income Tax Liability of Employees

In the absence of tax laws to the contrary, the amount of any compensation for which an employer receives an income tax deduction (including the payment of group insurance premiums) represents taxable income to the employee. However, Sec. 79 of the Internal Revenue Code provides favorable tax treatment to employer contributions for life insurance that qualifies as group term insurance.

Sec. 79 Requirements. In order to qualify as group term insurance under Sec. 79, life insurance must meet the following conditions:

- It must provide a death benefit excludible from federal income tax.
- It must be provided to a group of employees, defined to include all employees of an employer. If all employees are not covered, membership

must be determined on the basis of age, marital status, or factors relating to employment.

- It must be provided under a policy carried directly or indirectly by the employer. This includes (1) any policy for which the employer pays any part of the cost or (2) if the employer pays no part of the cost, any policy arranged by the employer if at least one employee is charged less than his or her cost (under Table I) and at least one other employee is charged more than his or her cost. If no employee is charged more than the Table I cost, a policy is not group term insurance for purposes of Sec. 79.

  A policy is defined to include a master contract or a group of individual policies. The term *carried indirectly* refers to those situations when the employer is not the policyowner but rather provides coverage to employees through master contracts issued to organizations such as negotiated trusteeships or multiple-employer welfare arrangements.

- The plan must be arranged in such a manner as to preclude individual selection of coverage amounts. However, it is acceptable to have alternative benefit schedules based on the amount an employee elects to contribute. Supplemental plans where an employee is given a choice, such as either 1, 1 1/2, or 2 times salary, are considered to fall within this category.

All life insurance that qualifies under Sec. 79 as group term insurance is considered to be a single plan of insurance, regardless of the number of insurance contracts used. For example, an employer might provide coverage for union employees under a negotiated trusteeship, coverage for other employees under an individual employer group insurance contract, and additional coverage for top executives under a group of individual life insurance policies. Under Sec. 79 these would all constitute a single plan. This plan must be provided for at least 10 full-time employees at some time during the calendar year. For purposes of meeting the 10-life requirement, employees who have not satisfied any required waiting periods may be counted as participants. In addition, employees who have elected not to participate are also counted as participants—but only if they would not have been required to contribute to the cost of other benefits besides group term insurance if they had participated. As will be described later, a plan with fewer than 10 full-time employees may still qualify for favorable tax treatment under Sec. 79 if more restrictive requirements are met.

Exceptions to Sec. 79. Even when all the previous requirements are met, there are some situations in which Sec. 79 does not apply. In some cases different sections of the Internal Revenue Code provide alternative tax treatment. For example, when group term insurance is issued to the trustees of a qualified pension plan and is used to provide a death benefit under the plan, the full amount of any life insurance paid for by employer contributions will result in taxable income to the employee.

There are three situations in which employer contributions for group term insurance will not result in taxable income to an employee, regardless of the amount of insurance: (1) if an employee has terminated employment because of disability, (2) if a qualified charity (as determined by the Internal Revenue Code) has been named as beneficiary for the entire year, or (3) if the employer has been named as beneficiary for the entire year.

Coverage on retired employees is subject to Sec. 79, and these persons are treated in the same manner as active employees. Thus they will have taxable income in any year in which the amount of coverage received exceeds $50,000. However, a grandfather clause to this new rule stipulates that it does not apply to group term life insurance plans (or to comparable successor plans or to plans of successor employers) in existence on January 1, 1984, for covered employees who (1) retired before 1984 or (2) were at least 55 years of age before 1984 and were employed by the employer any time during 1983. There is one exception to this grandfather clause; it does not apply to persons (either key or nonkey employees) retiring after 1986 if a plan is discriminatory. The factors that make a plan discriminatory are discussed later.

General Tax Rules. Under Sec. 79 the cost of the first $50,000 of coverage is not taxed to the employee. Since all group term insurance provided by an employer that qualifies under Sec. 79 is considered to be one plan, this exclusion applies only once to each employee. For example, an employee who has $10,000 of coverage that is provided to all employees under one policy and $75,000 of coverage provided to executives under a separate insurance policy would have a single $50,000 exclusion. The cost of coverage in excess of $50,000, less any employee contributions for the entire amount of coverage, represents taxable income to the employee. For purposes of Sec. 79 the cost of this excess coverage is determined by a government table called the Uniform Premium Table I. This table will often result in a lower cost than would be calculated using the actual premium paid by the employer for the coverage.

Uniform Premium Table I	
Age	Cost per Month per $1,000 of Coverage
29 and under	$ .08
30–34	.09
35–39	.11
40–44	.17
45–49	.29
50–54	.48
55–59	.75
60–64	1.17
65–69	2.10
70 and over	3.76

To calculate the cost of an employee's coverage for one month of protection under a group term insurance plan, the Uniform Premium Table I cost shown for the employee's age bracket (based on the employee's attained age at the end of the tax year) is multiplied by the number of thousands in excess of 50 of group term insurance on the employee. For example, if an employee aged 57 was provided with $150,000 of group term insurance, the employee's monthly cost (assuming no employee contributions) would be calculated as follows:

Coverage provided	$150,000
Less Section 79 exclusion	50,000
Amount subject to taxation	$100,000
Uniform Premium Table I monthly cost per $1,000 of coverage at age 57	$.75
Monthly cost ($.75 x 100)	$75

The monthly costs are then totaled to obtain an annual cost. Assuming no change in the amount of coverage during the year, the annual cost would be $900. Any employee contributions for the entire amount of coverage are deducted from the annual cost to determine the taxable income that must be reported by an employee. If an employee contributed $.30 per month ($3.60 per year) per $1,000 of coverage, the employee's total annual contribution for $150,000 of coverage would be $540. This reduces the amount reportable as taxable income from $900 to $360.

One final point is worthy of attention. When the Uniform Premium Table I was incorporated into the IRS regulations for Sec. 79, it resulted in favorable tax treatment for the cost of group term insurance, because the monthly costs in the table were always lower than the actual cost of coverage in the marketplace. Today group term insurance coverage can often be purchased at a lower cost than Table I rates. There are some who argue that in these instances the actual cost of coverage can be used in place of the Table I cost for determining an employee's taxable income. From the standpoint of logic and consistency with the tax laws this view makes sense. However, the regulations for Sec. 79 are very specific: only Table I costs are to be used.

Nondiscrimination Rules. Any plan that qualified as group term insurance under Sec. 79 is subject to nondiscrimination rules, and the $50,000 exclusion will not be available to key employees if a plan is discriminatory. Such a plan favors key employees in either eligibility or benefits. In addition, the value of the full amount of coverage for key employees, less their own contribution, will be considered taxable income, based on the greater of actual or Table I costs. A key employee of a firm is defined as any person who at any time during the current plan year or the preceding 4 plan years is any of the following:

- an officer of the firm who earns from the firm more than 50 percent of the Internal Revenue Code limit on the amount of benefits payable by a defined-benefit plan. This amount (50 percent of $115,641, or $57,820.50, for 1993) is indexed annually. For purposes of this rule the number of employees treated as officers is the greater of 3 or 10 percent of the firm's employees, subject to a maximum of 50. In applying the rule the following employees can be excluded: persons who are part-time, persons who are under 21, and persons with less than 6 months of service with the firm.
- one of the 10 employees owning the largest interests in the firm and having an annual compensation from the firm of more than $30,000
- a more-than-5-percent owner of the firm
- a more-than-one-percent owner of the firm who earns over $150,000 per year

- a retired employee who was a key employee when he or she retired or terminated service

Note that the definition of key employee includes not only active employees but also retired employees who were key employees at the time of retirement or separation from service.

Eligibility requirements are not discriminatory if (1) at least 70 percent of all employees are eligible, (2) at least 85 percent of all employees who are participants are not key employees, or (3) participants comprise a classification that the IRS determines is nondiscriminatory. For purposes of the 70 percent test employees with less than 3 years' service, part-time employees, and seasonal employees may be excluded. Employees covered by collective-bargaining agreements may also be excluded if plan benefits were the subject of good-faith bargaining.

Benefits are not discriminatory if neither the type nor amount of benefits discriminates in favor of key employees. It is permissible to base benefits on a uniform percentage of salary.

One issue that arose after the passage of the nondiscrimination rules in 1984 was whether they applied separately to active and to retired employees. A technical correction in the Tax Reform Act of 1986 clarified the issue by stating that the rules do apply separately to the extent provided in IRS regulations. However, such regulations have yet to be issued.

Groups with Fewer than 10 Full-time Employees. A group insurance plan that covers fewer than 10 employees must satisfy an additional set of requirements before it is eligible for favorable tax treatment under Sec. 79. These rules predated the general nondiscrimination rules previously described, and it was assumed that the under-10 rules would be abolished when the new rules were adopted. However, that was not done, so smaller groups are subject to two separate and somewhat overlapping sets of rules. It should again be noted that Sec. 79 applies to an employer's overall plan of group insurance, not to separate group insurance contracts. For example, an employer providing group insurance coverage for its 50 hourly employees under one group insurance contract and for its 6 executives under a separate contract is considered to have a single plan covering 56 employees and thus is exempt from the under-10 requirements. While the stated purpose of the under-10 requirements is to preclude individual selection, their effect is to prevent the group insurance plan from discriminating in favor of the owners or stockholder-employees of small businesses.

With some exceptions plans covering fewer than 10 employees must provide coverage for all full-time employees. For purposes of this requirement employees who are not customarily employed for more than 20 hours in any one week or 5 months in any calendar year are considered part-time employees. It is permissible to exclude full-time employees from coverage under the following circumstances:

- The employee has reached 65.
- The employee has not satisfied the waiting period under the plan. However, the waiting period may not exceed 6 months.
- The employee has elected not to participate in the plan, but only if the employee would not have been required to contribute to the cost of other benefits besides group term life insurance if he or she had participated.

- The employee has not satisfied the evidence of insurability required under the plan. An employee's eligibility for insurance (or the amount of insurance on the employee's life) may be subject to evidence of insurability. However, this evidence of insurability must be determined solely on the basis of a medical questionnaire completed by the employee and not by a medical examination.

The amount of coverage must be a flat amount, a uniform percentage of salary, or an amount based on different employee classifications. These employee classifications, which are referred to as coverage brackets in Sec. 79, may be determined in the manner described earlier in this chapter in the section on benefit schedules. The amount of coverage provided to each employee in any classification may be no greater than 2 1/2 times the amount of coverage provided to each employee in the next lower classification. In addition, each employee in the lowest classification must be provided with an amount of coverage that is equal to at least 10 percent of the amount provided to each employee in the highest classification. There must also be a reasonable expectation that there will be at least one employee in each classification. The following benefit schedule would be unacceptable for two reasons. First, the amount of coverage provided for the hourly employees is only 5 percent of the amount of coverage provided for the president. Second, the amount of coverage on the supervisor is more than 2 1/2 times the amount of coverage provided for the hourly employees.

Classification	Amount of Coverage
President	$100,000
Supervisor	40,000
Hourly employees	5,000

The following benefit schedule, however, would be acceptable:

Classification	Amount of Coverage
President	$100,000
Supervisor	40,000
Hourly employees	20,000

If a group insurance plan that covers fewer than 10 employees does not qualify for favorable tax treatment under Sec. 79, any premiums paid by the employer for such coverage will represent taxable income to the employees. The employer, however, will still receive an income tax deduction for any premiums paid in behalf of the employees as long as overall compensation is reasonable.

Taxation of Proceeds

In most instances the death proceeds under a group term insurance contract do not result in any taxable income to the beneficiary if they are paid in a lump sum. If the proceeds are payable in installments over more than one taxable year of the beneficiary, only the interest earnings attributable to the proceeds will be included in the beneficiary's income for tax purposes.

Under certain circumstances the proceeds are not exempt from income taxation if the coverage was transferred (either in whole or in part) for a valuable consideration. Such a situation will arise when the stockholder-employees of a corporation name each other as beneficiaries under their group term insurance coverage as a method of funding a buy-sell agreement. The mutual agreement to name each other as beneficiaries is the valuable consideration. Under these circumstances any proceeds paid to a beneficiary constitutes ordinary income to the extent that the proceeds exceed the beneficiary's tax basis, as determined by the Internal Revenue Code.

In many cases benefits paid by an employer to employees or their beneficiaries from the firm's assets receive the same tax treatment as benefits provided under an insurance contract. This is not true for death benefits. If they are provided other than through an insurance contract, the amount of the proceeds in excess of $5,000 will represent taxable income to the beneficiary. For this reason employers are less likely to use alternative funding arrangements for death benefits than for disability and medical expense benefits.

Proceeds of a group term insurance contract, even if paid to a named beneficiary, are included in an employees gross estate for federal estate tax purposes as long as the employee possessed incidents of ownership in the coverage at the time of death. However, no estate tax is levied on any amounts, including life insurance proceeds, left to a surviving spouse. In addition, taxable estates of $600,000 or less are generally free of estate taxation regardless of the beneficiary.

When an estate would otherwise be subject to estate taxation, an employee may remove the proceeds of group term insurance from his or her taxable estate by absolutely assigning all incidents of ownership to another person, usually the beneficiary of the coverage. Incidents of ownership include the right to change the beneficiary, to terminate coverage, to assign coverage, or to exercise the conversion privilege. For this favorable treatment, however, the Internal Revenue Code requires that such an assignment be permissible under both the group term insurance master contract and the laws of the state having jurisdiction. The absolute assignment is usually in the form of a gift, which is not without its own tax implications. The amount of insurance is considered a gift made each year by the employee to the person to whom the absolute assignment was granted. Consequently if the value of the gift is of sufficient size, federal gift taxes will be payable. Since the Internal Revenue Code and the Internal Revenue Service regulations are silent on the specific gift tax consequences of assigned group term insurance, there is disagreement about whether the gift should be valued at Table I costs or at the actual premium for the coverage.

The assignment of group term life insurance also results in the inclusion of some values in the employee's estate. If the employee dies within 3 years of making the assignment, the full amount of the proceeds will be included in the employee's estate. If death occurs more than 3 years after the assignment is made, only the premiums paid within the 3 years prior to death will be included in the employee's taxable estate. In the past a problem arose if the employer changed group insurance carriers, thus requiring the employee to make a new assignment and again be subject to the 3-year time limit. However, the Internal Revenue Service now considers this type of situation to be a continuation of the original assignment as long as the amount and provisions of the new coverage are essentially the same as those of the old coverage.

There has been some uncertainty about the taxation of accelerated benefits from a group term insurance policy. In the past such a benefit has not met the definition of a life insurance death benefit or any other income-tax-free benefit from a life insurance policy. However, at the time this book was being written, the IRS had just issued proposed regulations to clarify the situation. The regulations are subject to revision as a result of pubic comments, but it appears that accelerated benefits will be income tax free if made as the result of a terminal illness that is expected to result in death within 12 months of payment.

Treatment of Added Coverages

Supplemental life insurance can be written as either a separate contract or as part of the contract providing basic group term life insurance coverage. If it is a separate contract and if the supplemental group life insurance meets the conditions of qualifying as group term insurance under Sec. 79, the amount of coverage provided is added to all other group term insurance for purposes of calculating the Uniform Premium Table I cost. Any premiums paid by the employee for the supplemental coverage are included in the deduction used to determine the final taxable income. In all other ways supplemental life insurance is treated the same as group term insurance.

Many separate supplemental contracts are noncontributory, and the cost for each employee's coverage does not exceed Table I cost. In this case the supplemental contract does not qualify as group term life insurance under Sec. 79. As a result the value of the coverage is not included in an employee's income.

When supplemental life insurance coverage is written in conjunction with a basic group life insurance plan, employers have the option of treating the supplemental coverage as a separate policy of insurance as long as the premiums are properly allocated among the two portions of the coverage. There is no advantage in treating the supplemental coverage as a separate policy if it would still qualify by itself as group term insurance under Sec. 79. However, this election will minimize taxable income to employees if the cost of the supplemental coverage is paid totally by the employees and all employees are charged rates at or below Table I rates.

Premiums paid for accidental death and dismemberment insurance are considered to be health insurance premiums rather than group term insurance premiums. However, these are also deductible to the employer as an ordinary and necessary business expense the same as for group term insurance. Benefits paid to an employee under the dismemberment portion of the coverage are treated as benefits received under a health insurance contract and are received income tax free. Death benefits received under the coverage are treated like death benefits received under group term life insurance.

For federal tax purposes, survivor income benefit insurance is considered to be a group term insurance coverage. Under Sec. 79, the amount of the benefit is considered to be the commuted value of benefit payments that would have been received by eligible survivors if the employee had died during the year. This amount normally is provided annually by the insurance company. A commuted value is also used for estate tax purposes. In all other respects survivor income benefit insurance is treated the same as group term insurance.

Employer contributions for dependent life insurance coverage are fully deductible by the employer as an ordinary and necessary business expense if overall compensation of the employee is reasonable. Employer contributions do not result in taxable income to an employee as long as the value of the benefit is *de minimis*. This means that the value is so small that it is administratively impractical for the employer to account for the cost on a per-person basis. Dependent coverage of $2,000 or less on any person falls into this category. The Internal Revenue Service considers amounts of coverage in excess of $2,000 on any dependent to be more than *de minimis*. If more than $2,000 of coverage is provided for any dependent from employer contributions, the cost of the entire amount of coverage for that dependent (as determined by Uniform Premium Table I rates) will be considered taxable income to the employee.

Death benefits will be free of income taxation and will not be included in the taxable estate of the dependent for estate tax purposes.

State Taxation

In most instances state tax laws affecting group term insurance are similar to the federal laws. However, two major differences do exist. In most states the payment of group term insurance premiums by the employer will not result in any taxable income to the employee, even if the amount of coverage exceeds $50,000. In addition, death proceeds receive favorable tax treatment under the estate and inheritance tax laws of most states. Generally the proceeds are at least partially, if not totally, exempt from such taxation.

5

Group Life Insurance:
Postretirement Coverage

Group term insurance plans were traditionally designed to provide employees with preretirement life insurance coverage. At retirement an employee was then faced with the decision of whether to let coverage terminate or to convert to an individual policy at an extremely high premium rate. In recent years, however, an increasing number of group life insurance plans have been designed to provide postretirement as well as preretirement life insurance coverage. In some cases this has been accomplished by continuing group term insurance coverage, often at a reduced amount, after retirement. In other cases it has been done through life insurance that provides permanent benefits that have been funded during the working years of employees.

The popularity of various approaches for providing postretirement life insurance coverage has changed over time, primarily because of changes in tax laws. The first part of this chapter discusses three approaches that are currently and commonly used:

- current revenue funding to continue group term insurance coverage
- group universal life insurance
- group term carve-outs

The last part of the chapter is devoted to three older types of products that were once very popular but are not widely used in new plans. However, each of these products is still used to some degree with existing plans. These products are

- group paid-up insurance
- group ordinary insurance
- retired lives reserves

CURRENT REVENUE FUNDING TO CONTINUE GROUP TERM INSURANCE

Most postretirement life insurance coverage consists of the continuation of group term insurance. This requires the employer to make two important decisions: the amount of coverage to be continued and the method of paying the cost of the continued coverage. Although the full amount of coverage prior to retirement may be continued, the high cost of group term insurance coverage for older employees frequently results in a reduction in the amount of coverage. In some cases employees are provided with a flat amount of coverage (such as $2,000 or $5,000); in other cases employees are provided with a percentage (such as 50 percent) of the amount of coverage they had on the date of retirement.

The cost of providing postretirement life insurance is usually paid from current revenue, with each periodic premium the insurance company receives based on the lives of all employees covered, both active and retired. Since retired employees have no salary or wages from which payroll deductions can be made, most postretirement life insurance coverage is noncontributory.

The tax implications of providing postretirement group term insurance on a current-revenue basis are the same for both the employer and the employee as those discussed in chapter 4.

It was once popular, particularly for smaller employers, to prefund postretirement coverage through retired lives reserves, which are discussed later in this chapter. However, adverse changes in tax laws have significantly reduced this popularity.

GROUP UNIVERSAL LIFE INSURANCE

Beginning in the mid-1980s many of the large writers of group insurance started to sell group universal life insurance, a trend that has been greeted with much interest by insurers, employers, and even employees. This interest seems to stem primarily from five factors:

- the phenomenal success of universal life in the individual marketplace. Introduced in the 1970s, universal life insurance now accounts for about 25 percent of newly written individual life insurance premiums.
- tax legislation that resulted in employer-provided term life insurance in excess of $50,000 becoming taxable after retirement.
- the clarification of the tax treatment of universal life insurance. For the first few years after the introduction of universal life insurance, there was concern that the IRS would not grant it the same favorable tax treatment that was granted to traditional cash value life insurance policies. There was speculation that the interest paid on the cash value might become subject to taxation and also that the death benefit would be considered taxable income to the beneficiary. For the most part these fears have been laid to rest by tax legislation as long as a universal life insurance policy meets certain prescribed guidelines. Therefore the cash value of a universal life insurance policy accumulates tax free, and death benefits are free of income taxation.
- the interest of employers to contain employee benefit costs. Little needs to be said about the attempts of employers to minimize the costs of their employee benefit plans. Group universal life insurance plans can make life insurance available to employees with little cost to the employer.
- less favorable tax treatment for two formerly popular products for prefunding postretirement life insurance—Sec. 79 plans and retired lives reserves.

Group universal life insurance products are being marketed primarily as supplemental life insurance plans—either to replace existing supplemental group term life insurance plans or as additional supplemental plans. Some insurers are selling them as a way of providing the basic life insurance plan of the employee as well. Marketing efforts are touting group universal life insurance as having the following advantages to the employer:

- no direct cost other than those associated with payroll deductions and possibly enrollment, since the entire premium cost is borne by the employee. In this sense group universal life insurance plans are much like mass-marketed insurance plans (described in chapter 9).
- no ERISA filing and reporting requirement as long as the master contract is issued to a trust and as long as there are no employer contributions for the cost of coverage. The current products are marketed through multiple-employer trusts, with the trust being the policyowner.
- the ability of employees to continue coverage into retirement, alleviating pressure for the employer to provide postretirement life insurance benefits.

The following advantages are being claimed for employees:

- the availability of a popular life insurance product at group rates
- the opportunity to continue insurance coverage after retirement, possibly without any postretirement contributions
- flexibility in designing coverage to best meet the needs of the individual employee

The current plans being marketed are still evolving, and differences do exist among the plans being offered by competing insurance companies. Because of the flexibility given policyholders, the administrative aspects of a group universal plan are formidable, and most insurers originally designed their plans only for employers with a large number of employees, usually at least 1,000. However, most insurers that write the product now make it available for as few as 100 lives.

Skeptics, including employees of some insurance companies offering group universal life, wonder if the administrative aspects can be accomplished in such a manner that it can be offered at a cost that is significantly lower than coverage in the individual marketplace. In raising this question, they point out the administrative problems and costs that have arisen when universal life insurance has been included in mass-marketed individual insurance plans, as well as the highly competitive market for individual universal life insurance that has resulted in rates with extremely low margins for contributions to surplus. These drawbacks, coupled with the lack of employer contributions, make the potential for savings to employees through the group insurance approach less than for many other types of insurance. Other critics point out that the popularity of universal life insurance in general has decreased as interest rates have dropped over the last few years, and they wonder how successful universal life will be if interest rates drop further. However, plans that are installed are usually well received by employees, and participation generally meets or exceeds expectations.

General Nature

Group universal life insurance is a flexible-premium policy that, unlike traditional cash value life insurance, divides the pure insurance protection and the cash value accumulation into separate and distinct components. The employee is required to pay a specified initial premium, from which a charge is subtracted for one month's mortality. This mortality charge in effect is used to purchase the required amount of pure or term insurance (often referred to as the *amount at risk)* at a cost based on the insured's current age. Under some policies an additional deduction is made for expenses. The balance of the initial premium becomes the initial cash value of the policy, which, when credited with interest, becomes the cash value at the end of the period. The process continues in succeeding periods. New premiums are added to the cash value, charges are made for expenses and mortality, and interest is credited to the remaining cash value. Employees receive periodic disclosure statements showing all charges made for the period, as well as any interest earnings.

Group universal life insurance offers an employee considerable flexibility to meet several life-cycle financial needs with a single type of insurance coverage. The death benefit can be increased because of marriage, the birth of a child, or an increase in income. The death benefit can be reduced later when the need for life insurance decreases. Cash withdrawals can be made for the down payment on a home or to pay college tuition. Premium payments can be reduced during those periods when a young family has pressing financial needs. As financial circumstances improve, premiums can be increased so that an adequate retirement fund can be accumulated. The usual settlement options found in traditional cash value life insurance are available, so an employee can periodically elect to liquidate the cash accumulation as a source of retirement income.

Types of Group Universal Products

Two approaches have been used in designing group universal life insurance products. Under the first approach there is a single group universal life insurance plan. An employee who wants only term insurance can pay a premium equal to the mortality and expense charges so that there is no accumulation of cash values. Naturally an employee who wants to accumulate cash values must pay a larger premium.

Under the second approach there are actually two group insurance plans—a term insurance plan and a universal life insurance plan. An employee who wants only term insurance contributes to the term insurance plan, and an employee who wants only universal life insurance contributes to the universal life insurance plan. With this approach an employee purchasing universal life insurance must make premium payments that are sufficient to generate a cash value accumulation. Initially the employee may be required to make minimum premium payments, such as two or three times the cost of the pure insurance. If an employee who has only the term insurance coverage later wants to switch to universal life insurance coverage, the group term insurance certificate is cancelled, and the employee is issued a new certificate under the universal life insurance plan. An employee can also withdraw his or her cash accumulation under the universal life insurance plan and switch to the term insurance plan or can even have coverage under both plans. Typically an employee is eligible to purchase a maximum aggregate amount of coverage under the two plans. For example, if this amount is three times annual salary, the employee could purchase term insurance equal to two times salary and universal life insurance that has a pure insurance amount equal to one times salary.

Underwriting

Insurance companies that write group universal life insurance have underwriting standards concerning group size, the amounts of coverage available, and insurability.

Currently most group universal life insurance products are being limited primarily to employers who have at least 100 or 200 employees. However, a few insurers write coverage for even smaller groups. Some insurance companies also have an employee percentage-participation requirement, such as 20 or 25 percent, that must be satisfied before a group can be installed. Other insurance companies feel their marketing approach is designed so that adequate participation will result and therefore have no participation requirements.

Employees can generally elect amounts of pure insurance equal to varying multiples of their salaries, which typically start at one-half or one and range as high as three or five. There may be a minimum amount of coverage that must be purchased, such as $10,000. The maximum multiple an insurance company will offer is influenced by factors such as the size of the group, the amount of insurance provided under the employer's basic employer-pay-all group term insurance plan, and the percentage participation in the plan. In general the rules regarding the amounts of coverage are the same as those that have been traditionally applied to supplemental group term life insurance plans. The initial premium, which is a function of an employee's age and death benefit, is frequently designed to accumulate a cash value at age 65 equal to approximately 20 percent of the total death benefit.

Other approaches for determining the death benefit may be used, depending on insurance company practices and employer desires. Under some plans employees may elect specific amounts of insurance, such as $25,000, $50,000, or $100,000. Again an employee's age and the death benefit selected determine the premium. Some plans allow an employee to select the premium he or she wants to pay. The amount of the premium and the employee's age then automatically determine the amount of the death benefit.

The extent to which evidence of insurability is required of individual employees is also similar to that found under most supplemental group term life insurance plans. When an employee is initially eligible, coverage is usually issued on a guaranteed basis up to specified limits, which again are influenced by the size of the group, the amount of coverage provided under the employer's basic group term insurance plan, and the degree of participation in the plan. If an employee chooses a larger death benefit, simplified underwriting is used up to a second amount, after which regular underwriting is used. Guaranteed issue is often unavailable for small groups, in which case underwriting on the basis of a simplified questionnaire is used up to a specific amount of death benefit, after which regular underwriting is used.

With some exceptions future increases in the amount of pure insurance are subject to evidence of insurability. These exceptions include additional amounts resulting from salary increases as long as the total amount of coverage remains within the guaranteed issue limit. A few insurance companies also allow additional purchases without evidence of insurability when certain events occur, such as marriage or the birth of a child.

The Death Benefit

The policyowner under an individual group universal life insurance policy typically has a choice of two death benefit options. Option A provides a level death benefit in the early policy years. As the cash value increases, the amount of pure insurance decreases so that the total amount paid to a beneficiary upon the insured's death remains constant. Without any provision to the contrary, the cash value would eventually approach the amount of the total death benefit. To prevent this from occurring, and also to keep the policy from failing to qualify as a life insurance policy under existing tax regulations, it is provided that the amount of pure insurance will not decrease further once the cash value reaches a predetermined level. Thereafter the total death benefit will increase unless the cash value decreases. Figure 5-1 graphically demonstrates option A.

FIGURE 5-1
Universal Life Insurance—Death Benefit Option A

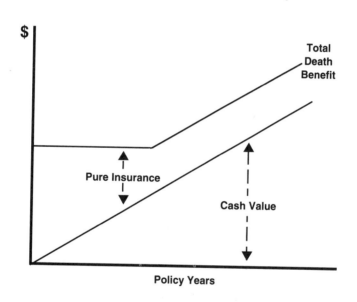

Under option B the amount of pure insurance is constant, and the death benefit increases each period by the change in the policy cash value. This is shown graphically in figure 5-2.

Under group universal life insurance products an employee usually has only one death benefit option available, and whether it is option A or option B depends on which one has been selected by the employer. In general there seems to be feeling that the availability of both options makes a plan more difficult to explain to employees and more costly to administer. Most employers have selected option B, which is generally more easily marketed to employees since the increasing total death benefit is a visible sign of any increase in their cash value or "investment." As a result several insurers now make only option B available with their group products.

FIGURE 5-2
Universal Life Insurance—Death Benefit Opion B

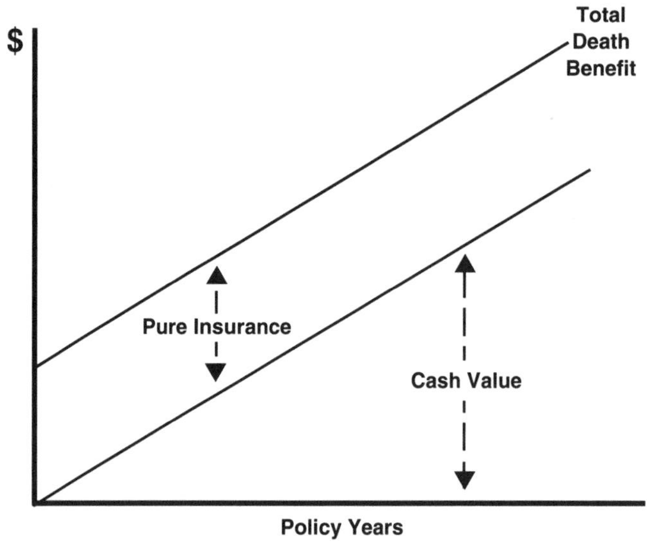

Universal life insurance products give the insured the right to increase or decrease the death benefit from the level originally selected as circumstances change. For example, the policyowner might have initially selected a pure death benefit of $100,000 under option B. Because of the birth of a child, this might be increased to $150,000. Increases, but not decreases, generally require that the insured provide evidence of insurability.

Mortality Charges

Most products have a guaranteed mortality charge for 3 years, after which the mortality charge will be based on the experience of each particular group. As with experience rating in general, the credibility given to a group's actual experience will be greater for larger groups. Most insurance companies guarantee that any future increases in the mortality charge will not exceed a stated maximum.

The products designed for small groups typically use pooled rates that apply to all groups insured through a particular trust. Therefore the mortality charge for any employer will vary, not with the employer's overall experience but rather with the overall experience of the trust.

Expense Charges

Probably the greatest variations among group life insurance products occur in the expense charges that are levied. Typically a percentage of each premium, such as 2 percent, is deducted for expenses. In addition, there is a flat monthly charge, normally ranging from $1 to $3, to maintain the accumulation account. Some insurance companies levy this charge against all certificate holders, even those who are contributing only enough to have the pure insurance coverage. Other insurance companies levy the charge only against those accounts that have a positive cash value accumulation. A few insurance companies also load their mortality charges for expenses. Finally many companies levy a transaction charge, such as $25, that often applies to withdrawals in early policy years. A transaction charge may also apply to policy loans and additional lump-sum contributions. In evaluating the expense charges of different insurers, one should remember that an insurer with a lower-than-average charge may be subtly compensating for this charge by having a higher mortality charge or crediting a lower interest rate to cash value accumulations than would otherwise be paid.

Interest Rates

Most insurance companies guarantee that the initial interest rate credited to cash value accumulations will be in effect for one year. After that time the rate is typically adjusted quarterly or semiannually but cannot be below some contractual minimum such as 4 or 4.5 percent. The interest rate credited is usually determined on a discretionary basis but is influenced by the insurance company's investment income and competitive factors. However, some insurers stipulate that it will be linked to some money market instrument, such as 3-month Treasury bills. In general the same interest is credited to all groups that an insurance company has underwritten.

Several insurance companies are exploring the possibility of establishing separate accounts for group universal life insurance accumulations and allowing individual employees to direct the types of assets in which their accumulations are invested. Such a change will give employees much of the investment flexibility that is currently available under many 401(k) plans.

Premium Adjustments

Employees are allowed considerable flexibility in the amount and timing of premium payments. Premiums can be raised or lowered and even suspended. In the latter case the contract will terminate if an employee's cash value accumulation is inadequate to pay current mortality and expense charges. Of course premium payments could be reinstated to prevent this from happening. Additional lump-sum contributions may also be made to the accumulation account.

Two restrictions are placed on premium adjustments. First, the premium payment cannot be such that the size of the cash value accumulation becomes so large in relationship to the pure protection that an employee's coverage fails to qualify as a policy of insurance under IRS regulations. Second, since changes in premium payments through payroll deductions are costly to administer, many employers limit the frequency with which adjustments are allowed.

Loans and Withdrawals

Employees are allowed to make loans and withdrawals from their accumulated cash values, but for administrative reasons the frequency of loans and withdrawals may be limited. There are also minimum loan and withdrawal amounts, such as $250 or $500. In addition, an employee is usually required to leave a minimum balance in the cash value account sufficient to pay mortality and expenses charges for some time period, possibly as long as one year. If an option A death benefit is in effect, the amount of the pure insurance is increased by the amount of the loan or withdrawal so that the total death benefit remains the same. With an option B death benefit the amount of the total death benefit is decreased.

The interest rate charged on policy loans is usually pegged to some index, such as Moody's composite bond yield. In addition, the interest rate credited to an amount of the cash value equal to the policy loan is reduced. This reduced interest rate may be the guaranteed policy minimum or may also be based on some index, such as 2 percent less than Moody's composite bond yield.

An employee can withdraw his or her entire cash value accumulation and terminate coverage. Total withdrawals are subject to a surrender charge during early policy years. The charge decreases with policy duration and is usually in addition to any transaction charge that might also be levied.

Dependent Coverage

Most products allow an employee to purchase a rider that provides term insurance coverage on his or her spouse and children. For example, one insurance company allows an employee to elect spousal coverage of $10,000 to $50,000 in $10,000 increments and coverage on children in the amount of either $5,000 or $10,000. Other insurers make varying amounts available.

Some insurance companies allow separate universal life insurance coverage to be elected, but usually only for the spouse. In such cases the coverage is provided under a separate group insurance certificate rather than a rider.

Accidental Death and Waiver of Premium

A group universal life insurance plan may provide accidental death benefits and a disability waiver of premium. These benefits are not optional for each employee; rather they are part of the coverage only if the employer has elected to include them in the plan. When a waiver of premium is included, all that is waived in case of disability is the portion of the premium necessary to pay the cost of the pure insurance protection for the employee and any dependents.

Employee Options at Retirement and Termination

Several situations may arise in which an employee is no longer actively working, or a group universal plan might be terminated by the employer.

Several options are available to the retiring employee. First, the employee can continue the group insurance coverage like an active employee. However, if premium payments are continued, the employee will be billed by the insurance company, probably on a quarterly basis. Because of the direct billing, the employee may also be subject to a higher monthly expense charge. Second, the employee can terminate the coverage and completely withdraw his or her accumulated cash value. Third, the employee can elect one of the policy settlement options for the liquidation of the cash value in the form of annuity income. Finally, some insurers allow the retiring employee to decrease the amount of pure insurance so that the cash value will be adequate to keep the policy in force without any more premium payments. In effect the employee then has a paid-up policy.

The same options are generally available to an employee who terminates employment prior to retirement. In contrast to most other types of group insurance arrangements, the continuation of coverage does not involve a conversion and the accompanying conversion charge; rather the employee usually remains in the same group. This ability to continue group coverage after termination of employment is commonly referred to as portability. If former employees who continue coverage have higher mortality rates, this will be reflected in the mortality charge for the entire group. However, at least one insurer places terminated employees into a separate group consisting of terminated employees from all plans. These persons will be subject to a mortality charge based solely on the experience of this group. Thus any higher mortality due to adverse selection will not be shared by the actively working employees.

If the employer terminates the group insurance arrangement, some insurance companies keep the group in force on a direct-bill basis, even if the coverage has been replaced with another insurer. Other insurance companies continue the group coverage only if the employer has not replaced the plan. If replacement occurs, the insurance company terminates the pure insurance amount and either gives the cash value to participants or transfers it to the trustee of the new plan.

Enrollment and Administration

Variations exist in the method by which employees are enrolled in group universal life insurance plans. Some early plans used agents who were compensated in the form of commissions or fees, but several insurance companies have dropped this practice. The actual enrollment is typically done by the employer with materials provided by the insurance company. However, salaried or commissioned representatives of the insurer usually meet with the employees in group meetings to explain the plan.

The employer's main administrative function is to process the payroll deductions associated with a plan. As previously mentioned, employee flexibility may be somewhat limited to minimize the costs of numerous changes in payroll deductions.

Other administrative functions are performed by the insurance company or a third-party administrator. These functions included providing employees with annual statements about their transactions and cash value accumulation under the plan. Toll-free telephone lines are often maintained to provide information and advice to employees.

Taxation

Group universal life insurance products are not designed to be policies of insurance under Sec. 79. In addition, each employee pays the full cost of his or her coverage. Therefore the tax treatment is the same to employees as if they had purchased a universal life insurance policy in the individual insurance marketplace.

GROUP TERM CARVE-OUTS

Prior to 1984 employees had no taxable income if they were provided with postretirement coverage under a group term life insurance plan. At that time coverage in excess of $50,000 became subject to the imputed income rules of Sec. 79, based on Table I costs. In 1989 Table I was revised, and these costs were raised significantly for persons aged 65 and older. As a result employers have increasingly turned to group term carve-outs. While carve-outs can be used for any employee with more than $50,000 of group term coverage, they typically apply only to shareholders and key executives.

Bonus Plans

In the simplest sense a carve-out works like this: The employer decides which employees will be covered under the carve-out plan and limits coverage for these employees under its group term plan to the $50,000 that can be received tax free. The employer then gives any premium savings to each "carved-out" employee in the form of a bonus, which is fully deductible to the employer as long as the employee's overall compensation is reasonable. The bonus amounts will be either paid directly to an insurance company for individual coverage on the lives of the participants in the carve-out plan or in some cases provided to the employees as compensation to pay life insurance premiums. In most cases the coverage purchased under the carve-out plan will be some form of permanent life insurance protection that will provide paid-up coverage at retirement. Traditional whole life insurance, universal life insurance, and variable life insurance are all viable alternatives. At retirement the employee can either keep the coverage in force (possibly at a reduced paid-up amount) or surrender the policy for its cash value.

The popularity of carve-out plans lies in the fact that a comparable or greater amount of life insurance coverage can often be provided to participants at a lower cost than if the participants had received all their coverage under the group term life insurance plan. Since the carve-out plan does not qualify as a plan of insurance under Sec. 79, each participant will have taxable income in the amount of the bonus. However, this income will be offset by the absence of any imputed income from Table I.

In reality carve-out plans are more complex. In many cases the cost of permanent coverage for an employee may actually be greater than the cost of group term coverage during the working years. However, this high cost is often more than compensated for by the cash value at retirement and the absence of imputed income after retirement. Under some carve-out plans participants must pay this increased premium cost with aftertax dollars. Under other plans the employer increases the bonus amount. In effect the employer is now paying more than if the carve-out plan did not exist, but this arrangement is often acceptable to the employer as a way of providing shareholders and key executives with a benefit that is not available to other employees. In many places the bonus is also increased to compensate the employee for any additional income taxes that must be paid because of the carve-out plan. Such an arrangement is commonly referred to as a zero-tax approach.

A carve-out plan can pose a potential problem if there are employees who are rated or uninsurable, but the problem is ameliorated if the plan has enough

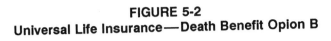

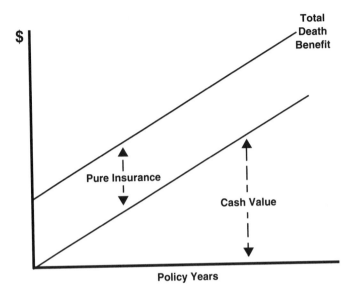

participants that the insurance company will use simplified underwriting or grant concessions on impaired risks. Any employee who is still uninsurable can be continued in the group term plan.

Other Types of Carve-Out Plans

While a bonus arrangement is the most common type of carve-out plan, other alternatives are available. Some carve-out plans are designed as death-benefit-only plans, under which the employer agrees only to pay a death benefit to the employee's beneficiary out of corporate assets. The employer often funds the plan with corporate-owned life insurance on the employee's life. With this approach the employee has no taxable income, but death benefits in excess of $5,000 will result in taxable income to the beneficiary. In addition, the employer is unable to deduct the premiums as a business expense but does receive the death proceeds tax free.

Some firms also use split-dollar life insurance in carve-out plans. The most common approach is to use a collateral assignment arrangement under which the employer pays most of the premium, and the employee collaterally assigns a portion of the cash value and death benefit to the employer equal to the employer's premium payments. At retirement (or any other predetermined time) the employee withdraws the cash value necessary to repay the employer, who then removes the collateral assignment. At that time the employee has full control of the policy, and the remaining cash value can be used to keep coverage in force. Many split-dollar arrangements are also used to provide nonqualified retirement benefits to key employees as a supplement to the benefits under the employer's qualified retirement plan.

Determining the Best Plan

In many instances carve-out plans are the most cost-effective approach for providing benefits to key employees. The best plan depends on the overall benefit objectives of the employer. A proper analysis of alternatives involves a complex consideration of many factors, including the employer's tax bracket, the effect on the employer's financial statements, the employee's tax bracket, premium costs, and the time value of money.

OTHER PRODUCTS FOR PROVIDING POSTRETIREMENT COVERAGE

Permanent insurance coverage that will continue after retirement has long been available under group versions of certain forms of life insurance that are more traditional than universal life insurance. While terminology may differ, the products used to provide this permanent protection after retirement have generally been placed in two categories: group paid-up insurance and group ordinary insurance. (These coverages should be distinguished from group permanent insurance, the term that normally describes cash value life insurance used to fund pension plans.) If properly designed, group insurance products that provide permanent life insurance coverage may qualify for favorable tax treatment under Sec. 79. Consequently such products, particularly those providing group ordinary insurance, are frequently referred to as Sec. 79 products.

Retired lives reserves may also be used to prefund the cost of continued group term life insurance coverage after retirement.

Group Paid-Up Insurance

Although once a popular type of group insurance coverage, relatively few group paid-up insurance plans have been written in recent years. However, a number of such plans, generally those of large employers, still exist. Under the typical group paid-up insurance plan the total amount of insurance coverage is determined the same way as it is for group term insurance plans (for example, a schedule related to earnings or a flat amount). The amount of insurance consists of accumulating units of single-premium whole life insurance and decreasing amounts of group term insurance, with the total amount of coverage remaining constant.

The typical plan is contributory, with employee contributions used to purchase the increments of single-premium whole life insurance. The employer pays the cost of the group term insurance, and the amount of the term coverage decreases as employee contributions are used to purchase additional units of whole life insurance. The amount of employee contributions is normally uniform for all employees, with a monthly contribution rate commonly ranging between $1.00 and $1.50 per $1,000 of insurance. These contributions are accumulated during each policy year and are used to purchase paid-up insurance on the anniversary date of the group insurance contract. Consequently an employee is provided with term insurance only from the date of initial participation until the next anniversary date of the contract. The following illustration is based on a monthly contribution of $1.00 per month for an employee entering a group paid-up plan at age 29.

Age	Annual Paid-Up Insurance Purchased by $1 Monthly Contribution	Accumulated Paid-Up Insurance Purchased by Employee's Contribution	Decreasing Amount of Term Insurance Paid by Employer	Total Amount of Life Insurance
29	$ 0	$ 0	$1,000.00	$1,000
30	44.10	44.10	955.90	1,000
31	43.20	87.30	912.70	1,000
32	41.88	129.18	870.82	1,000
.	.	.	.	.
.	.	.	.	.
.	.	.	.	.
63	18.96	948.48	51.52	1,000
64	18.60	967.08	32.92	1,000

If this employee retires on his or her 65th birthday, $967.08 of paid-up insurance can be continued in force with no further contribution required. Since the amount of paid-up insurance purchased by any employee is determined by the employee's attained age at the time a contribution is made, younger employees will accumulate more paid-up insurance for a given contribution than older employees. As a result, some plans provide for increased employee contributions for employees entering the plan at older ages.

While cash values (equal at least to an employee's aggregate contributions) accumulate under the policy, they are not available to employees during employment. At termination of employment an employee may surrender the policy for its cash value or maintain the paid-up portion in force without further premiums. In addition, a terminating employee has the right to convert the term insurance coverage to an individual policy the same way as does an employee for regular group term insurance. However, this conversion privilege may be available only if the employee continues the paid-up coverage.

Group Ordinary Insurance

Because of the many variations it is impossible to describe a typical group ordinary insurance product. However, it can be viewed essentially as dividing a whole life insurance policy into two segments: a term portion and a permanent or cash value portion. The total amount of coverage available to an employee is determined the same way it is in group term insurance. The cost of the term portion of the coverage is paid by the employer, and the permanent portion, which the employee may be able to decline, is generally paid by the employee.

There is no typical group ordinary product. Rather, the terminology is used to describe any product (except group paid-up insurance) that provides cash value life insurance to a group of employees and that will qualify for favorable income tax treatment under Sec. 79.

Some group ordinary products are not actually group insurance contracts but consist of single individual insurance policies for each employee, with premiums and coverage allocated between the term and permanent portions. Other group ordinary products consist of separate individual policies for each portion. Some group ordinary products are actually group term insurance policies with the permanent element added as a rider to the basic term coverage; other group ordinary products use individual contracts for the permanent portion of coverage but use a single group contract for the term portion. Under these various forms the product may be structured in one of several ways with respect to the allocation of premiums and coverage. These include

- decreasing term insurance with an increasing premium (to be paid by the employer) and increasing permanent insurance with a decreasing premium (probably to be paid by the employee). This will result in a level death benefit and a level total premium.
- decreasing term insurance with a level premium and increasing permanent insurance with a level total premium. This will also result in a level death benefit and a level premium.
- level term insurance with an increasing premium and increasing permanent insurance with a decreasing premium. This will result in a level total premium but an increasing death benefit, like a whole life insurance policy in which the "fifth dividend" option is used.

Upon termination of employment an employee may either surrender the policy for its cash value or continue coverage. If individual policies are used, the employee may continue paying the premium (regardless of whether this is already being done) to keep coverage in force. If group contracts are used, then the employee may convert coverage to an individual contract just as with group term insurance or group paid-up insurance.

Although group ordinary products were immensely popular in the 1970s, their popularity diminished rapidly after changes to Sec. 79 in 1979 (described below). However, there are still many plans funded with group ordinary products, and some coverage is still written.

Taxation of Group Paid-Up Insurance and Group Ordinary Insurance

With the exception of the income tax liability of employees, group paid-up insurance and group ordinary insurance are treated in essentially the same manner as group term insurance (described in chapter 4). Favorable tax treatment for the term portion of group insurance contracts that have permanent benefits (that is, cash value life insurance) has been available for many years to employees under Sec. 79, if certain requirements are satisfied. However, changes to Sec. 79 in 1979 resulted in a lessening of this favorable tax treatment and diminished the popularity of group insurance contracts that provide permanent benefits. No favorable tax treatment is given to the premium for the permanent portion of the coverage. If paid by an employer, the premiums for permanent coverage will be fully taxable to the employee as additional compensation.

The Sec. 79 regulation pertaining to group insurance with permanent benefits can be divided into three segments:

- the general requirements that a policy having permanent benefits must satisfy in order to have a portion of the policy considered as group term life insurance for purposes of Sec. 79
- a mandatory actuarial procedure for determining the cost of the permanent benefits
- the provisions for the tax treatment of dividends

General Requirements

The regulations define a *policy* as including two or more obligations of an insurer (or its affiliates) that are offered to a group of employees as a result of their employment relationship. The definition is broad enough to include a group of individual policies provided to a group of employees. In addition, term insurance benefits and permanent benefits provided under separate contracts can be considered a policy, even if one of the benefits is provided to employees who decline the other. The regulations also specify that a *permanent benefit* is an economic value extending beyond one policy year. This includes, for example, paid-up insurance or cash surrender values.

Before any part of a policy may be treated as group term life insurance, two requirements must be met:[1]

- The policy or the employer must designate in writing the portion of each employee's death benefit that is considered group term insurance.
- The portion of each employee's death benefit that is designated as group term insurance for any policy year must not be less than the difference between the total death benefit provided under the policy and the employee's *deemed death benefit*[2] at the end of the policy year.

If these requirements are met, the portion of the policy representing group term insurance will receive favorable income tax treatment under Sec. 79. When added to any other coverage that qualifies for Sec. 79 treatment, only the cost of the total term protection that exceeds $50,000 will represent taxable income to an employee. This cost is calculated by using Uniform Premium Table I rates and is reduced by the aggregate of any employee contributions for the entire term coverage but not for the permanent coverage.

The Cost of Permanent Benefits

The regulations also establish a mandatory allocation procedure for determining the cost of permanent benefits for an employee in a given policy year.[3] This cost represents taxable income to the employee to the extent that it is paid by the employer. It should be noted that the cost as determined by this formula is independent of the annual premium for permanent benefits actually specified in the policy. For example, if an employee is required to pay the cost of permanent benefits, and this cost is specified in the policy as $300, the employee will have taxable income to the extent that the mandatory allocation procedure yields a cost in excess of $300.

Treatment of Dividends

If the employer pays the entire cost of the permanent benefits, any dividends that are actually or constructively received by the employee must be included in the employee's income for federal income tax purposes. In all other cases the amount of dividends included in an employee's taxable income is determined by a formula specified in the regulations.[4] The effect of this formula is that any dividend will result in currently taxable income unless an employee has paid more than the aggregate costs (from the inception of coverage) for the permanent protection, as determined by the mandatory allocation formula.

Retired Lives Reserves

In the late 1970s and early 1980s increasing interest was shown in prefunding the cost of postretirement group term insurance coverage through retired-lives-reserve arrangements. Much of this interest stemmed from Internal Revenue Service regulations regarding Sec. 79 that made group paid-up and group ordinary products less attractive. The concept was not new; retired lives reserves, while not extensively used prior to that time, had been in existence for many years, primarily for very large employers. However, the trend in the 1970s was to establish them for smaller employers since the tax laws allowed the plans to be designed so that they often provided significant benefits to the firm's owners or key employees.

Because the Tax Reform Act of 1984 imposed more stringent requirements on retired lives reserves, there is no longer a great interest in establishing new plans. Nevertheless, many plans are still in existence, and under certain circumstances they remain a viable option for prefunding postretirement life insurance benefits.

A retired lives reserve is best defined as a fund established during the working years of employees for the purpose of paying all or a part of the cost of group term insurance for the employees after retirement. In some cases the term has been used to describe a fund that is designed to pay the cost of coverage for active as well as retired employees. However, the term *retired lives reserve* properly used refers only to that portion of the fund that applies to postretirement benefits. The fund may be established and maintained through a trust—either a tax-exempt Sec. 501(c)(9) trust or a nonexempt trust—or with an insurance company. If properly designed, a retired lives reserve (1) will enable an employer to make currently tax-deductible contributions to the fund during the working years of employees and (2) will not result in any taxable income to employees before retirement.

Tax Deductibility of Employer Contributions

An employer's contributions to a retired lives reserve are currently deductible for federal income tax purposes as long as certain conditions are met:

- The contributions must be an ordinary and necessary business expense.
- The balance in the reserve must be held solely for the purpose of providing life insurance coverage for currently retired employees or for active employees when they retire.
- The amount added annually to the reserve must be no greater than an amount that would be required to fairly allocate (on an actuarially level basis) the unfunded cost of the postretirement life insurance coverage over the remaining working lives of the employees involved. (There is no requirement that the entire permissible annual contribution be made. Any missed contributions may be made at a later date on an actuarially level basis only and not in a lump sum.)
- The employer must not have a right to recapture any portion of the assets in the reserve as long as any employees (either active or retired) covered under the plan are still alive. The effect of this condition is of considerable significance and is often the reason that a retired lives reserve is not established. Even if a retired lives reserve plan is discontinued, assets must be used to provide the promised postretirement benefits to active and retired employees previously covered under the plan, as long as such employees are living and the reserve has any assets.

Current deductions may be taken only for prefunding coverage that will be received tax free by retired employees under Sec. 79. This amount is generally $50,000 but may be higher for certain employees, subject to a grandfather clause. In addition, contributions on behalf of key employees cannot be deducted if the plan is discriminatory under Sec. 79.

Taxation to Employees

As long as an employee has no rights in a retired lives reserve except to receive postretirement group term insurance coverage until his or her death, the Internal Revenue Service has ruled that the employee will incur no income taxation as a result of either employer contributions to the reserve or investment earnings on the reserve.

Prior to the Tax Reform Act of 1984 the continuance of group term life insurance after retirement did not result in any income taxation to employees. As mentioned in chapter 4, this is no longer the case. Except for certain persons subject to a grandfather clause, the act now results in identical Sec. 79 treatment for both active and retired employees. Thus retired employees will be taxed on the amount of coverage that exceeds $50,000 in each year for which postretirement coverage is provided.

In those instances where death benefits are paid directly from trust assets, the tax consequences to the employee are the same as if death benefits were provided through group term insurance contracts, except that death proceeds in excess of $5,000 will represent taxable income to the beneficiary.

Methods for Funding

A retired lives reserve may be established and maintained through either a tax-exempt Sec. 501(c)(9) trust, a nonexempt trust, or an insurance company reserve account.

Tax-exempt Trust. A retired lives reserve that provides postretirement group term insurance may be funded through a tax-exempt Sec. 501(c)(9) trust (described further in chapter 12), which may either pay the premiums for group term insurance on retired employees or pay death benefits directly from trust assets. Because of its tax-exempt nature investment earnings of the trust are not subject to federal income taxation.

In order for a trust to qualify for tax-exempt status under Sec. 501(c)(9) of the Internal Revenue Code, certain requirements must be met:

- Benefits must be offered to all members of one or more classes of employees on a basis that does not limit membership to shareholders or highly compensated employees.
- Coverage must be voluntary.
- The trust must be operated only for the purpose of providing for the payment of life, health, or other benefits to employees or their dependents.
- No portion of the earnings of the trust may inure, other than by payment of benefits, to the benefit of any shareholder or other individual. Disproportionate benefits to highly compensated personnel and the return of contributions to an employer upon termination of the plan constitute inurement and will prevent a plan from qualifying.

It is generally felt that because of these restrictions (particularly the first and the fourth restrictions) a Sec. 501(c)(9) trust is better suited for large corporations than for small closely held corporations. In addition, an employee has no guarantee that the assets of the trust will be sufficient to either provide the annual premiums for group term insurance or pay death benefits.

The assets of the trust can also be used to provide paid-up insurance policies for each employee at retirement rather than to continue the group term coverage or to pay death benefits directly from the trust. However, the cost of such policies will not qualify for the income tax exemption for Sec. 79.

Nonexempt Trust. A nonexempt or taxable trust allows more flexibility than a Sec. 501(c)(9) trust as to which employees may be covered and the amount of insurance that may be provided for each employee. Consequently it allows a small closely held corporation to provide disproportionate benefits as well as to offer benefits to a more select group of employees. However, the plan of group insurance must satisfy Sec. 79 requirements if employees are to receive favorable income tax treatment for the benefits provided.

One disadvantage of a nonexempt trust is that investment earnings are taxable to the trust. However, taxation can be avoided if the trust assets are invested in tax-exempt securities. Moreover, taxation can be deferred until the date of surrender or until benefit payments begin if the assets are invested in cash value life insurance or annuity contracts. As with a Sec. 501(c)(9) trust, employees have no guarantee that the assets of the trust will be adequate to meet all future obligations.

Insurance Company Reserve Account. If a retired lives reserve is maintained with an insurance company, Internal Revenue Service regulations provide that any investment income credited to the reserve will not result in income taxation to the reserve, the employer, the employees, or the insurance company.

A retired lives reserve maintained with an insurance company is usually established in conjunction with a preretirement group term insurance plan. It is then used to pay the cost of continued coverage (possibly at a different level) for employees after retirement. In past years the typical approach has been to use a group term insurance contract with a deposit administration fund rider. The deposit administration fund is the retired lives reserve. However, some retired lives reserve products use individual term insurance contracts with a separate retired lives reserve fund. Under either approach the retired lives reserve is not allocated to any particular employee. Thus if an employee terminates employment prior to retirement, any contributions made in anticipation of continuing his or her coverage remain in the fund and can be used to provide benefits to other employees who do remain until retirement. After an employee retires, funds are withdrawn from the reserve as needed to pay the cost of postretirement benefits provided by the term insurance contract. Under the earliest products neither the future group term insurance rates nor the sufficiency of the retired lives reserve to pay the cost of promised benefits was guaranteed by insurance companies. The lack of guarantees was particularly unattractive to smaller businesses. Consequently many insurance companies modified their retired lives reserve products to provide guaranteed rates in future years for the group term coverage.

Many retired lives reserve products are also designed so that at retirement an employee's future benefits can be guaranteed. Essentially the retired lives reserve is divided into two accounts: an accumulation account and a retired life account. The accumulation account is not allocated to individual employees. However, at retirement a lump-sum amount (as determined by insurance company rates) can be transferred to the retired life account. Once this transfer takes place the funds are allocated to that particular employee and are used with accruing interest to pay the premium for the employee's coverage as needed. If the employee dies before the funds are depleted, any excess funds belong to the insurance company; if the funds are insufficient, the insurance company guarantees continued coverage without any additional premium payments.

The following illustration is typical of a retired lives reserve product offered by any insurance company. As mentioned earlier, most of these products provide both preretirement and postretirement coverage.

Assumptions

Amount of preretirement insurance: $100,000
Amount of postretirement insurance: $50,000
Current age of employee: 45
Retirement age of employee: 65
Sex of employee: male
Current assumed interest rate for retired lives reserve deposits: 6 percent
Minimum guaranteed interest rate for retired lives reserve deposits: 4 percent

Age	Annual Cost of $100,000 Term Insurance	Annual Retired Lives Reserve Deposit	Annual Total Employer Cost (Before Tax)	Accumulated Retired Lives Reserve Fund (End of Year)
45	$ 468	$760	$1,228	$ 25
46	582	760	1,342	390
47	628	760	1,388	795
.	.	.	.	.
.	.	.	.	.
.	.	.	.	.
62	2,264	760	3,024	17,284
63	2,506	760	3,266	19,632
64	2,778	760	3,538	22,250
Total at age 65	$26,606	$15,200	$41,806	

This illustration is based on a target figure of $22,250 as the amount needed in the retired lives reserve to guarantee the postretirement insurance to an employee at age 65. Many insurance companies will guarantee that the amount that must be transferred from the accumulation account to the retired life account upon the retirement of an employee will not exceed the target figure. In fact, it may actually be lower at that time because of insurance company actuarial assumptions. It is important to note in this example that the annual deposit of $760 to the retired lives reserve is based on a current assumed interest rate of 6 percent. Most insurers will guarantee such rates for only one year. Consequently if interest rates drop in the future, increased retired lives reserve deposits will be necessary to reach the targeted accumulation. Conversely rising interest rates will lower the annual deposits. It should be noted, however, that the current interest rate is subject to a minimum guarantee (4 percent in this case) below which it cannot fall.

Two other points are worthy of mention. First, even though the illustration is for a single employee, amounts in the accumulation account are not allocated to individual employees. If the employee in the illustration terminates employment, any amounts deposited in anticipation of his retirement will remain in the reserve and can be used to reduce the contributions otherwise necessary for employees who do remain until retirement. Second, the first-year accumulation of $25 in the retired lives reserve fund indicates a heavy front-end load in early years, which in turn reflects administrative and acquisition charges, including the agent's commission.

In some cases retired lives reserve products are sold to supplement existing group term insurance plans. While such products are occasionally sold to provide only postretirement coverage, additional preretirement coverage is usually also included. These products are often referred to as either superimposed (or supplemental) plans or wraparound plans. Under a superimposed plan (figure 5-3), The retired lives reserve only continues the preretirement coverage added by the retired lives product. Under a wraparound plan (figure 5-4), an amount equal to both the existing and the added preretirement coverage is continued. However, the full amount of this continued coverage is provided under the retired lives reserve product.

A group insurance plan may use a retired lives reserve to continue coverage after retirement for all employees or only for selected employees. However, the nondiscrimination rules of Sec. 79 will apply.

TWO PLANS USING RETIRED LIVES RESERVE PRODUCTS TO PROVIDE ADDITIONAL INSURANCE COVERAGE

FIGURE 5-3
Superimposed Plan

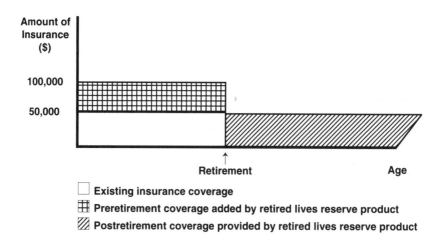

FIGURE 5-4
Wraparound Plan

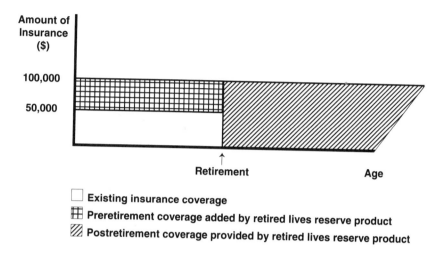

Existing insurance coverage

Preretirement coverage added by retired lives reserve product

Postretirement coverage provided by retired lives reserve product

NOTES

1. In addition, plans covering fewer than 10 lives and providing permanent protection must also satisfy the same requirements described in chapter 4 for group term life insurance plans covering fewer than 10 lives.

2. The deemed death benefit for a given policy year is defined as R/Y where

   R = the net level premium reserve at the end of that policy year for all benefits provided to the employee by the policy or, if greater, the cash value of the policy at the end of the policy year

   Y = the net single premium for insurance (the premium for one dollar of paid-up whole life insurance) at the employee's age at the end of that policy year

   R and Y are based on the 1958 CSO Mortality Table and a 4 percent interest rate.

3. The cost of permanent benefits for any employee is X (DDB^2-DDB^1) where

   DDB^2 = the employee's deemed death benefit at the end of the policy year

   DDB^1 = the employee's deemed benefit at the end of the preceding policy year

   X = the net single premium for insurance (the premium for one dollar of paid-up whole life insurance) at the employee's attained age at the beginning of the policy year

   X is based on the 1958 CSO Mortality Table and a 4 percent rate.

4. The amount included in an employee's income is $(D+C)-(PI+DI+AP)$ where

   D = the total amount of dividends actually or constructively received under the policy by the employee in the current and all preceding tax years of the employee

   C = the total cost of the permanent benefits for the current and all preceding tax years of the employee (determined under the formulas above)

PI   =   the total amount of premium included in the employee's income under the formulas for the current and all preceding tax years of the employee

DI   =   the total amount of dividends included in the employee's income under this dividend formula in all preceding tax years of the employee

AP   =   the total amount paid for permanent benefits by the employee in the current and all preceding taxable years of the employee

6

Group Disability
Income Insurance

The purpose of disability income insurance is to partially (and sometimes totally) replace the income of employees who are unable to work because of sickness or accident. While an employee may miss a few days of work from time to time, there is often a tendency to underestimate both the frequency and severity of disabilities that last for longer periods. At all working ages the probability of being disabled for at least 90 consecutive days is much greater than the chance of dying. One out of every three employees will have a disability that lasts at least 90 days during his or her working years, and one out of every ten employees can expect to be permanently disabled prior to age 65.

In terms of its financial impact on the family, permanent disability is more severe than death. In both cases income ceases. In the case of permanent disability, however, family expenses—instead of decreasing because of one less family member—may actually increase because of the cost of providing care for the disabled person.

Employers are less likely to provide employees with disability income benefits than with either life insurance or medical expense benefits. It is difficult to estimate the exact extent of disability coverage because benefits often are not insured and workers are sometimes covered under overlapping plans. However, a reasonable estimate would be that no more than two-thirds of all employees have some form of short-term employer-provided protection, and only about one-third have protection for long-term disabilities. This does not mean that almost all employees have some sort of disability income coverage, because many employees have both short-term and long-term protection and thus are included in both estimates. These estimates are also somewhat misleading because most employees have long-term disability income coverage under social security as well as coverage for certain types of disabilities under other government programs.

Group disability income insurance consists of two distinct products:

- short-term disability income insurance (often referred to as accident and sickness insurance or weekly indemnity insurance), which provides benefits for a limited period of time, usually 6 months or less
- long-term disability income insurance, which provides extended benefits (possibly for life) after an employee has been disabled for a period of time, frequently 6 months.

Two important tasks in designing and underwriting insured group disability income plans are to coordinate them with each other (if both a short-term and a long-term plan are provided for employees) and to coordinate them with other benefits to which employees might be entitled under social insurance programs or uninsured salary continuation plans. A lack of coordination can lead to such a generous level of benefits for employees that absences from work because of disability might be either falsified or unnecessarily prolonged.

Before examining group disability income insurance, therefore, this chapter will discuss the disability benefits available under social insurance programs and salary continuation plans. It will conclude with a discussion of the relevant tax laws affecting disability income insurance.

SOCIAL INSURANCE PROGRAMS

One major goal of many social insurance programs has been to provide protection for income lost as a result of disability. The vast majority of employees are covered under both the federal social security program and state workers' compensation laws. In addition, a few states have enacted compulsory temporary disability laws that provide benefits to employees with short-term nonoccupational disabilities. While a detailed discussion of social insurance programs is beyond the scope of this book, their eligibility requirements for disability benefits, as well as the levels of such benefits, will be briefly described.

Social Security

Most employees are engaged in employment covered under the social security program. Benefits under the program are financed by a payroll tax on both the employee and the employer, as well as on self-employed persons. This tax is subject to periodic adjustments, and in addition to disability benefits, it is used to finance survivor, retirement, and certain medicare benefits.

Eligibility

Eligibility for social security disability benefits is contingent upon an employee's having the proper insured status, meeting the definition of disability, and satisfying a waiting period.

Insured Status. An employee must be both fully insured and disability insured to qualify for disability benefits under the social security program. To be *fully insured* an employee must have the lesser of (1) 40 quarters[1] of social security coverage or (2) one quarter of coverage for the number of years after 1950 (or after the year the employee turned 21, if later), subject to a minimum of 6 quarters. To be *disability insured* an employee aged 31 or older must have credit for coverage under social security for at least 20 of the 40 quarters, ending with the quarter in which the disability commenced. This requirement is reduced for employees under age 31.

Definition of Disability. To collect social security disability benefits an employee must be unable to engage in any kind of gainful work because of a medically determinable physical or mental condition that has lasted or is expected to last at least 12 months or to result in death. These requirements are more stringent than those found in other social insurance programs and in the vast majority of disability income insurance contracts.

Waiting Period. In general benefits start with the sixth full calendar month of disability and are not retroactive to the date of disablement. However, if a

Benefits

Benefits under social security are based on an employee's *average indexed monthly earning* or those earnings (adjusted for changes in the level of covered wages) on which social security taxes have been paid. While higher average earnings will result in a larger absolute benefit, lower-paid workers, other things being equal, will receive a greater percentage of their predisability income than higher-paid workers.

Each disabled worker is entitled to a benefit for himself or herself. Additional family benefits (which are a function of the worker's benefit) may also be received if a worker has eligible dependents. These include dependent unmarried children under age 18 (or older if they are disabled) and a spouse who is caring for a child (or children) under age 16. Ignoring additional family benefits, a disabled employee who has been earning $20,000 per year can expect a social security benefit of approximately 41 percent of earnings at the time of disability. However, an employee who has been paying the maximum social security tax can expect a benefit of only about 25 percent of predisability earnings that were subject to social security taxation. If family benefits are received, these figures will be approximately 62 percent and 38 percent, respectively.

Benefits cease when the employee reaches age 65, dies, or is no longer disabled. At age 65 the disability benefits are replaced by social security retirement benefits. At death family benefits will continue as survivor benefits. Benefits will continue for an adjustment period of 3 months if an employee no longer satisfies the definition of disability.

If an employee under age 65 also receives disability benefits under other federal, state, or local programs, social security benefits are reduced to the extent that the total benefit from all programs exceeds 80 percent of the employee's *average current earnings* prior to disability. Average current earnings are defined as the largest of (1) the average monthly earnings used in computing the disability benefit, (2) 1/60 of total wages and self-employment income for the 5 consecutive years after 1950 with the highest total income, or (3) 1/12 of the total wages and self-employment income earned in the year of disability or any one of the 5 preceding years, whichever is highest. However, there are some exceptions. Benefits will not be reduced because of (1) a service-connected disability benefit from the Veterans' Administration, (2) a public-employee pension based on employment covered under social security, or (3) a needs-based public benefit.

Workers' Compensation Laws

Workers' compensation laws were enacted to require employers to provide benefits to employees for losses resulting from work-related accidents or diseases. In addition to providing benefits to employees for medical expenses, rehabilitation services, and lost income, benefits are also given to survivors of deceased employees. These laws are based on the principle of liability without fault. Essentially an employer is absolutely liable for providing the benefits prescribed by the workers' compensation law regardless of whether the employer would be considered legally liable in the absence of the workers' compensation law. However, these benefits, with the possible exception of medical expense benefits, are subject to statutory maximums.

considered legally liable in the absence of the workers' compensation law. However, these benefits, with the possible exception of medical expense benefits, are subject to statutory maximums.

All states have workers' compensation laws. In addition, several similar laws have been enacted by the federal government. The Federal Workmen's Compensation Act provides benefits for the employees of the federal government and the District of Columbia. Railroad employees and seamen aboard ships are covered under the Federal Employer's Liability Act; and stevedores, longshoremen, and workers that repair ships are covered under the United States Longshoremen's and Harbor Workers' Act.

Substantial variations exist among the state laws. Most are compulsory, but a few are elective. In states with elective workers' compensation laws, the majority of employers do elect coverage. If they do not, their employees are not entitled to workers' compensation benefits and must sue for damages resulting from occupational accidents or diseases. No workers' compensation law covers all employees. Many exclude certain agricultural, domestic, and casual employees. Some laws also exclude employers with a small number of employees.

Most states allow employers to comply with the workers' compensation law by purchasing coverage from insurance companies. Several of these states also have competitive state funds from which coverage may be obtained, but these funds usually provide coverage for fewer employees than insurance companies. Six states have monopolistic state funds that are the only source for obtaining coverage under the law.

Almost all states, including some with monopolistic state funds, allow employers to self-insure their workers' compensation exposure. These employers must generally post a bond or other security and receive the approval of the agency administering the law. While the number of firms using self-insurance for workers' compensation is small, these firms account for approximately half the employees covered under such laws.

Eligibility

Before an employee can be eligible for disability benefits under a workers' compensation law, he or she must work in an occupation covered by the law, be disabled by a covered injury, meet the definition of disability, and satisfy a waiting period.

Covered Injury. The typical workers' compensation law provides coverage for *accidental occupational injuries arising out of and in the course of employment.* In all states this includes injuries arising out of accidents, which are generally defined as sudden and unexpected events that are definite in time and place. Most workers' compensation laws exclude self-inflicted injuries and accidents resulting from an employee's intoxication or willful disregard of safety rules.

Every state has some coverage for injuries that result from occupational diseases. While the trend is toward full coverage for occupational diseases, some states cover only those diseases that are specifically listed in the law.

Definition of Disability. For an employee to collect disability benefits under workers' compensation laws his or her injuries must result in one of the following four categories of disability:

- temporary total. The employee cannot perform any of the duties of his or her regular job. However, full recovery is expected. Most workers' compensation claims are paid for this type of disability.
- permanent total. The employee will never be able to perform any of the duties of his or her regular job or any other job. Several states also list in their laws certain disabilities (such as loss of both eyes or both arms) that result in an employee's automatically being considered permanently and totally disabled even though future employment might be possible.
- temporary partial. The employee can only perform some of the duties of his or her regular job but is neither totally nor permanently disabled. For example, an employee with a sprained back might be able to work part-time.
- permanent partial. The employee has a permanent injury, such as the loss of an eye, but may be able to perform his or her regular job or may be retrained for another job.

Waiting Period. Most workers' compensation laws have a waiting period for disability benefits that varies from 2 to 7 days. However, benefits are frequently paid retroactively to the date of the injury if an employee is disabled for a specified period of time or is confined to a hospital.

Benefits

Disability income benefits under workers' compensation laws are a function of an employee's average weekly wage over some period of time, commonly the 13 weeks immediately preceding the disability. For total disabilities benefits are a percentage (usually 66 2/3 percent) of an employee's average weekly wage, subject to maximum and minimum amounts that vary substantially by state. Benefits for temporary total disabilities continue until an employee returns to work; benefits for permanent total disabilities usually continue for life but have a limited duration (such as 10 years) in a few states.

Benefits for partial disabilities are calculated as a percentage of the difference between an employee's wages before and after the disability. In most states the duration of these benefits is subject to a statutory maximum. Several states also provide lump-sum payments to employees whose permanent partial disabilities involve the loss of an eye, arm, or other body member. These benefits, which are determined by a schedule in the law, may be in lieu of or in addition to periodic disability income benefits.

All states have provisions in their workers' compensation laws for rehabilitative services for disabled workers. Benefits are included for medical rehabilitation as well as for vocational rehabilitation, including training, counseling, and job placement.

Temporary Disability Laws

At their inception state unemployment insurance programs were usually designed to cover only unemployed persons who were both willing and able to work. Benefits were denied to anyone who was unable to work for any reason, including disability. Some states amended their unemployment insurance laws to provide coverage to the unemployed who subsequently became disabled. However, five states—California, Hawaii, New Jersey, New York, and Rhode Island—and Puerto Rico went one step further by enacting temporary disability laws, under which employees can collect disability income benefits regardless of whether their disability begins when they are employed or when they are unemployed. While variations exist among the states, these laws (often referred to as nonoccupational disability laws since benefits are not provided for disabilities covered under workers' compensation laws) are generally patterned after the state unemployment insurance law and provide similar benefits.

In the six jurisdictions with temporary disability laws most employers must provide coverage to their employees. In most jurisdictions except Rhode Island, which has a monopolistic state fund, coverage may be obtained from either a competitive state fund or private insurance companies. Private coverage must at least provide the benefits prescribed under the law but may be more comprehensive. As with workers' compensation insurance, self-insurance is generally permitted. Depending on the jurisdiction the cost of an employer's program may be borne entirely by employee contributions, entirely by employer contributions, or by contributions from both parties.

Eligibility

Before an employee is eligible for benefits under a temporary disability law, the employee must satisfy (1) an earnings or employment requirement, (2) the definition of disability, and (3) a waiting period.

Earnings or Employment Requirement. Every jurisdiction requires that an employee must have worked for a specified period of time and/or have received a specified amount of wages within some period prior to disability in order to qualify for benefits.

Definition of Disability. Most laws define disability as the inability of the worker to perform his or her regular or customary work because of a nonoccupational injury or illness. New Jersey has the most stringent definition of disability, requiring that an employee be unable to perform any work for remuneration. As with workers' compensation laws, certain types of disabilities are not covered. In most jurisdictions these include disabilities caused by self-inflicted injuries or illegal acts.

Waiting Period. The usual waiting period for benefits is 7 days. However, in some jurisdictions it is waived if the employee is hospitalized.

Benefits

Benefits typically are a percentage, ranging from 50 percent to 66 2/3 percent, of the employee's average weekly wage for some period prior to disability, subject to a maximum and a minimum amount. Benefits are generally paid up to 26 weeks if the employee remains disabled that long.

SALARY CONTINUATION PLANS

Two approaches are used by employers to provide short-term disability benefits to employees: salary continuation plans and short-term disability income insurance plans. Salary continuation plans (often called sick-leave plans) are uninsured and generally fully replace lost income for a limited period of time, starting on the first day of disability. In contrast, short-term disability income insurance plans (which are covered in the next section of this chapter) usually provide benefits that replace only a portion of an employee's lost income and often contain a waiting period before benefits start, particularly for sickness.

Traditionally many salary continuation plans were informal, with the availability, amount, and duration of benefits for an employee being discretionary on the part of the employer. Some plans used by small firms or used for a limited number of executives still operate this way. However, the vast majority of salary continuation plans are now formalized and have specific written rules concerning eligibility and benefits.

Eligibility

Almost all salary continuation plans are limited to permanent full-time employees, but benefits may also be provided for permanent part-time employees. Most plans also require an employee to satisfy a short probationary period (1 to 3 months being common) before being eligible for benefits. Salary continuation plans may also be limited to certain classes of employees, such as top management or nonunion employees. The latter is common when the union employees are covered under a collectively bargained, but insured, plan.

Benefits

Most salary continuation plans are designed to provide benefits equal to 100 percent of an employee's regular pay. Some plans, however, provide a reduced level of benefits after an initial period of full pay.

Several approaches are used in determining the duration of benefits. The most traditional approach credits eligible employees with a certain amount of sick leave each year, such as 10 days. The majority of plans using this approach allow employees to accumulate unused sick leave up to some maximum amount, which rarely exceeds 6 months (sometimes specified as 130 days or 26 weeks). A variation of this approach is to credit employees with an amount of sick leave, such as one day, for each month of service. The following is an example of a benefit schedule that uses this variation:

Length of Service	Amount of Sick Leave*
Less than 3 months	None
3 or more months	1 day at full pay for each month of service (retroactive to date of employment)
*Maximum unused sick leave: 130 days	

Another approach, as illustrated below, bases the duration of benefits on an employee's length of service:

Length of Service	Maximum Days of Sick Leave per Year
Less than 3 months	0
3 months to 1 year	5
2 years	10
3 years	15
5 years	20
7 years	25
10 years	30

An alternative to this approach provides benefits for a uniform duration of time to all employees, except possibly those with short periods of service. However, benefits are reduced to a level less than full pay after some period of time that is related to an employee's length of service. The following is an illustration of this increasingly common approach:

Length of Service	Weeks of Sick Leave per Disability		Total Weeks
	100% of Pay	50% of Pay	
Less than 6 months	0	0	0
6 months to 1 year	2	0	2
1 year	4	22	26
2 years	8	18	26
3 years	12	14	26
4 years	16	10	26
5 years	20	6	26
6 years or more	26	0	26

In some instances an employee is not eligible for salary continuation benefits if he or she is eligible for benefits under social insurance plans, such as workers' compensation. However, most salary continuation plans are coordinated with social insurance programs. For example, if an employee is entitled to 100 percent of pay and receives 60 percent of pay as a workers' compensation benefit, the salary continuation plan will pay the remaining 40 percent.

A problem for the employer is how to verify an employee's disability. In general, the employee's word is accepted for disabilities that last a week or less. Under most salary continuation plans there is a provision that benefits for longer periods will be paid only if the employee is under the care of a physician, and the physician certifies that the employee is unable to work.

INSURED DISABILITY INCOME PLANS

As mentioned, insured disability income plans consist of two distinct products: short-term coverage and long-term coverage. Approximately twice as many employees have short-term coverage as have long-term coverage. However, over the last few years the number of employees with insured benefits for short-term disability has remained almost constant, while the number of employees with insured benefits for long-term disability has increased.

In many respects the contractual provisions of both short-term and long-term disability income contracts are the same or very similar. In other respects — notably, the eligibility requirements, the definition of disability, and the amount and duration of benefits — there are significant differences.

Eligibility

The eligibility requirements contained in group disability income insurance contracts are similar to those found in group term insurance contracts. In addition to being in a covered classification, an employee must usually work full-time and be actively at work before coverage will commence. Any requirements concerning probationary periods, insurability, and premium contributions must also be satisfied.

Short-term and long-term disability income insurance plans frequently differ in both the classes of employees that are eligible for coverage and the length of the probationary period. Employers are more likely to provide short-term benefits to a wider range of employees, and it is not unusual for short-term plans to cover all full-time employees. However, these plans may be a result of collective bargaining and apply only to union employees. In this situation other employees frequently have short-term disability benefits under uninsured salary continuation plans.

Long-term disability plans often limit benefits to salaried employees. Claims experience has traditionally been less favorable for hourly paid employees for a number of reasons. Claims of hourly paid employees tend to be more frequent, particularly in recessionary times when the possibility of temporary layoffs or terminations increases. Such claims also tend to be of longer duration, possibly because of the likelihood that these employees hold repetitive and nonchallenging jobs. Some long-term plans also exclude employees below a certain salary level since this category of employees, like hourly paid employees, is considered to have a reasonable level of benefits under social security.

Long-term disability income plans tend to have longer probationary periods than short-term disability income plans. While the majority of short-term disability plans (as well as group term insurance plans and medical expense plans) either have no probationary period or have a probationary period of 3 months or less, it is common for long-term disability plans to have probationary periods ranging from 3 months to 1 year. While short-term plans only require that an employee be actively at work on the date he or she is otherwise eligible for coverage, long-term plans sometimes require that the employee be on the job for an extended period (such as 30 days) without illness or injury before coverage will become effective.

Definition of Disability

Benefits are paid under disability income insurance contracts only if the employee meets the definition of disability as specified in the contract. Virtually all short-term disability income insurance contracts define disability as *the total and continuous inability of the employee to perform any and every duty of his or her regular occupation.* A small minority of contracts use a more restrictive definition, requiring that an employee be unable to engage in any occupation for compensation. Partial disabilities are not covered. In addition, the majority of short-term contracts limit coverage to nonoccupational disabilities, since employees have workers' compensation benefits for occupational disabilities. This limitation tends to be most common when benefits under the short-term contract are comparable to or lesser in amount than those under the workers' compensation law. In those cases where workers' compensation benefits are relatively low and the employer desires to provide additional benefits, coverage may be written for both occupational and nonoccupational disabilities.

A few long-term disability income contracts use the same liberal definition of disability that is commonly used in short-term contracts. However, the term *material duties* often replaces the term *each and every duty.* A few other contracts define disability as *the total and continuous inability of the employee to engage in any and every gainful occupation for which he or she is qualified or shall reasonably become qualified by reason of training, education, or experience.* However, the majority of long-term disability contracts use a dual definition that combines these two. Under a dual definition benefits will be paid for some period of time (usually 24 or 36 months) as long as an employee is unable to perform his or her regular occupation. After that time benefits will only be paid if the employee is unable to engage in any occupation for which he or she is qualified by reason of training, education, or experience. The purpose of this combined definition is to require and encourage a disabled employee, if that employee becomes able after a period of time, to readjust his or her life-style and earn a livelihood in another occupation.

A more recent definition of disability found in some long-term contracts contains an occupation test and an earnings test. Under the occupation test a person is totally disabled if he or she meets the definition of disability as described in the previous paragraph. However, if the occupation test is not satisfied, a person will still be considered totally disabled as long as an earnings test is satisfied. This means that the person's income has dropped by a stated percentage, such as 50 percent, because of injury or sickness. This newer definition makes a group insurance contract similar to an individual disability income policy that provides residual benefits.

The definition of disability in long-term contracts may differ from that found in short-term contracts in two other respects. Long-term contracts occasionally provide benefits for partial disabilities in a manner similar to that described for workers' compensation insurance. However, the amount and duration of such benefits may be limited when compared with those for total disabilities, and the receipt of benefits is usually contingent upon a prior period of disability. In addition, most long-term contracts provide coverage for both occupational and nonoccupational disabilities.

Exclusions

Under certain circumstances disability income benefits will not be paid even if an employee satisfies the definition of disability. Common exclusions under both short-term and long-term disability income contracts specify that no benefits will be paid

- for any period during which the employee is not under the care of a physician
- for any disability caused by an intentionally self-inflicted injury
- unless the period of disability commenced while the employee was covered under the contract. For example, an employee who previously elected not to participate under a contributory plan cannot obtain coverage for an existing disability by deciding to pay the required premium.
- if the employee is engaged in any occupation for remuneration. This exclusion applies in those situations when an employee is totally disabled with respect to his or her regular job but is engaged in other employment that can be performed despite the employee's condition.

Until the 1978 amendment to the Civil Rights Act it was common for disabilities resulting from pregnancy to be excluded. Such an exclusion is now illegal under federal law if an employer has 15 or more employees. Employers with fewer than 15 employees may still exclude pregnancy disabilities unless they are subject to state laws to the contrary.

Additional exclusions are often found in long-term contracts. These commonly deny benefits for disabilities resulting from

- war, whether declared or undeclared
- participation in an assault or felony
- mental disease, alcoholism, or drug addiction. However, some contracts provide benefits if an employee is confined in a hospital or institution specializing in the care and treatment of such disorders; other contracts provide benefits but limit their duration (such as for 24 months).
- preexisting conditions

The exclusion for preexisting conditions is designed to counter the adverse selection and potentially large claims that could occur if an employer established a group disability income plan or if an employee elected to participate in the plan because of some known condition that is likely to result in disability. While variations exist, a common provision for preexisting conditions excludes coverage for any disability that commences during the first 12 months an employee is covered under the contract if the employee received treatment or medical advice for the disabling condition both (1) prior to the date the employee became eligible for coverage and (2) within 90 consecutive days prior to the commencement of the disability.

When coverage is transferred from one insurance company to another, it is not unusual, particularly in the case of large employers, for the new insurance company to waive the limitation for preexisting conditions for those employees who were insured under the previous contract. In some instances the provision is modified so that benefits are limited to those that would have been provided under the previous contract, possibly for a specified duration, such as one year.

Benefits

A discussion of the benefits under disability income contracts is more complex than a discussion of the benefits under group life insurance contracts. A similarity exists in that there are benefit schedules that classify employees and specify the amount of disability income to be provided. However, the relationship between an employee's earnings and the employee's potential benefits is more important in disability income insurance than in group life insurance. In addition, disability benefits are subject to several provisions not found in group life insurance contracts. These pertain to the length of time that benefits will be paid and the coordination of benefits with other available types of disability income.

Benefit Schedules

As in group life insurance, there is a variety of benefit schedules found in group disability income contracts. Benefits may be available to all employees or limited to specific groups of employees. In addition, benefits may be expressed as either flat-dollar amounts, varying dollar amounts by classification, or a percentage of earnings.

A major difficulty in disability insurance is determining the appropriate level of benefits to provide. Absenteeism is encouraged and the incentive to return to work is diminished if a disabled employee is given a level of income that is comparable to his or her regular earnings. In general disability income plans are designed to provide a level of benefits that replaces between 50 and 70 percent of an employee's gross income. While this may appear to represent a substantial reduction of regular earnings, it should be remembered that a disabled employee does not have the usual expenses associated with working, such as transportation costs. In addition, disability income benefits are not subject to social security taxation after a period of time and, depending on the source and amount, may be free of income taxation. Despite the logic in providing a reduced level of income, some short-term disability income plans provide employees with 100 percent of their predisability earnings. In most cases this level of benefits is either a result of collective bargaining or an effort by employers to provide nonunion employees with a level of benefits that is comparable to that of union employees.

Many short-term disability income plans and the majority of long-term plans base benefits on a single percentage of regular earnings (excluding bonuses and overtime). This percentage varies widely for short-term plans, and benefits as low as 50 percent or as high as 100 percent are not unusual. However, many insurers are reluctant to underwrite plans that provide benefits higher than 70 percent of earnings. In some instances short-term plans, like salary continuation plans, may use different percentages, such as 100 percent of earnings for 4 weeks and 70 percent of earnings for the remaining benefit period. The length of time that the higher level of benefits will be provided may also be a function of the length of an employee's service.

Long-term plans typically provide benefits that range from 50 to 70 percent of earnings, with 60 and 66 2/3 being the most prevalent percentages. Some plans also use a sliding scale, such as 66 2/3 percent of the first $4,000 of monthly earnings and 40 percent of earnings in excess of $4,000.

It is common for plans that determine benefits as a percentage of earnings to also place a maximum dollar amount on the benefit that will be provided, regardless of earnings. For example, a short-term plan covering hourly employees may have a benefit equal to 70 percent of earnings that might be subject to a maximum of $250 per week. Similarly a long-term plan may provide benefits equal to 66 2/3 percent of earnings, but might be subject to a monthly maximum that varies from $1,000 for some small groups to $4,000 or $5,000 (and sometimes higher) for large groups. The purpose of such a maximum is to prevent the absolute benefit from being so high that an employee, by adjusting his or her life-style, could live comfortably on the disability income benefit and thus have no financial incentive to return to work.

Other types of benefit schedules are found in short-term disability income plans, particularly when these plans are designed for hourly paid employees. If the weekly earnings of most employees fall within a narrow range, the benefit might be expressed as a flat-dollar amount. For example, if all employees earn between $300 and $400 per week, a benefit of $225 per week might be used. If earnings vary widely, a benefit schedule such as the following might be used:

Weekly Earnings	Weekly Benefit
$221 to $260	$170
$261 to $300	200
$301 to $340	220
$341 to $380	250
Over $380	280

A similar approach is occasionally used in long-term disability income plans, as shown by the following benefit schedule for salaried employees earning in excess of $18,000 per year:

Monthly Earnings	Monthly Benefit
$1,500 to $2,500	$1,200
$2,501 to $3,500	1,500
$3,501 to $4,500	2,400
Over $4,500	3,000

Period of Benefits

To determine the period for which disability income benefits will be paid, it is necessary to determine when benefits will begin and how long they will be paid. In both respects differences exist between short-term and long-term plans.

Short-term Plans. Short-term disability income contracts commonly contain a waiting period (referred to as an elimination period in disability income contracts). The waiting period is the length of time that an employee covered under the contract must be disabled before benefits begin. In the typical short-term contract there is no waiting period for disabilities resulting from accidents, but a waiting period ranging from 1 to 7 days is used for disabilities resulting from sicknesses. However, in some plans there is a single waiting period that applies to disabilities from either accidents or sicknesses; in a few plans there are no waiting periods for either cause. Waiting periods longer than 7 days are occasionally used, particularly when there is a salary continuation plan to provide benefits during the initial portion of a disability. In addition to lowering the cost of a disability income plan, the waiting period discourages unwarranted absences from work because of sickness. In a few cases benefits are paid retroactively to the date of disability if the disability lasts for a predetermined period of time. However, it is generally felt that retroactive benefits cause employees to prolong their return to work in order to receive benefits for the full period of their disability.

Once an employee begins to receive benefit payments under a short-term disability contract, the benefits continue until the end of the benefit period specified in the contract, if the employee remains disabled for that length of time. Although short-term contracts may provide benefits up to 2 years (with long-term contracts providing benefits for periods in excess of 2 years), it is unusual for benefits to continue for more than one year. In fact, the majority of short-term contracts stipulate that benefits will be paid for either 13 or 26 weeks, with the latter period being most prevalent. It is also common for short-term plans to be described in terms of their elimination period and their duration of benefits. For example, a "1-8-26" plan pays benefits for a maximum of 26 weeks beginning with the first day of disability in the case of an accident and with the eighth day of disability in the case of a sickness.

In a few cases the maximum period of benefits applies to a specified duration of time (such as any consecutive 12 months) regardless of the number of separate disabilities. However, in most plans both the maximum benefit period and the elimination period apply to each separate disability. Moreover, successive periods of disability caused by the same accident or the same or related sickness are generally considered to be a single disability unless they are separated by a period (normally 2 weeks) of continuous resumption of active employment. This provision prevents an employee from briefly returning to work in order to obtain a second maximum period of benefits for the same disability.

Even though a reduction in short-term disability income benefits for older employees can probably be justified on a cost basis, few plans have incorporated such a reduction.

Long-term Plans. While waiting periods in long-term disability income plans may be as short as 30 days or as long as one year or more, the vast majority of plans contain elimination periods ranging from 3 to 6 months, with 6 months most common. In many cases the length of the waiting period will correspond to the length of time benefits will be paid under a firm's short-term disability income plan or salary continuation plan. In contrast to short-term plans, there is no difference between the waiting periods for sicknesses and accidents.

Long-term disability income benefits may be paid for as short a period as 2 years or as long as the lifetime of the disabled employee. In a few cases the length of the benefit period may differ, depending upon whether the disability was a result of an accident or a sickness. Prior to the amending of the Age Discrimination in Employment Act it was common for long-term disability income benefits to cease at age 65. Since that time several different approaches have been used for older employees. In a few cases benefits are paid until age 70 for any disability that occurred before that age. For disabilities occurring at age 70 or later, benefits are paid for a reduced duration. A more common approach is to provide benefits to age 65 for employees who are disabled prior to a specified age. Employees disabled after the specified age are given benefits for a limited time. For example, a plan may provide the following:

Age at Commencement of Disability	Benefit Duration
59 and younger	To age 65
60–64	5 years
65–69	To age 70
70–74	1 year
75 and older	6 months

A similar approach uses a sliding level of benefit durations after a certain age. For example, a plan may provide that employees disabled prior to age 60 will receive benefits until age 65. The following schedule might then be used for employees who are disabled at age 60 or older:

Age at Commencement of Disability	Benefit Duration (in Years)
60	5
61	4
62	3 1/2
63	3
64	2 1/2
65	2
66	2
67	1
68	1
69	1

As in short-term disability income plans, provisions are made in long-term plans for successive disabilities. The majority of contracts stipulate that successive periods of disability that are separated by less than some period (usually varying from 3 to 6 months) of continuous, active full-time employment will be considered a single disability, unless the subsequent disability (1) arises from an unrelated cause and (2) begins after the employee has returned to work.

Coordination with Other Benefits

To minimize the possibility that an employee will receive total benefits higher than his or her predisability earnings, disability income plans commonly stipulate that benefits will be integrated with other sources of disability income. The effect of this integration is to reduce (either totally or partially) the benefits payable under the disability income contract to the extent that certain other benefits are available. In general the insurance laws or regulations of most states allow such reductions to be made as a result of benefits from social insurance programs and group insurance or retirement plans provided by the employer, but not as a result of benefits from individual disability income contracts unless they were purchased by the employer. Employers and employees often resent the fact that disability income benefits that they have "paid for" may be reduced. However, such reductions are considered in determining the rates charged for disability income insurance. In effect, the employer is purchasing a contract that is only a supplement to these other available sources of disability income rather than being penalized because these resources are available.

For various reasons, including the limited duration of benefits and the desire for simplified operating procedures, integration with other benefits is less likely to exist in short-term plans than in long-term plans. If a short-term plan covers only nonoccupational disabilities, there is no need for integration with workers' compensation benefits; and unless benefits are provided for disabilities lasting longer than 5 months, there is no need to integrate benefits with social security. In general benefits under short-term plans are integrated with (1) workers' compensation benefits, if the plan covers occupational disabilities; (2) temporary disability laws, if they are applicable; and (3) social security benefits, if the maximum benefit period is longer than 5 months.

Some insurance companies will sell long-term disability income coverage without any provision for coordination with other disability income benefits. However, the availability and potential magnitude of other benefits will be an underwriting factor in determining the maximum amount of coverage that will be written. Long-term disability income benefits, however, are usually integrated with benefits provided under the following:

- social security
- workers' compensation laws
- temporary disability laws
- other insurance plans for which the employer makes a contribution or payroll deduction
- pension plans for which the employer has made a contribution or payroll deduction to the extent that the employee elects to receive retirement benefits because of disability
- salary continuation plans
- earnings from employment, either with the employer of from other sources

The integration with social security may be based solely on the benefit a disabled worker receives for himself or herself (referred to as the employee's primary insurance amount). It may also be based on the employee's total family benefit if the employee has eligible dependents.

Two basic approaches to integration are used: a full-integration approach and a dual-percentage approach. Under the *full-integration approach,* long-term disability income benefits are reduced to the extent that any benefits subject to integration are received. For example, assume that an employee earning $2,500 per month is entitled to a disability income benefit of 60 percent, or $1,500 per month. In addition, suppose the employee is entitled to a disability benefit of

$900 under social security, as well as additional family benefits of $450 (a total of $1,350). If the long-term disability income benefit plan provides for integration with total family benefits, the employee will receive $1,500 ($1,350 from social security and the remaining $150 from the long-term plan). However, if full integration is provided only with respect to the primary insurance amount (in other words, the $450 of family benefits is not considered), the employee will receive $1,950 ($1,350 from social security and $600 from the long-term disability plan).

Under the *dual-percentage approach* two percentages are used: one that is applicable to benefits that will be provided under the long-term plan when there are no other benefits subject to integration, and another higher percentage that is applicable to total benefits payable from the long-term plan and other sources subject to integration. For example, an insured plan might provide benefits equal to 60 percent of earnings in the absence of other benefits subject to integration. If there are benefits subject to integration, benefits under the insured plan will be reduced to the extent that the sum of the benefits under the long-term disability plan and the benefits subject to integration exceed another percentage, such as 70 percent. Using these percentages and the previous example, 70 percent of earnings will be $1,750. Since the long-term disability benefit and all the social security benefits total $2,850, the long-term disability benefit will be reduced by $1,100 if the plan provides for integration with total family benefits. Therefore the employee will receive a total benefit of $1,750 ($1,350 from social security and $400 from the long-term plan).

It is possible for the integration with other benefits to totally eliminate a long-term disability benefit. To prevent this from happening, many plans provide (and some states require) that a minimum benefit, such as $25 or $50 per month, be paid. Most plans also contain a provision freezing the amount of any social security reduction at the initial level that was established when the claim began. For example, assume an employee is entitled to receive $1,000 per month in disability income benefits under a long-term plan that contains a provision for full integration with social security. If the employee initially receives $400 from the long-term plan and $600 from social security, the $400 will continue to be paid under a provision that freezes the offset even if social security benefits are increased. If a 5 percent increase is later granted in social security benefits, the employee will receive a total benefit of $1,030. Without such a provision the intended effect of increases in social security benefits would be erased by equivalent reductions in other disability income benefits provided to the employee. This is seen by some regulators as being contrary to public policy and thus a reason for requiring insured plans to contain a freeze in the amount of the social security offset.

Other Contract Provisions

Many provisions contained in group disability income contracts are similar to those contained in group term insurance contracts and will not be discussed further in this chapter. These include provisions pertaining to incontestability, a grace period, the entire contract, and the payment of premiums. The provisions that will be discussed either are unique to group disability income benefit contracts or differ in certain respects from similar provisions found in group term insurance contracts.

Claims

The provisions concerning claims under both short-term and long-term disability income contracts are essentially the same. The insurance company must be notified within a relatively short time period, 20 or 30 days (or as soon as is reasonably possible), after the disability for which benefits are being claimed begins. A formal proof of loss must then be filed with the insurance company, usually within 90 days after the commencement of the disability or after the end of the week, month, or other time period for which benefits are payable. The proof of loss normally consists of a statement by the employee concerning the disability, a statement by the attending physician, and a statement by the employer indicating the date and reason that active employment ceased. Provisions are also included that require periodic reports from the attending physician or that permit the insurance company to request such reports at reasonable intervals. The insurance company also has the right to have the employee examined by a physician of its own choice (and at its own expense) at reasonable time periods during the duration of the claim.

Payment of Benefits

The insurance company is not obligated to make benefit payments until a proof of loss has been filed. In general benefits are payable to the employee. However, a facility-of-payment provision is included to allow payments to a guardian if the employee is physically, mentally, or otherwise incapable of giving a valid release for any payment received. Benefits may be assigned to another party if such an assignment is permissible under state law and the insurance contract.

Rehabilitation

As an incentive to encourage disabled employees to return to active employment as soon as possible, but possibly at a lower-paying job, most insurance companies include a rehabilitation provision in their long-term disability income contracts. This provision permits the employee to enter a trial work period of 1 or 2 years in rehabilitative employment. During this time disability benefits will continue but will be reduced by some percentage (varying from 50 to 80 percent) of the earnings from rehabilitative employment. For example, with a 50 percent reduction, an employee who is otherwise entitled to a disability benefit of $1,500 per month will have this benefit reduced by only $600 if he or she can earn $1,200 in the new job. If the trial work period indicates that the employee is unable to perform the rehabilitative employment, the original long-term benefits will be continued and the employee will not be required to satisfy a new waiting period.

While there are no other provisions in long-term disability income contracts that require the insurance company to aid in the rehabilitation of disabled employees, it is not unusual for insurance companies to provide benefits for rehabilitation when it is felt that the cost of these benefits will be offset by shortening an employee's disability period. These benefits may be in the form of physical therapy, job training, adaptive aids to enable a disabled person to perform job functions, or even the financing of a business venture.

Termination

For the most part the provisions in disability income contracts concerning either the termination of the master contract or an employee's coverage are the same as those found in group life insurance. However, there is one notable exception—a conversion privilege is rarely included. The rationale for not including such a provision is based on the theory that the termination of employment will also terminate an employee's income and thus the need for disability income protection.

One other situation should be mentioned. When an employee meets the definition of total disability under a disability income contract, the employee is considered to have terminated employment by reason of ceasing to be an active, full-time employee. Without some provision to the contrary, an employee who resumes work is then required to resatisfy any eligibility requirements, including a new probationary period. However, most group disability income contracts allow the employer to consider disabled employees as not having terminated employment for insurance purposes. The employer may continue coverage as long as it is done on a nondiscriminatory basis and as long as the required premiums are paid. In short-term contracts coverage is generally continued by the payment of premiums on the same basis as for active employees. However, it is common for long-term contracts to contain a waiver-of-premium provision.

It should be noted that the only practical effect of continuing coverage on a disabled employee is to guarantee that the employee will again be eligible for disability income benefits after he or she has returned to active employment. The continuation of coverage (or termination of coverage) has no effect on the future disability income benefits to an employee who is currently disabled and therefore entitled to receive benefits.

Supplemental Benefits

Three types of supplemental benefits that are occasionally found under long-term disability income contracts are a cost-of-living adjustment, a pension supplement, and a survivors' benefit.

Some disability income plans have cost-of-living adjustments (COLAs) so that the purchasing power of disability income benefits being received is not eroded by inflation. Under the typical COLA formula, benefits increase annually along with changes in the consumer price index.

Many firms make provisions in their pension plan for treating disabled employees as if they were still working and accruing pension benefits. Such a provision requires that contributions on behalf of disabled employees be made to the pension plan. In most cases these are paid from the current revenues of the employer. However, some disability income contracts stipulate that the contributions necessary to fund a disabled employee's accruing pension benefits be paid from the disability income contract.

It should also be noted that some pension plans provide disability income benefits by allowing disabled employees to begin receiving retirement benefits when they are totally and permanently disabled. It is common, however, to limit these early retirement benefits to employees who have satisfied some minimum period of service or who have reached some minimum age. In recent years the feeling among employee benefit consultants seems to be that it is preferable to have separate retirement and disability income plans.

Some long-term contracts provide a benefit to survivors in the form of continued payments after the death of a disabled employee. In effect the disability income payments will be continued, possibly at a reduced amount, for periods ranging up to 24 months. Payments are generally made only to eligible survivors, who commonly are the spouse and unmarried children under age 21.

FEDERAL TAXATION

While the following discussion focuses on the effect of the tax laws on disability income plans (either insured plans or salary continuation plans), the tax treatment of social insurance programs that provide disability income benefits will also be mentioned.

Contributions by an employer for social insurance programs are tax deductible to the employer, but contributions by the employees are not deductible. Social security benefits paid to a disabled worker are received income tax free unless the worker (and his or her spouse) has a moderately high adjusted gross income. Then up to one-half of the social security benefit may be subject to taxation. Any workers' compensation benefits received by an employee are free of income taxation. Temporary disability benefits received by employed persons are treated the same as insured disability income benefits (discussed below). In those jurisdictions where benefits can also be received by unemployed persons, any benefits paid to unemployed persons are considered unemployment insurance and are taxed accordingly.

Deductibility of Premiums

As with group life insurance, employer contributions for an employee's disability income insurance are fully deductible to the employer as an ordinary and necessary business expense if the overall compensation of the employee is reasonable. Salary continuation payments are similarly tax deductible. Contributions by an individual employee are considered payments for personal disability income insurance and are not tax deductible.

Income Tax Liability of Employees

In contrast to group life insurance, for which employer contributions may result in some taxable income to an employee, employer contributions for disability income insurance result in no taxable income to an employee. However, the payment of benefits under an insured plan or salary continuation plan may or may not result in the receipt of taxable income. In order to make this determination, it is necessary to look at whether the plan is fully contributory, noncontributory, or partially contributory.

Fully Contributory Plan

Under a fully contributory plan the entire cost is paid by employee contributions and benefits are received free of income taxation.

Noncontributory Plan

Under a noncontributory plan the entire cost is paid by the employer and benefits are included in an employee's gross income. However, the Internal Revenue Code provides a tax credit to persons who are permanently and totally disabled. This credit is subtracted from an individual's federal income tax liability rather than deducted from gross income, as was the $100 per week sick-pay exclusion that existed prior to 1984. For purposes of this tax credit the IRS uses the social security definition of disability; that is, an employee must be unable to engage in any kind of gainful work because of a medically determinable physical condition that has lasted or is expected to last at least 12 months or to result in death.

The maximum credit is $750 for a single person, $1,125 for a married person filing jointly, and $562.50 for a married person filing separately. The credit cannot exceed the taxable disability benefit actually received. The maximum credit is reduced if a single individual has an adjusted gross income (including the disability benefit) over $7,500, if a married person filing jointly has an adjusted gross income over $10,000, or if a married person filing separately has an adjusted gross income over $5,000. The reduction is equal to 7 1/2 percent of any income over the limit. In addition, the credit is reduced by 15 percent of any tax-free income received as a pension, annuity, or disability benefit from certain government programs, including benefits from social security. Since disability income plans are usually integrated with social security, the tax credit available to most persons who receive disability benefits from employer plans will be substantially reduced or eliminated altogether.

Partially Contributory Plan

Under a partially contributory plan benefits attributable to employee contributions are received free of income taxation. Benefits attributable to employer contributions are includible in gross income, but employees are eligible for the tax credit described previously.

The portion of the benefits attributable to employer contributions (and thus subject to income taxation) is based on the ratio of the employer's contributions to the total employer-employee contributions for an employee who has been under the plan for some period of time. For example, if the employer paid 75 percent of the cost of the plan, 75 percent of the benefits would be considered attributable to employer contributions and 25 percent to employee contributions. This time period used to calculate this percentage varies, depending upon the type of disability income plan and the length of time that the plan has been in existence. Under group insurance policies the time period used is the 3 policy years ending prior to the beginning of the calendar year in which the employee is disabled. If coverage has been in effect for a shorter time, IRS regulations specify the appropriate time period to use. Similar provisions pertain to contributory salary continuation plans, the major exception being that the time period is based on calendar years rather than policy years. If benefits are provided under individual disability income insurance policies, the proportion is determined on the basis of the premiums paid for the current policy year.

Tax Withholding and Social Security Taxes

Benefits paid directly to an employee by an employer under a salary continuation plan are treated like any other wages for purposes of tax withholding. Disability income benefits paid by a third party (such as an insurance company or a trust) are subject to the withholding tax rules and regulations only if the employee requests that taxes be withheld. In both cases benefits that are attributable to employer contributions are subject to social security taxes. However, social security taxes are payable only during the last calendar month in which the employee worked and the 6 months that follow.

STATE TAXATION

For income tax purposes some states consider an individual's taxable income to be the figure shown on the individual's federal income tax return, and those states treat disability income and salary continuation benefits as the federal government does. While considerable variations exist in other states, disability income and salary continuation benefits are generally treated more favorably than under the federal tax laws and are often totally exempt from state income taxation.

NOTE

1. To receive credit for one (calendar) quarter of coverage, a worker must have a specified amount of earnings under covered employment during a calendar year. This amount, $590 in 1993, is adjusted annually on the basis of changes in the national level of wages. For each $590 earned in 1993 an employee would have received credit for one quarter of coverage up to a maximum of 4 quarters of coverage for the year. Therefore $2,360 in covered earnings at any time during the year would have resulted in the maximum quarters of credit for the year.

7

Group Medical Expense Insurance: Providers and Basic Coverages

Medical expense insurance is the most significant type of group insurance in terms of both the number of persons covered and the dollar outlay. With the exception of employers with a very small number of employees, virtually all employers offer some type of medical expense plan. In almost all cases coverage identical to that offered for employees is also available for eligible dependents. In the absence of employee contributions the cost of providing medical coverage for employees will be several times greater for most employers than the combined cost of providing life insurance and disability income insurance.

Group medical expense contracts are not as standardized as group life insurance and group disability income insurance. Coverage may be provided through Blue Cross and Blue Shield plans, health maintenance organizations (HMOs), and preferred-provider organizations (PPOs) as well as insurance companies. In addition, a large and increasing percentage of the benefits is provided under plans that are partially or totally self-funded (self-insured). An overall medical expense plan may be limited to specific types of medical expenses, or it may be broad enough to cover almost all medical expenses. Even when broad coverage is available, benefits may be provided either under a single contract or under a combination of contracts. Furthermore, in contrast to other types of group insurance already discussed, benefits may be in the form of services rather than in form of cash payments. Finally, the skyrocketing cost of providing medical expense benefits in recent years has led to many changes in coverage and plan design aimed at controlling these costs. Many of these changes have resulted in more similarities among the providers of medical expense coverage than existed in the past.

Chapter 7 will discuss the providers of medical expense coverage and the *basic* coverages that are available for specific types of medical expenses. *Major medical* coverages that provide more comprehensive benefits, the contractual provisions of medical expense contracts, and the relevant tax laws will be discussed in chapter 8. Alternative methods of funding medical expense benefits will be covered in chapter 12, but other attempts at cost containment will be examined extensively throughout chapters 7 and 8.

COST CONTAINMENT

Since 1970 the average annual increases in the cost of medical care have been approximately twice the average annual increases in the consumer price index. No single factor accounts for these increases. Rather, it is a combination of reasons that include the following:

- technological advances. In the last few years many exciting technological advances have taken place. Numerous lives are now being saved by such techniques as CAT scans, fetal monitoring, and organ transplants. As miraculous as many of these techniques are, they are also very expensive.
- increasing malpractice suits. The providers of care are much more likely to be sued than in the past, and malpractice awards have outpaced the general rate of inflation. This has resulted in higher malpractice premiums, which are ultimately passed on to consumers. The increase in malpractice suits has also led to an increase in defensive medicine, with routine tests likely to be performed more often.
- increases in third-party payments. A growing portion of the country's health care expenditures is now paid by private health insurers or the government. Patients and providers of health care often have no financial incentives to economize on the use of health care service.
- undercapacity of medical facilities. Currently the United States has an overabundance of hospital beds, and a surplus of physicians is also beginning to develop. Empty hospital beds are expensive to maintain, and an oversupply of physicians tends to drive up the average costs of medical procedures so that physicians' average income does not drop.
- design of medical expense plans. Many medical expense plans now provide first-dollar coverage for many health care costs. There is often little incentive for patients to avoid the most expensive forms of treatment.
- AIDS. The continuing increase in the number of AIDS cases over the last 10 years has resulted in increasing costs to employers. Costs in excess of $100,000 for an employee with AIDS are not unusual.

Increasing health care costs have become the concern of almost everyone—government, labor, employers, and consumers. In this introduction to cost containment many of the measures used by employers are enumerated. Some of the following measures will be discussed in more detail throughout the next two chapters; others will be discussed later in the book:

- benefit plan design
- alternative providers
- alternative funding methods
- claims review
- health education and preventive care
- encouragement of external cost-control system
- managed care

Rarely will a single cost-containment technique produce great savings by itself, but a combination of these techniques, often referred to as managed care, may lead to significant cost reductions or a slowing of cost increases.

Benefit Plan Design

Numerous design features of a medical expense plan can control costs. These have traditionally been in the form of contractual provisions that shift costs to employees. Examples include

- deductibles
- coinsurance
- exclusions and limitations
- maximum benefits

In recent years design features have been aimed at reducing costs rather than shifting them. In fact, benefit plans are often designed to provide a higher level of benefits if less costly alternatives are used. Examples of these cost-containment features include

- preadmission testing
- second surgical opinions
- coordination of benefits
- the use of alternatives to hospitals—such as skilled nursing facilities, home health care, hospice care, birthing centers, and ambulatory care centers

Alternative Providers

The use of HMOs and PPOs has been popular for some years as a cost-containment method. These methods have now been joined by point-of-service plans. Each is described in more detail later in this chapter.

Alternative Funding Methods

Employers are increasingly turning to funding methods that are alternatives to the traditional insurance company plan or Blue Cross–Blue Shield plan. Chapter 12 is devoted to a discussion of these techniques.

Claims Review

There is no doubt that claims review can generate substantial cost savings. In general this review is done not by the employer but by the provider of medical expense benefits, a third-party administrator, or some independent outside organization. At a minimum claims should be reviewed for patient eligibility, eligibility of the services provided, duplicate policies, and charges that are in excess of usual, customary, and reasonable amounts. Many medical expense plans routinely audit hospital bills, particularly those that exceed some amount, such as $5,000 or $10,000. They check for errors in such items as length of stay, services performed, and billed charges. Many insurance companies have found that each dollar spent on this type of review results in two or three dollars of savings.

A newer trend in claims review is utilization review or case management. This may be done on a prospective basis, a concurrent basis, a retrospective basis, or a combination of the three. A prospective review involves analyzing a case to see what type of treatment is necessary. Hospital preadmission authorization, second surgical opinions, and predetermination of dental benefits (see chapter 9) fall into this category. However, when a patient is hospitalized, concurrent review can lead to shorter stays and the use of less expensive facilities. Concurrent review is normally carried out by a registered nurse and typically begins with precertification of a hospital stay for an initial specified length of time. The nurse then works with the patient's physician to monitor the length of stay and to determine whether other alternatives to hospitalization—such as hospices or home health care—can be used. Many providers of medical expense benefits will pay for these alternative forms of treatment even if they are not specifically covered under the medical expense plan—as long as their cost is lower than the cost of continued hospitalization.

A retrospective review involves an analysis of care after the fact to determine if it was appropriate. Such a review may lead to a denial of claims, but its purpose is often to monitor trends so that future actions can be taken in high-cost areas. For example, a retrospective review may lead to the establishment of a concurrent review program for a hospital with excessive lengths of stay.

Health Education and Preventive Care

There is little doubt that persons who lead healthy life-styles will tend to have fewer medical bills, particularly at younger ages. It is also evident that healthier employees save an employer money by taking fewer sick days and having fewer disability claims. For these reasons employers are increasingly establishing wellness programs and employee-assistance plans. Both of these programs are discussed in chapter 13. With an increasing health awareness among the general population the existence of these programs has a positive side effect—the improvement of employee morale.

The Encouragement of External Cost-Control Systems

While a certain degree of cost containment is within the control of employers, the proper control of costs is an ongoing process that requires participation by consumers (both employers and individuals), government, and the providers of health care services. At the national level the National Council on Health Planning and Development, an advisory body to the secretary of health and human services, identifies needs, monitors resources, establishes priorities, recommends courses of action, and oversees laws pertaining to health care. The council, which was created by the National Health Planning and Resources Development Act of 1974, oversees state and local activities that are carried out by state health planning and development agencies and local health system agencies (HSAs). Many employers encourage and are actively involved with these agencies.

At the state and local level many employers are active in coalitions whose purpose is to control costs and improve the quality of health care. These groups—which may also involve unions, providers of health care, insurance companies, and regulators—are often the catalyst for legislation such as laws authorizing PPOs and establishing hospital budget-review programs.

Managed Care

The current buzz word with respect to cost containment is *managed care*. In a general sense the term can be defined to include any medical expense plan that attempts to contain costs by controlling the behavior of participants. However, in practice the term is used by many persons to mean different things. At one extreme are traditional indemnity plans that require second opinions and/or hospital precertification. At the other extreme are HMOs and PPOs that limit a participant's choice of medical providers, negotiate provider fees, and use case management.

Managed care plans have evolved over the last few years. Today it is generally felt that a true managed care plan should have five basic characteristics:

- *controlled access of providers.* It is difficult to control costs if participants have unrestricted access to physicians and hospitals. Managed care plans attempt to encourage or force participants to use predetermined providers. Because a major portion of medical expenses results from referrals to specialists, managed care plans tend to use primary care physicians as gatekeepers to determine the necessity and appropriateness of specialty care.
- *comprehensive case management.* Successful managed care plans perform utilization review at all levels.
- *preventive care.* Managed care plans encourage preventive care and the attainment of healthier life-styles.
- *risk sharing.* Managed care plans are most successful if providers share in the financial consequences of medical decisions. Newer managed care plans have contractual guarantees to encourage cost-effective care. For example, a physician who minimizes diagnostic tests may receive a bonus. Ideally such as arrangement will eliminate unnecessary tests, not discourage tests that should be performed.
- *high-quality care.* A managed care plan will not be well received and selected by participants if there is a perception of inferior or inconvenient medical care. In the past too little attention was paid to this aspect of cost containment. Newer managed care plans not only select providers more carefully but also monitor the quality of care on a continuing basis.

There seems to be a reasonable consensus among employers and benefit specialists that there is a negative correlation between benefit costs and the degree of managed care. That is, the greater the degree of managed care, the lower the cost. For example, studies generally rank benefit plans in the following order (from highest to lowest) with respect to annual benefit costs:

- traditional insurance company and Blue Cross and Blue Shield plans without case management
- traditional insurance company and Blue Cross and Blue Shield plans with case management
- preferred-provider organizations
- open-ended HMOs
- independent practice association HMOs
- closed-panel HMOs

It is interesting to note that the degree of managed care increases as one goes down the list. In addition, there seems to be a high correlation between annual benefit costs and the rate of cost increases. For example, the cost of traditional benefit plans has been increasing recently at an annual rate in excess of 20 percent; closed-panel HMO costs have been increasing at an annual rate of about 10 percent.

ALTERNATE PROVIDERS OF MEDICAL EXPENSE COVERAGE

When providing death benefits and disability income benefits to their employees, employers have a limited number of choices. Coverage can be purchased from an insurance company, provided on a self-funded basis, or funded by a combination of these two approaches. However, when providing medical expense benefits, an employer has more options. Many employers purchase coverage from Blue Cross and Blue Shield associations (which compete vigorously with insurance companies), while some employers also provide benefits through health maintenance organizations or preferred-provider organizations. In most cases coverage under an HMO or PPO is not offered to employees as the only plan available but as an alternative to a more traditional insurance company plan or Blue Cross–Blue Shield plan.

Precise statistics indicating the relative significance of these alternate providers of medical expense coverage are difficult to obtain, particularly for group insurance. For example, many Blue Cross and Blue Shield associations and health maintenance organizations report only the total number of persons covered and make no distinction between individual coverage and group coverage. Many persons receive portions of their coverage from different types of providers, such as hospital coverage from a Blue Cross plan and other medical expense coverages from an insurance company under a supplemental major medical contract. In addition, self-funded plans may purchase stop-loss coverage and/or utilize preferred-provider organizations.

Even though precise statistics cannot be obtained, there is no doubt that a significant change has taken place over the last decade. In 1980 approximately 90 percent of all insured workers were covered under "traditional" medical expense plans, and 5 percent were covered under health maintenance organizations. *Traditional* means that if a worker or family member was sick, he or she had complete freedom in choosing a doctor or a hospital. Medical bills were paid by the plan, and no attempts were made to control costs or the utilization of services. It is estimated that between 10 and 15 percent of the employees under these traditional plans were in plans that were totally self-funded by the employer; the remainder of the employees were split fairly evenly between plans written by insurance companies and the Blues.

By the early 1990s the figures had changed dramatically, with the majority of employees now covered under plans that control costs and the access to medical care. It is now estimated that approximately 50 percent of employees are enrolled in managed-care plans—either HMOs, PPOs, or point-of-service plans. Of the remaining employees few are in traditional plans. Many are still with insurance companies and the Blues, but under plans that incorporate varying degrees of managed care.

One important change is hidden in these statistics—the increasing trend toward self-funding of medical expenses by employers. It is estimated that over 50 percent of all workers are covered under plans that are totally or substantially self-funded. Self-funding is more prevalent as the number of employees increases, with between 80 and 90 percent of persons who work for employers with more than 20,000 employees being covered under self-funded plans. However, self-funded is also used by employers with as few as 25 to 50 employees. It should be noted that the way benefits are provided under a self-funded plan can vary. The employer may design the plan to provide benefits on an indemnity basis or as an HMO or PPO.

Blue Cross–Blue Shield Plans

Prior to the Great Depression "health" insurance contracts provided by insurance companies were primarily designed to give income benefits to individuals who were disabled by accidents and, to a limited degree, illnesses. However, it was generally accepted that individuals should pay their own medical expenses from their savings. During the depression the savings of many individuals disappeared, unemployment was severe, and most insurance companies ceased writing disability income contracts. Faced with financial difficulties arising from the inability of many patients to pay their bills, many hospitals established plans for the prepayment of hospital expenses. By paying a monthly fee to the hospital a subscriber (the term used to describe persons covered by such plans) was entitled to a limited number of days of hospitalization per year. The early plans were limited to a single hospital, but by the mid-1930s many plans had become communitywide or statewide operations, offering subscribers the choice of using any participating hospital. Much of this expansion resulted from actions by the American Hospital Association to promote and control this type of plan. In the late 1930s the American Hospital Association adopted the Blue Cross name and emblem and permitted them to be used only by plans that met standards established by the association. As a general rule only one plan within a geographic area was allowed to use the Blue Cross name. Eventually the Blue Cross activities of the American Hospital Association were transferred to a separate national organization, the Blue Cross Association.

The success of the early Blue Cross plans and the inability of physicians to collect bills for their services during the depression resulted in the development of Blue Shield plans, established by local medical associations for the purpose of prepaying physicians' charges. The evolution of Blue Shield plans has paralleled that of Blue Cross plans, with the American Medical Association acting similarly to the American Hospital Association. Eventually the role of the American Medical Association was transferred to the National Association of Blue Shield Plans, which then became the national coordinating body.

To a large extent the persons covered by Blue Shield plans were the same ones whose hospital charges were covered by Blue Cross plans, and in many geographic regions this led to a close working relationship between the two. For many years in some areas of the country, one plan administered the other. However, this administration was typically on a fee-for-administration basis, with the two plans being separate legal entities. In recent years there has been a consolidation of more than half of the Blue Cross and Blue Shield plans. In most cases this consolidation has taken the form of a complete merger; in other cases the consolidation has only been partial. These partial consolidations have resulted in Blue Cross–Blue Shield plans that operate under a single staff but with separate governing boards.

There has been consolidation at the national level also. In 1978 the staffs of the two national organizations were merged, and a new organization—the Blue Cross and Blue Shield Associations—was formed to act on matters of mutual interest to both Blue Cross plans and Blue Shield plans. It was governed by members of the boards from both the Blue Cross Association and the National Association of Blue Shield Plans. In 1982 a complete merger took place with the resulting organization called the Blue Cross and Blue Shield Association.

As of mid-1992 there were 53 plans in existence that jointly wrote Blue Cross and Blue Shield coverage. In addition, there were 8 separate Blue Cross plans and 12 separate Blue Shield plans. Most states are served by a single joint plan or only one separate Blue Cross–Blue Shield plan. However, in a few states there is more than one plan, each operating within a specific geographic region. In a few sparsely populated states plans may cover more than one state. Only in rare instances is there any overlapping of the geographic areas served by individual plans.

Each local Blue Cross, Blue Shield, or Blue Cross–Blue Shield plan is a legally separate entity operated by a governing board, which establishes specific practices for the plan in accordance with the broad standards of the national Blue Cross and Blue Shield Association. Consequently individual plans may differ substantially from one another. The boards of these plans used to be dominated by the providers of coverage, but now the boards of most plans are dominated by "nonproviders," including representatives of consumer organizations, foundations, labor unions, businesses, and the general public.

A Comparison of the Blues and Insurance Companies

Perhaps the best way to describe the characteristics of Blue Cross–Blue Shield plans is to compare them with the characteristics of insurance companies. Traditionally the similarities between the Blues and insurance companies were overshadowed by their differences. Over time, however, intense competition has often caused one type of provider to adopt the more popular, but differing, practices of the other. As a result insurance companies and the Blues are becoming increasingly similar, in spite of their many distinctly different characteristics.

Regulation and Taxation

In a few states Blue Cross–Blue Shield plans are regulated under the same laws that apply to insurance companies. However, in most states the Blues are considered nonprofit organizations and are regulated under special legislation. Typically this regulation is carried out by the same body that regulates insurance companies. In some respects the Blues receive preferential treatment over insurance companies. Probably the most significant example of this treatment is their exemption from premium taxation and income taxation by the majority of states. Since premium taxes (usually about 2 percent of premiums) are passed on to consumers, this gives the Blues a cost advantage. In many other respects, however, the Blues are subject to more stringent regulation than insurance companies. For example, in most states their rates are subject to regulatory approval. With recent trends toward consumerism, this approval has become more burdensome and expensive.

In addition, the Blues are also accorded favorable tax treatment under the federal income tax laws. Prior to the Tax Reform Act of 1986 the Blues (except for the few plans that were incorporated as insurance companies) were exempt from federal income taxation. The tax act eliminated this complete exemption. Because of various deductions that can be taken, however, the average effective tax rate for the Blues is significantly below the average tax rate for insurance companies.

Form of Benefits

Traditionally the Blues have offered benefits in the form of services, while insurance companies have offered benefits on an indemnity (or reimbursement) basis. Under the service-benefit concept, benefits are expressed in terms of the services that will be provided by the hospitals or physicians participating in the plan rather than in terms of dollar maximums. For example, a Blue Cross plan might provide up to 90 days of hospitalization per year in semiprivate accommodations. In contrast, an insurance company might provide reimbursement for hospital charges subject to both dollar and duration limits, such as $400 per day for 90 days. In both cases, however, any charges in excess of the benefits must be borne by the covered person.

Blue Cross−Blue Shield plans involve two separate types of contractual relationship: a plan promises to provide specified services to a subscriber for whom a premium has been paid, and it has contracts with providers of services whereby the providers are reimbursed for the cost of services rendered to subscribers. In general subscribers are not billed for the cost of covered services or required to file claim forms. Rather, this is negotiated between the plan and the providers. This type of arrangement generally requires that subscribers receive their services from providers participating in the plan; however, most hospitals and physicians are participants. If nonparticipating providers can be used (such as for emergencies), benefits are usually paid on an indemnity basis, as is done by insurance companies.

In contrast, an insurance company agrees only to reimburse a covered person for medical expenses up to the limits specified in the insurance contract. There is no contractual relationship between the providers of medical services and the insurance company. Thus covered persons must file the appropriate claim forms. While covered persons have a legal obligation to pay their medical bills, the insurance company's obligation (unless benefits are assigned) is only to reimburse the covered person, not to actually pay the providers. However, most hospitals and many other providers require that any potential insurance benefits be assigned to them by a patient before they will render services. In effect, such an assignment requires the insurance company to pay benefits directly to the provider on behalf of the covered person.

In the past insurance companies incorporated maximum daily room and board limits into their contracts that did not cover medical expenses in full. However, to compete with the Blues, many insurance companies now frequently write contracts that provide full reimbursement for certain medical expenses. Even though a covered person may see little difference in the benefits received from either type of provider, the traditional distinction still exists: the Blues are providing services while insurance companies are providing reimbursement for the cost of services.

Types of Benefits

Over the years the Blues have specialized in providing basic medical benefits, with Blue Cross providing coverage for hospital expenses and Blue Shield providing coverage for surgical expenses and physicians' visits. Major medical benefits were rarely available. However, competition from insurance companies and increased cooperation between Blue Cross and Blue Shield have resulted in the Blues' now offering virtually the same coverages as insurance companies. It is interesting to note that as the Blues have expanded the scope of benefits offered, they have frequently included deductible and coinsurance provisions similar to those used by insurance companies. When there is a deducible, a covered person is required to pay expenses up to some limit (such as $100 per year or per illness) out of his or her own pocket before benefits will be paid. When coinsurance is used, a covered person is required to pay a percentage (such as 20 percent) of some or all expenses, the remaining portion being covered under the medical expense plan.

The advantage many insurance companies have had over the Blues has been their ability to offer a wide variety of group benefits, including life insurance coverage and disability income coverage. Until a few years ago most states had laws and regulations that prevented the Blues from offering any coverage other than medical expense benefits. However, because of changes in these laws and regulations, the Blues can now offer a wider range of group benefits to their subscribers. While competition between the Blues and insurance companies over writing these other benefits is increasing, the Blues currently write relatively little coverage other than medical expense benefits.

Reimbursement of Providers

The method by which the Blues reimburse the providers often results in their having a competitive advantage over insurance companies. Most Blue Cross plans pay participating hospitals on a per diem basis for each day a subscriber is hospitalized. Periodic negotiations with Blue Cross determine the amount of this payment (which includes room-and-board charges as well as other covered charges) for each hospital. For example, if the per diem amount is $600, the hospital will receive $600 for each day a subscriber is hospitalized, regardless of what the actual charges might be. While this per diem amount will be adequate on the average, the hospital will "lose money" on some patients but "make money" on others.

In addition to the administrative simplicity of this method of reimbursement, the per diem amount is often less than the average daily hospital charges. Frequently it is determined by excluding such hospital costs as bad debts, charity care, and nursing school costs. These costs, however, are used in determining charges for patients who are not Blue Cross subscribers. Therefore Blue Cross subscribers in effect receive a discount on the charges made to other patients, including those whose benefits are provided by insurance companies. This discount (except to the extent that it results from administrative savings) has not been allowed in some states and has come under increasing criticism where it is the normal practice. In general its size has been reduced in recent years, often due to legislation or regulation. It is interesting to note that there have been some experimental attempts by insurance companies to lower their cost of claims handling by using a similar reimbursement procedure with hospitals.

Under some Blue Shield plans physicians may also be reimbursed at less than their actual charges, as will be discussed later in this chapter.

National Coverage

While Blue Cross–Blue Shield plans operate in precise geographic regions, many insurance companies operate on a national basis. Therefore the Blues have had a more difficult time competing with insurance companies for the group insurance business of employers whose employees are located in areas served by various Blue Cross–Blue Shield plans. Even though the Blues have developed procedures for providing coverage to these "national accounts," most benefits specialists seem to feel that insurance companies have the competitive advantage in this regard.

Flexibility

There also seems to be a feeling among benefit consultants that insurance companies have a greater degree of flexibility in modifying their group contracts to meet the needs and desires of employers. Blue Cross–Blue Shield contracts have traditionally been quite standardized, with few, if any, variations allowed. One major reason for this rigidity is that changes in the benefits promised to subscribers also have an effect on the contracts between the Blues and the providers. However, with employers increasingly wanting new approaches to medical expense benefits, often for cost-containment reasons, many Blue Cross–Blue Shield plans have taken a more flexible approach. Considerable variations exist among plans, and some have been very innovative in meeting the demands of the marketplace, even going as far as to administer benefit plans that are self-funded by employers.

Rating

In their early years the Blues used only a "community-rating" approach in determining what premium rates to charge. Under this approach each plan uses the same rate structure for all subscribers, regardless of their past or potential loss experience and regardless of whether coverage is written on an individual or group basis. Usually the only variations in the rate structure result from variations in coverage: whether it is for an individual, a couple without children, or a family. The philosophy behind the community-rating approach is that coverage should be available to the widest range of persons possible at an affordable cost. Charging lower premium rates to segments of the community with better-than-average loss experience is thought to result in higher, and possibly unaffordable, premium rates for other segments of the community.

The use of community rating placed Blue Cross and Blue Shield at a competitive disadvantage when insurance companies began to aggressively market group medical expense insurance and use experience rating. With experience rating, insurance companies were frequently able to charge certain employer groups considerably lower premiums than those charged by the Blues. As a result by the mid-1950s insurance companies surpassed the Blues in the number of persons covered. Faced with the increasing dilemma that rate increases necessary to compensate for the loss of better-than-average business tended to drive even more business to the insurance companies, the Blues initiated the use of experience rating for groups. Today there is little difference in this regard between these two major providers with respect to group business. However, the Blues still use community rating in pricing products for smaller employers and for the individual marketplace.

Marketing

The Blues tend to have lower acquisition expenses than insurance companies, and most coverage is marketed by salaried employees. However, more than half of the plans also market coverage through agents and/or brokers in addition to their own sales forces. In general the commissions paid to agents or brokers are below the commissions paid by insurance companies.

Health Maintenance Organizations

Since the early 1970s the concept of health maintenance organizations (HMOs) has received considerable attention. Because the nature of these organizations varies, a precise definition is difficult. However, HMOs are generally regarded as organized systems of health care that provide a comprehensive array of medical services on a prepaid basis to voluntarily enrolled persons living within a specified geographic region. HMOs act like insurance companies and the Blues in that they finance health care. However, unlike insurance companies and the Blues, they also deliver medical services.

Even though the term *health maintenance organization* is relatively new, the concept of the HMO is not. For many years prepaid group practice plans (as they were called) have operated successfully in many parts of the country. However, growth was relatively slow until the passage of the Health Maintenance Organization Act of 1973. This act resulted from a belief on the part of the federal government that HMOs were a viable alternative method of financing and delivering health care and thus should be encouraged. In fact, the act has also resulted in many employers' being required to offer their employees the option of coverage by an HMO instead of by a more traditional medical expense plan. As of 1992 there were approximately 600 HMOs in existence.

Characteristics of HMOs

HMOs have several characteristics that distinguish them from insurance companies and the Blues.

Comprehensive Care. HMOs offer their subscribers a comprehensive package of health-care services, generally including benefits for outpatient services as well as for hospitalization. These services are usually provided to subscribers at no cost except the periodically required premium (referred to as a capitation payment). However, in some cases a modest copayment, such as $5 per physician's visit or $3 per drug prescription, may be imposed. HMOs emphasize preventive care and provide such services as routine physicals and immunizations. The cost of such preventive care is usually not covered under the contracts of insurance companies or the Blues, even when major medical coverage is provided. (A comparison of an HMO plan with a major medical plan of an insurance company is presented in chapter 8.)

Delivery of Medical Services. HMOs provide for the delivery of medical services, which in many cases are performed by salaried physicians and other personnel employed by the HMO. This is in contrast of the usual fee-for-service delivery system of medical care. However, some HMOs do contract with providers on a fee-for-services basis.

Subscribers are required to obtain their care from providers of medical services who are affiliated with the HMO. Since HMOs rarely operate in a geographic region any larger than a single metropolitan area, this may result in limited coverage for subscribers if treatment is received elsewhere. Most HMOs do have "out-of-area coverage" but only in the case of medical emergencies.

HMOs emphasize treatment by primary-care physicians to the greatest extent possible. These practitioners provide a gatekeeper function and control access to specialists. The HMO covers benefits provided by a specialist only if the specialist is recommended by the primary-care physician. This specialist may be a fellow employee in a group-practice plan or a physician who has a contract with the HMO. The subscriber has little or no say regarding the specialist selected, which has been one of the more controversial aspects of HMOs and one that has discouraged larger enrollment. However, some newer forms of HMOs (called point-of-service plans) do allow more freedom of choice. These plans are discussed later.

Cost Control. A major emphasis of HMOs is the control of medical expenses. By providing and encouraging preventive care, HMOs attempt to detect and treat medical conditions at an early stage, thereby avoiding expensive medical treatment in the future. There has also been an attempt by HMOs to provide treatment on an outpatient basis whenever possible. Because insurance companies and the Blues have in the past provided more comprehensive coverage for a hospitalized person, less expensive outpatient treatments were often not performed. This emphasis on outpatient treatment and preventive medicine has resulted in a much lower hospitalization rate for HMO subscribers than for the population as a whole. However, it appears that some of this decreased hospitalization rate is a result of younger and healthier employees' being more likely to elect HMO coverage.

The use of salaried employees by many HMOs may also result in lower costs since the physician or other provider of care has no financial incentive to prescribe additional, and possibly unnecessary, treatment. In fact, the physicians and other medical professionals in some HMOs may receive bonuses if the HMO operates efficiently and has a surplus from the capitation payments received.

Sponsorship of HMOs

Traditionally most HMOs were operated as nonprofit organizations, and these organizations currently have the majority of subscribers. However, the majority of new HMOs are profit making. While many subscribers are covered by HMOs that have been sponsored by consumer groups, a sizable and increasing portion is covered by plans sponsored by insurance companies or the Blues. Sponsorship may also come from physicians, hospitals, or labor unions.

The issue of whether insurance companies should be involved with HMOs has been a source of disagreement within the industry. Some insurance companies view HMOs as competitors with the potential of putting them out of the health insurance business. Other insurance companies view them as a viable alternative method of financing and delivering health care that can be offered to employers as one of the products in their portfolio. In addition to actually sponsoring and owning HMOs, some insurance companies are actively involved with HMOs in a variety of ways. These include

- consulting on such matters as plan design and administration
- administrative services, such as actuarial advice, claims monitoring, accounting, and computer services
- marketing assistance, such as designing sales literature. In a few cases the agents of insurance companies have been used to market HMOs. This has been done in conjunction with the marketing of the insurance company's hospitalization plan when the HMO does not provide hospitalization coverage to its subscribers.
- providing hospitalization coverage. HMOs that do not control their own hospital facilities may provide this benefit by purchasing coverage for their subscribers.
- providing emergency out-of-area coverage. An insurance company operating on a national basis may be better equipped to administer these claims than an HMO.
- providing financial support in a variety of ways, including reinsurance if an HMO experiences greater-than-expected demand for services and agreements to bail out financially troubled HMOs

Types of HMOs

There are three basic types of HMOs—group-practice plans, individual practice association plans, and open-ended plans.

The earliest type of HMO is the group-practice plan. While this type of plan accounts for only about 15 percent of the total number of HMOs, slightly more than half of HMO subscribers are covered under group-practice plans. Under this arrangement physicians (and other medical personnel) are either (1) employees of the HMO, which pays their salary, or (2) employees of another legal entity that has a contractual relationship with the HMO to provide medical services for its subscribers. The first approach is often referred to as a staff model and the second approach as a group model when the contractual arrangement is with one group of providers and a network model when the contractual relationship is with two or more provider groups. The physicians participating in group practice

HMOs are normally general practitioners and medical specialists who practice as a group, sharing facilities and support personnel. The plan may have a single facility for physicians that is frequently located in or near a hospital owned by the HMO or with which the HMO has an agreement to provide the necessary care for subscribers. Some of the larger group practice plans may also have other facilities, often staffed only by general practitioners, that are located throughout the geographic area served by the plan. If a plan or the legal entity contracting with the plan is not large enough to justify the hiring of certain types of specialists on a salaried basis, the HMO frequently makes contractual agreements with such specialists to provide their services to subscribers as needed. These specialists tend to be paid on a fee-for-service basis.

Group practice plans are often referred to as closed-panel plans since subscribers must use physicians employed by the plan or by the organization with which it contracts. With most plans having several general practitioners, subscribers may usually select their physician from among those accepting new patients and make medical appointments just as if the physician were in private practice. However, there is frequently little choice among specialists since a plan may employ or have a contract with only one physician in a given specialty.

In individual practice association plans participating physicians practice individually or in small groups at their own offices. In most cases these physicians accept non-HMO patients on a traditional fee-for-service basis, as well as HMO subscribers. Individual practice association plans are often referred to as open-panel plans since subscribers choose from a list of participating physicians. The number of physicians participating in this type of HMO is frequently larger than the number participating in group practice plans and may include several physicians within a given specialty. In some geographic areas most physicians may participate; in other geographic areas only a relatively small percentage of the physicians may participate. Most of the newer HMOs are individual-practice associations, and therefore the percentage of HMO subscribers served by these plans is growing.

Several methods may be used to compensate physicians participating in an individual-practice association. The most common is a fee schedule based on the services provided to subscribers. To encourage physicians to be cost effective, it is common for plans to have a provision for reducing payments to physicians if the experience of the plan is worse than expected. In addition, the physicians may receive a bonus if the experience of the plan is better than expected. Particularly with respect to general practitioners, some individual-practice association plans pay each physician a flat annual amount for each subscriber who has elected to use that physician. For this annual payment the physician must see these subscribers as often as necessary during the year.

It is unusual for individual-practice association plans to own their own hospitals. Rather, they enter into contracts with local hospitals to provide the necessary services for their subscribers.

The newest type of HMO is the open-ended plan, often called a point-of-service plan. These plans are described later in this chapter.

Extent of HMO Use

It is estimated that approximately 40 million employees and dependents are covered under health maintenance organizations. However, this percentage varies considerably by geographic region and by employer. Except in rare instances employees covered by HMO plans have elected this form of coverage as an alternative to their employer's insurance company plan or Blue Cross—Blue Shield plans. Although many employers are required by state and/or federal law to offer an HMO option, other employers voluntarily make the option available. The administrative details of such an option may be burdensome and expensive for small employers, but they seem to pose few problems for large employers with specialized employee benefit staffs. In many cases the financial consequences to the employer of such an option are insignificant since the employer will make the same contribution on an employee's behalf regardless of which plan is selected. Until recently the general attitude of employers toward HMOs seems to have been somewhat ambivalent: some employers have been in favor of them, others against, and the majority indifferent. However, according to several recent studies, most employers feel that HMOs have been a very effective technique for controlling benefit costs. On the other hand, some employers feel that HMOs may actually increase the cost of providing medical care. HMOs have tended to attract the younger, healthier employees. In fact, many HMOs have designed their plans to appeal most to this group by providing benefits popular to the group, such as well-baby care. When these younger, healthier persons leave the insurance company plan or Blue Cross plan, its average cost per remaining employee will increase if the plan is experience rated. Unless the employer's cost for the HMO coverage drops correspondingly, the employer's aggregate medical expense premiums will increase.

Most employees do not elect an HMO option. However, studies have revealed that employees who have elected HMOs are for the most part satisfied with their choice and are unlikely to switch back to an insurance company plan or Blue Cross—Blue Shield plan as long as the HMO option remains available. The success of an HMO in attracting subscribers seems to be primarily related to the following factors:

- the reputation of the HMO. To some extent this is a function of the experience of the HMO. In those areas where HMOs have been established for many years, a larger percentage of employees participate.
- the extent to which employees have established relationships with physicians. Employees are reluctant to elect an HMO option if it requires them to give up a physician with whom they are satisfied. However, in some cases this physician may also participate in the HMO. In general new employees are more likely to elect an HMO option if they are now residents of the area or are just entering the labor force.
- the attitude of the employer. Employees are more likely to elect HMO coverage if the HMO option is effectively and enthusiastically communicated by their employer.
- costs. HMOs are obviously more attractive to employers when they offer a less expensive alternative to coverage under insurance company plans. However, in some cases an HMO option will be more expensive to an

employee, but the expense may be more than offset by broader coverage and the lack of deductibles and coinsurance. The more that employees view an HMO alternative as being less expensive in the long run, the greater the employee participation will be.

The Health Maintenance Organization Act of 1973

The Health Maintenance Organization Act of 1973 has had a significant influence on both the interest in and the growth of HMOs. The act introduced the concept of the *federally qualified* HMO. Most HMOs formed since the passage of the act have been organized to take advantage of this federal qualification, which entitles them to federal grants for feasibility studies and development (including grants to solicit subscribers) and federal loans (or loan guarantees) to assist them in covering initial operating deficits. In addition, employers may be required to offer the HMO as a "dual option" to employees. Most of the older HMOs have also become federally qualified, primarily because of this dual-choice provision of the act.

Federal Qualification

To become federally qualified an HMO must meet certain requirements (set forth in the act) to the satisfaction of the secretary of health and human services. In return for a periodic prepaid fee an HMO must provide the following basic benefits to its subscribers at no cost or with nominal copayments:

- physicians' services, including consultant and referral services, up to 10 percent of which may be provided by physicians who are not affiliated with the HMO
- inpatient and outpatient hospital services
- medically necessary emergency health services
- short-term (up to 20 visits) outpatient mental health services
- medical treatment and referral services for alcohol or drug abuse or addiction
- diagnostic laboratory services and diagnostic and therapeutic radiologic services
- home health services
- preventive health services, such as immunizations, well-baby care, periodic physical examinations, and family-planning services
- medical social services, including education in methods of personal health maintenance and in the use of health services

The HMO may also provide the following supplemental benefits either as part of its standard benefit package or as optional benefits for which an additional fee may be charged:

- services of intermediate and long-term care facilities
- vision care
- dental care
- additional mental health services

- rehabilitative services
- prescription drugs

In addition to the benefits that either are required or may be included, an HMO must meet other requirements with respect to its operations. These include

- a fiscally sound operation, including provisions against the risk of insolvency
- annual open enrollment periods
- an ongoing quality assurance program

Prior to 1988 the HMO Act required HMOs to determine their rates on the basis of community rating for all employer groups. This provision of the act decreased the attractiveness of HMOs to employers whose employees had lower-than-average benefit claims. Since a 1988 amendment to the act HMOs can establish advance rates based on an employer's past and projected claims experience if a group has 100 or more employees. Experience rating can also be used for groups of fewer than 100 employees, but the advance rate cannot be more than 10 percent higher than the HMO's community rates. In contrast to the usual practice of experience rating (see chapter 11), HMOs are *not* allowed to make retrospective rate adjustments if claims turn out to be higher or lower than expected.

Dual-Choice Provision

Under the act an employer must offer one or possibly more federally qualified HMOs to its employees as an option to its insurance company, Blue Cross–Blue Shield, or self-funded health care plan if all the following circumstances exist:

- The employer is required to pay its employees the minimum wage specified by the Fair Labor Standards Act.
- The employer has 25 or more employees, including both full-time and part-time employees.
- The employer covers eligible employees with a health-care plan for which the employer makes a monetary contribution.
- The employer has received a request to make coverage available to its employees from one or more federally qualified HMOs operating in a defined geographic area where at least 25 employees reside.

The request by an HMO must be in writing and contain specific information, such as a current financial report, the geographic area to be served, the facilities to be used, and rates to be charged. In addition, the request must be received by an employer at least 180 days prior to the expiration or renewal date of any existing health benefit plans. If employees are represented by a collective-bargaining unit, the HMO option must first be offered to the union for its acceptance or rejection. If the union rejects the option, the employer is under no further obligation with respect to union employees. However, if the union accepts the option or if some employees are not subject to collective bargaining, the employer must make the HMO option available to employees who reside in the service area of the HMO.

The dual-choice option applies separately to group-practice plans and to individual-practice association plans. Thus an employer may be required to offer one of each type. Furthermore, an employer must also offer the option of coverage in other qualified HMOs to its employees, provided the other HMOs request inclusion and serve areas that include the residences of at least 25 employees who either (1) do not reside in the service area of a qualified HMO that is already offered as an option or (2) cannot obtain coverage because the current HMO is no longer accepting new subscribers. Again, the employer is not required to offer more than one of each type of HMO covering the same geographic area.

When an employer is initially contacted by a federally qualified HMO serving an area in which eligible employees reside, the employer may deal with any qualified HMO of the same type serving that area and is not limited to the one making the initial contact. The decision of which HMO to include as an option is up to the employer.

This dual-choice provision as previously described is subject to a sunset provision of October 1, 1995. After that date no employer will be required to offer an HMO to its employees.

Once an HMO option is made available, an employer must provide for a group enrollment period of at least 10 working days each year in which eligible employees may transfer between any available health insurance plans without the application of waiting periods, exclusions, or limitations based on health status. During this open enrollment period and at least 30 days prior to it, an employer must allow any participating HMOs to have fair and reasonable access to eligible employees for purposes of presenting and explaining their programs.

Prior to a 1988 amendment to the HMO Act an employer was required to contribute as much toward the cost of an employee's coverage under an HMO as would have been paid for medical expense benefits if the employee had elected the employer's insurance company plan or Blue Cross—Blue Shield plan. Employers are now required only to make nondiscriminatory contributions to HMOs. This charge allows an employer to make the same percentage contribution toward an HMO's premium as is made toward premiums of other medical expense plans.

Some states also have laws requiring employers to offer HMO coverage under certain circumstances. In general these laws apply to any HMO within the state, regardless of whether it is federally qualified. In at least one state coverage must be offered and administered on a payroll-deduction basis even if the employer does not have an existing medical expense plan.

A problem may arise if an HMO ceases operations because of financial difficulties. Unfortunately this has occurred in several cases, even among those HMOs that have met the standards for federal qualification. Unless the cessation of HMO coverage coincides with an open enrollment period, these employees may not be able to join or rejoin their employer's insurance company plan or Blue Cross—Blue Shield plan without showing evidence of insurability. However, under these circumstances many insurance companies and Blue Cross—Blue Shield plans will include provisions in their contracts for coverage without evidence of insurability for these employees.

Preferred-Provider Organizations

A concept that continues to receive considerable attention from employers and insurance companies is the preferred-provider organization (PPO). A few PPOs have existed on a small scale for many years, but since the early 1980s PPOs have grown in number and begun to be viewed as a new weapon to control increased medical care costs. In 1992 approximately 1,000 PPOs were in existence, and an estimated 90 million employees and dependents had the option of using them for medical care.

While many variations exist, PPOs can basically be described as groups of health-care providers that contract with employers, insurance companies, union trust funds, third-party administrators, or others to provide medical care services at a reduced fee. PPOs may be organized by the providers themselves or by other organizations such as insurance companies, the Blues, or groups of employers. Like HMOs they may take the form of group practices or separate individual practices. They may provide a broad array of medical services, including physicians' services, hospital care, laboratory costs, and home health care, or they may be limited only to hospitalization or physicians' services. Some PPOs are very specialized and provide specific services such as dental care, mental health benefits, substance abuse services, maternity care, or prescription drugs.

PPOs typically differ from HMOs in two major respects. First, they rarely provide benefits on a prepaid basis. The participants in the PPO are generally paid on a fee-for-service basis as their services are used. However, fees are usually subject to a schedule that is the same for all participants in the PPO, and participants may have an incentive to control utilization through bonus arrangements. Second, employees are not required to use the practitioners or facilities of PPOs that contract with their group insurance company, Blue Cross–Blue Shield plan, or employer; rather, a choice can be made each time medical care is needed. However, employees are offered incentives to use the PPO, including lower or reduced deductibles and copayments as well as increased benefits such as preventive health care.

Employers were disappointed with some of the early PPOs. While discounts were received, they seemed to have little effect on benefit costs because discounts were from higher-than-average fees or providers were more likely to perform diagnostic tests or prolong hospital stays to generate additional fees to compensate for the discounts. Needless to say, these PPOs seldom lasted long.

The successful PPOs today emphasize quality care and utilization review. In selecting physicians and hospitals, PPOs look not only at the type of care provided but also at the cost-effectiveness of the provider. In this era of fierce competition among medical care providers, these physicians and hospitals are often willing to accept discounts in hopes of increasing patient volume. It is also important for a PPO to monitor and control utilization on an ongoing basis. In some cases bonuses are provided if the quantity of care is below specified utilization targets. However, there is always the risk that a low quantity of care may also be associated with a low quality of care.

Over time PPOs have continued to evolve, as have HMOs. Some PPOs provide benefits on a prepaid basis, while others perform a gatekeeper function. If a specialist is not recommended by a subscriber's primary-care physician, benefits may be reduced. With these changes it is sometimes difficult to determine the exact form of a managed-care organization. However, those that operate as traditional HMOs generally provide medical expense coverage at a slightly lower cost than those that operate as traditional PPOs. However, it must be pointed out that there are wide variations among HMOs as well as among PPOs. Therefore a careful analysis of quality of care, cost, and financial stability is necessary before a particular HMO or PPO is selected.

Point-of-Service Plans

While many employees have been attracted to the minimal out-of-pocket costs associated with HMOs, there has been considerable reluctance to join because of the limited choice of medical-care providers in case of a serious illness. As a result a number of newer HMOs have been designed as point-of-service plans (also referred to as open-ended HMOs). When a subscriber needs medical care, he or she may use the HMO physicians and facilities or elect to go elsewhere. Expenses for treatment received outside the HMO network are reimbursed as if the subscriber were covered under an indemnity plan. However, the deductibles and copayments tend to be higher than those in many indemnity plans. For example, one plan has a $300 annual deductible for outside office visits, and only 70 percent of the costs above the deductible are reimbursed.

Employers that use point-of-service plans hope that these plans will encourage a greater number of older and illness-prone employees to leave more expensive traditional benefit plans and join HMOs, which are viewed as being better able to control escalating medical costs. The early experience has shown this to be the case. One interesting result is that while new HMO subscribers still have the security of occasionally seeing an outside specialist, most subscribers have confined their visits solely to HMO physicians.

Multiple-Option Plans

Until recently an employer who wanted to make an HMO option available to employees had to enter into a separate contractual arrangement with the HMO. Unless a PPO was sponsored by the insurance company or Blue Cross–Blue Shield plan of an employer, a similar contractual arrangement was also required. Several insurance companies and Blue Cross–Blue Shield plans are now providing all these options under a single medical expense contract. For example, one insurer is marketing a so-called triple-option plan that gives employees the choice of a traditional fee-for-service indemnity plan, an indemnity plan using a PPO, or an HMO. In most cases the HMOs and PPOs used in such arrangements have been formed or purchased by the insurance company or Blue Cross–Blue Shield plan, but occasionally a contractual relationship has been established with an existing HMO or PPO.

These plans offer certain advantages to the employer. First, administration is easier since all elements of the plan are purchased form a single provider. Second, costs may be lower since the entire plan, including the HMO, is normally subject to experience rating. Because federally qualified HMOs cannot fully use experience rating, only nonfederally qualified HMOs are typically used in multiple-option plans.

Self-Funded Plans

It should be obvious from the first few pages of this chapter that self-funding of medical expense plans is becoming increasingly common. Self-funding, which is discussed in detail in chapter 12, may not only result in cost savings but also improve an employer's cash flow.

The remainder of this chapter and the discussion of major medical benefits in the following chapter focus primarily on insured plans. However, it is important to remember that a self-funded plan must be properly designed. Most self-funded plans have "borrowed" liberally from insured plans and contain similar if not identical provisions.

BASIC MEDICAL EXPENSE COVERAGES

Traditionally medical expense coverage has consisted of separate benefits for hospital expenses, surgical expenses, and physicians' visits. Coverage was limited, and many types of medical expenses were not covered. In this environment two developments took place: basic coverages for other types of medical expenses were developed, and a vast majority of employers began to provide more extensive benefits to employees than had previously been available through the commonly written basic coverages. While this broader coverage is increasingly being provided through a single comprehensive contract, a significant number of employees are still covered under medical expense plans that consist of selected basic coverages supplemented by a major medical contract. This is particularly true for large employers. Small employers are much more likely to use a single major medical contract. The remainder of this chapter will describe these basic coverages. They consist of the three traditional coverages for

- hospital expense benefits
- surgical expense benefits
- physicians' visits expense benefits

as well as the following newer coverages for

- extended care facilities
- home health care
- hospice care
- ambulatory care
- birthing centers
- diagnostic X-ray and laboratory services
- radiation therapy
- supplemental accident benefits
- prescription drugs
- vision care

While many of these coverages can be written separately, it is not unusual for them to be incorporated into a single contract. During the remainder of this chapter it should be remembered that many of the medical expenses for which basic benefit coverage is either limited or excluded would be covered under a supplemental major medical contract.

Hospital Expense Benefits

Hospital expense coverage provides benefits for charges incurred in a hospital by a covered person (that is, the employee or his or her dependents) who is an inpatient or, in some circumstances, an outpatient. Every medical expense contract defines what is meant by a hospital. While the actual wording may vary among insurance companies and in some states, the following definition is typical:

> The term *hospital* means (1) an institution that is accredited as a hospital under the hospital accreditation program of the Joint Commission on Accreditation of Hospitals or (2) any other institution that is legally operated under the supervision of a staff of physicians and with 24-hour-a-day nursing service. In no event should the term *hospital* include a convalescent nursing home or include any institution or part thereof that (1) is used principally as a convalescent facility, rest facility, nursing facility, or facility for the aged; or (2) furnishes primarily domiciliary or custodial care, including training in the routines of daily living; or (3) is operated primarily as a school.

Inpatient Benefits

Hospital inpatient benefits fall into two categories: coverage for room-and-board charges and coverage for "other charges."

Room and Board. Coverage for room-and-board charges includes the cost of the hospital room, meals, and the services normally provided to all inpatients, including routine nursing care. Separate charges for such items as telephones and televisions are usually not covered. Benefits are normally provided for a specific number of days for each separate hospital confinement, a time period that may vary from 31 days to 365 days. Some contracts provide coverage for an unlimited number of days. For purposes of this time period as well as for other benefits, most contracts stipulate that successive periods of hospital confinement will be treated as a single hospital confinement unless they (1) arise from entirely unrelated causes or (2) are separated by the employee's return to continuous full-time active employment for some period of time, such as 2 weeks. For dependents this latter requirement is replaced by one specifying that they must completely recover or remain out of the hospital for some period of time, such as 3 months.

The amount of the daily room-and-board benefit may be expressed in one of two ways: either a flat-dollar maximum or the cost of semiprivate accommodations. Under the first approach benefits are provided for actual room-and-board charges up to a maximum daily amount, such as $400. Employers using this approach may have different maximum benefits for employees in different locations to reflect geographic variations in hospital costs.

The majority of hospital expense contracts cover actual room-and-board charges up to the cost of semiprivate accommodations (that is, two-person rooms) in the hospital in which the covered person is confined. This is the traditional approach used by Blue Cross plans and is increasingly used by insurance companies. The cost of a private room may be covered in full if it is medically necessary. If a private room is not medically necessary, covered persons electing such accommodations must usually pay any charges above the normal semiprivate room rate. However, a few insurance plans provide additional coverage, usually a fixed daily dollar amount, for elective private room occupancy.

Many hospital expense contracts include additional room-and-board benefits for confinement in an intensive care unit. In some cases, particularly when normal room-and-board benefits are subject to a dollar maximum, intensive care benefits are expressed as some multiple (commonly two) of the normal room-and-board benefit. In those cases where benefits are provided for the cost of semiprivate accommodations, intensive care charges are frequently covered in full. However, in both cases intensive care benefits may be subject to either a time limit or an overall dollar maximum.

Other Charges. Coverage for "other charges" (often referred to as miscellaneous charges, ancillary charges, or hospital extras) provides benefits for certain services and supplies ordered by a physician during a covered person's hospital confinement, such as drugs, operating room charges, laboratory services, and X rays. However, with a few exceptions only the hospital portion of these charges is covered; any associated charges for professional services such as physicians' fees are not covered. The exceptions often include charges for anesthesia and ambulance services. Traditionally anesthesia and its administration were provided and billed by the hospital and considered a covered expense. As anesthesia came to be administered and separately billed by physicians not employed by the hospital, many hospital expense benefit contracts were altered to cover anesthesia if it was administered in a hospital, whether the patient was billed by the hospital or by a physician. Recently, however, the trend has been toward covering anesthesia as a surgical expense benefit instead of a hospital expense benefit.

The amount of the benefit for other charges is usually expressed in one of the following three ways:

- full coverage up to a dollar maximum. This approach is most commonly found in contracts when the daily room-and-board benefit is also subject to a dollar limit. In most cases this maximum is some multiple (often 20) of the daily room-and-board benefit. For example, a contract with a daily room-and-board benefit of $400 might have an $8,000 maximum for other charges.
- full coverage up to a dollar maximum (again, often expressed as a multiple of the room-and-board benefit) and partial coverage for a limited amount of additional expenses. For example, a contract might cover the first $2,000 of charges in full and 75 percent of the next $3,000 in charges.
- full payment subject only to the duration for which room-and-board benefits are payable. While this approach is normally associated with contracts that provide room-and-board benefits equal to the cost of semiprivate accommodations, it may also be used when room-and-board benefits are subject to a daily maximum.

When coverage for ambulance services is provided, it is common to limit the benefit to a dollar maximum, such as $50 per hospital confinement. A few plans have a mileage limit in lieu of a dollar limit.

Preadmission Certification. As a method of controlling costs medical expense plans are increasingly adopting utilization review programs. One aspect of these programs, which were discussed earlier in this chapter, is preadmission certification. Such a program requires that a covered person or his or her physician obtain prior authorization for any nonemergency hospitalization. Authorization usually must also be obtained within 24 to 48 hours of admissions for emergencies.

The initial reviewer, typically a registered nurse, determines whether hospitalization or some type of alternative care is most appropriate and what the appropriate length of stay for the medical condition should be. If the preapproved length of stay is insufficient, the patient's physician must obtain prior approval for any extension.

Most plans reduce benefits if the preadmission certification procedure is not followed. Probably the most common reduction is to pay only 50 percent of the benefit that would otherwise be paid. If a patient enters the hospital after a preadmission certification has been denied, many plans will not pay for any hospital expenses. Other plans will provide a reduced level of benefits.

Outpatient Benefits

Traditionally hospital expense contracts did not cover outpatient expenses. However, it is not unusual today to find coverage for hospital outpatient expenses arising from the following:

- surgery. When broader coverage exists for surgery performed on inpatients than on outpatients, there is no question that unnecessary hospitalization is encouraged. The purpose of this benefit is to provide comparable coverage and thus lower hospital utilization (when surgical procedures can be performed on an outpatient basis). It should be noted that this benefit covers only hospital charges (such as the use of operating facilities), not the surgeon's fee.
- preadmission testing. The first day or two of hospital confinements, particularly for surgical procedures, are often devoted to the performance of necessary diagnostic tests and X rays. This benefit encourages the performing of these procedures on an outpatient basis prior to hospitalization by covering the costs as if the person were an inpatient. For benefits to be paid these procedures must generally be (1) performed after a hospital confinement for surgery has been scheduled, (2) ordered by the same physician who ordered the hospital confinement, (3) performed in the hospital where the confinement will take place, and (4) accepted by the hospital in lieu of the same tests that would normally be performed during confinement. Benefits are paid even if the preadmission testing leads to a cancellation of the scheduled confinement. Even when benefits for preadmission testing are available, they are sometimes not used because physicians and patients find it easier to have such testing performed on an inpatient basis.

- emergency room treatment. Hospital expense contracts commonly provide coverage for emergency room treatment of accidental injuries within some specified time period (varying from 24 to 72 hours) after an accident. In a few cases similar benefits are also provided for sudden and serious illnesses. It should be noted that any emergency room charges incurred immediately prior to hospitalization are considered inpatient expenses.

In most cases these outpatient expenses are treated like other charges, but in some hospital expense plans, separate benefits may apply to outpatient surgery and emergency room treatment.

Exclusions

While variations exist among the providers of hospital coverage (some of which result from state legislation), most hospital expense contracts do not usually cover expenses resulting from the following:

- occupational injury or disease to the extent that benefits are provided by workers' compensation laws or similar legislation. Many contracts exclude coverage for benefits available through workers' compensation laws. Thus work-related hospital expenses are excluded even if the employer has not purchased workers' compensation coverage.
- cosmetic surgery unless such surgery is to correct a condition resulting from an accidental injury incurred while the covered person is insured under the contract
- physical examinations (including diagnostic tests and X rays) unless such examinations are necessary for the treatment of an injury or illness
- convalescent, custodial, or rest care
- private-duty nursing
- services furnished by or on behalf of government agencies unless there is a requirement for either the patient or the patient's medical expense plan to pay for the services. Prior to the passage of the Consolidated Omnibus Budget Reconciliation Act of 1985, it was common for employee benefit plans to exclude payment for medical services received in a Veterans' Administration or military hospital since the patient had no legal obligation to pay. Under provisions of the act medical expense plans must generally pay benefits to the government on the same basis as they would have paid if care had been received elsewhere. However, if a plan does not pay charges in full because of deductibles, coinsurance, or plan limitations, the patient is not responsible for the balance. With respect to VA hospitals the provisions of the act apply only to non-service-connected disabilities. The rules for military hospitals apply to retired (but not active) members of the armed services and most spouses and dependent children of active or retired military persons.

Hospital expense contracts may also exclude (or only provide limited coverage for) expenses arising from mental illness, alcoholism, and drug addiction unless these exclusions are prohibited by law. Until the amendment in the Civil Rights Act in 1978 it was not unusual to exclude maternity-related expenses from hospital expense contracts. However, the act now requires that benefit plans or employers with 15 or more employees treat pregnancy, childbirth, and related conditions the same as any other illness. (See chapter 3.)

In the absence of state laws to the contrary, pregnancy may be and often is excluded under group insurance contracts written for employers with fewer than 15 employees. If these employers wish to provide such coverage, it can usually be added as an optional benefit. In some cases pregnancy is treated like any other illness covered under the contract. In other cases benefits are determined in accordance with a schedule that most commonly provides an all-inclusive benefit for hospital, surgical, and certain other expenses associated with delivery. Regular physician visits and diagnostic tests may or may not be covered. The following is an example of a maternity schedule:

Type of Pregnancy	Benefit
Normal Delivery	$1,500
Cesarean	3,000
Miscarriage	750

A variation of this schedule that is often used by Blue Cross–Blue Shield plans provides a surgical benefit (possibly including visits prior to delivery) but covers hospital expenses on a semiprivate room basis.

An expense associated with maternity is the nursery charge for a newborn infant. In most cases this will be equal to at least 50 percent of a hospital's normal room-and-board charge. This expense is not covered as part of a maternity benefit and is not covered under many hospital expense contracts if the infant is healthy (since the contract covers only expenses associated with accidents and illnesses). However, some contracts do cover nursery charges, and a number of states require that they be covered.

Deductibles and Coinsurance

It is common for deductibles and coinsurance to apply to major medical expense coverages. In contrast, hospital expenses under basic hospital expense coverage (and benefits under other basic medical expense coverages as well) are usually not subject to deductibles or coinsurance. Rather, any limitations that exist are most likely to be in the form of maximum amounts that will be paid.

Surgical Expense Benefits

Surgical expense coverage provides benefits for physicians' charges associated with surgical procedures. While one tends to think of a surgical procedure as involving cutting, insurance contracts typically define the term broadly to include such procedures as suturing, electrocauterization, removal of a stone or foreign body by endoscopic means, and the treatment of fractures or dislocations.

Even though surgical expense coverage is frequently sold in connection with hospital expense coverage, surgical expense coverage normally provides benefits for surgery performed not only in the hospital (either as an inpatient or an outpatient), but also as an outpatient in a free-standing (that is, separate from a hospital) ambulatory surgical center and in a physician's office. To discourage unnecessary hospitalization, some surgical expense benefit contracts actually provide larger benefits if a procedure is performed as outpatient surgery.

Outpatient surgery also results in charges for medical supplies, nurses, and the use of facilities. As mentioned, these charges are often covered if surgery is performed on an outpatient basis in a hospital. However, neither hospital expense coverage nor surgical expense coverage usually provides such benefits if the surgery is performed in a physician's office or in an ambulatory surgical center. Even though not specifically covered, costs of alternate facilities are paid by some insurance companies (and required by some states) when their use has clearly prevented hospital expenses from being incurred. As will be discussed later in this chapter, benefits for ambulatory care centers are sometimes included as an additional basic coverage.

Benefits

Surgical expense coverage traditionally provided benefits only for the fee of the primary surgeon. However, newer contracts often provide separate benefits for assistant surgeons and anesthesiologists as well. Since both hospital expense coverage and surgical expense coverage often cover anesthesia, it is important that an overall medical expense plan be properly designed to make sure this benefit is neither omitted nor overlapping. The major difficulty in this regard occurs when different providers are used for the hospital and surgical benefits.

Benefit amounts may be expressed in several ways, ranging from a schedule of fees to the full payment of actual charges.

Fee Schedule. In providing basic surgical expense benefits, some insurance companies and some Blue Shield plans use either a fee schedule or a relative value schedule in which charges are paid up to the maximum amounts specified in the schedule of surgical procedures contained in the master contract. It is common to refer to a fee schedule by the maximum amount that will be paid for the most expensive procedure, even though for the vast majority of procedures the benefits that will be paid are less, reflecting the relatively lower costs for such procedures. The following is an excerpt from a *$2,000 schedule:*

Surgial Procedure	Maximum Benefit
Cardiovascular system:	
Aortic valve replacement	$2,000
Pericardiectomy	1,200
Digestive system:	
Adenoidectomy	100
Appendectomy	400
Tonsillectomy, under age 18 years	150
Tonsillectomy, over age 18 years	200
Respiratory system:	
Pneumonectomy	1,000
Tracheotomy	200

The benefit specified in the schedule of surgical procedures is the maximum amount that will be paid to the primary surgeon for all charges, including follow-up visits. To the extent that the charges of the primary surgeon are below this amount, the balance can generally be applied to charges of assistant surgeons and possibly anesthesiologists. If separate benefits are provided for an assistant surgeon, they are usually a percentage, commonly 20 percent, of this amount. If benefits are provided for an anesthesiologist, a separate dollar maximum also varying by procedure will usually be specified. The typical fee schedule contains between 100 and 200 of the more common surgical procedures. When other surgical procedures are performed, payment is based on an amount determined by the insurance company but consistent with the fee schedule. For example, if the charge for an unlisted procedure is typically the same as for an appendectomy, the benefit maximum for that procedure will most likely be used. If more than one surgical procedure is performed at the same time, the total benefit is normally limited to the maximum benefit payable for the most expensive procedure plus 50 percent of the maximum benefit payable for any other procedures. However, no additional amounts will usually be paid for the second procedure if it is considered incidental and if it is performed through the same incision.

Relative-Value Schedule. A variation of the fee schedule is the relative-value schedule in which the value of each surgical procedure is expressed in unit values that are relative to each other. For example, a surgical procedure with the unit value of 50 is considered to be twice as expensive as one with a unit value of 25. These relative values are based on statistics from insurance companies or state medical associations and may vary depending on the source of the statistics. The following is an excerpt from a relative-value schedule:

Surgical Procedure	Relative Value Units
Skin:	
Biopsy	3
Excision of pilonidal cyst	30
Stomach:	
Excision of ulcer or tumor	60
Total gastrectomy	100

To determine the actual maximum benefit that will be paid, it is necessary to multiply the relative value by a dollar-conversion factor selected by the policy-owner and specified in the master contract. For example, with a $20 conversion factor $60 would be paid for a skin biopsy and $1,200 for the removal of a stomach ulcer. Providers using relative-value schedules usually have the same schedule in all contracts but vary the levels of benefits for different policyowners by using different dollar-conversion factors. Employers can also take geographic variations in surgical costs into consideration by using different dollar-conversion factors for employees in different locations.

Reasonable-and-Customary Charges. The majority of surgical expense plans follow the approach used in major medical contracts and provide benefits to the extent that surgical charges are reasonable and customary. Unfortunately insurance contracts are vague as to the precise meaning of these terms, and each company determines what it considers reasonable and customary. In general reasonable-and-customary charges (sometimes referred to as usual, customary, and reasonable charges or prevailing charges) are considered to be those that fall within the range of fees normally charged for a given procedure by physicians of similar training and experience within a geographic region.

The usual practice of insurance companies is to pay charges in full as long as the charges do not exceed some percentile (usually ranging from the 85th to the 95th) of the range of charges for a specific surgical procedure within a certain geographic region. For example, if an insurance company uses the 90th percentile and if for a certain procedure 90 percent of the charges are $300 or less, this is the maximum amount that will be paid. The covered person will be required to absorb any additional charges if he or she uses a more expensive physician. Through the use of computers insurance companies now have statistics that categorize expenses by geographic regions that are as small as the zip codes of medical-care providers. Thus while $300 may be the maximum reasonable-and-customary amount in one part of a metropolitan area, $350 may be considered reasonable and customary in another part of the same metropolitan area.

Blue Shield plans often use a somewhat modified approach in determining the maximum amount that will be paid. Each year physicians file their charges for the coming year with the Blue Shield plan. During that year the association will pay charges in full up to some percentile of these filed charges. Under some plans the physicians agree not to charge Blue Shield patients amounts in excess of their filed fees. In addition, participating physicians in other Blue Shield plans agree to accept any Blue Shield payment as payment in full, particularly for employees with an income level below a certain amount, such as $10,000 for an individual and $15,000 for a family.

Second Surgical Opinions

In an attempt to control medical costs by eliminating unnecessary surgery, many medical expense plans, both basic and major medical, now provide benefits for second surgical opinions. There is no question that as a result of such opinions some patients will decide against surgery. However, it is still unclear whether the cost savings of second surgical opinions might be illusionary. For example, surgery may still be required at a later date, or long-term costs may be incurred for alternative treatment.

A voluntary approach for obtaining second surgical opinions is often used. If a physician or surgeon recommends surgery, a covered person can seek a second opinion and the cost will be borne by the medical expense plan. In some instances the benefit is limited to a specific maximum, but in most cases the costs of the second opinion, including X rays and diagnostic tests, are paid in full. Some plans will also pay for a third opinion if the first two opinions disagree. When there are divergent opinions, the final choice is up to the patient, and the regular benefits of the plan will usually be paid for any resulting surgery. As an incentive to encourage second opinions, some plans actually provide larger benefits for a covered person who has obtained a second opinion, even if it does not agree with the first opinion.

In the last few years it has become increasingly common for medical expense plans to require mandatory second opinions. These provisions may apply to any elective and nonemergency surgery but frequently apply only to a specified list of procedures. In most cases the second opinion must be performed by a surgeon selected by the insurance company or other provider of benefits. If conflicting opinions arise, a third opinion may be obtained. The costs of the second and third opinions are paid in full. In contrast to voluntary provisions, mandatory provisions generally specify that benefits will be paid at a reduced level if surgery is performed either without a second opinion or contrary to the final opinion.

The trend toward mandatory second opinions has had an interesting result. Since many employers felt money was being saved under their voluntary programs, wouldn't it be logical to save more money by making the program mandatory? Unfortunately the opposite situation has often been the case: people who voluntarily seek a second opinion are frequently looking for an alternative to surgery while those who obtain a second opinion only because it is required are more likely to accept surgery as the best alternative. Employers have also found that a second opinion by a surgeon is still likely to call for surgery. As a result there seems to be a growing feeling that the cost of mandatory second opinions may exceed any decrease in surgical benefits paid. Consequently some employers have returned to voluntary programs or stopped providing coverage for second opinions altogether.

Exclusions

As with hospital expense coverage and virtually all other types of medical expense coverage, exclusions exist under basic surgical expense contracts for occupational injuries or disease, certain services provided by government agencies, and cosmetic surgery. All surgical expense contracts have an exclusion for certain types of dental surgery. However, the extent of the exclusion varies and care must be taken in properly integrating any dental coverage with other basic coverages. At one extreme some contracts exclude virtually any procedures associated with the teeth or disease of the surrounding tissue or bone structure. At the other extreme a more common exclusion eliminates coverage for most dental procedures but does provide surgical benefits if a covered person is hospitalized for the removal of impacted teeth or for surgery of the gums or bone structure surrounding the teeth. It is interesting to note that although benefits for oral surgery may not be paid even if a covered person is hospitalized, the hospital expenses are often covered under hospital expense contracts.

Physicians' Visits Expense Benefits

Physicians' visits expense coverage (often referred to as medical expense coverage or regular medical expense coverage) provides benefits for fees of attending physicians other than surgeons (since the charges of the latter are paid under surgical expense benefits coverage). Benefits are usually provided only for physicians' visits while a covered person is hospitalized. However, coverage may also include office and home visits.

In-Hospital Coverage

In-hospital coverage is designed to provide benefits for physicians' charges when a covered person is hospitalized as an inpatient. Three general approaches are used to determine the amount and duration of benefits. Under one approach physicians' fees are paid on a reasonable-and-customary basis, up to a specific number of visits per hospitalization. In most cases this will correspond to the period of time for which hospital expense benefits are provided. Under the second approach benefits are limited to a daily maximum, again up to a specified period of time. The daily maximum may be expressed as a dollar amount (such as $30) or in terms of a relative value (such as 1.5) that is generally multiplied by the same dollar conversion factor applicable to surgical expense benefits. However, a separate conversion factor might be used. A difficulty with this approach is that physicians often charge more for initial hospital visits. Consequently the daily maximum in some contracts is increased for the first day (or for 2 or 3 days) of hospitalization. The third approach expresses the total benefit as a lump-sum amount equal to the daily benefit times the number of days hospitalized. For example, if the daily benefit is $25 and the covered person is hospitalized for 10 days, physicians' charges would be paid in full up to $250, regardless of the charges incurred on any specific day or the number of visits made by the physician.

Three additional types of benefits are sometimes included when in-hospital coverage is provided:

- coverage for physicians' visits when a covered person is in an intensive care unit. If benefits are paid on a reasonable-and-customary basis, these charges will be covered in the same manner. Under plans with a daily maximum the maximum may be increased to reflect the more expensive charges normally associated with intensive care.
- coverage for consultation services. Most plans cover only the charges of attending physicians. However, some plans provide benefits for the consultation services of other physicians. This benefit may be subject to a dollar maximum or paid on a reasonable-and-customary basis.
- coverage for physicians' visits in other types of medical care facilities, such as extended care centers. This benefit is most commonly provided when room-and-board charges for these alternative facilities are also covered.

In-Hospital and Out-of-Hospital Coverage

In addition to the benefits previously described, coverage for physicians' visits may also include physicians' charges incurred in a physician's office or in a covered person's home. This broader coverage is usually not written as a separate and distinct benefit but rather as a single overall coverage for all types of physicians' visits. Benefits may be paid on a reasonable-and-customary basis or be subject to a dollar maximum per visit. In the latter case it is not unusual to have two different dollar maximums: one for hospital visits and home visits and a lesser one for office visits. Benefits will be subject to some overall maximum limit, which may be expressed as either a dollar amount (such as $1,000) or a specified number of visits (such as 60). This limit may be applied on an annual basis or for any single illness or injury. Most plans contain a waiting period, commonly ranging from one to five visits, before benefits for home and office visits will be paid. However, this waiting period is often waived in the case of an accident.

Some plans also provide coverage for well-baby care. This includes benefits for inoculations and physicians' examinations (both in and out of the hospital) of healthy infants for a limited period of time, such as 3 months after birth. In addition, coverage sometimes includes benefits for hospital nursery charges. Some states require that medical expense contracts cover these benefits for newborns only until the infant is discharged from the hospital.

Exclusions

Most of the exclusions mentioned previously in connection with surgical expense coverage also apply to physicians' visits expense coverage. In addition to these exclusions, there are usually no benefits for physical examinations, eye examinations, or dentistry. Fees charged when a physician did not actually see a patient (such as for a telephone consultation) are also often excluded. Finally charges made by a physician who is a salaried staff member of a hospital are frequently not covered.

Other Benefits

When medical expense plans consist of basic coverages supplemented by major medical insurance, it is not unusual for the basic benefits to cover only hospital expenses, surgical expenses, and sometimes physicians' visits. Other types of basic benefits might also be provided, which in most cases cover expenses that either are included or may be included in a supplemental major medical contract. However, providing such coverage in the form of separate basic benefits may result in a greater reimbursement to an employee since deductibles and coinsurance often do not apply.

Extended Care Facility Benefits

Many hospital patients recover to a point where they no longer require the full level of medical care provided by a hospital, but they cannot be discharged because they still require a period of convalescence under supervised medical care. Extended care facilities (often called convalescent nursing homes or skilled nursing facilities) have been established in many areas to provide this type of care. To the extent that patients can be treated in these facilities (which are often adjacent to hospitals), daily room-and-board charges can be reduced—often substantially. Obviously this type of care is discouraged if it is not covered on a comparable basis with confinement in a hospital. However, even when comparable coverage is provided, there seems to be a reluctance on the part of both patients and physicians to use such facilities. It becomes an additional facility for physicians to visit, and patients often express concern about the quality of care provided.

Extended care facility coverage provides benefits to the person who is an inpatient in an extended care facility, which is typically defined as an institution that furnishes room and board and 24-hour-a-day skilled nursing care under the supervision of a physician or a registered professional nurse. It does not include facilities that are designed as a place for rest or domiciliary care for the aged. In addition, facilities for the treatment of drug abuse and alcoholism are often excluded from the definition.

To receive benefits the following conditions must usually be satisfied:

- The confinement must be recommended by a physician.
- Twenty-four-hour-a-day nursing care must be needed.
- The confinement must commence within (1) 14 days after termination of a specified period of hospital confinement (generally 3 days) for which room-and-board benefits were payable or (2) 14 days of a previous confinement in an extended care facility for which benefits were payable. A few but increasing number of contracts include benefits for situations where extended care facilities are used in lieu of hospitalization.
- The confinement must be for the same or a related condition for which the covered person was hospitalized.

Benefits are provided in much the same manner as under hospital expense coverage. If hospital expense benefits are on a semiprivate accommodation basis, extended care facility benefits are generally paid on the same basis. If hospital expense benefits are subject to a daily dollar maximum, extended care facility benefits are usually likewise subject to a daily dollar maximum, most typically equal to 50 percent of the daily hospital benefit. The maximum length of time for which extended care benefits will be paid may be independent of the period of time for which a person is hospitalized, in which case a maximum of 60 days' coverage is fairly common. Alternatively the benefit period may be related to the number of unused hospital days. The most common approach in this instance is to allow 2 days in an extended care facility for each unused hospital day. For example, if a hospital expense plan provides benefits for a maximum period of 90 days and if a covered person is hospitalized for 50 days, the 40 unused hospital days can be exchanged for 80 days of benefits in an extended care facility. Other charges incurred in an extended care facility may be treated in one of several ways. They may be covered in full, subject to a separate dollar limit, or treated as part of the maximum benefit payable for other charges under hospital expense coverage.

Home Health Care Benefits

Home health care coverage is similar to extended care facility benefits but designed for those situations when the necessary part-time nursing care ordered by a physician following hospitalization can be provided in the patient's home. Coverage is for (1) nursing care (usually limited to a maximum of 2 hours per day) under the supervision of a registered nurse; (2) physical, occupational, and speech therapy; and (3) medical supplies and equipment, such as wheelchairs and hospital beds.

In most cases the benefits payable are equal to a percentage, frequently 80 percent, of reasonable-and-customary charges. Benefit payments are limited to either a maximum number of visits (such as 60 per calendar year) or to a period of time (such as 90 days after benefits commence). In the latter case the time period may be a function of the unused hospital days, such as 3 days of home visits for each unused hospital day.

Hospice Benefits

Hospices for the treatment of terminally ill persons are a recent development in the area of medical care. Hospice care does not attempt to cure medical conditions but rather is devoted to easing the physical and psychological pain associated with death. In addition to providing services for the dying patient, a hospice may also offer counseling to surviving family members. While a hospice is usually thought of as a separate facility, this type of care can also be provided on an outpatient basis in the dying person's home. Where hospice care is available, the cost of treating terminally ill patients is usually much less than the cost of traditional hospitalization. Currently few benefit plans provide hospice coverage, but considerable interest in such coverage has been generated among employers as a means of controlling medical costs.

Ambulatory Care Expense Benefits

Recent years have seen the development of ambulatory care centers, often called surgicenters. These centers, designed for the purpose of outpatient surgery, are separate from hospitals. Since these facilities fail to meet the definition of a hospital, benefits for their use are not included under hospital expense coverage. Consequently some basic medical expense plans provide benefits for ambulatory care expenses. Ambulatory care centers are generally defined as permanent facilities that (1) are operated primarily for the purpose of performing surgical procedures, (2) have continuous physician services and professional nursing services, and (3) do not provide services or other accommodations for patients to stay overnight. In most cases benefits are paid as if the covered person were an inpatient in a hospital. However, to encourage the use of such facilities as a less expensive alternative to hospitals, benefits may be paid at a higher level or even in full. Benefits cover any charges for use of the facility as well as other charges, such as medical supplies, X rays, and diagnostic tests.

Birthing Centers

Another recent development in medical care is birthing centers, which are designed to provide a homelike facility for the delivery of babies. Like ambulatory care centers, they are separate from hospitals.

The cost of using birthing centers is considerably less than using hospitals. Deliveries are performed by nurse-midwives, and mothers and babies are released shortly after birth. Benefits may be paid as if the mother used a hospital and obstetrician but are frequently paid in full as an incentive to use these lower-cost facilities.

Diagnostic X-ray and Laboratory Expense Benefits

In recent years the use of diagnostic X rays and laboratory services has increased substantially (often because of defensive medicine practiced by physicians). Under the previous coverages mentioned benefits include the cost of these services if a covered person is an inpatient. However, outpatient benefits cover only costs connected with surgery at a hospital or ambulatory care center or preadmission testing. Diagnostic X-ray and laboratory coverage provides benefits for the cost of these services (including physicians' charges) when performed on an outpatient basis and when not otherwise covered under other portions of a basic medical expense plan. While benefits are usually provided for both illnesses and injuries, they may be provided only for illnesses if a medical expense plan contains a separate supplemental accident expense benefit (as will be described later in this chapter).

Several approaches are used to provide diagnostic X-ray and laboratory coverage. One approach includes a schedule of procedures (similar to a surgical schedule) with maximum benefits specified for each procedure. Plans taking this approach usually contain a single overall maximum benefit or possibly separate overall maximum benefits for X rays and laboratory services. This maximum benefit may apply on a per-illness or per-injury basis or on an annual basis. A second approach covers all charges in full up to a specified maximum amount per procedure. A third approach pays benefits as if the X rays and laboratory examinations had been performed while the covered person was an inpatient in a hospital. In this situation the maximum benefit specified for other charges under hospital expense coverage applies to the aggregate of these outpatient charges and any other miscellaneous charges (associated with the same illness or injury) that are incurred while the covered person is hospitalized.

Since diagnostic X-ray and laboratory expense coverage is designed to complement other basic coverages, benefits that might be provided under these other coverages are generally excluded from diagnostic X-ray and laboratory expense coverage. In addition, exclusions generally exist for routine physical examinations and dentistry.

Radiation Therapy Expense Benefits

The widespread use of radiation therapy is a relatively new but common form of treatment for some illnesses, particularly cancer. Under the traditional basic coverages, benefits are provided under hospital expense coverage only as long as a covered person is hospitalized. Therefore the primary purpose of radiation therapy expense benefits is to cover the cost of these treatments when performed on an outpatient basis. However, coverage may also be written to supplement any such benefits under hospital expense coverage. The use of radiation for diagnostic purposes is not covered because such coverage is provided by diagnostic X-ray and laboratory expense benefits. Coverage is often provided for the treatment of both malignant and benign conditions, but sometimes it is limited to cancerous conditions only.

Benefits are generally provided for the administration of the therapy, the use of facilities, and any materials and their preparation. Some insurance companies treat radiation therapy as a single category of benefits, while others divide it into two categories: treatments involving the use of X-ray machines and treatments involving the use of radioactive isotopes, radioactive iodine, or other radioactive substances that are applied to the body or taken internally. Benefits may be paid on a reasonable-and-customary basis or in accordance with a fee or relative-value schedule. An overall maximum limit (or limits if two categories of benefits are used) may also apply. This limit may be based on some time period, such as 12 months, or it may apply to the entire course of treatment for a condition, regardless of duration.

Prescription Drug Expense Benefits

With the exception of drugs administered in a hospital or in an extended care facility, the cost of prescription drugs is covered as a basic benefit only if prescription drug expense coverage is purchased. The cost of prescription drugs has typically been covered under major medical insurance. However, separate prescription drug plans are often a result of collective bargaining even when there is a major medical plan. This benefit is highly visible to employees who periodically have prescriptions that must be filled either for themselves or for members of their family. Some benefit consultants also feel that a separate prescription drug plan may result in cost savings since the large number of relatively small claims lends itself to more economical methods of administration and processing of claims.

The typical basic prescription drug plan covers the cost of drugs (except those dispensed in a hospital or in an extended care facility) that are required by either state or federal law to be dispensed by prescription. Drugs for which prescriptions are not required by law are usually not covered even if they are ordered by the physician on a prescription form. One frequent exception to this general rule is injectable insulin, which is generally covered despite the fact that in many states it is a nonprescription drug. No coverage is provided for charges to administer drugs or the cost of the therapeutic devices or appliances, such as bandages or hypodermic needles. It is common to exclude benefits for a quantity of drugs in excess of a specified amount. In some plans this quantity is expressed as the amount normally prescribed by physicians; in other plans it is expressed as a supply for a certain time period, often 34 days. However, refills are considered new prescriptions.

Some plans cover maintenance drugs, such as medicine for the treatment of high blood pressure; other plans exclude them. Excluding these drugs, however, may be a false economy. Although the current cost of a prescription drug plan will be lower, medical conditions may remain untreated and preventable surgical and hospital expenses may result. Contraceptive drugs may also be covered or excluded. Some prescription drug plans take a middle approach by covering these drugs only when they are prescribed for treating some medical condition rather than for preventing conception.

Most prescription drug plans have a deductible (often referred to as a copayment) that must be paid by a covered person for any prescriptions filled. In most cases this is a flat amount varying from $3 to $5 per prescription. Some plans have two copayments—one for generic drugs and a higher one for name brand drugs.

Two basic methods are used to provide prescription drug coverage: a reimbursement approach and a service approach. Under plans using a reimbursement approach, a covered individual personally pays the cost of prescription drugs, using any pharmacy he or she chooses. A claim for reimbursement is then filed with the provider of benefits. Reimbursement (subject to any copayments) is made to the covered person on the basis of either billed charges or reasonable-and-customary charges.

While coverage for prescription drugs under major medical plans is often on a reimbursement basis, the majority of basic medical plans use a service approach. Under this approach drugs are provided to covered persons by participating pharmacies upon receipt of a prescription, proper identification (usually a card issued by the plan), and any required copayments. The pharmacy then bills the provider of coverage for the remaining cost of any prescription filled. This provider may be a Blue Cross–Blue Shield association, an insurance company, or a third-party administrator acting on behalf of either an insurance company or an employer with a self-insured plan. Because of the specialization that can be used in handling many small claims and the need to establish a system of participating pharmacies, most insurance companies, except for a few large ones, use third-party administrators for their prescription drug plans.

Under virtually all service plans the provider of coverage or the third-party administrator negotiates a contract with participating pharmacies to provide the drugs at a reduced cost, usually equal to the wholesale cost of the drug plus a flat dispensing fee, such as $3 for each prescription. Prescriptions filled at nonparticipating pharmacies are generally covered but handled on a reimbursement basis. In addition, reimbursement in these cases is typically less than the cost of the prescription. The usual provision under Blue Cross–Blue Shield plans is to pay 75 percent of the cost of a prescription drug purchased at a nonparticipating pharmacy (less any copayment), while insurance companies usually pay up to the amount that would have been paid to a participating pharmacy.

Vision Care Expense Benefits

The previous coverages discussed do not provide benefits for the cost of eyeglasses and only rarely cover the cost of routine eye examinations. Vision care expense coverage is designed to provide benefits for these expenses. Coverage may be provided by insurance companies, Blue Cross–Blue Shield plans, plans of state optometric associations patterned after Blue Shield, close-panel HMO-type plans established by local providers of vision services, vision care PPOs, or third-party administrators.

Benefits are occasionally provided on a reasonable-and-customary basis or are subject to a flat benefit per year that may be applied to any covered expenses. Normally, however, a benefit schedule will be used that specifies the type and amounts of benefits and the frequency with which they will be provided. An example of one such schedule appears below. Under some plans most benefits are provided on a service basis rather than being subject to a maximum benefit. However, these plans usually cover only the cost of basic frames, which the covered persons can upgrade at an additional expense.

Type of Benefit	Maximum Amount
Any 12-month period:	
Eye examination	$ 45
Lenses, pair	
single vision	45
bifocal	75
trifocal	125
lenticular	200
contact (when medically necessary)	300
contact (when not medically necessary)	125
Any 24-month period:	
Frames	60

Exclusions commonly exist for any extra charge for plastic lenses or the cost of safety lenses or prescription sunglasses. Benefits are generally provided for eye examinations by either an optometrist or an ophthalmologist. Larger benefits are sometimes provided if the latter is used. Vision care plans do not pay benefits for eye surgery or treatment of eye diseases since these are covered under other basic coverages or major medical coverage.

Supplemental Accident Expense Benefits

Some basic medical expense plans (as well as an occasional major medical plan) include a supplemental accident expense benefit. The purpose of this benefit is to cover expenses associated with accidents to the extent that they are not provided under other medical expense coverages. There would probably be little need for this type of coverage if a basic medical expense plan included all the coverages previously described in this chapter. Most basic medical expense plans consist only of hospital, surgical, and physicians' visits coverage, however, and little coverage exists for the treatment of accidental injuries except on an inpatient basis.

Benefits usually apply to expenses incurred within 90 days after an accident and pay for such items as professional fees, diagnostic X rays, laboratory examinations, and physical therapy. In addition, benefits are subject to a maximum limit, with $300 and $500 limits most commonly used.

Supplemental accident coverage has been the subject of controversy inasmuch as there seems to be no logical reason for providing different benefits for accidental injuries than for illnesses. However, the benefit is popular among employees and its cost is relatively small.

8

Group Medical Expense Insurance: Major Medical, Contract Provisions, and Taxation

MAJOR MEDICAL COVERAGE

Most employees have some type of major medical expense coverage that provides substantial protection against catastrophic medical expenses, with relatively few exclusions or limitations. However, the employee must frequently pay a portion of the cost of these medical expenses in the form of a deductible and/or coinsurance.

Types of Major Medical Coverage

There are two general types of plans for providing major medical coverage—supplemental (or superimposed) plans and comprehensive plans. In supplemental plans major medical coverage is coordinated with various basic medical expense coverages. One example of this kind of coordinated medical expense plan is shown in figure 8-1.

Subject to its own limitations and exclusions, a supplemental major medical plan covers expenses that are not included under the basic coverages. These include

- expenses not within the scope of the basic coverages. For example, benefits for office visits to a physician may be included if the basic coverages only provide benefits for in-hospital visits.
- expenses no longer covered under the basic coverages because those benefits have been exhausted. For example, if the basic coverages provide room-and-board benefits in full, but only for a maximum of 60 days, the cost of room and board will be covered by the major medical plan beginning on the 61st day.
- expenses in excess of the dollar maximum provided under the basic coverages. For example, if the basic coverages list a maximum benefit of $500 for a specific surgical procedure, and the cost of the procedure is $700, the remaining $200 will be covered by the major medical plan.
- expenses specifically excluded under the basic coverages. For example, if the basic coverages exclude hospital charges for the treatment of alcoholism, the major medical coverage may provide benefits. However, expenses that are excluded under the basic coverages are often excluded under the major medical plan.

Figure 8-1

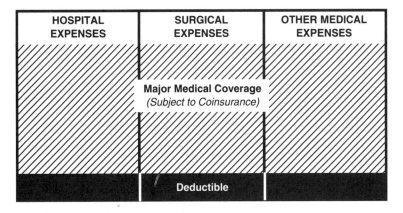

In the comprehensive type of major medical coverage a single major medical contract covers all medical expenses. This is illustrated is figure 8-2. In this example once the deductible is satisfied, most medical expenses are covered subject to a coinsurance provision. Although this illustration shows a comprehensive major medical plan in its purest form, most comprehensive medical expense contracts contain modifications that either eliminate or reduce the deductible or coinsurance provision for certain expenses. These variations will be discussed later in this chapter.

Figure 8-2

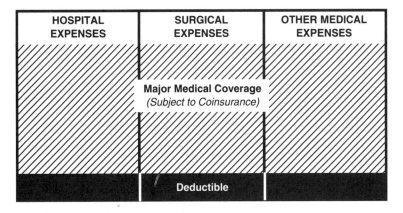

Supplemental versus Comprehensive

At first glance it might appear that the simplicity of a comprehensive major medical plan makes it preferable to a supplemental plan. However, supplemental plans continue to cover the majority of employees, even though most newly written plans are of the comprehensive type. In a few instances the continued use of supplemental plans has been based on tradition. When some firms with basic medical plans found it necessary to expand that coverage, they added a supplemental plan instead of redesigning the entire medical expense plan itself. In most cases, however, there have been a number of more valid reasons for choosing separate coverages. These include the employer's desire to (1) use more than one provider of coverage, (2) offer first-dollar coverage, or (3) use different contribution rates for the basic and supplemental coverages. However, there are also disadvantages to using supplemental plans, including more difficult administration and communication.

More than One Provider of Coverage

Frequently the provider of a supplemental major medical plan is different from the provider of the underlying basic coverages. Usually Blue Cross or Blue Cross–Blue Shield provides the basic coverages and an insurance company provides the supplemental coverage. In the past only a few of the Blues offered major medical coverage because (1) some of them felt such coverage was not within the scope of their traditional benefit structure, (2) some states legally prohibited it, and (3) some Blues experienced administrative difficulties over the effective and efficient coordinating of these broader benefits. Although most Blue Cross–Blue Shield plans now offer major medical coverage (often referred to as extended benefits), insurance companies are still by far the largest providers of major medical benefits.

The most common type of supplemental plan is the one shown in figure 8-1, but occasionally a major medical plan is designed to supplement only a basic Blue Cross plan, as shown in figure 8-3. This type of plan is most common in those geographic areas where the Blues do not operate jointly and thus cannot offer a single coordinated basic plan.

Figure 8-3

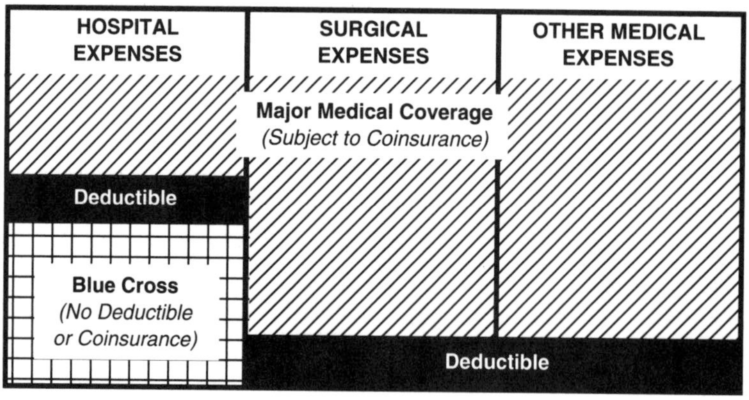

First-Dollar Coverage

Under the traditional comprehensive major medical plan a deductible and coinsurance apply to all covered expenses. However, because of competition or labor negotiations, employers frequently offer their employees *first-dollar coverage* for certain medical expenses. With first-dollar coverage there is no deductible and usually no coinsurance, and the basic medical expense plan will consist only of those benefits provided on a first-dollar basis. Because first-dollar coverage has been characteristic of the Blues, they are frequently used as the providers of basic coverages. Therefore in order to compete with them, most insurance companies now offer comprehensive major medical plans that are modified to provide similar first-dollar coverage.

It should be emphasized that, all other things being equal, first-dollar coverage will increase the cost of a medical expense plan. Employers have become increasingly concerned with the cost of providing medical expense coverage and are less likely than in the past to provide first-dollar coverage.

Different Contribution Rates

Some employers still maintain separate basic medical and major medical expense plans, since different employer contributions are made for each plan. The most common arrangement under these circumstances has the employer paying the entire cost of the basic coverages for the employee (and possibly his or her dependents) and the employee paying a portion, if not all, of the costs of the major medical coverage. The current trend, however, is to have a single plan even when the contribution rates for the basic and major medical coverages differ.

Administration and Communication

Most employers want to have benefit plans that minimize administrative problems and that can be easily communicated to employees. In both regards comprehensive plans have the advantage. With supplemental plans the employer must often deal with two providers of coverage. Therefore two plans must be properly coordinated so that no undesired gaps in coverage exist. In addition, the processing of claims also becomes more burdensome for both the employer and the employees. The complexity of medical expense plans in general makes them difficult to communicate to employees, and the task becomes even more complex when two plans are used.

Even when a single provider supplies both the basic medical expense plan and a supplemental major medical plan, the same problems may exist. The employer must often negotiate the plans with separate divisions of the provider's organization, and separate claims forms and claims departments are frequently used.

Characteristics of Major Medical Coverage

The distinguishing features of major medical expense plans—either supplemental or comprehensive—include a broad range of covered expenses, deductibles, coinsurance, and high overall maximum benefits.

Covered Expenses

Major medical plans give broad coverage for necessary expenses incurred for medical services and supplies that have been ordered or prescribed by a physician. These services and supplies, which are specified in the contract, generally include

- hospital room and board. Coverage has not traditionally been provided either for confinements in extended care facilities or for home health care. However, major medical plans now often include such coverage. Some plans also provide benefits for room and board in alternative facilities such as birthing centers.
- other hospital charges
- charges of outpatient surgical centers
- anesthetics and their administration
- services of doctors of medicine or osteopathy. Coverage for the services of other medical practitioners (such as chiropractors or podiatrists) may also be included.
- private-duty nursing by a registered nurse. The services of a licensed practical nurse may also be covered.
- prescription drugs
- physical and speech therapy
- diagnostic X-ray and laboratory services
- radiation therapy
- blood and blood plasma
- artificial limbs and organs
- pacemakers
- casts, splints, trusses, braces, and crutches
- rental of wheelchairs, hospital beds, or iron lungs
- ambulance services

The expenses of dental care may also be included as a major medical benefit. However, dental benefits (see chapter 9) are usually provided under a separate dental expense plan.

Even though coverage is broad, major medical contracts contain certain exclusions and limitations.

Exclusions. Common exclusions found in major medical contracts include charges arising from the following:

- occupational injuries or diseases to the extent that benefits are provided by workers' compensation laws or similar legislation
- services furnished by or on behalf of government agencies, unless there is a requirement for the patient or the patient's medical expense plan to pay
- cosmetic surgery, unless such surgery is to correct a condition resulting from either an accidental injury or a birth defect (if the parent has dependent coverage when the child is born)
- physical examinations, unless such examinations are necessary for the treatment of an injury or illness. While most major medical plans contain this exclusion, it should be noted that some employers provide coverage for physical examinations. In most cases, however, benefits will be provided under a separate, and often self-funded, plan and not as part of the major medical coverage.
- convalescent, custodial, or rest care
- dental care except for (1) treatment required because of injury to natural teeth and (2) hospital and surgical charges associated with hospital

confinement for dental surgery. This exclusion will not be included if dental coverage is provided under the major medical contract.

- eye refraction, or the purchase or fitting of eyeglasses or hearing aids. Like the dental care exclusion, this exclusion will not be included if the major medical coverage provides benefits for vision and hearing care. These benefits, however, are most likely to be provided under a separate plan.
- expenses either paid or eligible for payment under medicare or other federal, state, or local medical expense programs
- benefits provided by any other benefit program to which the employer makes a contribution. This includes any benefits provided under basic medical expense plans if a supplementary major medical plan is used.

To minimize the problem of adverse selection, most major medical plans also contain an exclusion for preexisting conditions. However, this exclusion applies only for a limited time, after which the condition will no longer be considered preexisting and will be covered in full, subject to any other contract limitations or exclusions. It is interesting to note that a preexisting-conditions clause is common in major medical contracts, but it is rarely found in basic medical expense contracts.

A *preexisting condition* is typically defined as any illness or injury for which a covered person received medical care during the 3-month period prior to the person's effective date of coverage. Usually the condition is no longer considered preexisting after the earlier of (1) a period of 3 consecutive months during which no medical care is received for the condition or (2) 12 months of coverage under the contract by the individual.

Some insurance companies provide limited coverage rather than exclude coverage for preexisting conditions. During the time a condition is considered preexisting, benefits may be paid subject to limitations, such as a 50 percent coinsurance provision or a calendar-year maximum of $1,000. It is also not unusual, particularly with large employers, for the preexisting-conditions clause to be waived for persons who are eligible for coverage on the date a master contract becomes effective. However, future employees will be subject to the provision.

Limitations. Major medical plans also contain "internal limits" for certain types of medical expenses. Although the expenses are covered, the amounts that will be paid under the contract are limited. Benefits are not paid (with rare exceptions) for charges that exceed what is reasonable and customary. In addition, limitations are often placed on the following expenses:

- hospital room and board. Benefits are generally limited to the charge for semiprivate accommodations unless other accommodations are medically necessary. However, in some cases a flat-dollar maximum is placed on the daily semiprivate accommodation rate.
- extended care facilities, home health care benefits, and hospice benefits (if provided). Benefits for extended care facilities are often subject to a dollar limit per day for room-and-board charges as well as a time limit on the number of days that coverage will be provided. Similarly home health care benefits are often subject to a maximum daily benefit and limited to

a certain number of visits within a specific time period. Hospice benefits are usually limited to a specified maximum amount, such as $5,000.

● surgery. Although most major medical contracts pay surgical expenses on a reasonable-and-customary basis, some use a surgical schedule as was described in chapter 7.

● dental care, vision and hearing care, and physical examinations. When these are covered under major medical contracts, benefits are frequently subject to schedules and annual limitations.

It has been common for major medical plans to provide limited benefits for treatment for mental and nervous disorders, alcoholism, and drug addiction. Unless state laws require that such conditions be treated like any other medical condition, inpatient coverage is often limited to a specific number of days each year (commonly 30 or 60). Outpatient benefits are even more limited. Benefits are usually subject to 50 percent coinsurance and to a specific dollar limit per visit. An annual maximum benefit (such as $1,000) may also be imposed. In addition, it is not unusual to have an overall maximum lifetime benefit (for example, $25,000).

One unfortunate effect of this type of limitation is that the low coinsurance percentage for outpatient care encourages many persons to seek inpatient treatment, which is significantly more expensive but no more effective in the eyes of many medical experts. As a result some plans have started to carveout coverage from the major medical plan. Benefits are then coordinated by a managed-care plan that specializes in mental health and/or substance abuse problems. These plans provide more generous benefits but control costs by emphasizing outpatient treatment. In addition, case management has been successful in encouraging more people to actually begin prescribed treatment and finish treatment once it has started. This type of carve-out approach is being tried not only by indemnity plans but also by HMOs and PPOs.

Deductibles

A deductible is the initial amount of covered medical expenses an individual must pay before he or she will receive benefits under a major medical plan. For example, if a plan has an annual deductible of $200, the covered person is responsible for the first $200 of medical expenses incurred each year. Covered expenses in excess of $200 are then paid by the major medical plan, subject to any limitations or coinsurance. In addition to the different types of deductibles there are variations in (1) the amounts of the deductible, (2) the frequency with which it must be satisfied, and (3) the expenses to which it applies.

Types of Deductibles. Probably the simplest form of deductible is the *initial deductible* commonly used in comprehensive major medical plans (see figure 8-2). Essentially a covered person must satisfy this deductible before any insurance benefits will be paid by the plan.

Most supplemental medical expense plans use a *corridor deductible* (see figure 8-1), under which no benefits are paid by the major medical plan until an individual has incurred a specific amount of covered expenses above those paid under his or her basic coverages. For example, assume an individual incurs $4,000 of covered medical expenses, $2,500 of which are paid by the basic coverages. If the supplemental major medical plan has a $200 corridor deductible, the plan will pay $1,300 of the expenses, subject to any limitations or coinsurance. This is determined as follows:

Covered expenses	$4,000
Less expenses covered under basic protection	2,500
	$1,500
Less deductible	200
	$1,300

In those situations when no benefits are paid under the basic coverages, the corridor deductible operates as if it were an initial deductible.

Some supplemental major medical expense plans contain an *integrated deductible*, which tends to be large (at least $500), but any amounts paid under the basic coverages can be used to satisfy it. For example, assume the specified deductible is $1,000 per year. If an individual incurs $1,000 or more of covered expenses under the basic coverages, the annual deductible is satisfied. As another example, assume a person incurs $1,500 of medical expenses, $800 of which is for hospital charges that are covered in full under the individual's basic coverages and $700 of which consists of noncovered outpatient expenses. The $800 for hospital charges can be used toward satisfying the deductible. However, the individual must pay the next $200 of medical expenses out of his or her own pocket in order to satisfy the remaining deductible amount. Therefore in this case only $500 of the $700 of outpatient charges would be paid, subject to any other limitations and coinsurance, under the major medical coverage.

Although the integrated deductible was once quite common, its complexity has precluded its being as popular as the corridor deductible. Currently it is found in only a few supplemental major medical expense plans.

Deductible Amounts. With the exception of the integrated deductible, deductible amounts for any covered person tend to be relatively small. Most deductibles are fixed-dollar amounts that apply separately to each person and usually fall within the range of $100 to $250. A few major medical expense plans contain deductibles that are based on a percentage of an employee's salary (such as 1 or 2 percent), possibly subject to a maximum annual limit (such as $250).

In most major medical expense plans the deductible must be satisfied only once during any given time period (usually a calendar year), regardless of the number of causes from which medical expenses arise. This type of deductible is often referred to as an *all-causes deductible*. However, a few plans have *per-cause deductibles* (also referred to as *per-disability* deductibles) under which the deductible amount must be satisfied for each separate accident or illness before major medical benefits will be paid.

Deductibles apply to each covered individual, including the dependents of an employee. However, to minimize the family's burden of satisfying several deductibles, most major medical expense plans also contain a *family deductible.* Once the family deductible is satisfied, future covered medical expenses of all family members will be paid just as if every member of the family had satisfied his or her individual deductible.

Two basic types of family deductibles are found in major medical expense plans. The most common type waives any deductible requirements for other family members once a certain number of family members (generally two or three) have satisfied their individual deductibles. However, two important points should be noted. First, major medical benefits will be paid for each individual family member once his or her individual deductible is satisfied, even though the family deductible has not been met. Second, the waiver of any deductible requirements that results from the satisfaction of the family deductible does not apply to medical expenses incurred prior to the date the deductible is satisfied. For example, assume a family deductible is satisfied when each of three family members incurs $200 in covered medical expenses. If a fourth family member has had $60 in medical expenses up to that point, future medical expenses for that person will be paid under the major medical coverage. The $60, however, will not be covered. In effect the satisfaction of the family deductible freezes the deductible for each family member at the lesser of the individual deductible or the amount of medical expenses incurred up to that time.

Another approach taken in some major medical plans is to have a fixed-dollar amount for the family deductible (such as $500). In addition, each family member has to meet an individual deductible (such as $200). Major medical benefits will be paid for any given family member once his or her deductible is satisfied, and future deductible requirements for all family members will be waived once the family maximum has been reached. Although the same expenses can satisfy both the family deductible and an individual deductible, any amount that is applied toward the family deductible cannot exceed the individual deductible. For example, if a family has deductibles of $200 for an individual and $500 for the family and if one family member incurs $1,000 in covered medical expenses, the $800 exceeding the individual deductible will be paid under the major medical plan, subject to any limitations and coinsurance. The $200 used to satisfy the individual deductible, but no more, can also be applied to the family deductible. However, the family deductible will not be completely satisfied until other family members incur another $300 in covered expenses (but no more than $200 from any one family member).

Most major medical expense contracts contain a *common accident provision,* whereby if two or more members of the same family are injured in the same accident, the covered medical expenses for all family members will at most be subject to a single deductible, usually equal to the individual deductible amount. In effect this deductible establishes the maximum amount of medical expenses that must be borne by an employee for his or her family before major medical benefits will be paid. In some cases the employee may actually bear a smaller portion of the medical expenses if the amount satisfies the family or individual deductibles. For example, if each of the three family members incurs $300 of medical expenses in an accident under a plan that contains a $200 deductible, at least $700 of these expenses will be covered under the major medical coverage. However, if because of previous medical expenses only $40 is needed to satisfy the family deductible, then $860 of these expenses will be covered under the major medical plan.

Deductible Frequency. An all-causes deductible usually applies to medical expenses incurred within a 12-month period, which is usually a calendar year (January 1 to December 31). Under such a *calendar-year deductible* expenses incurred from January 1 apply toward the deductible, and once the deductible has been satisfied, the balance of any covered expenses incurred during the year will then be paid by the major medical plan, subject to any limitations and coinsurance.

Most plans with a calendar-year deductible also have a carryover provision that allows any expenses (1) applied to the deductible and (2) incurred during the last 3 months of the year to also be applied to the deductible for the following year. For example, assume an individual satisfies only $150 of a $200 deductible prior to October 1. If less than $50 of covered expenses are incurred in the last 3 months of the year, the deductible will not be totally satisfied for the year, but this amount can be applied to the deductible for the following year. If $50 or more of covered expenses are incurred in this 3-month period, not only will the deductible be satisfied for the year but this amount ($50) can also be applied to the deductible for the following year. No carryover is allowed if the deductible for the year is satisfied prior to the last 3 months of the year.

A rarely used variation of the calendar-year deductible allows expenses incurred during any 12-month period to satisfy the deductible. Once an individual incurs covered medical expenses equal to the deductible in any consecutive 12-month period, major medical benefits will be paid for the remainder of the period.

The example below illustrates these two types of deductibles. Assume an individual incurs the following covered medical expenses:

Year 1

January 15	$40.00
March 9	40.00
August 20	40.00
December 1	60.00

Year 2

May 5	100.00
May 20	40.00
July 11	60.00
September 8	80.00
October 15	120.00

If the person has a $200 calendar-year deductible, it will not be satisfied during year one, because only $180 of expenses have been incurred. However, if the individual's plan contains a carryover provision, the deductible for year two will be satisfied on May 20, since $60 of expenses can be carried over from the first year. Consequently the expenses in July, September, and October will be paid subject to any limitations and coinsurance. If, however, the plan does not contain a carryover provision, the deductible will not be satisfied until July 11, and only the September and October expenses will be covered.

If this same individual has a deductible based on any consecutive 12-month period, it will be satisfied on May 5 of the second year (the date on which $200 of expenses will have been incurred within a consecutive 12-month period). Since the first expense included in the period occurred on August 20 of year one, any expenses between May 5 and August 19 of year two will be paid (that is, the May 20 and July 11 expenses totaling $100). After August 19 the individual must incur covered expenses of $200 or more within another consecutive 12-month period before a deductible will again be satisfied. In this example a second deductible will be satisfied with the October 15 expense. Since the first expense toward the satisfaction of this second deductible occurred on September 8, major medical benefits will be paid from October 16 of year two to September 7 of year three. Because this type of deductible is more difficult to explain to employees and more burdensome administratively than a calendar-year deductible, it is rarely used.

With a per-cause deductible, a different approach is normally taken. Medical expenses used to satisfy the deductible for each illness or accident must be incurred within a specified *accumulation* period. Although the accumulation period can be a calendar-year or some other 12-month period, most accumulation periods consist of any consecutive 2-, 3-, or 6-month periods. Once the deductible for an accumulation period has been met, benefits will be paid for a *benefit period,* which usually begins when the deductible is satisfied, but sometimes begins on the date the first expense toward the deductible is incurred. (In the latter case expenses used to satisfy the deductible are not paid by the major medical plan.) The benefit period typically lasts until the earlier of (1) 2 years or (2) the end of some time period (usually 60 or 90 days) in which covered medical expenses from that cause are less than a small but specified dollar amount (such as $25 or $50). Once the benefit period ends, an individual must again satisfy the deductible before a new benefit period will begin.

Expenses to Which the Deductible Applies. Most major medical plans have a single deductible that applies to all medical expenses. However, some plans have two (or more) deductibles that apply separately to different categories of medical expenses. While many variations exist, the most common plan of this type has a small deductible (such as $50) that applies to those expenses over which individuals have the least control (for example, hospital charges, surgical charges, and charges resulting from accidents). A larger deductible (such as $100) applies to all other medical expenses.

In some major medical plans the deductible does not apply to certain expenses. In effect this gives the covered person first-dollar coverage for these charges. Insurance companies sometimes write comprehensive major medical expense plans without any deductible for hospital and/or surgical expenses as their way of competing with the first-dollar coverage offered by the Blues. In addition, these expenses are often not subject to a coinsurance provision. Rather, a dollar maximum may be placed on the amount of benefits that will be paid in full. Above this maximum, coinsurance will apply.

Coinsurance

Major medical expense plans contain a coinsurance provision, whereby the plan will pay only a specified percentage (in most cases 80 percent) of the covered expenses that exceed the deductible. The term *coinsurance* as used in this book refers to the percentage of covered expenses paid by a medical expense plan. Thus a plan with 80 percent coinsurance, sometimes referred to as an 80/20 plan, will pay 80 percent of covered expenses while a person who receives benefits under the plan must pay the remaining 20 percent. In some plans the term *coinsurance* is not used, but rather a percentage participation, such as 20 percent, is specified. As commonly used, a percentage participation (sometimes also referred to as a copayment) refers to the percentage of covered medical expenses that will not be paid by a medical expense plan and that must be paid by a person receiving benefits.

If a medical expense plan has a $200 calendar-year deductible and an 80 percent coinsurance provision that applies to all expenses, an individual who incurs $1,200 of covered medical expenses during the year (assuming no limitations) will receive an $800 reimbursement under a comprehensive major medical expense plan. This is calculated as follows:

Covered expenses	$1,200
Less deductible	200
Times coinsurance	$1,000
percentage	.80
	$ 800

The individual will have to pay the remaining $400 from his or her own pocket (that is, the deductible plus 20 percent of those expenses exceeding the deductible). It has been argued that having such provisions is a financial incentive for employees to control their use of medical care, since they must bear a portion of the cost of any expenses incurred.

Just as deductibles vary, so do coinsurance provisions. Sometimes different coinsurance percentages apply to different categories of medical expenses. For example, outpatient psychiatric charges may be subject to 50 percent coinsurance, while other covered medical expenses are subject to 80 percent coinsurance. In addition, certain medical expenses may be subject to 100 percent coinsurance (and usually no deductible), which in effect means that the expenses are paid in full, subject to any limitations. Such full coverage is most likely to exist (1) for those expenses over which an individual has little control, (2) when there is a desire to provide first-dollar coverage for certain expenses, or (3) when there is a desire to encourage the use of the most cost-effective treatment (such as outpatient surgery, preadmission testing, or birthing centers).

Figures 8-4 through 8-7 show how the deductible and coinsurance provisions might be modified in a comprehensive major medical expense plan.

Figure 8-4 illustrates a medical expense plan that has both the deductible and the coinsurance provision waived for hospital expenses, surgical expenses, and certain other expenses up to specified limits. This type of modification results in a plan similar to a Blue Cross–Blue Shield plan that has supplemental major medical coverage but no corridor deductible. Figure 8-5 shows a comprehensive major medical expense plan that is designed to provide first-dollar coverage for hospital expenses only. Notice the similarity between this plan and a Blue Cross plan that has supplemental major medical coverage (figure 8-3). Figures 8-6 and 8-7 illustrate two other possible variations. In figure 8-6 the deductible and the coinsurance provision are completely waived for certain medical expenses. In figure 8-7 only the coinsurance provision—and not the deductible—is waived.

Figure 8-4

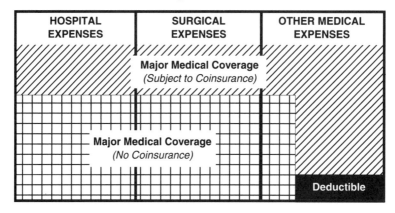

Figure 8-5

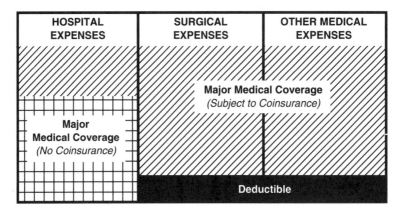

In the case of catastrophic medical expenses the coinsurance provision could result in an individual's being required to assume a large dollar amount of his or her own medical expenses. Consequently many major medical expense plans place a limit (often referred to as a stop-loss or coinsurance limit or cap) on the amount of out-of-pocket expenses that must be borne by a covered person during any time period. It is sometimes specified that the coinsurance provision only applies to a limited amount of expenses and that expenses in excess of this limit will be paid in full. For example, the plan may have a $200 deductible, an 80 percent coinsurance provision that applies to the next $3,000 of covered expenses, and full coverage for any remaining covered expenses. Therefore the most an individual will have to pay out of his or her own pocket in any year is the $200 deductible and 20 percent of $3,000 (for a total of $800). Occasionally this type of plan is modified to allow a gradual increase in the coinsurance percentage, such as 80 percent of the first $2,000 of covered expenses above the deductible, 90 percent of the next $2,000, and 100 percent of the remainder.

Figure 8-6

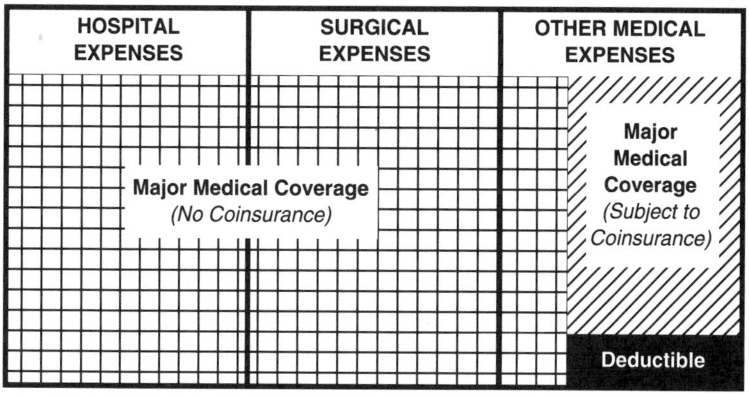

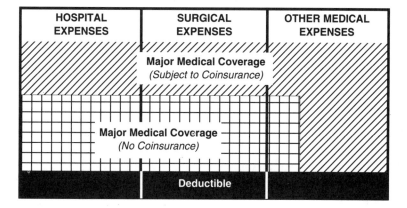

Figure 8-7

Another way of limiting coinsurance states the maximum dollar amount of expenses that must be borne by any individual (or a family) during a specific period. Once this limit is reached, by paying either deductibles or a percentage of medical expenses, additional expenses will be paid in full. For example, under a plan with a $200 deductible and an 80 percent coinsurance provision, a limit of $1,000 will be met if total medical expenses reach $4,200. Of this amount the individual will be responsible for the $200 deductible and 20 percent of the remaining $4,000 (for a total of $1,000). Any medical expenses in excess of $4,200 will be paid in full.

Maximum Benefits

The maximum benefits that will be paid for any covered person under a major medical contract may be determined in one of two ways. Although the use of a *lifetime maximum* is most common, a few contracts contain a *per-cause maximum*. In both instances the benefit maximum applies separately to each employee and each dependent covered under the contract.

Lifetime Maximum. When a lifetime maximum is used, the specified overall maximum applies to all medical expenses paid (after the application of deductibles and coinsurance) during the entire period an individual is covered under the contract. It is no longer common to find benefit maximums of less than $100,000, and most benefit maximums fall within the range of $250,000 to $1 million. In some instances the benefit amount is unlimited.

In the absence of any provisions to the contrary, the lifetime maximum will be reduced by the amount of any benefits paid. For example, an individual with a $200 calendar-year deductible, an 80 percent coinsurance provision, and a $100,000 lifetime maximum, who incurs $4,000 of medical expenses in his or her first year of coverage (assuming it corresponds with the calendar year), will receive benefits of $3,040 (that is, 80 percent of $3,800). This will reduce the remaining lifetime benefit to $96,960.

Major medical contracts commonly contain provisions for restoring (either partially or totally) the lifetime maximum to its original level. Most contracts stipulate that on some date each year (often January 1) the entire deficit in the lifetime maximum will be automatically restored, subject to a maximum annual restoration that may vary from $1,000 to $5,000. However, the overall maximum cannot be increased above its original limit. If the plan in the previous example has a $1,000 automatic annual restoration, the amount of the remaining benefit will initially be increased to $97,960. Ignoring any future reductions for benefits paid, this limit will continue to increase by $1,000 each year until the original $100,000 maximum is restored.

Most contracts also state that after a covered person has used up a specified amount (often $1,000 or $2,000), he or she may have the maximum benefit restored to its original level upon supplying satisfactory evidence of insurability to the insurance company. Although insurance contracts are silent on what constitutes evidence of insurability, most insurance companies use the same standards and procedures that apply to applicants for individual medical expense insurance.

In addition to the overall lifetime maximum *internal maximums* are sometimes found in major medical contracts. For example, a plan may have a $1 million overall lifetime maximum, but a $10,000 lifetime maximum for mental and nervous disorders. In other words only $10,000 of the $1 million will be paid for expenses relating to these conditions. This is probably the most common type of an internal maximum, but a few plans do contain calendar-year or per-disability maximums. The provision for restoring benefits does not apply to the calendar-year or per-disability maximums and may or may not apply to the mental and nervous disorder maximum.

Per-Cause Maximum. A few plans contain maximum limits for each cause of medical expenses, but in general this type of maximum limit is used only when the deductible is also applied on a per-cause basis. Most plans of this type do not have an automatic restoration-of-benefits provision but do allow benefits to be reinstated upon satisfactory evidence of insurability. If this evidence is not (or cannot be) provided, coverage will terminate for any cause for which the maximum benefits have been paid. However, coverage will remain in force for expenses arising from other causes.

HMO COVERAGE AS AN ALTERNATIVE TO MAJOR MEDICAL

Most health maintenance organization also provide broad protection for medical expenses. In fact, federally qualified HMOs often give more comprehensive protection than most major medical plans, since in addition to covering such items as routine examinations and immunizations, they tend to require less out-of-pocket expenses by the members. HMOs that meet the requirements for federal qualification are allowed to use copayments for services (1) if the copayment for any single service does not exceed 50 percent of the cost for that service, and (2) if the total of all copayments does not exceed more than 20 percent of the cost of supplying all basic health services. In practice copayments (if used at all) are usually substantially below these permissible limits. In addition, no subscriber is required to copay more than 50 percent of the annual subscriber fee that would have been charged if coverage had been written without any copayments.

The chart on the following pages compares the major medical plan and two HMOs that are offered to the employees of one organization. All three plans are reasonably representative of their respective plan type.

OTHER CONTRACT PROVISIONS COMMON TO BOTH BASIC AND MAJOR MEDICAL EXPENSE CONTRACTS

Many of the provisions found in both basic and major medical expense contracts are similar—if not identical—to those found in group term life insurance (discussed in chapter 4). However, certain provisions are either unique to medical expense insurance contracts or differ substantially from those found in other types of group insurance. These pertain to eligibility, managed-care provisions, coordination of benefits, the effect of medicare, termination, and claims.

Eligibility

The eligibility requirements for medical expense insurance are essentially the same as those discussed for group term insurance in chapter 4—an employee must usually be in a covered classification, must satisfy any probationary period, and must be full-time. Coverage is rarely made available to part-time employees. In addition, medical expense contracts often contain an actively-at-work provision. This may be waived for larger employers for whom adverse selection tends to be less of a problem than for smaller groups, since any adverse selection for a large group will be reflected in future premiums through the experience-rating process.

Eligibility requirements may vary somewhat if an employer changes insurance companies. Even though it has been adopted by only a few states, most insurance companies follow the procedures established by the NAIC Model Regulation on Group Coverage Discontinuance and Replacement for medical expense coverage (and possibly other group coverages). This regulation stipulates that coverage will be provided (but possibly limited) under a new plan to anyone who (1) was covered under the prior plan at the date it was discontinued and (2) is in an eligible classification of the new plan. Employees actively at work on the date coverage is transferred are automatically covered under the new plan and are exempt from any probationary periods. If the new plan contains a preexisting-conditions

A Comparison: Insured Plan versus HMOs

	Insured Comprehensive Major Medical Expense Plan	Group Practice HMO	Individual Practice Association HMO
Choice of Physician	Member may select any licensed physician or surgeon.	Member selects a personal physician from the medical group, who coordinates and directs all health care needs including referrals to specialists.	Members select a personal primary-care physician from among the health plan physicians.
Where Primary Care and Specialty Care Are Available	Care is provided in physician's office or outpatient facility.	Care is provided at four multi-specialty centers.	Care is provided in participating private physicians' offices.
Choice of Hospitals	Member may select any accredited hospital—choice depends on where physician has admitting privileges.	Selection is from participating hospitals.	Selection is from participating hospitals.
Annual Deductible and Coinsurance	There is a $200 deductible. The plan has no coinsurance for hospitalization, but it does have 80% coinsurance for other covered services. There is no coinsurance on covered services after $3,000 in benefits is paid.	There is no deductible and no coinsurance (except small copayments for home visits and outpatient mental health).	There is no deductible and no coinsurance (except small copayments for home visits, outpatient mental health, and a deductible for prescription drugs).

Maximum Benefit	$1 million lifetime maximum	No overall maximum limit	No overall maximum limit
Preventive Care			
Routine physicals	Not covered	Covered in full	Covered in full
Well-baby care	Not covered	Covered in full	Covered in full
Pap smears	Routine exams not covered	Covered in full	Covered in full
Immunizations	Not covered	Covered in full	Covered in full
Eye exam	Not covered	Covered in full, including written prescriptions for lenses	Paid in full for children up to age 18
Hearing exam	Not covered	Covered in full	Covered in full
Health education	Available through some physicians' offices	Periodic classes held on diet, prenatal care, physical fitness, etc.	Covered in full through participating hospital programs
Physician Care			
Surgery	Covered at 80% after satisfying deductible	Covered in full	Covered in full
Inpatient visits	Covered at 80% after deductible	Covered in full	Covered in full
Office and home	Covered at 80% after deductible	Office visits covered in full, home visits covered in full, charge of $3 per allied health professional home visit	Office visits covered in full; charge of $5 per doctor's home visit
X rays and lab	Covered at 80% after deductible	Covered in full	Covered in full

A Comparison: Insured Plan versus HMOs

	Insured Comprehensive Major Medical Expense Plan	Group Practice HMO	Individual Practice Association HMO
Hospital Services			
Room and board	Covered in full for unlimited days in semiprivate room after satisfying deductible	Covered in full for unlimited days in semiprivate room	Covered in full for unlimited days in semiprivate room
Supplies, tests, medication, etc.	Covered in full for covered benefit days	Covered in full	Covered in full
Private-duty nurse	Covered in full while hospitalized (outpatient licensed practical nurse services covered at 50% up to $250 per year)	Covered in full	Covered in full
Emergency Care	Covered in full for care received in hospital outpatient department within 24 hours of an accident	Covered in full for around-the-clock emergency care by plan physicians and in participating hospitals. Emergency care by nonplan physicians or hospitals is also covered when obtaining plan care is not reasonable because of distance and urgency.	Covered in full for around-the-clock emergency care by participating physicians and in participating hospitals. Emergency care by non-participating physicians or hospitals is also covered when obtaining plan care is not reasonable because of distance and urgency.
Ambulance service	Covered in full for local transportation after satisfying deductible	Covered in full	Covered in full

Maternity Care			
Hospital	Covered in full after deductible	Covered in full	Covered in full
Physician	Covered at 80% after deductible	Covered in full	Covered in full
Mental Health Care			
Hospital	Covered as regular hospitalization, i.e., 365 day/lifetime limitation	Covered in full for 45 days per year	Covered in full for 30 days during 12-month period
Inpatient physician	Covered as regular inpatient physician care	Covered in full for 45 days per year	Covered in full for 30 days during 12-month period
Outpatient physician	Covered at 50% up to $20 per visit and $1,000 per year	Covered for 30 visits per year; first 3 visits covered in full, next 27 visits member pays $10 per visit	Covered for 20 visits per period; first 3 visits covered in full, next 7 visits member pays 25% of regular fee, next 10 visits member pays 50% of regular fee
Alcohol and drug addiction	Covered like other mental health services	No special limits, covered as other medical and mental health services	After detoxification treatment, covered as for mental health problems
Dental Care			
Hospital	Covered for hospital costs when confinement is necessary for dental care	Covered for hospital costs when confinement is necessary for dental care	Covered for hospital costs when confinement is necessary for dental care
Dentist or dental surgeon	Covered for treatment of accidental injury to natural teeth	Covered for treatment of accidental injury to natural teeth and certain oral surgical procedures (e.g., impacted wisdom teeth)	Covered for treatment of diseases and injuries to the jaw and removal of impacted wisdom teeth

A Comparison: Insured Plan versus HMOs

	Insured Comprehensive Major Medical Expense Plan	Group Practice HMO	Individual Practice Association HMO
Outpatient Medication Prescription drugs	Covered at 80% after deductible, if related to treatment of nonoccupational illness or injury	Not covered	Covered in full after $50 deductible per person per contract year
Injections	Covered at 80% after deductible, if related to treatment of nonoccupational illness or injury	Covered in full	Covered in full
Prescribed Home Health Services	Covered at 80% after deductible	Covered in full	Covered in full
Allergy Care	Covered at 80% after deductible	Covered in full	Covered in full
Eligibility	Spouse and unmarried dependent children to age 19 or age 23 if a full-time student	Spouse and unmarried dependent children to age 19 or 23 if a full-time student	Spouse and unmarried dependent children through age 19 or 23 if a full-time student
Conversion	Conversion to individual coverage available	Conversion to nongroup coverage available	Conversion to individual enrollment available at same benefit level

provision, benefits applicable to an individual's preexisting conditions are limited to the lesser of (1) the maximum benefits of the new plan (ignoring the preexisting conditions) or (2) the maximum benefits of the prior plan.

Employees who are not actively at work on the date coverage is discontinued under the old plan (such as employee disabled by illness or injury or those suffering temporary interruptions of employment) must be included in the new plan. However, their benefits can be limited to the old plan's level until they meet the actively-at-work requirement of the new plan. Two other points should be made concerning the transfer of coverage. First, the new plan will not pay benefits for expenses covered by the old plan under an extension-of-benefits provision (discussed later), and second, when applying any deductibles or waiting periods under the new plan, credit is usually given for the satisfaction (or partial satisfaction) of the same or similar provisions during the last 3 months of the old plan. For example, assume that coverage is transferred in the middle of a calendar year and the new plan contains the same $200-a-year calendar deductible as the old plan. If an employee has already satisfied the deductible under the old plan, no new deductible would be required for the remainder of the calendar year provided that (1) the expenses used to satisfy the deductible under the old plan would satisfy the deductible under the new plan, and (2) the expenses were incurred during the last 3 months of the old plan. If only $140 of the $200 was incurred during those last 3 months, an additional $60 deductible would be required under the new plan for the remainder of the calendar year.

Dependent Eligibility

The same medical expense benefits that are provided for an eligible employee usually will also be available for that employee's dependents. Dependent coverage is rarely available unless the employee also has coverage. As long as any necessary payroll deductions have been authorized, dependent coverage is typically effective on the same date as the employee's coverage. If coverage under a contributory plan is not elected within 31 days after dependents are eligible, future coverage will be available only during an open enrollment period or when satisfactory evidence of insurability can be provided. However, if an employee was previously without dependents (and therefore had no dependent coverage), any newly acquired dependents (by birth, marriage, or adoption) will be eligible for coverage as of the date they gain dependent status.

The term *dependents* most commonly refers to an employee's spouse who is not legally separated from the employee and any unmarried dependent children (including stepchildren and adopted children) under the age of 19. However, coverage is usually provided for children to age 23 if they are full-time students. In addition, coverage may also continue (and is required to be continued in some states) for children who are incapable of earning their own living because of a physical or mental infirmity. Such children will be considered dependents as long as this condition exists, but periodic proof of the condition may be required by the insurance company. If an employee has dependent coverage, all newly acquired dependents (by birth, marriage, or adoption) are automatically covered.

The plans of a few employers define the term *dependent* broadly enough to include unmarried domestic partners. For example, one plan covers unmarried couples as long as they live together, show financial interdependence and joint responsibility for each other's common welfare, and consider themselves life partners. Most plans provide benefits to domestic partners engaged in either heterosexual or homosexual relationships. Some plans provide benefits only to persons of the opposite sex of the employee, and a small number of plans limit benefits only to persons of the same sex. The rationale for the latter is that persons of opposite sexes can obtain benefits by marrying, whereas this option is not available to persons of the same sex.

Some persons that meet the definition of a dependent may be ineligible for coverage because they are in the armed forces or they are eligible for coverage under the same plan as employees themselves. This latter restriction, however, may not apply to a spouse unless the spouse is actually covered under the plan. Some plans also exclude coverage for any dependents residing outside the United States or Canada.

Most medical expense plans contain a "nonconfinement" provision for dependents, which is similar to the actively-at-work provision for employees. Under this provision a dependent is not covered if he or she is confined for medical care or treatment in a hospital or at home at the time of eligibility. Coverage, however, will become effective when the dependent is released from such confinement.

When coverage is transferred, dependents are treated the same as employees, except that any actively-at-work provision is usually replaced by a nonconfinement provision.

Utilization-Management Provisions

Traditional medical expense plans have contained few provisions aimed at managing the care of covered persons, but this situation continues to change. Some of these changes have already been discussed. Requirements for hospital certification and second surgical opinions have existed for several years. The carve-out of benefits for mental illness and substance abuse is much newer. Other recent changes include maternity management and the preapproval of visits to specialists. These programs are distinct from standard precertification and utilization review.

Maternity Management

The identification of high-risk pregnancies and proper medical treatment can result in significant cost savings to a benefit plan. For example, the expenses associated with premature birth can amount to several hundred thousand dollars. As a result many plans have begun to incorporate maternity management. In contrast to many cost-containment efforts maternity management focuses on low-frequency, high-cost claims. While there is a charge for this coverage, its cost will usually be more than offset if only one large claim is avoided.

A maternity-management provision requires an employee to notify the organization providing utilization management within some prescribed time period after confirmation of pregnancy. Failure to obtain this *precertification* may result in a reduction of benefits. A case manager, usually a registered nurse, works closely with the expectant mother and her physician throughout the pregnancy to see that a complete assessment of the mother's health is made so that unfavorable risk factors can be monitored. Individualized maternity education will be provided through brochures and telephone contact. This education focuses on prenatal care with respect to items such as nutrition, alcohol use, and smoking.

Preapproval of Visits to Specialists

Many persons elect to bypass primary-care physicians, such as family physicians and pediatricians, and use specialists and the emergency room as their primary access to medical care. This results in additional costs but does not improve medical outcome in the opinion of much of the medical community. To counter this practice, some medical expense plans require that a visit to a specialist be preceded by a visit to a primary-care physician. It is not necessary for the primary-care physician to actually certify that a trip to a specialist is necessary, only that he or she has been told that the patient plans to make such a visit. The rationale for this procedure is that the primary-care physician may convince the patient that he or she is able to treat the condition and that a specialist is unnecessary, at least at that time. If a specialist is needed, the primary-care physician is also in a better position to recommend the right type of specialist and to coordinate health care for persons seeing multiple specialists.

Failure to use the primary-care physician as a quasi-gatekeeper will result in a reduction in benefits. Usually benefits will still be paid but at a lower level.

Coordination of Benefits

In recent years the percentage of individuals having duplicate group medical expense coverage has increased substantially. Probably the most common situation is the one in which a husband and wife both work and have coverage under their respective employers' noncontributory plans. If the employer of either spouse also provides dependent coverage on a noncontributory basis, the other spouse (and other dependents if both employers provide such coverage) will be covered under both plans. If dependent coverage is contributory, it will be necessary for a couple with children to elect such coverage under one of their plans. However, because a spouse is considered a dependent, he or she will also have duplicate coverage when the election is made. Duplicate coverage may also arise when

- an employee has two jobs
- children are covered under both a parent's and a stepparent's plans
- an employee elects coverage under a contributory plan even though he or she is covered as a dependent under another plan. This could result from ignorance or from an attempt to collect double the amount if a claim should occur. In many cases this coverage is elected because it is broader, even though it still results in an element of duplicate coverage.

Duplicate coverage can also occur if an individual has coverage under a group plan that is not provided by an employer. A common example involves children whose parents have purchased accident coverage for them through their schools.

In the absence of any provisions to the contrary, group insurance plans are obligated to provide benefits in cases of duplicate coverage as if no other coverage exists. However, to prevent individuals from receiving benefits that exceed their actual expenses, most group insurance plans contain a *coordination-of-benefits (COB) provision,* under which priorities are established for the payment of benefits by each plan covering an individual.

Most COB provisions are based on the 1991 Model Group Coordination of Benefits Regulation promulgated by the National Association of Insurance Commissioners. This regulation updates earlier regulations, and all or portions have now been adopted by the majority of states. As with all NAIC model legislation and regulations, some states have adopted the COB provisions with variations.

Although some flexibility is allowed, virtually all COB provisions apply when other coverage exists through the group insurance plans or group benefit arrangements (such as the Blues, HMOs, or self-funded plans) of another employer. They may also apply to no-fault automobile insurance benefits and to coverage for students that is either sponsored or provided by educational institutions. However, these provisions virtually never apply (and cannot in most states) to any other coverages provided under contracts purchased on an individual basis outside of the employment relationship.

Determination of Primary Coverage

The usual COB provision stipulates that any other plan without the COB provision is primary and that any plan with it is secondary. If more than one plan has a COB provision, the following priorities are established:

- Coverage as an employee is usually primary to coverage as a dependent. The exception to this rule occurs if a retired person is covered by medicare, under a retiree plan of a former employer, and as a dependent of a spouse who is an active employee. In this case coverage as a dependent is primary, medicare is secondary, and the retiree plan pays last.
- If the parents of dependent children are neither separated nor divorced, the plan covering the parent whose birthday falls earlier in the year is primary. (Prior to the 1985 provisions the policy of the father was primary to the policy of the mother. If the plan of one parent uses the birthday rule, and the plan of the other parent still uses the male/female rule, the latter rule is to be followed.)
- If the parents of dependent children are separated or divorced, the following priorities apply:
  - The plan of the parent with custody is primary.
  - The plan of the spouse of the parent with custody (the stepparent) is secondary.
  - The plan of the parent without custody pays last.
  However, if the specific terms of a court decree state that one of the parents is responsible for the child's health care expenses, the plan of that parent is primary as long as the insurance company or other entity obligated to provide the benefits has actual knowledge of the terms of the

court decree. If benefits are paid under another plan before this knowledge is obtained, the "court-decree rule" does not apply during the remainder of the plan or policy year.

● Coverage as an active employee (or as that person's dependent) is primary to coverage as a retired or laid-off employee (or as that person's dependent). However, this rule is ignored unless both plans contain the rule.

● Coverage as an active employee (or that person's dependent) is primary to a plan that provides COBRA continuation benefits. This rule is also ignored unless both plans contain the rule.

● If none of the previous rules establishes a priority, the plan covering the person for the longest period of time is primary.

Determination of Benefits Payable

The actual mechanics of the previously described COB provision are demonstrated in the following example, which assumes that a person has coverage under the plans of two employers:

Plan A has basic benefits with a maximum of (1) $300 per day for semiprivate hospital accommodations up to 31 days, (2) $1,000 for hospital extras, and (3) $1,500 for surgery. It has no deductibles or coinsurance.

Plan B has comprehensive major medical expense coverage with (1) a $200-per-year calendar deductible, (2) 80 percent coinsurance, and (3) a $250,000 maximum. Hospital benefits are limited to the cost of semiprivate accommodations.

Assume also that this person incurs the following expenses:

Semiprivate room for 8 days at $500 per day	$4,000
Other hospital charges	1,200
Surgeon's fees	2,000
Total expenses	$7,200

If there were no COB provision in either plan, plan A would pay $4,900 ($2,400 for hospital room and board, $1,000 for hospital extras, and $1,500 for surgery), and plan B would pay $5,600 (assuming no portion of the deductible had previously been satisfied). This latter amount consists of 80 percent of covered expenses that exceed the $200 deductible. Consequently the person would collect benefits totaling $10,500, or $3,300 in excess of his or her actual expenses.

Before the COB provision is used, it must first be determined whether the provision applies to a given claim. It will apply only if the sum of the benefits under the plans involved (assuming there is no provision) exceeds an individual's allowable expenses. *Allowable expenses* are defined as any necessary, reasonable, and customary items of expense, all or a portion of which are covered under at least one of the plans that provides benefits to the person for whom the claim is made. However, the amount of any benefit reductions under a primary plan because a covered person failed to comply with the plan's provisions (such as second opinions or precertification) is not considered an allowable expense. In addition, the difference between the cost of a private hospital room and the cost of a semiprivate hospital room is not considered an allowable expense unless the patient's stay in a private room is medically necessary. When the allowable expenses are determined, any deductibles, coinsurance, and plan maximum are ignored.

In the previous example the entire $7,200 is considered allowable expenses. Because the sum of the benefits otherwise payable under the two plans ($10,500) exceeds this amount, the COB provision applies. If the sum of the benefits did not exceed the allowable expenses, the COB provision would not apply, and each plan would pay its benefits as if it were the only existing plan.

When the COB provision applies, a person receives benefits equal to 100 percent of his or her allowable expenses and no more. The primary plan pays its benefits as if no other coverage exists, and the secondary plan (or plans) pays the remaining benefits. If plan A in this example is primary, it will pay $4,900, and plan B will pay the remaining $2,300 of expenses. If plan B is primary, it will pay $5,600, and plan A will pay the remaining $1,600.

The Preservation of Deductibles and Coinsurance. The preservation of deductibles and coinsurance was acceptable under 1985 NAIC provisions. The major rationale for such a provision was that the traditional approach negated the cost-containment effects of deductibles and coinsurance since most persons will be indemnified for 100 percent of their expenses even if both plans contained these cost-saving features. However, most states did not adopt this portion of the provisions, and it was deleted in 1987 by the NAIC. However, a few states do allow the preservation of deductibles and coinsurance and permit one of two approaches to be used.

The first approach is similar to the traditional approach but allows the secondary plan to pay the difference between 80 percent (or more if the plan so provides) of total allowable expenses actually incurred less whatever was paid by the primary plan. In the example 80 percent of allowable expense is $5,760. If plan A is primary and pays $4,900, plan B will be required to pay only $860 if it used the 80 percent figure.

The secondary approach for preserving deductibles and coinsurance does not use the concept of allowable expense. Rather, the secondary plan pays the difference, if any, between (1) the amount it would have paid if it had been primary and (2) the amount paid by the primary plan. This approach maintains the benefit provisions of the secondary plan — deductibles, coinsurance, and any other policy limitations or exclusions. In the example plan B will pay $5,600 if it had been primary. If plan A is actually primary, it will pay $4,900 and plan B will pay an additional $700.

When it is permissible to preserve deductibles and coinsurance, most states require a plan to comply with certain rules that were contained in the deleted portion of the NAIC provisions:

- Covered persons must be given prior notice that they will not receive 100 percent of their expenses if duplicate coverage exists. This gives them the opportunity to discontinue coverage under one of the plans if that is possible and is in their best interest.

- The plan must allow a person who is otherwise eligible for coverage under the plan but not enrolled in it to enroll if his or her coverage under another group plan terminates for any reason and cannot be replaced. The rationale for this provision is that the COB provision tends to encourage working families to drop duplicate coverage. This rule prevents a total loss of protection if coverage under the plan that was not dropped is later terminated.
- If a plan uses the second approach (the one without the concept of allowable expense), it cannot have a coinsurance factor of less than (1) 50 percent for mental or nervous disorders or alcohol and drug abuse treatments, (2) 50 percent for benefits if a covered person fails to obtain or follow cost-containment provisions, such as second surgical opinions or preadmission certification, and (3) 75 percent for other covered expenses. The latter restriction, however, does not apply to dental care, vision care, hearing care, or prescription drugs.

Always-Secondary Plans

In most states insured medical expenses plans (including the Blues, HMOs, and PPOs) are not required to use a coordination-of-benefits provision. However, when such a provision is used, it must comply with the appropriate state rules. Self-funded plans, on the other hand, are not bound by these rules and can use any type of coordination-of-benefits provision. As a rule a self-funded plan will use a provision that is identical or similar to that imposed on insured plans. Unfortunately some self-funded plans have been designed so that they are excess or "always secondary" to any other medical expense plan.

The most extreme situation occurs if a person is covered under two self-funded plans, each of which takes an always-secondary approach. Each plan will pay as if it was secondary. In the previous example this means that Plan A will pay $1,600 and Plan B will pay $2,300. This total of $3,900 is less than either plan would pay if it were primary. This issue has been the subject of several court cases, and some (but not all) courts have stated that the always-secondary position cannot prevail. While these courts have ordered an equitable payment of benefits to the covered person, that person has been forced to take the matter to court.

A similar situation exists if a person is covered under a self-funded plan that is always secondary (but would be primary if the state's rules applied) and an insured plan that is legitimately secondary because of the state's coordination-of-benefits rules. However, the results are usually somewhat different. In most states the insured plan must pay two amounts to the covered person. The first amount is what the insured plan is obligated to pay as the secondary plan. The second amount is the difference between what the self-funded plan pays on a secondary basis and what it would have paid if it had settled the claim as the primary payer of benefits. This amount is considered an advance to the covered person, and the insured plan receives a right of subrogation. This means that the insured plan has the right to take legal action to recover the amount of the advance from the self-funded plan. If the amount is recovered, the advance is in effect repaid. If there is no recovery, the covered person has no obligation to repay the insured plan.

The Relationship with Medicare

Since most employees and their dependents will be eligible for medicare upon reaching age 65 (and possibly under other circumstances), a provision that will eliminate any possible duplication of coverage is necessary. The simplest solution would be to exclude any person eligible for medicare from eligibility under the group contract. However, in most cases this approach would conflict with the Age Discrimination in Employment Act, which prohibits discrimination in welfare benefit plans for active employees.

Medicare Secondary Rules

As mentioned in chapter 3, employers with 20 or more employees must make coverage available under their medical expense plans to active employees aged 65 or older and to active employees' spouses who are eligible for medicare. Unless an employee elects otherwise, the employer's plan is primary and medicare is secondary. Except in plans that require large employee contributions, it is doubtful that employees will elect medicare to be primary since employers are prohibited from offering active employees or their spouses either a medicare carve-out or a medicare supplement.

Medicare is the secondary payer of benefits in two other situations. The first situation involves persons who are eligible for medicare benefits to treat end-stage renal disease with dialysis or kidney transplants. Medicare provides these benefits to any insured workers (regardless of age) and to their spouses and dependent children, but the employer's plan is primary during the first 18 months of treatment only; after that time medicare is primary and the employer's plan is secondary. It should be noted that the employer's plan could totally exclude dialysis and/or kidney transplants, in which case medicare would pay. However, the employer is prevented by law from excluding these benefits for the first 18 months if they are covered thereafter. This rule for renal disease applies to medical expense plans of all employers, not just those with 20 or more employees.

Medicare is also the secondary payer of benefits to disabled employees (or the disabled dependents of employees) under age 65 who are eligible for medicare and who are covered under the medical expense plan of large employers. It should be noted, however, that medicare does not pay anything until a person has been eligible for social security disability income benefits for 2 years. This rule, which applies only to the plans of employers with 100 or more employees, will expire in September 1995, unless it is extended. The rule applies only if an employer continues medical expense coverage for disabled persons; there is no requirement for such a continuation.

Medicare Carve-Outs and Supplements

An employer's plan may cover certain persons aged 65 or older who are not covered by the provisions of the Age Discrimination in Employment Act. These include retirees and active employees of firms with fewer than 20 employees.

There is nothing to prevent an employer from terminating coverage for these persons. However, many employers provide them with either a medicare carve-out or medicare supplement.

With a *medicare carve-out* plan benefits are reduced to the extent that benefits are payable under medicare for the same expenses. (Medicare may also pay for some expenses not covered by the group plan.) For example, if a person who incurs $1,000 of covered expenses is not eligible for medicare, $720 in benefits will be paid under a medical expense plan that has a $100 deductible and an 80 percent coinsurance provision. However, if the same person is eligible for medicare, and if medicare pays $650 for the same expenses, the employer's plan will pay only $70, for a total benefit of $720.

Some medical expense plans use a more liberal carve-out approach and reduce covered expenses (rather than benefits payable) by any amounts received under medicare. In the previous example the $650 paid by medicare would be subtracted from the $1,000 of covered expenses, which would leave $350. After the deductible and coinsurance are applied to this amount, the employer's plan will pay $200. Therefore the covered person will receive a total of $850 in benefits, or $130 more than a person not eligible for medicare.

As an alternative to using a carve-out approach, some employers use a *medicare supplement* that provides benefits for certain specific expenses not covered under medicare. These include (1) the portion of expenses that is not paid by medicare because of deductibles, coinsurance, or copayments, and (2) certain expenses excluded by medicare, such as prescription drugs. Such a supplement may or may not provide benefits similar to those available under a carve-out plan.

Termination of Coverage

In the absence of any provisions for continuation or conversion, group insurance coverage on an employee generally ceases on the earliest of the following:

- the date on which employment terminates. In some contracts coverage ceases on the last day of the month in which employment terminates.
- the date on which the employee ceases to be eligible
- the date on which the master contract terminates
- the date on which the overall maximum benefit of major medical coverage is received
- the end of the last period for which the employee has made any required contribution

Coverage on any dependent usually ceases on the earliest of the following:

- the date on which he or she ceases to meet the definition of dependent
- the date on which the coverage of the employee ceases for any reason except the employee's receipt of the overall maximum benefit
- the date on which the overall maximum benefit of major medical coverage is received by the dependent

- the end of the last period for which the employee has made any required contribution for dependent coverage

However, coverage often continues past these dates because of federal legislation or employer practices.

The Continuation of Coverage under COBRA

The Consolidated Omnibus Budget Reconciliation Act of 1985 (COBRA) requires that group health plans allow employees and certain beneficiaries to elect to have their current health insurance coverage extended at group rates for up to 36 months following a "qualifying event" that results in the loss of coverage. The term *group health plan* as used in the act is broad enough to include medical expense plans, dental plans, vision care plans, and prescription drug plans, regardless of whether benefits are self-insured or provided through other entities such as insurance companies or HMOs. COBRA applies even if the cost of a plan is paid solely by employees as long as the plan would not be available at the same cost to an employee if he or she were not employed. However, there is one exception to this rule: mass-marketed plans under which the employer's only involvement is to process payroll deductions are not subject to COBRA.

The act applies only to employers that had 20 or more employees on a typical business day during the preceeding calendar year. (However, church and government plans are exempt from the act.) Failure to comply with the act will result in an excise tax of up to $100 per day for each person denied coverage. The tax can be levied on the employer as well as on the entity (such as an insurer or HMO) that provides or administers the benefits.

Under the act each of the following is a qualifying event if it results in the loss of coverage by an employee or the employee's spouse or dependent child:

- the death of the covered employee
- the termination of the employee for any reason except gross misconduct. This includes quitting, retiring, or being fired for anything other than gross misconduct.
- a reduction of the employee's hours so that the employee or dependent is ineligible for coverage
- the divorce or legal separation of the covered employee and his or her spouse
- for spouses and children, the employee's eligibility for medicare
- a child's ceasing to be an eligible dependent under the plan

The act specifies that the beneficiary—any employee, spouse, or dependent child who loses coverage because of any of these events—is entitled to elect continued coverage without providing evidence of insurability. The beneficiary must be allowed to continue coverage identical to that provided to employees and dependents to whom a qualifying event has not occurred. If a medical expense plan includes such items as dental care or vision care as an integral part of the plan, the beneficiary must also be allowed to continue coverage without these benefits, even though such an option is not available to active employees or their dependents.

Coverage for persons electing continuation can be changed when changes are made to the plan covering active employees and their dependents. The continued coverage must extend from the date of the qualifying event to the earliest of the following:

- 18 months for employees and dependents when the employee's employment has terminated or coverage has been terminated because of a reduction in hours. This period is extended to 29 months if the Social Security Administration determines that an employee met the social security definition of total disability at the time of the qualifying event.
- 36 months for other qualifying beneficiaries
- the date the plan terminates for all employees
- the date the coverage ceases because of a qualifying beneficiary's failure to make a timely payment of premium
- the date a qualifying beneficiary becomes entitled to medicare or becomes covered (as either an employee or dependent) under another group health plan, provided the group health plan does not contain an exclusion or limitation with respect to any preexisting condition. If the new plan does not cover a preexisting condition, the COBRA coverage can be continued until the earlier of (1) the remainder of the 18- or 36-month period or (2) the time when the preexisting-conditions provision no longer applies.

If a second qualifying event occurs during the period of continued coverage (such as the divorce of a terminated employee), the maximum period of continuation is usually 36 months. One exception is if the second event is a former employee's eligibility for medicare. In this case other family members can continue COBRA coverage for an additional 36 months. For example, an employer retires at age 64, creating a qualifying event entitling beneficiaries to 18 months of continued coverage. Twelve months later when the retiree becomes entitled to medicare, the dependents have a new qualifying event and can continue coverage for 36 more months.

At the termination of continued coverage a qualified beneficiary must be offered the right to convert to an individual insurance policy if a conversion privilege is generally available to employees under the employer's plan.

Notification of the right to continue coverage must be made at two times by a plan's administrator. The first time is when a plan becomes subject to COBRA or when a person becomes covered under a plan subject to COBRA. Notification must be given to an employee as well as to his or her spouse. The second time is when a qualifying event occurs. In this case the employer must notify the plan administrator, who then must notify all qualifying beneficiaries within 14 days. In general the employer has 30 days to notify the plan administrator. However, an employer may not know of a qualifying event if it involves divorce, legal separation, or a child's ceasing to be eligible for coverage. In these circumstances the employee or family member must notify the employer within 60 days of the event, or the right to elect COBRA coverage will be lost. The time period for the employer to notify the plan administrator begins when the employer is informed of the qualifying event as long as this occurs within the 60-day period.

The continuation of coverage is not automatic; it must be elected by a qualifying beneficiary. The election period starts on the date of the qualifying event and may end not earlier than 60 days after actual notice of the event to the qualifying beneficiary by the plan administrator. Once coverage is elected, the beneficiary has 45 days to pay the premium for the period of coverage prior to the election.

Under COBRA the cost of the continued coverage may be passed on to the qualifying beneficiary, but the cost cannot exceed 102 percent of the cost to the plan for the period of coverage for a similarly situated active employee to whom a qualifying event has not occurred. The extra 2 percent is supposed to cover the employer's extra administrative costs. The one exception to this rule occurs for months 19 through 29 if an employee is disabled, in which case the premium can then be as high as 150 percent. Qualifying beneficiaries must have the option of paying the premium in monthly installments. In addition, there must be a grace period of at least 30 days for each installment.

COBRA has resulted in significant extra costs for employers. Surveys indicate that coverage is elected by approximately 20 percent of those persons who are entitled to a COBRA continuation. The length of coverage averages almost one year for persons eligible for an 18-month extension and almost 2 years for persons eligible for a 36-month extension. While significant variations exist among employers, claim costs of persons with COBRA coverage generally run between 150 percent and 200 percent of claim costs for active employees and dependents. In addition, administrative costs are estimated to be about $20 per month for each person with COBRA coverage.

The Continuation of Coverage in Addition to COBRA

Even before the passage of COBRA it was becoming increasingly common for employers (particularly large employers) to continue group insurance coverage for certain employees—and sometimes their dependents—beyond the usual termination dates. Obviously when coverage is continued now, an employer must, at a minimum, comply with COBRA. However, an employer can be more liberal than COBRA by paying all or a portion of the cost, providing continued coverage for additional categories of persons, or continuing coverage for a longer period of time. Some states have continuation laws for insured medical expense plans that might require coverage to be made available in situations not covered by COBRA. One example is coverage for employees of firms with fewer than 20 employees; another is coverage for periods longer than those required by COBRA.

Retired Employees. Even though not required to do so by the Age Discrimination in Employment Act, many employers continue coverage on retired employees. Although coverage can also be continued for retirees' dependents, it is often limited only to spouses. Retired employees under age 65 usually have the same coverage as the active employees have. However, coverage for employees aged 65 or older (if included under the same plan) may be provided under a carve-out plan that includes medicare or a medicare supplement. The lifetime maximum for persons eligible for medicare is often much lower (such as $5,000 or $10,000) than for active employees. In addition, this maximum is not usually subject to any provision that restores benefits that have been paid.

The subject of retiree benefits has become a major concern to employers since the Financial Accounting Standards Board (FASB) issued a proposal in 1989 for the accounting for postretirement benefits other than pensions. Final rules were issued in 1990. Under the FASB rules, to be phased in between 1993 and 1997, employers are required to do the following:

- recognize the present value of future retiree medical expense benefits on the firm's balance sheet with other liabilities
- record the cost for postretirement medical benefits in the period when an employee performs services. This is comparable to the accounting for pension costs.
- amortize the present value of the future cost of benefits accrued prior to new rules

These new rules are in contrast to the long-used practice of paying retiree medical benefits or premiums out of current revenue and recognizing these costs as expenses when paid. Although the rules are probably logical from a financial accounting standpoint, the effect on employers will be staggering. Estimates are that as many as half of the Fortune 500 companies will be required to report lower earnings, and some could even have their net worths wiped out completely.

The new FASB rules will result in two major changes by employers. First, many employers will lower and possibly eliminate retiree benefits. This has already started to occur. A few employees have announced plans to eliminate retiree benefits completely for both existing and future retirees. However, there are legal uncertainties as to whether benefits that have been promised to retirees can be eliminated or reduced. Many employers also feel that there is a moral obligation to continue these benefits. As a result most employers are not altering plans with respect to current retirees or active employees who are eligible to retire. Rather the changes apply to future retirees only. These changes, which seem to be running the gamut, include the following:

- the elimination of benefits for future retirees
- the shifting of more of the cost burden to future retirees by reducing benefits. This reduction may be in the form of lower benefit maximums, fewer types of expenses being covered, or increased copayments.
- adding or increasing retiree sharing of premium costs after retirement
- shifting to a defined-contribution approach to funding retiree benefits. For example, an employer might agree to pay $5 per month toward the cost of coverage after retirement for each year of service by an employee. Thus an employer would make a monthly contribution of $150 for an employee who retired with 30 years of service, but a contribution of only $75 for an employee with 15 years of service. Many plans of this nature have been designed so that the employer's contribution increases with changes in the consumer price index, subject to maximum increases such as 5 percent per year.

A second change is that employers will increasingly explore methods to prefund the benefits. However, there are no alternatives for prefunding that are as favorable as the alternatives for funding pension benefits. One alternative is the use of a 501(c)(9) trust (or VEBA). As discussed in chapter 12, there are limitations on the deductibility of contributions to a 501(c)(9) trust. In addition, a 501(c)(9) trust can be used to fund retiree benefits only if it is currently being used to fund benefits for active employees.

Another alternative is to prefund medical benefits within a pension plan. Contributions are tax deductible, and earnings accumulate tax free. The IRS rules for qualified retirement plans permit the payment of benefits for medical expenses from a pension plan if certain requirements are satisfied:

- The medical benefits must be subordinate to the retirement benefits. This rule is met if the cost of the medical benefits provided does not exceed 25 percent of the employer's aggregate contribution to the pension plan. For many employers this figure is too low to allow the entire future liability to be prefunded.
- A separate account must be established and maintained for the monies allocated to medical benefits. This can be an aggregate account for nonkey employees, but individual separate accounts must be maintained for key employees and medical benefits attributable to a key employee (and family members) can be made only from his or her account.
- The employer's contributions for medical benefits must be ascertainable and reasonable.

Although the rules for funding retiree medical benefits in a pension plan are restricted and administratively complex, they offer an employer the greatest opportunity to deduct the cost of prefunded benefits. It should also be noted that Congress is aware of the prefunding issue, and there have been proposals to change the pension rules to allow a more liberalized approach to the prefunding of retiree medical benefits, including long-term care. One change, effective in 1991, allows employers to transfer pension assets from an overfunded defined-benefit plan to the account used to pay retiree medical benefits. However, such transfers are allowed only through 1995. A transfer can occur only once a year, and any amounts transferred must be used to provide retiree health benefits for the current year only.

Surviving Dependents. Coverage can also be continued for the survivors of deceased active employees and/or deceased retired employees. However, coverage for the survivors of active employees is not commonly continued beyond the period required by COBRA. In addition, coverage for the survivors of retired employees may be limited to surviving spouses. In both instances the continued coverage is usually identical to what was provided prior to the employee's death. It is also common for the employer to continue the same premium contribution level.

Laid-off Employees. Medical expense coverage can be continued for laid-off workers, and large employers frequently provide such coverage for a limited period. Few employers provide coverage beyond the period required by COBRA, but some employers continue to make the same premium contribution, at least for a limited period of time.

Disabled Employees. As with group term life insurance, medical expense coverage can be continued for an employee (and dependents) when he or she has a temporary interruption of employment, including one arising from illness or injury. Many employers also cover employees who have long-term disabilities or who have retired because of a disability. In most cases this continuation of coverage is contingent upon satisfaction of some definition of total (and possibly permanent) disability.

Extension of Benefits

When coverage is terminated rather than continued, most medical expense plans extend benefits for any covered employee or dependent who is totally disabled at the time of termination. However, the disability must have resulted from an illness or injury that occurred while the person was covered under the group contract. Generally the same level of benefits will be provided as before termination. Although some contracts will cover only expenses associated with the same cause of disability, other contracts will cover any expenses that would have been paid under the terminated coverage, regardless of cause.

Under basic medical expense contracts the extension of benefits generally ceases after 3 months, or when the individual is no longer totally or continuously disabled, whichever comes first. A similar provision is used in major medical contracts, but the time period is longer (generally 12 months or the end of the benefit period following the one in which termination took place).

Conversion

Except when termination results from the failure to pay any required premiums, medical expense contracts usually contain (and are often required to contain) a conversion provision, whereby most covered persons whose group coverage terminates are allowed to purchase individual medical expense coverage without evidence of insurability and without any limitation of benefits for preexisting conditions. Covered persons commonly have 31 days from the date of termination of the group coverage to exercise this conversion privilege, and coverage is then effective retroactively to the date of termination.

This conversion privilege is typically given to any employee who has been insured under the group contract (or under any group contract it replaced) for at least 3 months, and it permits the employee to convert his or her own coverage as well as any dependent coverage. In addition, a spouse or child whose dependent coverage ceases for any other reason may also be eligible for conversion (for example, a spouse who divorces or separates, and children who reach age 19).

A person who is eligible for both the conversion privilege and the right to continue the group insurance coverage under COBRA has two choices when eligibility for coverage terminates. He or she can either elect to convert under the provisions of the policy or elect to continue the group coverage. If the latter choice is made, the COBRA rules specify that the person must again be eligible to convert to an individual policy within the usual conversion period (31 days) after the maximum continuation-of-coverage period ceases. Policy provisions may also make the conversion privilege available to persons whose coverage terminates prior to the end of the maximum continuation period.

The insurance company has the right to refuse the issue of a "conversion" policy to anyone (1) who is covered by medicare or (2) whose benefits under the converted policy, together with similar benefits from other sources, would result in overinsurance according to the insurance company's standards. These similar benefits may be found in other coverages that the individual has (either group or individual coverage) or for which the individual is eligible under any group arrangement.

The use of the word *conversion* is often a misnomer. In actuality a person whose coverage terminates is only given the right to purchase a contract on an individual basis at individual rates. Most Blue Cross–Blue Shield plans offer a conversion policy that is similar or identical to the terminated group coverage. However, most insurance companies offer a conversion policy (or a choice of policies) that contains a lower level of benefits than existed under the group coverage. Traditionally the conversion policy contained only basic hospital and surgical coverages even if major medical coverage was provided under the group contract. Now many insurance companies provide (and are required to provide in many states) a conversion policy that includes major medical benefits, which do not necessarily have to be as broad as those under the former group coverage.

Claims

Medical expense contracts that provide benefits on a service basis generally do not require covered persons to file claim forms. Rather, the providers of services perform any necessary paperwork and are then reimbursed directly.

Medical expense contracts that provide benefits on an indemnity basis require that the insurance company (or other provider) be given a written proof of loss (that is, a claim form) concerning the occurrence, character, and extent of the loss for which a claim is made. This form typically contains portions that must be completed and signed by the employee, a representative of the employer, and the provider of medical services.

The period during which an employee must file a claim depends upon the insurance company and state requirements. An employee generally has at least 90 days (or as soon as is reasonably possible) after medical expenses are incurred to file. Some insurance companies require that they be notified within a shorter time (such as 20 days) about any illness or injury on which a claim may be based, even though they give a longer time period for the actual filing of the form itself.

Individuals have the right under medical expense plans to assign their benefits to the providers of medical services. Such an assignment, which authorizes the insurance company to make the benefit payment directly to the provider, may generally be made by completing the appropriate portion of the claim form. In addition, the insurance company has the right (as it does in disability income insurance) to examine any person for whom a claim is filed at its own expense and with the physician of its own choice.

FEDERAL TAXATION

In many respects the federal tax treatment of group medical expense premiums and benefits parallels that of other group coverage if they are provided through an insurance company, a Blue Cross–Blue Shield plan, a health maintenance organization, or a preferred-provider organization. Contributions by the employer for an employee's coverage are tax deductible to the employer as long as the overall compensation of the employee is reasonable. Employer contributions do not create any income tax liability for an employee. In addition, benefits are not taxable to an employee except when they exceed any medical expenses incurred.

One major difference between group medical expense coverage and other forms of group insurance is that a portion of an employee's contribution for coverage may be tax deductible as a medical expense if that individual itemizes his or her income tax deductions. Under the Internal Revenue Code individuals are allowed to deduct certain medical care expenses (including dental expenses) for which no reimbursement was received. This deduction is limited to expenses (including amounts paid for insurance) that exceed 7.5 percent of the person's adjusted gross income.

Under provisions of the Tax Reform Act of 1986 sole proprietors and partners can deduct 25 percent of the cost of any medical expense coverage provided to them or their families under a plan carried by their proprietorship or partnership. However, the deduction cannot exceed the taxpayer's earned income for the year. Under previous law the proprietorship or partnership could deduct the cost of medical expense coverage for the proprietor or any partner, but the amounts deducted constituted fully taxable income to the proprietor or partner. The 25 percent deduction now allowable may be taken only if the proprietor or partner is not eligible to participate in any subsidized medical expense plan of another employer of the proprietor or partner or of an employer of the proprietor's or partner's spouse. It should be noted that this is not an itemized deduction, but rather a deduction in arriving at adjusted gross income. In addition, any amount deducted cannot be used to determine whether the 7.5 percent threshold for the regular medical expense deduction has been satisfied.

The tax situation may be different if an employer provides medical expense benefits through a self-funded plan (referred to in the Internal Revenue Code as a self-insured medical reimbursement plan), under which employers either (1) pay the providers of medical care directly or (2) reimburse employees for their medical expenses. If a self-funded plan meets certain nondiscrimination requirements for highly compensated employees, the employer can deduct benefit payments as they are made, and the employee will have no taxable income. If a plan is discriminatory, the employer will still receive an income tax deduction. However, all or a portion of the benefits received by "highly compensated individuals," but not by other employees, will be treated as taxable income. A highly compensated individual of a company is (1) one of the five highest-paid officers of the firm, (2) a shareholder who owns more than 10 percent of the firm's stock, or (3) one of the highest-paid 25 percent of all the firm's employees. There are no nondiscrimination rules if a plan is not self-funded and provides benefits through an insurance contract, a Blue Cross–Blue Shield plan, an HMO, or a PPO.

To be considered nondiscriminatory a self-funded plan must meet certain requirements regarding eligibility and benefits. The plan must provide benefits (1) for 70 percent or more of "all employees," or (2) for 80 percent or more of all eligible employees if 70 percent or more of all employees are eligible. Certain employees can be excluded from the all-employees category without affecting the plan's nondiscriminatory status. These include

- employees who have not completed 3 years of service
- employees who have not attained age 25

- part-time employees. Anyone who works fewer than 25 hours per week is automatically considered a part-time employee. Persons who work 25 or more hours, but fewer than 35 hours per week, may also be counted as part-time as long as other employees in similar work for the employer have substantially more hours.
- seasonal employees. Anyone who works fewer than 7 months of the year is automatically considered a seasonal employee. Persons who work between 7 and 9 months of the year may also be considered seasonal as long as other employees have substantially more months of employment.
- employees who are covered by a collective-bargaining agreement if accident-and-health benefits were a subject of collective bargaining

Even if a plan fails to meet the percentage requirements regarding eligibility, it can still qualify as nondiscriminatory as long as the IRS is satisfied that the plan benefits a classification of employees in a manner that does not discriminate in favor of highly compensated employees. This determination is made on a case-by-case basis.

To satisfy the nondiscrimination requirements for benefits, the same type and amount of benefits must be provided for all employees covered under the plan, regardless of their compensation. In addition, the dependents of other employees cannot be treated less favorably than the dependents of highly compensated employees. However, because diagnostic procedures are not considered part of a self-funded plan for purposes of the nondiscrimination rule, a higher level of this type of benefit is permissible for highly compensated employees.

If a plan is discriminatory in either benefits or eligibility, highly compensated employees must include the amount of any "excess reimbursement" in their gross income for income tax purposes. If highly compensated employees receive any benefits that are not available to all employees covered under the plan, then these benefits are considered an excess reimbursement. For example, if a plan pays 80 percent of covered expenses for employees in general, but 100 percent for highly compensated employees, the extra 20 percent of benefits constitutes taxable income.

If a self-funded plan discriminates in the way it determines eligibility, then highly compensated employees will have excess reimbursements for any amounts they receive. The amount of this excess reimbursement is determined by a percentage that is calculated by dividing the total amount of benefits received by highly compensated employees (exclusive of any other excess reimbursements) by the total amount of benefits paid to all employees (exclusive of any other excess reimbursements). Using the previous example, assume a highly compensated employee receives $2,000 in benefits during a certain year. If other employees receive only 80 percent of this amount (or $1,600), then the highly compensated employee will have received an excess reimbursement of $400. If the plan also discriminates in the area of eligibility, the highly compensated employee will incur additional excess reimbursement. For example, if 60 percent of the benefits (ignoring any benefits already considered excess reimbursement) are given to highly compensated employees, then 60 percent of the remaining $1,600 ($2,000 − $400), or $960, will be added to the $400, for a total excess reimbursement of $1,360.

If a plan provides benefits only for highly compensated employees, then all benefits received will be considered an excess reimbursement, since the percentage is 100 percent.

9

Additional Group Insurance Benefits

So far the three traditional types of group insurance have been discussed: life insurance, disability income insurance, and medical expense insurance. This chapter will focus on three of the newer and/or less common types of group insurance coverage: group dental insurance, group long-term care insurance, and group legal expense insurance. It will also cover mass-marketed individual life and health insurance programs. While these are not technically group insurance, they are marketed primarily on a group basis. Finally, there is a brief discussion of property and liability insurance as a group benefit.

GROUP DENTAL INSURANCE

Since the early 1970s group dental insurance has been one of the fastest-growing employee benefits. It has been estimated that in the last 20 years the percentage of employees who have dental coverage has grown from about 5 percent to over 60 percent. Many employee benefit consultants feel that by the end of the century most employees, except for those who work for small employers, will have dental coverage.

To a great extent group dental insurance contracts have been patterned after group medical expense contracts, and they contain many similar, if not identical, provisions. Like group medical expense insurance, however, group dental insurance has many variations. Dental plans may be limited to specific types of expenses or they may be broad enough to cover virtually all dental expenses. In addition, coverage can be obtained from alternative types of providers, and benefits can be in the form of either services or cash payments.

Providers of Dental Coverage

Like medical expense coverage, dental coverage can also be purchased by employers from several sources. The three most common ones are insurance companies, dental service plans, and the Blues. Dental benefits may also be self-funded.

Insurance Companies

Approximately half the coverage for dental expenses is written by insurance companies, often on an indemnity basis. Coverage is usually offered independently of other group insurance coverages, but it may be incorporated into a major medical contract. However, if it is part of a major medical contract, the coverage is often referred to as an *integrated dental plan,* and the benefits are frequently subject to the same provisions and limitations as benefits that are available under a separate dental plan.

Many insurance companies now offer managed-care plans to provide dental care. In some cases these plans are insurer-sponsored HMOs or PPOs. In other cases these plans are hybrid models that may have some features found in traditional HMOs and PPOs, but also have unique features.

One model that has enjoyed considerable success has preferred-provider networks of dentists. If an employee elects to use a preferred-provider network, he or she selects a dentist who is paid a preestablished monthly fee by the plan. The dentist must then provide a specified level of treatment, including coverage at no cost to the patient for diagnostic, preventive, and basic dental services. However, there are copayments for major dental services. If the employee does not elect to use the preferred-provider network, reimbursement levels are lower for all services other than diagnostic and preventive care. In addition, there is an annual deductible. One unique feature about this model is that the employee has the option to periodically switch in and out of the preferred-provider network, possibly as soon as the beginning of the following month.

Dental Service Plans

Most states have dental service plans, often called *Delta Plans,* that write approximately one-quarter of the dental coverage along with the Blues. However, the extent of their use varies widely by state, and western states generally have larger and more successful plans than states in other parts of the country. The majority of these plans are nonprofit organizations that are sponsored by state dental associations. In addition, they are patterned after Blue Shield plans, and dentists provide service benefits on a contractual basis. Also like Blue Shield, state Delta Plans are coordinated by a national board, Delta Dental Plans, Inc.

Blue Cross—Blue Shield

Many Blue Cross—Blue Shield plans also provide dental coverage. In some cases the Blues have contractual arrangements with dentists that are similar to those of dental service plans; in other cases benefits are paid on an indemnity basis just as if an insurance company were involved. Finally, a few of the Blues market dental coverage through Delta Plans in conjunction with their own medical expense plans.

Other Sources

Although a few health maintenance organizations offer dental benefits, this practice is not very common. Any benefits that are provided (primarily checkups, preventive services, and routine fillings) are often limited to children.

Coverage may also be obtained from dental maintenance organization (DMO) plans, which operate like health maintenance organizations but provide only dental care. In addition, dental PPOs have become more common in recent years. While the number of DMOs and dental PPOs is still modest, they are growing at a rapid rate and may become major providers of dental care in the near future. Several factors would seem to make this growth logical. Dental expenses are more predictable than medical care expenses, and the preventive nature of much dental care provides a real potential to hold down future dental costs.

Employers are increasingly turning to self-funding of dental benefits. An employer may either self-administer the plan or use the services of a third-party administrator.

Contractual Provisions

Although group dental insurance contracts have been patterned after group medical expense contracts, some of their provisions are different, and others are unique to dental coverage. These provisions pertain to eligibility, benefits, exclusions, benefit limitations, predetermination of benefits, and termination.

Eligibility

In contributory plans most employers use the same eligibility requirements for dental coverage as they use for medical expense coverage. However, some employers have different probationary periods for the two coverages. Probationary periods are used because members of a group who previously had no dental insurance usually have a large number of untreated dental problems. In addition, many dental care expenditures are postponable, and they will be postponed by an employee who anticipates coverage under a dental plan in the future. Depending on the group's characteristics, the number of first-year claims for a new plan or for new employees and their dependents under an existing dental plan can be expected to run between 20 and 50 percent more than long-run annual claims. Therefore to counter this higher-than-average number of claims, some employers use a longer probationary period for dental benefits than for medical expense benefits. Other employers may have the same probationary period for both types of coverage but will impose waiting periods before certain types of dental expenses will be covered (such as 12 months for orthodontics).

Longer-than-usual probationary periods or waiting periods will initially minimize claims, but unless an organization has a high turnover rate, it may be false economy. Many persons who do not have coverage will merely postpone treatment until they do have coverage. This postponement may actually lead to increased claims, because existing dental conditions will only become more severe and will then require more expensive treatment. For this reason some benefit consultants feel that dental plans should at most contain relatively short probationary and waiting periods.

Another method of countering high first-year claims is to require evidence of insurability. For example, an insurance company might require any person who desires coverage from the dental plan to undergo a dental examination. If major dental problems are disclosed, the person must have them corrected before insurance coverage will become effective.

Since dental expenditures are postponable and somewhat predictable, the problem of adverse selection under contributory plans is more severe for dental insurance than for other types of group insurance. To counter this adverse selection, insurance companies impose more stringent underwriting (including eligibility) requirements on contributory dental plans than they do on other types of group insurance. In addition, most insurance companies insist on a high percentage of participation (such as 80 or 85 percent), and a few will actually not write contributory coverage. Many insurance companies will also insist on having other business besides dental coverage from the employer.

The problem of adverse selection is particularly severe when persons desire coverage after the date on which they were initially eligible to participate. These persons most likely want coverage because they or someone in their family needs dental treatment. Several provisions that try to minimize this problem are contained in dental insurance contracts. They include one or a combination of the following:

- reducing benefits (usually by 50 percent) for a period of time (such as one year) following the late enrollment
- reducing the maximum benefit to a low amount (such as $100 or $200) for the year following the late enrollment
- excluding some benefits for a certain period (such as one or 2 years) following the late enrollment period. This exclusion may apply to all dental expenses except those that result from an accident, or it may apply only to a limited array of benefits (such as orthodontics and prosthetics).

Benefits

Most dental insurance plans pay for almost all types of dental expenses, but a particular plan may provide more limited coverage. One characteristic of dental insurance that is seldom found in medical expense plans is the inclusion of benefits for both routine diagnostic procedures (including oral examinations and X rays) and preventive dental treatment (including teeth cleaning and fluoride treatment). In fact, a few dental plans actually require periodic oral examinations as a condition for continuing eligibility. There is clear evidence that the cost of providing these benefits will be more than offset by the avoidance of the expensive dental procedures that are required when a condition is not discovered early or when a preventive treatment has not been given.

In addition to benefits for diagnostic and preventive treatment, benefits for dental expenses may be provided for the following categories of dental treatment:

- restoration (including fillings, crowns, and other procedures used to restore the functional use of natural teeth)
- oral surgery (including the extraction of teeth as well as other surgical treatment of diseases, injuries, and defects of the jaw)
- endodontics (treatment for diseases of the dental pulp within teeth, such as root canals)
- periodontics (treatment of diseases of the surrounding and supporting tissues of the teeth)
- prosthodontics (the replacement of missing teeth and structures by artificial devices, such as bridgework and dentures)
- orthodontics (the prevention and correction of dental and oral anomalies through the use of corrective devices, such as braces and retainers)

Most dental plans will usually cover any expenses that arise from the first five categories listed above, and they may or may not include benefits for orthodontics.

Whatever benefits are provided may be on a schedule basis, on a nonscheduled basis, or on some combination of the two.

Scheduled Plans. A schedule dental plan is similar to a surgical expense plan in which benefits are paid up to the amount specified in the fee schedule. The following is an excerpt from one such dental schedule:

Dental Services	Maximum Benefit
Diagnostic	
Initial oral examination	$ 15.00
Periodic oral examination	10.00
Preventive	
Prophylaxis (14 years of age or older)	30.00
Prophylaxis (under 14 years of age)	20.00
Prosthodontics	
Complete upper denture	400.00

Most scheduled dental plans provide benefits on a first-dollar basis and contain no deductibles or specified coinsurance percentage. However, benefit maximums are often lower than the usual-and-customary charges of dentists, thereby forcing employees to bear a portion of the costs of their dental services. For example, if a schedule is designed to provide maximum benefits that are equal to approximately 80 percent of the usual-and-customary charges, employees are in effect subject to an 80 percent coinsurance provision. In order to encourage diagnostic and preventive services, some dental schedules are designed so that the fees for these services are almost completely covered, while benefits for other dental services are paid at a lower level.

Unlike a surgical schedule, which lists only the more common surgical procedures, a dental schedule is essentially an all-inclusive list of the covered dental services. If a service is not on the list, most contracts will cover it, but only if the schedule contains what could be considered a suitable substitute. In addition, any benefits paid will be limited to the amount specified for the substitute service.

Although once common, scheduled dental plans are now used less frequently than either nonscheduled plans or combination plans.

Nonscheduled Plans. Nonscheduled dental plans, often called comprehensive dental plans, are the most common type of dental coverage. They resemble major medical expense contracts because dental expenses are paid on a reasonable-and-customary basis, subject to any exclusions, limitations, or copayments contained in the contract. The use of the term *nonscheduled* is somewhat of a misnomer, since many nonscheduled plans actually do contain a schedule of the covered dental services, but they do not list specific benefit amounts for individual services.

Nonscheduled dental plans usually contain both deductibles and coinsurance provisions. Although a single deductible and a single coinsurance percentage may apply to all dental services, the more common practice is to treat different classes of dental services in different ways. The typical nonscheduled dental plan breaks dental services into three broad categories: diagnostic and preventive services, basic services (such as fillings, oral surgery, periodontics, and endodontics), and major services (such as inlays, crowns, dentures, and orthodontics).

Diagnostic and preventive services are typically covered in full and are not subject to a deductible or coinsurance. (They are, however, subject to any other contract limitations.) The other two categories, however, are generally each subject to an annual deductible (usually between $25 and $50 per person). In addition to the deductible, the cost of basic services may be reimbursed at a higher percentage (such as 80 percent), while major services are subject to a lower percentage (often 50 percent).

Combination Plans. Combination plans contain features of both scheduled and nonscheduled plans. The typical combination plan covers diagnostic and preventive services on a usual-and-customary basis but uses a fee schedule for other dental services.

Exclusions

Exclusions are found in all dental plans, but their number and type vary. Some of the more common exclusions include charges for the following:

- services that are purely cosmetic, unless necessitated by an accidental bodily injury while a person is covered under the plan. (Orthodontics, although often used for cosmetic reasons, can usually also be justified as necessary to correct abnormal dental conditions.)
- replacement of lost, missing, or stolen dentures, or other prosthetic devices
- duplicate dentures or other prosthetic devices
- oral hygiene instruction or other training in preventive dental care
- services that do not have uniform professional endorsement
- occupational injuries to the extent that benefits are provided by workers' compensation laws or similar legislation
- services furnished by or on behalf of government agencies, unless there is a requirement to pay
- certain services that began prior to the date that coverage for an individual became effective (for example, a crown for which a tooth was prepared prior to coverage)

Limitations

Dental insurance plans also contain numerous limitations that are designed to control claim costs and to eliminate unnecessary dental care. In addition to deductibles and coinsurance, virtually all dental plans contain overall benefit maximums. Most plans contain a calendar-year maximum (varying from $500 to $2,000) but no lifetime maximum. However, some plans have only a lifetime maximum (such as $1,000 or $5,000), and a few plans contain both a calendar-year maximum and a large lifetime maximum. These maximums may apply to all dental expenses, or they may be limited to all expenses except those that arise from orthodontics (and occasionally periodontics). In the latter case benefits for orthodontics will be subject to a separate, lower lifetime maximum, typically between $500 and $2,000.

Most dental plans limit the frequency with which some benefits will be paid. Routine oral examinations and teeth cleaning are usually limited to once every 6 months, and full mouth X rays to once every 24 or 36 months. The replacement of dentures may also be limited to one time in some specified period (such as 5 years).

The typical dental plan also limits benefits to the least expensive type of accepted dental treatment for a given dental condition. For example, if either a gold or silver filling can be used, benefit payments will be limited to the cost of a silver filling, even if a gold filling is inserted.

Predetermination of Benefits

The majority of dental contracts provide for a pretreatment review of certain dental services by the insurance company. Although this procedure is usually not mandatory, it does allow both the dentist and the patient to know just how much will be paid under the plan before the treatment is performed. In addition, it enables the insurance company (or other provider of benefits) to have some control over the performance of unnecessary or more-costly-than-necessary procedures, by giving patients an opportunity to seek less costly care (possibly from another dentist) if they learn that benefits will be limited.

In general, the predetermination-of-benefits provision (which goes by several names, such as precertification or prior authorization) applies only in nonemergency situations and when a dentist's charge for a course of treatment exceeds a specified amount (varying from $100 to $300). The dentist in effect files a claim form (and X rays if applicable) with the insurance company just as if the treatment had already been performed. The insurance company reviews the form and returns it to the dentist. The form specifies the services that will be covered and the amount of reimbursement. If and when the services are actually performed, payment is made to the dentist by the insurance company after the claim form has been returned with the appropriate signatures and the date of completion.

When the predetermination-of-benefits provision has not been followed, benefits will still be paid. However, neither the dentist nor the covered person will know in advance what services will be covered by the insurance company or how much the insurance company will pay for these services.

Termination

Coverage under dental insurance plans typically terminates for the same reasons it terminates under medical expense coverage (described in chapter 8). Rarely is there any type of conversion privilege for dental benefits, even when the coverage is written as part of a major medical contract. However, dental coverage is subject to the continuation rules of COBRA.

Benefits for a dental service received after termination may still be covered as long as (1) the charge for the service was "incurred" prior to the termination date, and (2) treatment is completed within 60 or 90 days after termination. For example, the charge for a crown or bridgework is incurred once the preparation of the tooth (or teeth) has begun, even though the actual installation of the crown or bridgework (and the billing) does not take place until after the coverage terminates. Similarly charges for dentures are incurred on the date the impressions for the dentures are taken, and charges for root canal therapy are incurred on the date the root canal is opened.

GROUP LONG-TERM CARE INSURANCE

In the 1980s insurance companies started to market long-term care insurance policies to individuals. Many of the earlier policies had limited benefits and expensive premiums. As the products have evolved, benefits have improved while premiums have remained stable or decreased. As with universal life insurance, success in the individual marketplace led to interest in group long-term care insurance as an employee benefit. The first group long-term plan was written in 1987, and a small but growing number of employers, mostly large ones, now make coverage available. The number of insurance companies writing coverage has also grown, but the number still remains relatively small and is primarily limited to the largest group insurance carriers.

At best the growth of group long-term care insurance can be described as slow and cautious for several reasons. First, the individual long-term care insurance market is still in an evolving state, due partially to the lack of adequate actuarial data to design and price coverage. The situation is not unlike the early days of disability income insurance. Second, the tax status of group long-term coverage is uncertain. It appears that employer-provided benefits, unlike medical expense benefits, will result in taxation to employees. To the extent that employers want to spend additional benefit dollars, they want to spend them on benefits for which employees receive favorable tax benefits. As a result almost all group long-term care plans are financed solely by employee contributions. Third, there is uncertainty about whether long-term care can be included in a cafeteria plan on a tax-favored basis. Finally, participation in group plans has been modest because older employees who feel they have a need for the coverage often find it too expensive. A surprise, however, with many of the early plans has been the higher-than-expected participation by employees in the 40-to-50 age bracket.

Before a description of the existing plans is undertaken, it is important to discuss the need for long-term care protection and the sources already available to meet this need.

The Need for Long-term Care

The need for long-term care arises from the following factors:

- an aging population
- increasing costs
- the inability of families to provide full care
- the inadequacy of insurance protection

An Aging Population

Long-term care has traditionally been thought of as a problem primarily for the older population. The population aged 65 or over is the fastest-growing age group; today it represents about 11 percent of the population, a figure that is expected to increase to between 20 and 25 percent over the next 50 years. The segment of the population aged 85 and over is growing at an even faster rate. While less than 10 percent of the over-65 group is over 85 today, this percentage is expected to double over the next two generations.

An aging society presents changing problems. Those who needed long-term care in the past were most likely to have suffered from strokes or other acute diseases, but with longer life spans a larger portion of the elderly will be incapacitated by chronic conditions such as Alzheimer's disease, arthritis, osteoporosis, and lung and heart disease—conditions that often require continuing assistance with day-to-day needs. The likelihood that a nursing home will be needed increases dramatically with age. One percent of persons between the ages of 65 and 74 reside in nursing homes, and the percentage increases to 6 percent between the ages of 75 and 84. At age 85 and over, the figure rises to approximately 25 percent.

It should be noted that the elderly are not the only group of persons who need long-term care. Many younger persons are unable to care for themselves because of handicaps resulting from birth defects, mental conditions, illnesses, or accidents.

Increasing Costs

Nearly $50 billion is spent each year on nursing home care. This cost is increasing faster than inflation because of the growing demand for nursing home beds and the shortage of skilled medical personnel. The cost of complete long-term care for an individual can also be astronomical, with annual nursing home costs of $30,000 to $50,000 not being unusual.

The Inability of Families to Provide Full Care

Traditionally long-term care has been provided by family members, often at considerable personal sacrifices and great personal stress. However, it is becoming more difficult for families to provide long-term care for the following reasons:

- the geographic dispersion of family members
- increased participation in the paid work force by women and children
- fewer children in the family
- more childless families
- higher divorce rates
- the inability of family members to provide care because they themselves are growing old

The Inadequacy of Insurance Protection

Private medical expense insurance policies (both group and individual) almost always have an exclusion for convalescent, custodial, or rest care. Some policies, particularly group policies, do provide coverage for extended-care facilities and for home health care. In both cases the purpose is to provide care in a manner that is cheaper than care in a hospital. However, coverage is provided only if a person also needs medical care; benefits are not provided if a person is merely "old" and needs someone to care for him or her.

Medicare is also inadequate because it does not cover custodial care unless this care is needed along with the medical or rehabilitative treatment provided in skilled nursing facilities or under home health care benefits.

Sources of Long-term Care

There are several sources other than insurance that are available for providing long-term care. However, there are drawbacks associated with each source.

One source is to rely on personal savings. Unless a person has substantial resources, however, this approach may force an individual and his or her dependents into poverty. It may also mean that the financial objective of leaving assets to heirs will not be met.

A second source is to rely on welfare. The medicaid program in most states will provide benefits, which usually include nursing home care, to the "medically needy." However, a person is not eligible unless he or she is either poor or has exhausted most other assets (including those of a spouse). There is also often a social stigma associated with the acceptance of welfare.

Life-care facilities are growing in popularity as a source of meeting long-term care needs. With a life-care facility residents pay an "entrance fee" that allows them to occupy a dwelling unit but usually does not give them actual ownership rights. The entrance fee is typically not refundable if the resident leaves the facility voluntarily or dies. (There may be some partial refund if a person leaves within a specified time period.) Residents pay a monthly fee that includes meals, some housecleaning services, and varying degrees of health care. If a person needs long-term care, he or she must give up the independent living unit and move to the nursing home portion of the facility, but the monthly fee normally remains the same. The disadvantages of this option are that the cost of a life-care facility is beyond the reach of many persons, and a resident must be in reasonably good health and able to live independently at the time the facility is entered. Therefore the decision to use a life-care facility must be made in advance of the need for long-term care. Once such care is needed or is imminent, this approach is no longer viable.

A few insurers now include long-term care benefits in some cash value life insurance policies. Essentially an insured can begin to use these accelerated benefits while still living. For example, if the insured is in a nursing home, he or she might receive a benefit equal to 25 or 50 percent of the policy face. However, any benefits reduce the future death benefit payable to heirs.

Group Long-term Care Policies

Most of the early group long-term care policies were designed for specific large employers, and much variation existed. Today, however, most insurance companies have a standard group long-term care product, which in virtually all cases is consistent with the provisions in the Long-Term Care Insurance Model Act of the National Association of Insurance Commissioners. The result is that group policies tend to be comparable to the broader policies that are sold in the individual marketplace.

Eligibility for Coverage

The typical eligibility rule (that is, full time, actively at work, and so on) apply to group long-term care policies. At a minimum, coverage can be purchased for an active employee and/or spouse. Some policies also provide coverage to retirees and to other family members such as children, parents, parents-in-law, and possibly adult children. There is a maximum age for eligibility, but it may be as high as 80.

Cost

As previously mentioned, the cost of group long-term care coverage is almost always borne by the employee. Initial premiums are usually in 5-year age brackets and increase significantly with age. For example, one plan has an annual premium of $200 for persons aged 40−44 and $850 for persons aged 60−65. Once coverage is elected, premiums remain level and do not increase when a person enters another age bracket. Coverage is guaranteed renewable, so premiums can be increased by class.

Under some plans premiums are payable until a covered person either dies or starts to receive benefits. Under other plans premiums are higher but cease at retirement age. Such a plan is analogous to a life insurance policy that is paid up at age 65.

Level of Care

There are several levels of care that can be provided by long-term care policies:

- *skilled nursing care,* which consists of daily nursing and rehabilitative care that can be performed only by, or under the supervision of, skilled medical personnel and must be based on a doctor's orders
- *intermediate care,* which involves occasional nursing and rehabilitative care that must be based on a doctor's orders and can be performed only by, or under the supervision of, skilled medical personnel
- *custodial care,* which is primarily to handle personal needs such as walking, bathing, dressing, eating, or taking medicine and can usually be provided by someone without professional medical skills or training
- *home health care,* which is received at home and includes part-time skilled nursing care, speech therapy, physical or occupational therapy, part-time

services from home health aides, and help from homemakers or chore-workers

- *adult day care,* which is received at centers specifically designed for the elderly who live at home, but whose spouses or families cannot be available to stay home during the day. The level of care received is similar to that provided for home health care. Most adult day-care centers also provide transportation to and from the center.

Most policies cover at least the first three levels of care, and many cover all five. One problem with some individual long-term care policies is that eligibility for one level of care is preconditioned on prior long-term care at a higher level. For example, custodial care in a nursing home can be received only if a person has already received skilled nursing care or intermediate care. There are no benefits if a person enters a nursing home and needs only custodial care. Group policies, on the other hand, are much broader than individual policies because most of them pay for at least the first three levels of care and usually have no requirement that a prior higher level of long-term care has been received.

Some policies also provide benefits for respite care, which allows occasional full-time care at home for a person who is receiving home health care. Respite-care benefits enable family members who are providing much of the home care to take a needed break.

Benefits

Benefits are usually limited to a specific dollar amount per day, with $50 to $100 being common. A few plans allow participants to select varying benefit levels (for example, $50, $75, or $100 per day) when coverage is initially elected. Benefits may vary by level of care, with the highest benefits being provided for skilled nursing care and the lowest level for home health care and/or adult day care if they are covered. For example, home health care benefits are often paid at one-half the level of custodial care benefits. Annual respite care benefits are usually limited to some multiple, such as 20, of the maximum daily benefit. Some plans have protection against inflation, with benefits increasing periodically with some index like the consumer price index. However, inflation increases are often capped at some annual maximum, such as 3 percent.

While a few group long-term care plans provide benefits for an unlimited duration, most limit benefits to a period of time, ranging from 3 to 7 years, or to some equivalent dollar maximum. It should be noted that most persons who enter nursing homes either are discharged or die within 2 years. However, it is not unusual for stays to last 7 years or longer. As in the case of disability income insurance, benefits are often subject to a waiting period, which may vary from 10 to 150 days with 90 days being most common.

Eligibility for Benefits

Until recently most group long-term care policies required a prior hospitalization in order to qualify for benefits. Almost all insurance companies now use a new criterion, which specifies several so-called activities of daily living. While variations exist, these activities often include eating, bathing, dressing, transferring from bed to chair, using the toilet, and maintaining continence. In order to receive benefits, there must be independent certification that a person is totally dependent on others to perform a certain number of these activities. For example, one insurer lists seven activities and requires total dependence for any three of them; another insurer requires dependence for two out of a list of six.

Because eligibility for benefits often depends on subjective evaluations, most insurance companies use some form of case management. Case management may be mandatory, with the case manager determining eligibility, working with the physician and family to determine an appropriate type of care, and periodically reassessing the case. Or case management may be voluntary, with the case manager making recommendations about the type of care needed and providing information about the sources for care.

Preexisting Conditions

Almost all group long-term care policies have a preexisting-conditions provision. Benefits typically are not paid during the first 6 months of plan participation for care needed for a condition that was treated within 6 months prior to participation.

Exclusions

Several exclusions are found in group long-term care policies:

- war
- institutional care received outside the United States
- treatment for drug or alcohol abuse
- intentionally self-inflicted injury
- attempted suicide
- confinement or care for which benefits are payable under workers compensation or similar laws
- confinement or care for which the insured or the insured's estate is not required to pay

In contrast to many older individual policies, group contracts have not been written to exclude organic-based mental diseases such as Alzheimer's.

Renewability and Portability

Group long-term care plans are guaranteed renewable. If a participant leaves, the group coverage can usually be continued on a direct-payment basis, under either the group contract or an individual contract.

GROUP LEGAL EXPENSE INSURANCE

Plans that cover the legal expenses of employees have been a common benefit in several European countries for many years. However, until the mid-1970s the concept was not widely used in the United States. The plans that did exist were almost always established by unions and were financed from general union funds.

Usually the legal services were provided by attorneys who were employed by the unions, and the only legal services covered were those limited to job-related difficulties, such as suspensions or workers' compensation disputes.

The limited extent of legal expense plans was due to the existence of several obstacles, all of which have been substantially reduced or eliminated in recent years. Prior to 1971 all states had laws that made it illegal for insurance companies (or other organizations) to market group legal insurance plans under which contributions were paid in advance by the covered persons or by anyone else on their behalf. (However, self-funded plans, whose benefits were paid from the general revenues of unions or employers as reimbursement for legal expenses, did not usually come under these limitations.) In 1971 the U.S. Supreme Court declared that these laws were unconstitutional, and the states have replaced them with laws that allow group legal benefits to be provided (subject to some restrictions) by a plan that is funded in advance.

The Supreme Court ruling actually did little to encourage the growth of legal expense plans, since federal tax laws did not give favorable treatment to legal expense benefits, and the Taft-Hartley Act did not allow legal expense benefits to be a subject of collective bargaining. However, in 1973 the Taft-Hartley Act was amended to make legal expense benefits a new subject of collective bargaining, and the Tax Reform Act of 1976 gave favorable tax treatment to certain legal expense plans by providing that neither the premiums paid by employers nor the benefits received under the plans constitute taxable income to employees. As a result of these changes the number of legal expense plans has grown considerably, and several thousand employers now provide these benefits to their employees. However, most of these employers offer group legal benefits only to union employees (as a result of collective bargaining) through negotiated trusteeships that provide the benefits on an uninsured basis. Some employers have established voluntary plans under which an employee can elect to participate if he or she desires. In many cases this is part of a cafeteria plan, and the employee pays the full cost of the coverage on an after-tax basis.

Although some insurance companies market group plans that include legal expense benefits, few plans of this type are in existence.

Requirements for Favorable Tax Treatment

Favorable tax treatment is given to group legal expense plans under Sec. 120 of the Internal Revenue Code only if they qualify as "prepaid legal services plans." In order to obtain this qualification, a plan that provides benefits for legal expenses must meet the following requirements:

- The plan must be established under a separate written document that specifies the benefits that will be provided.
- The plan must be for the exclusive benefit of employees, their spouses, or dependents.
- Contributions to the plan or benefits under the plan must not discriminate in favor of highly compensated employees.
- No more than 25 percent of the annual contributions to the plan may be made in behalf of the "owners" (or their spouses or dependents) of the organization that established the plan. An owner is defined as any person

who owns more than 5 percent of the stock of the organization at any time during the year or who has more than a 5 percent interest in either the capital or profits of the organization.

- Amounts contributed under the plan must be paid to either (1) an insurance company in the form of a premium, (2) another organization or person that provides personal legal services or indemnification against the cost of legal services in exchange for a prepayment or the payment of a premium, or (3) a trust that is permitted by Section 501(c) of the Internal Revenue Code to receive contributions for a legal services plan.

This last requirement is broadly written so that contributions can be made to negotiated trusteeships or to organizations that provide legal services on a prepaid basis. Self-funded plans of the employer are also permitted, as long as an appropriate trust is established and benefits are funded with contributions paid in advance. Self-funded plans with benefits paid from the general revenue of the employer cannot qualify, and any benefits paid to employees will result in taxable income.

Benefits from a prepaid legal services plan are tax free. In addition, Sec. 120 provides that the first $70 of annual contributions to a plan in behalf of an employee do not result in taxable income. If, for example, an employer pays $100 per year for each employee to a trust or as an insurance premium, the $30 excess must be reported as income for the employee.

(Note: At the time this book was revised, Sec. 120 was scheduled to expire for taxable years beginning after June 30, 1992. The section has been extended before and will probably be extended again. If an extension does not occur, the amount of any insurance premiums or trust contributions will be included in an employee's income.)

Types of Plans

The types of group legal expense plans vary widely in the ways they provide legal services. When an employer or negotiated trusteeship establishes a group legal expense plan, benefits can be self-funded or purchased from another organization. In addition to insurance companies, these other organizations include prepaid plans that are sponsored by state bar associations, groups of attorneys, or other organizations (either profit or nonprofit) formed for this purpose.

Benefits can be provided on a closed-panel basis, on an open-panel basis, or on some combination of these two. By far the most common are closed-panel plans, under which covered persons must obtain legal services from lawyers who are selected by the provider of benefits. These may be lawyers who are full-time employees of the plan or lawyers who provide benefits for plan members but who also have other clients. Under an open-panel plan covered persons may be able to choose their own lawyer, or they may have to select one from a limited list of lawyers who have agreed to the terms and conditions of the plan (such as agreeing to charge no more than the plan's suggested fee schedule). When these two plan types are combined, the resulting plan will usually have its own lawyers provide routine legal services on a closed-panel basis but will use an open-panel approach when covered persons have more serious legal problems.

Like medical or dental expense benefits, legal expense benefits can be provided either as services or as reimbursements for actual expenses. Virtually all closed-panel plans use a service approach and provide full benefits without requiring any copayments by the covered persons. Open-panel plans may also provide benefits on a service basis, primarily when eligible lawyers agree to the fee structure paid by the plan. When benefits are paid on the basis of actual charges incurred by a covered person, deductibles and coinsurance are sometimes used.

Benefit Schedules

Benefits under legal expense plans can be provided on either a scheduled basis or on a comprehensive basis. *Scheduled legal expense plans* list the specific types of legal expenses for which benefits will be paid. While significant variations exist among plans, most at least cover the following:

- consultation and advice on any legal matter
- preparation of legal documents, such as deeds, wills, and powers-of-attorney
- adoption
- personal bankruptcy
- defense of civil suits
- juvenile delinquency proceedings
- domestic problems, such as separation, divorce, or annulment
- criminal defense

When benefits are provided on an indemnity basis, the maximum benefit for each covered legal service is usually limited to a flat amount or to a maximum hourly fee. In addition, there may be an overall maximum annual benefit (such as $1,000). Whether it provides benefits on a service or an indemnity basis, a scheduled legal expense plan may also limit the frequency with which benefits will be paid for each covered service. Under some plans the participating lawyers also agree to provide—at a discount—services that are not otherwise included in the plan.

Comprehensive legal expense plans are like major medical expense plans in that all legal expenses are covered except for those that are specifically excluded. Common exclusions include legal expenses that arise from the following:

- business activities or transactions
- class action suits
- cases that have contingent fees
- actions against the legal expense plan
- actions against the employer
- actions against the union
- Internal Revenue audits

In addition, these plans generally exclude expenses that are not charged by a lawyer (such as court costs and fines). These plans usually provide benefits on a closed-panel basis and have no overall benefit maximums or internal dollar limitations.

MASS-MARKETED INDIVIDUAL LIFE AND HEALTH INSURANCE

Some employers offer their employees individual insurance on a payroll-deduction basis. Although this type of benefit has existed for many years, its character has changed in recent years.

Originally such coverage was designed for employers who were ineligible for group insurance because of their small number of employees. Often referred to as wholesale life insurance or franchise health insurance, these plans were similar to group insurance in their plan design and in the types of coverage they provided. In addition, amounts of insurance were predetermined, and coverage under the plan ceased at termination of employment. However, these plans differed from group insurance in that individual policies and individual underwriting were used. In contrast to group insurance plans that insure a number of persons under one policy, these arrangements can best be described as quasi-group plans that insure a number of persons under individual policies. Since group insurance coverage is available for most small groups (often through multiple-employer welfare arrangements), this type of mass-marketed individual insurance is not commonly written today.

While many variations exist, the majority of mass-marketed individual insurance plans currently made available to employees fall into one of two broad categories:

- salary allotment (or salary reduction) plans involving individual underwriting
- money-purchase plans with simplified underwriting

Under either type of plan the employer agrees to withhold premiums from participating employees' paychecks each pay period and submit them to the insurance company. Only in rare cases does the employer pay any portion of the premium. Arrangements are also made between the employer and the insurance company concerning how employees will be solicited. While the plan may be serviced by agents or company representatives, sales to individual employees are almost always done by regular agents of the insurance company. Each employee can determine the amount of coverage purchased, within limits, and coverage can be continued after termination of employment (normally at the same premium) as long as the employee continues paying the premium directly to the insurer. However, a less frequent mode of premium payment may be required. For example, instead of the previous payroll deduction each month, an annual premium of 12 times the monthly deduction may be required.

Salary Allotment Plans

Under salary allotment plans employees have the option of purchasing some or all of the insurance products normally offered by the insurance company in the individual insurance market. Plans offered by life insurance companies are usually designed for executives or higher-paid employees. Policies with cash values are always available, but term insurance, long-term disability income insurance, and other products may be offered. The premium per policy period is normally calculated by dividing the insurance company's regular annual rate-book premium by the number of payroll periods for which deductions will be made. For example, if the annual rate-book premium is $240, the monthly premium on a payroll-deduction basis will be $20. This is in contrast to the somewhat higher monthly premium that would be charged by most insurance companies if a policyowner paid the premium directly to the insurance company. In most cases regular individual underwriting is used, and regular commission scales are paid.

Some life insurance companies either will offer salary allotment plans at a discount from regular rate-book premiums or will use liberalized underwriting. To compensate for such practices, these insurers are generally more restrictive in making the plans available or employ cost-saving features, such as lower commission scales.

Money-Purchase Plans

Money-purchase plans represent the fastest-growing form of mass-marketed individual insurance available to employees. Initially these plans were primarily marketed to small employers with meager employee benefit plans, so that they could make life insurance coverage available to their employees with little cost to the employer other than the costs of publicizing the plan and administering the payroll deductions. However, a significant number of large firms now also offer such plans to their employees as a method of making additional insurance available.

To a large extent money-purchase plans have been designed to meet the insurance needs of the lower-paid employees, who tend to purchase rather small amounts of insurance. Consequently these plans are sometimes made available only to hourly paid employees. The main goal of most insurance companies in offering money-purchase plans is to market cash value life insurance, and hence this coverage is always offered. The term money-purchase comes from the fact that amounts of coverage are sold on the basis of what can be purchased with a given premium, such as $1, $2, or $5 per week. An employee must select one of the given premiums, with a maximum of $5 per week common. Since the amount of coverage is a function of the employee's attained age, larger amounts of coverage are available to younger employees than to older employees. Furthermore, the cash value policy used by an insurance company in its money-purchase plan may be a form normally sold in the individual market or may be one designed specifically for mass marketing. In some plans this will be a whole life policy on which an employee can continue paying premiums after retirement or that can be converted to a paid-up policy with a lower face amount. In other plans a limited-payment policy is used, enabling coverage to continue after retirement without reduction in amount and without the need to continue premium payments.

A rider that provides term life insurance coverage on an employee's children and possibly the employee's spouse is usually available. The coverage is normally a set amount, such as $1,000 per person, and results in either an additional premium, such as 10 cents per month, or a reduction in the amount of cash value life insurance otherwise available at the premium selected by the employee. Term life insurance coverage for an employee is available under some plans, but its availability is often contingent on the employee's purchase of cash value life insurance. Most plans also make cash value life insurance available to an employee's children and spouse. Again, the amount of coverage is determined by what can be purchased with a given weekly premium. Some plans also offer deferred annuities by which an employee can supplement pension and social security benefits.

In most cases coverage under money-purchase plans can be purchased at a cost lower than that for comparable benefits in the regular individual market. While there is individual underwriting, the underwriting standards of most insurers result in making at least 95 percent of all employees eligible for coverage. Many insurance companies use the same commission scales that are normally paid on individual insurance, but some companies use a reduced scale.

As in group insurance, insurance companies impose underwriting standards on money-purchase plans. These plans are not normally made available to employers who have high employee turnover or who are in industries characterized by a high turnover. In addition, employers in business for less than a minimum period of time are often ineligible. Employees must typically complete a waiting period of six months to one year before coverage may be purchased. Most insurance companies will insist on a minimum number of participants (such as 5) and/or a minimum percentage participation. In addition, money-purchase plans may be available to employers with fewer than 25 employees only if there has been some type of prescreening to determine the suitability of the employer and the group of employees.

Variations for Universal Life Insurance

Universal life insurance is commonly sold in mass-marketed individual insurance plans, and for some insurance companies it may be the only product marketed in this manner. Some insurers market it on a money-purchase basis as previously described.

Other insurers take a different approach with respect to the determination of the amount of insurance and the periodic premium. Rather than selecting the desired premium, employees choose the amount of pure death protection. Several options—such as $10,000, $25,000, and $50,000—may be offered, and the available options may vary by salary level or position. A minimum periodic premium will then be specified for each option and a given employee's age. The premium will be sufficient to generate a cash value at retirement age if the current interest assumptions of the insurer are met. Employees, however, can elect to pay higher premiums so that a larger cash value will develop. Some insurers set the initial premium at a multiple (such as twice) of the pure insurance cost; others make it an amount that will generate a cash value equal to a percentage (such as 50 percent) of the original amount of insurance. After the policy has been in force for some time period, employees typically have flexibility with respect to premium levels similar to what is available to persons purchasing group universal life insurance (discussed in chapter 5). Except for this difference in premium determination, most mass-marketed universal life insurance products have the other characteristics of a money-purchase plan.

PROPERTY AND LIABILITY INSURANCE AS A GROUP BENEFIT

In the mid 1960s it was thought that property and liability insurance, especially automobile insurance, would be the next major employee benefit. However, by the late 1970s most of the insurance companies that had entered this market were no longer willing to write property and liability coverage as an employee benefit. In fact, many began to dismiss this benefit as an idea whose time might never come. The current status of property and liability insurance as an employee benefit is that for several years it has been offered by a few large employers. Detailed statistics from the insurance industry are difficult to obtain since most coverage is actually mass-marketed individual insurance and is not reported as a group benefit. However, estimates indicate that no more than about one percent of personal property and liability insurance is provided as the result of an employer-arranged plan.

Reasons for Slow Growth

The slow growth of group property and liability plans can be traced to several factors. These include unfavorable tax treatment, a low potential for cost savings, a lack of employer enthusiasm, and regulatory restrictions.

Unfavorable Tax Treatment

The Internal Revenue Code specifically exempts employer contributions for certain employee benefits from being included in the taxable income of employees. This exemption does not apply to property and liability insurance. Although the employer is allowed an income tax deduction, an employee must report as taxable income any contributions made in his or her behalf for property and liability coverage. Note, however, that the portion of any premium that applies to medical or no-fault benefits is treated as health insurance and is not included in income.

In general, employers, unions, and employees prefer that employer dollars be used to provide nontaxable benefits. Therefore without employer contributions it is often difficult to offer employees property and liability insurance at a substantial enough saving to encourage significant participation.

Lower Potential for Cost Savings

The potential for savings under group property and liability insurance plans is typically less than it is under group insurance plans that provide life insurance, disability income, or medical expense benefits. Under these latter plans there is a substantial reduction in agents' commissions when compared to commissions received on individual coverage. Such savings do not occur in property and liability insurance, because commissions scales for individual insurance are lower as a percentage of premium. The main reason for this lower scale is that a less intense marketing effort is required by agents, since consumers are more likely to seek out property and liability coverage on their own, rather than be solicited by agents. Therefore a higher portion of commissions are for services that are performed for the client, rather than for the agents' marketing efforts. These services (for example, financial responsibility filings, automobile changes, and certificates of insurance for mortgagees) must still be performed for coverage that is provided on a group basis.

A second source of savings under most types of group insurance coverage results from the reduction or elimination of individual underwriting, which, together with other savings, more than offsets the cost of covering poor risks at group rates. However, this is not the case in property and liability insurance, particularly in automobile insurance. Not only are savings lower, but there are proportionately many more substandard drivers who must pay surcharged premiums in the individual property and liability insurance marketplace than there are persons with poor health in the individual life and health insurance marketplace. The lack of individual underwriting in property and liability insurance will usually mean that the average rate for the group members is higher than some persons would pay in the individual marketplace. Consequently to avoid getting only the poor risks, group property and liability insurance plans generally use individual—but possibly liberalized—underwriting. As a result poorer risks are charged a higher premium or are ineligible for coverage in some cases.

Under the most successful group property and liability plans savings have averaged only between 5 and 15 percent when compared with the same insurance company's rates for individual coverage. However, property and liability rates vary widely among insurance companies, and this group rate may still be higher than many employees are paying for their individual coverage. Without a significant cost advantage there is little incentive for an employee to switch to a group property and liability plan, except perhaps for the simplicity of paying premiums on a payroll-deduction basis. This is particularly true when the employee has an established relationship with his or her current property and liability insurance company or agent. Consequently it may be difficult to enroll the minimum percentage (usually 30 or more) of employees required by the insurance company.

Lack of Employer Enthusiasm

In addition to the unfavorable tax treatment of employer contributions to the employee, many employers feel that group property and liability plans will place a strain on the relationship with their employees. While the magnitude of the problem varies among employers that offer group property and liability plans, it is an undisputed fact that dissatisfaction with the plan and the employer does occur when employees (1) are ineligible for coverage because of underwriting considerations, (2) find the coverage more expensive than their current individual coverage, or (3) have disputes over claims. In spite of this dissatisfaction, however, many employers view property and liability insurance as a very desirable benefit because of high visibility.

Regulatory Restrictions

Once common in almost all states, some type of regulation or statute that hinders the marketing of group property and liability insurance still exists in several states. These *fictitious group insurance statutes,* or similar regulations, prohibit the grouping of individual risks in order to give them favorable treatment in underwriting, coverage, or rates, with the possible exception of rate reductions that are the result of savings in expenses. In effect, what is done for group life insurance, medical expense, and disability coverages cannot be done for property and liability insurance. These laws apply only to true group insurance products; mass-marketed plans are not affected. In addition, the laws of some states effectively prohibit true group insurance products because there is no specific statute that allows these products to be written.

Many states also have regulations that prohibit any person who is not a licensed insurance agent from advising in the sale of property and liability insurance. This prevents the employer from performing any other functions besides those of a purely administrative nature, such as accepting applications or deducting premiums from payroll.

Federal regulatory restrictions are another reason for the lack of union interest, since the Federal Labor Code prohibits a negotiated trusteeship from providing property and liability coverage. However, this is no prohibition against bargaining for this benefit and having it provided under a plan established by the employer.

Types of Plans

Most employer-provided property and liability insurance plans are not true group insurance but are mass-marketed plans of individual insurance similar to the salary allotment plans described earlier in this chapter. The cost of these plans is usually borne entirely by the participating employees. Besides handling the payroll deductions, the employer has little, if any, responsibility for the administration of the plan. Employees are solicited by representatives of the insurance company, usually by mail or phone. Some insurance companies may actually have agents located on or near the employer's premises, but the majority of insurance companies give group members toll-free numbers for contacting their representatives.

Mass-marketed property and liability insurance plans are usually not experience rated but are offered at a slight discount because of the administrative savings associated with mass marketing. Premiums for employees vary because they are based on the same factors as individual property and liability insurance (such as age, driving record, or value of the home), which also means that some employees may be ineligible for coverage. Most plans offer automobile insurance, and a few also offer other coverages, such as homeowners insurance and umbrella liability insurance. Employees usually have the same choices regarding the amount and type of coverage that they would have in the individual marketplace, and the contracts offered are usually identical. However, modifications that attempt to decrease the cost of the mass-marketed coverage are sometimes made. These include larger deductibles and provisions in the automobile insurance policy that eliminate coverage for medical expenses to the extent that they are paid under the employer's medical expense plan.

A few companies offer property and liability insurance on a true group basis and use both a master contract and experience rating for the group. All employees are usually eligible. The coverages offered to the employees are usually the same as those offered under quasi-group plans, but the rating structure tends to be less refined, particularly for automobile insurance. Instead of having several dozen classifications that are based on factors such as age, sex, and driving record, there may only be three or four classifications that are based only on driving record. In virtually all cases when true group property and liability plans are made available, the insurance company will insist on employer contributions of between 25 and 50 percent of the cost of the coverage and on participation by a large percentage of employees, possibly as high as 75 percent.

10

Employee Benefit Marketing

The marketing of employee benefits is a complex and specialized process that is subject to frequent changes as a result of the influences of employers, organized labor, and federal and state regulations. Competition is intense, and the buyer often uses competitive bidding. Also many employers continually review benefit plans for ways to contain cost increases and to improve the services received from insurance companies or from other providers of benefits or services. Therefore it is essential for agents, brokers, consultants, third-party administrators, and insurance companies to maintain a high level of technical competence and to provide continuous service.

In this chapter group insurance marketing will be described with respect to (1) the types of buyers, (2) the types of sellers and their representatives, and (3) the marketing process.

THE BUYERS

The buyers of group benefits can be categorized by both the type and the size of their group. The buyers of coverage for employees consist primarily of employers, trustees, and associations. (These and other types of eligible groups were discussed in chapter 3.) While it is difficult to precisely categorize the group benefit market by the size of groups, certain generalizations can be made. Approximately one-half of all employee benefit plans are established for groups of fewer than 25 employees. However, these groups account for only between 10 and 15 percent of the total dollar volume of employee benefits. In most cases the person making group insurance decisions for these small groups (unless the decisions are dictated by collective bargaining) is the owner or chief executive officer of the organization.

The next largest segment of the market (25 to 30 percent of all groups) consists of groups from organizations that have 25 to 100 employees. These groups also represent only between 10 and 15 percent of the total employee benefit premium volume. Again, the person making group insurance decisions tends to be the owner or chief executive of the organization.

Groups of 100 to 500 employees account for only about 10 percent of group benefit plans, but they represent approximately 25 percent of the total dollars spent on employee benefits. Because of the greater flexibility available in plan design (including the consideration of alternative funding methods) and the various ways in which the plan can be administered, there is the need to devote more time to group insurance matters than the owner or chief executive of an organization can afford to spend. Therefore while possibly retaining the final decision-making authority, this person usually delegates the actual task of benefit planning to some employee in the organization. This employee is frequently the personnel director, but he or she may also be an administrative or financial vice president.

Groups of more than 500 employees account for only a small percentage of the group benefit plans in existence, but these plans represent approximately half of the benefit dollars spent by employers. Firms of this size usually have one or more persons who devote their full time to group insurance matters. These persons may be in a separate "insurance" or "benefit" department, or they may be part of a personnel, financial, or administrative department.

THE SELLERS

The sellers of employee benefit products and services consist primarily of insurance companies, the Blues, HMOs, PPOs, and third-party administrators. Just as certain generalizations were made about who makes employee benefit decisions within an organization, some generalizations can be made about where products and services are purchased. However, the breakdown by size is different.

Employers with fewer than 10 employees, who have more limited choices than larger employers, usually purchase coverage from MEWAs or the Blues. However, there are significant geographic differences with respect to the purchase of medical expense coverage. In some areas the Blues, because of large discounts and community rating, have a significant cost advantage and are the primary providers of coverage. In other areas the Blues are minor players and provide little coverage to employers of this size. In still other areas a very competitive marketplace exists.

The choice of products and services increases for employers with 10 to 25 employees. Not only is coverage available from MEWAs and the Blues, but it can also frequently be obtained from HMOs and PPOs. For this size group insurance companies also have products that are sold directly to employers rather than through MEWAs.

If an employer has more than 25 employees, the possibility of self-funding of benefits, particularly medical expense benefits, becomes a real possibility. In this marketplace there is a significant demand for the purchase of administrative services from insurance companies and third-party administrators.

The functions and methods of compensation for each of the participants in the group benefit sales process are discussed below.

Agents

Insurance company agents play a major role in marketing group insurance, particularly to groups that have fewer than 100 employees. Agents usually locate the prospective group insurance cases, but the extent of their further involvement in the sales process varies depending on the size of the group. For very small groups virtually all sales activities are conducted by the agent. For larger groups the agent is likely to call on the group representative of the insurance company for assistance in selling, installing, and servicing the case. To many agents the selling of group insurance is not a specialty but is rather the selling of just another product in the portfolio of their insurance company. While some agents limit their activities to group insurance sales, most specialists in this area need to sell the products of more than one company and therefore operate as brokers.

Agents are compensated in the form of commission payments from the insurance company. When compared with the commission rates for individual insurance, the commission rates for group insurance are considerably lower. In general, this reflects the fact that the premium on a group insurance contract is usually much larger than the premium on an average-sized individual policy. In addition, for all but the smallest cases the agent typically relies on a group representative of the insurance company to perform many of the sales and service activities pertaining to the case.

For multiple-employer trusts the commission rate is normally 10 percent of the initial annual premium, and this rate usually remains the same in renewal years, although it may drop slightly.

For other groups two approaches are used. The larger the group, the more common it is for commissions to be determined by negotiation between the policyowner, the agent, and the insurance company. However, commissions are also frequently determined by one of two basic types of commission schedules. The *standard (or regular) schedule* has high first-year commission rates and lower rates in renewal years. The *level schedule* has the same commission rates for both the first year and any renewal years. These two schedules are designed so that over some period of time (often 10 years) the same overall commission will be paid for a given amount of premium, regardless of which schedule is used. While variations exist among insurance companies, most of the major group insurance writers use schedules that are fairly uniform. The following schedules are typical:

Annual Premium		Standard Schedule First Year	Renewal Years	Level Schedule
First	$1,000	20.0%	5.00%	6.50%
Next	4,000	20.0	3.00	4.70
"	5,000	15.0	1.50	2.85
"	10,000	12.5	1.50	2.60
"	10,000	10.0	1.50	2.35
"	20,000	5.0	1.50	1.85
"	200,000	2.5	1.00	1.15
"	250,000	1.0	0.50	0.55
"	2,000,000	0.5	0.25	0.25
Over	2,500,000	0.1	0.10	0.10

It is important to note that these are sliding scales based on additional increments of premium volume, not on the total premium volume. For example, using the regular scale, the first-year commission on a group case with an annual premium volume of $40,000 is calculated as follows:

$$
\begin{array}{rcl}
\$\ 1,000 \times 20.0\% &=& \$\ 200 \\
4,000 \times 20.0 &=& 800 \\
5,000 \times 15.0 &=& 750 \\
10,000 \times 12.5 &=& 1,250 \\
10,000 \times 10.0 &=& 1,000 \\
\underline{10,000 \times\ \ 5.0} &=& \underline{\ \ \ 500} \\
\$40,000 & & \$4,500 \ (\text{or } 11.25\% \text{ of the total} \\
& & \text{premium})
\end{array}
$$

After the first year the commission under either of these schedules may be further subdivided into selling commissions and service commissions, with the agent who sold the case receiving the latter only if he or she continues to service the case. An agent may voluntarily terminate his or her relationship with the case. In addition, most insurance companies allow the client to request a change in the servicing agent.

In most cases the agent may choose either commission schedule. The standard schedule obviously produces a higher income for the agent in early years and will generate a larger total income if the case is cancelled after a short period of time. However, the level schedule should be more beneficial if substantial increases in premium volume are expected in the renewal years of a case. Insurance companies are concerned about using the standard commission schedule when there is a high probability that a group insurance case will either change insurers or lapse. Consequently many insurers require that the level schedule be used for transferred business, reinstated cases, fully contributory plans, or groups below a certain size. In addition, the level schedule may also be mandatory for very large groups when competitive bidding requires that expenses be held to a minimum and be recoverable in the early years of a contract.

Brokers and Consultants

The majority of large group insurance buyers retain a broker or employee benefit consultant to provide professional advice on group insurance matters and to aid them in dealing with insurance companies. Brokers and consultants are agents of the buyers and owe their allegiance to the buyers rather than to the insurance companies through which they place their clients' coverages. Traditionally the major distinction between brokers and consultants was that brokers were compensated on a commission basis for the coverages they placed in behalf of clients, while consultants were compensated by fees charged to the clients. From a practical standpoint, the distinction between brokers and consultants has become blurred and is more semantic than real. Generally those persons or organizations that call themselves brokers operate on a commission basis, but they also charge fees for advice and services that do not result in the sale of a product. While some consulting firms still operate solely on a fee basis, many receive commissions from insurance companies for business they have placed for their clients. This may be their sole compensation for placing the coverage (with fees charged for other services), or it may offset the higher fee that a client is charged for this service. The commission schedules used by insurance companies for brokers and benefit consultants are usually the same as those used for agents. However, for large cases it is common for the commission to be a negotiated amount.

Some group insurance business is placed by brokers who specialize in other types of insurance. For example, a broker who handles a client's property and liability insurance may also have the opportunity to place group insurance coverages. However, the majority of brokers and consultants who become involved in group sales are specialists in the area of group insurance. These range from individuals or small local firms to very large national and international firms (or departments or divisions of these firms). These large firms, which often also handle the property and liability insurance needs of their clients, account for the majority of premium volume that is placed through brokers and consultants, and they are well suited to serving the needs of clients whose organizations are geographically widespread. Many of the employees of these firms are former group representatives.

Group Representatives

The group representative is an employee of the insurance company who is generally located outside the home office and specializes in the selling and servicing of his or her company's group insurance products. The group representative's sales activities are conducted through the agents, brokers, and consultants whom the group representative educates and motivates to place group insurance business with his or her company. In addition, the group representative aids the agents, brokers, or consultants in prospecting, securing necessary underwriting data, designing plans and preparing and presenting group insurance proposals. After a plan is sold, the group representative is frequently involved in the enrolling of eligible employees, the administrative procedures of installing the case, and the providing of services necessary to keep the case in force. Group representatives almost always receive a salary, and most are eligible for bonuses that are based on performance. Significant variations exist among companies, and some pay a low salary but offer the potential for a bonus that exceeds the salary, while others pay a much higher salary and give a much smaller bonus. The bonus is frequently a function of the commissions paid the agents, brokers, or consultants with whom the group representative has dealt. In addition, it may also be a function of the persistency and profitability of the group insurance cases with which the group representative has been involved.

Service Plans

Intense competition exists among insurance companies, the Blues, and HMOs for the sale of medical expense coverage. With rare exceptions the Blues and HMOs have traditionally marketed their products and services through employees who receive a salary (and possibly a bonus) rather than through agents, brokers, and consultants who are paid a commission. One competitive advantage enjoyed by these organizations is that the compensation paid to their salespersons is usually lower than the commissions that are paid by insurance companies to agents, brokers, or consultants who produce a comparable volume of business. However, in recent years many Blue Cross–Blue Shield associations have started marketing their products through insurance agents as well as through their own salaried employees. The Blues, like the group representatives of insurance companies, have also developed close working relationships with the larger brokerage or employee benefit consulting firms in order to encourage their consideration of the Blues as a source for placing their clients' coverages. If coverage is placed with the Blues, brokers or consultants will charge their clients fees, except in those instances when the Blues pay commissions.

Third-Party Administrators

Third-party administrators are persons or organizations who are hired to provide certain administrative services to group benefit plans. Traditionally their primary role has been to administer plans that are written for associations or negotiated trusteeships. The functions of these administrators include receiving employee reports and contributions, keeping track of employee eligibility, preparing any reports required by state and federal laws, and handling complaints and grievances. In addition, the administrator will be involved in certain aspects of the claims process. At a minimum this will probably involve the certification of eligibility and the processing of claims forms for submission to an insurance company, but it may also include paying claims from the trust's funds. Besides professional administrators, third-party administrators may be banks and insurance companies.

Many multiple-employer welfare arrangements, including those of insurance companies, are administered by third-party administrators. As described in chapter 3 the functions that are performed by the administrator vary and are subject to negotiations between the administrator and the sponsor of the trust.

The increasing use of alternative funding methods, including total self-funding, has resulted in the need for employers to provide many of the services (such as claims handling) that are performed by an insurance company when traditional fully insured contracts are purchased. (See chapter 12 for a discussion of self-funding.) When employers have been unable to provide these services themselves in a cost-effective manner, they have often turned to third-party administrators. In some cases these third-party administrators are professionals who specialize solely in these tasks; in other cases they are brokers, consultants, or insurance companies that market these services to their clients as additional products. Over the last decade the use of third-party administrators has increased dramatically, particularly for medical expense benefits.

THE MARKETING PROCESS

While the main goal of employee benefit marketing is to "close the sale," the process can be divided into two broad categories of activities: those that precede the sale and those that follow the sale. Presale activities include prospecting and the development and presentation of the group insurance proposal; postsale activities include the enrollment of employees and the actual installation, servicing, and renewal of the group insurance plan.

Prospecting

Prospecting is the first step in the marketing process. It involves persuading the employer (or the employer's broker or consultant) to accept a group insurance proposal from the insurance company (or Blue Cross–Blue Shield organization, HMO, PPO, or other provider of benefits or services). To be successful (that is, to actually present a proposal), prospecting also involves convincing the employer to provide the information necessary for the preparation of the proposal.

The process of prospecting tends to vary for different segments of the group insurance market. For very small groups (under 10 or 15 employees), the plans marketed are usually provided through multiple-employer welfare arrangements rather than through the traditional group insurance arrangements of insurance companies. Some of the sales activities in this segment are conducted by agents who specialize in group insurance, but a large portion of the sales activities is conducted by agents or brokers whose primary sales activities take place in the individual marketplace. (In fact, the multiple-employer trusts of many insurance companies are actually considered for marketing purposes to be part of the product line of the individual insurance department rather than part of the group insurance department.) In many cases the agent or broker will have had previous contacts with the employer in regard to his or her personal or business insurance. However, it is also in the marketing to small groups that prospecting without known contacts (cold canvasing) is most likely to take place. Because of the modest premiums that are generated by these small groups, all the sales activities (not just prospecting) are usually carried out by the agent or broker with little direct involvement by representatives from the insurance company. Because of the limited and relatively inflexible products available for these small groups, training of agents or brokers in this market is often oriented toward what products are available rather than toward group insurance planning in general.

As the size of groups increases, the chance of successful prospecting diminishes rapidly unless the agent or broker (1) has a known contact who is a key person in an organization's decision-making process for group insurance matters and (2) has a more sophisticated understanding of group insurance. In these segments of the group insurance market, group representatives spend considerable time training agents or brokers in the intricacies of group insurance and motivating them to develop prospects. For medium-size groups the agent or broker may do the actual prospecting alone or with the group representative, or he or she may give qualified leads to the group representative who will perform this function. For large groups the situation is usually different since most large firms retain brokers or employee benefit consultants to advise them on employee benefit programs and to aid them in the implementation of any decisions that are made, including the placing of insurance coverages. Therefore in this segment of the employee benefit market, prospecting can be viewed as a two-part process. On one hand there is intense competition among brokers and consultants to obtain the large firms as clients. On the other hand, since the clients are seldom successfully approached except through the broker or consultant, the prospecting consists of group representatives (and representatives of the Blues and third-party administrators) who develop a close working relationship with the brokers or consultants to encourage the consideration of the group representatives' organization as a provider of group insurance or other employee benefit products or services.

Developing the Proposal

In the broadest sense the development of a benefit plan proposal involves designing the benefit plan, calculating the premium rate or rates, and putting the proposal in its final form for presentation.

It is at this stage of the marketing process that the majority of the underwriting will be done for a case that is ultimately written. In effect, most insurance companies are saying that the benefit plan presented to the employer will probably be acceptable to the company at the rates specified if the proposal leads to an application for coverage. However, most insurance companies "hedge" their positions and will not make an absolute commitment to write the coverage at this stage, except possibly for very large groups that have already been reviewed by the senior underwriting personnel. In many cases the preliminary underwriting is done in field offices and the proposal specifies that home office approval will be necessary. In addition, the proposal will include any assumptions made in the preliminary underwriting that must be verified before the case is finally accepted. Finally, any underwriting conditions that must be met before coverage will be written (such as a certain percentage participation) are listed in the proposal. Obtaining the necessary information for underwriting is often difficult for insurance companies, particularly when the agent or broker primarily sells individual insurance. In the individual marketplace the agent or broker is accustomed to obtaining much of the necessary underwriting information from the client at the time an application is written rather than prior to the sales presentation. Furthermore, the small employers that are approached by these agents or brokers tend to be less sophisticated in group insurance matters than large employers, and they often fail to see the necessity for providing detailed information at this point in the sales process. Consequently for the sales process to continue past the prospecting stage, it is necessary that agents and brokers recognize the importance of obtaining underwriting information and that they be willing and able to convey this importance to the employer.

The premium rates presented in the group insurance proposal are based on the employee census that is provided prior to the development of the proposal, and thus they are usually only tentative rates, a fact that is clearly stated in the proposal. The final premium rates will usually be determined at the time a group insurance plan is installed and will be based on the census of employees covered under the plan at its inception.

While variations exist among insurance companies and the amount of detail tends to increase as the size of the group insurance case becomes larger, most proposals contain at least the following information:

- a description of each coverage included in the plan
- a schedule of the tentative premium rates and total premium for each coverage
- a description of the persons eligible for coverage under the plan
- any underwriting assumptions or conditions
- details for servicing the plan, such as the procedures and facilities for administering claims
- general information about the insurance company, including its size, financial strength, and products and services

For large group insurance cases detailed information will usually be provided concerning the insurance company's retention and how premium rates and reserves are calculated.

As with prospecting, the process of developing a proposal differs depending on whether coverage is written for a small group, a large client that is controlled by a broker or benefit consultant, or a group that falls somewhere between these two extremes. For small groups that are written through multiple-employer welfare arrangements, the preparation of a proposal is usually a relatively simple matter. Since little or no flexibility is available for the coverages offered, the plan design consists primarily of an agent or broker describing the available options and determining the employer's preferences. The preliminary underwriting is typically carried out by the agent or broker in the sense that it is his or her responsibility to determine whether the employer meets the trust's relatively rigid underwriting criteria. Since the rate structure is fairly simplified, the agent or broker will also usually determine the tentative premium based on the census data provided by the employer. The proposal typically consists of (1) a standard brochure or packet of information that describes the trust and its benefits and (2) a brief premium-calculation presentation that contains a list of the employees to be covered and the tentative premium to be paid by the employer for the initial period of coverage.

It should be pointed out that under some multiple-employer welfare arrangements, particularly when they are being used to write coverage for groups larger than 10 or 15 employees, the underwriting, premium calculations, and preparation of the proposal are carried out by the insurance company or the administrator of the trust. Furthermore, as the size of the group written through the trust increases, additional underwriting information (such as past claims history) may also be requested.

The situation is quite different for large groups. For group insurance cases that are not controlled by large brokers or benefit consultants, the group representative will play a major role in the development of the proposal. It is usually the group representative, possibly along with the agent or broker, who will meet with the employer. Depending on the relationship between the employer and the agent or broker, the group representative may have to put considerable effort into convincing the employer that it is worth the time to proceed with the proposal. This will include countering any of the employer's objections and convincing the employer that the insurance company can provide the products and services necessary to meet his or her needs. It is also at this time that the group representative must determine whether the employer is a serious prospect (that is, whether there is some possibility that the employer will add coverages or change insurers). In addition, the group representative must assess whether the employer is likely to meet the underwriting standards of the insurance company. For example, an insurance company may be unwilling to prepare a proposal for an employer that has a history of frequently changing insurers.

If the development of the proposal proceeds beyond the initial contact stage, the group representative must (1) determine the employer's objectives (see chapter 14), (2) aid the employer in designing the benefit plan for which the proposal will be made, and (3) obtain the information required to complete the development of the proposal. The data from the employer will then be provided to the insurance company, usually through a field office. The rating and actual design of the proposal will normally be conducted at the field office but, except for small cases, the underwriting function is likely to be performed at the home office or, in the case of large insurance companies, at a regional office. However, for very large cases it is common for the entire process, not just the underwriting, to be completed at some level higher than the field office.

To complete the proposal the insurance company obviously needs a description of the benefit plan desired and a census of covered employees containing any information that will impact on underwriting or premium calculations. At a minimum this information will probably include age and sex, but it may also include marital status, geographic location, income, and an indication of whether there are dependents. This census may contain an actual list of employees by name or it may consist of aggregate data. In addition, the following information will commonly be requested by most insurance companies from the prospect or the prospect's agent, broker, or consultant:

- the reason for transferring (unless it is a new case)
- the nature of the employer's industry
- a history of changes in the number of employees
- a statement indicating whether the plan is contributory and, if so, the amount of the employer's contribution
- the length of time with the current insurer
- premiums, rates, and claims experience with the current insurer for each line of coverage (usually for the prior 3 years)
- a statement indicating whether collective bargaining is involved
- copies of information pertaining to the current plan (such as benefit booklets or certificates of insurance)
- the most recent premium statement from the current insurer
- any renewal information from the current insurer

When a group insurance case is controlled by a large broker or benefit consultant, the broker or consultant will design the benefit plan in conjunction with the employer. In some cases the business will be placed with the existing insurance company or with a company that is either wanted by the employer or recommended by the broker or consultant. In other cases bids will be requested from several sources based on specifications prepared by the broker or consultant. In general, the bidding process is not open to every insurance company (or other provider of benefits) but is done on an invitation basis. The decision about which insurance companies are invited to bid may be made at the discretion of the consultant or may be determined by the employer. For example, some employers may want bids only from companies headquartered in the same state.

The bidding specifications are accompanied by a cover letter that invites the insurance company to bid and states the last date on which bids may be received or postmarked. This date is usually from 45 to 90 days prior to the date coverage will become effective. The specifications typically consist of a description of the plan desired, a census of employees, and any information the insurance company will need to properly underwrite and rate the case (see the previous list). Based on this data the insurance company is asked to present a bid in the form of monthly and annual premiums for the coverage desired. In addition, a "net cost illustration" or "retention exhibit" will usually be requested for a 2- to 5-year period. This illustration must show the projected premiums, incurred claims, retention, and dividends for each year, and it is often required to be based on assumptions listed in the specifications.

The insurance company is typically confronted with a rigid set of specifications on which it must bid. However, some specifications are flexible and allow an insurance company to suggest changes in the specifications and to present a bid that is based on these suggestions. Furthermore, the specifications will contain numerous questions about the insurance company's practices and ability to service the case. The list of questions may be quite lengthy and the following are only a few of the ones that are commonly asked:

- How are incurred claims defined?
- How is retention defined?
- How is the level of reserves determined?
- What is the interest rate credited to reserves?
- How are catastrophic losses handled in the experience-rating process?
- What charges are levied against the group's experience when coverage is converted?
- For what period of time are rates guaranteed?
- How much notice of rate changes is given at renewal?
- What is the procedure for handling claims?
- What services are provided in the area of cost containment?
- If you are selected to provide coverage, on what date will the master contract and certificates of insurance be delivered?

Presenting the Proposal

The successful presentation of a proposal will lead to a sale that is closed when the employer submits a signed application and the first periodic premium. For small groups the presentation of the proposal will be made directly to the employer by the agent or broker. In general there is little room for negotiations and the employer will either accept or reject the initial proposal.

For large groups when the employer is dealt with directly, the agent or broker may also present the proposal. However, because of the technical expertise necessary, the group representative will probably be involved, and will either present the proposal or assist the agent or broker in this task. It is at this point that further negotiation on plan design and revision of the proposal are most likely to take place.

When a group insurance case is put out to bid by a large broker or benefit consultant, there is usually no direct contact between the insurance company and the employer in the initial stages of the presentation. Rather, the presentation is made, usually by the group representative, to the broker or consultant, who then evaluates the proposals and makes a recommendation to the employer. This recommendation may be for the employer to select a specific proposal, but it often consists of presenting an employer with two or three proposals that best meet the employer's objectives. In this latter instance the group representatives of the insurance companies involved are typically asked to meet with both the broker or consultant and the employer to further discuss the proposals. At this stage of the process it is not unusual to give each company in contention a copy of the proposals that have been submitted by their competitors.

Enrollment

The first step in the postsale activities of group marketing involves the enrollment of employees in the plan. If the plan is noncontributory, the employer must provide the insurance company with enrollment cards or a list of all employees to be covered and a certification that they have met all eligibility requirements, such as being actively at work or having satisfied a probationary period. If a plan is contributory, it must be properly marketed to the employees in order to encourage the maximum enrollment. In fact, unless the solicitation of employees is effective, the actual installation of the plan may never occur because of insufficient enrollment. Usually the insurance company prepares the solicitation materials, such as letters or benefit booklets. For small employers these may be standardized materials, but for large employers they will be custom designed. If a group is large enough, the insurance company may even prepare audiovisual presentations. Although the actual solicitation will always involve the employer, it may consist only of the employer's providing these materials to the employees. However, it is common for the employer to allow group meetings to be held (during normal working hours) in which the agent, broker, or group representative can explain the plan to the employees and answer their questions.

The actual enrollment of employees either shortly follows or takes place simultaneously with the solicitation process. It consists of requesting the employees to complete enrollment forms that are supplied by the insurance company. These enrollment forms are usually brief, but they will be more detailed if the plan involves any individual underwriting of employees in addition to the usual group underwriting. While the actual enrollment may be conducted by the agent, broker, or group representative, it is common for the employer's supervisory personnel to carry out this activity.

While proper marketing of a contributory plan to employees is crucial, a noncontributory plan must also be properly presented to employees if they are to fully understand and appreciate its provisions. In many cases this means that the plan will be presented to employees in virtually the same manner as if it were contributory.

Installation

When the enrollment procedure is completed, the insurance company calculates the final premium rates and prepares the master contract (or joinder agreement in the case of a multiple-employer trust) and any other administrative materials for the employer as well as the certificates of insurance for the employees. The agent or broker usually delivers these materials to small employers, but in larger cases the task is most often performed by the group representative who is accompanied by the agent or broker. It is at this point that the agent, broker, or group representative thoroughly reviews the plan with the employer and explains its administrative aspects, such as premium billings, claims procedures, and the enrollment and termination of employees. The importance of this meeting with the employer should not be ignored since the future success of a group insurance case is often a function of how well these administrative procedures are explained and thus understood by the employer.

Servicing the Case

Similarly the importance of properly servicing a group insurance case cannot be overlooked. Good service will not only increase the satisfaction of the employer, but it will also minimize the possibility that the case will be transferred to another insurance company at the time of renewal. In addition, it may also lead to other business for the insurance company or the agent or broker when the employer adds a new coverage or renews an existing coverage.

The process of servicing a case begins when the initial sale is made and continues throughout its life. Except for small groups, the servicing is usually conducted by the group representative. However, some insurance companies have trained personnel whose sole function is to service group insurance cases. This allows the group representative to devote more of his or her time to sales activities. Most requests for service relate to routine administrative matters that involve billing, claims, or enrollment procedures. As previously mentioned, these requests will be minimized if a case is properly installed. To discover if there is any difficulty with a group insurance case at its earliest stage, the group representative must develop a close working relationship with other functional departments of the insurance company. For example, correspondence between the employer and claims personnel may be the first indication of any potential dissatisfaction.

Even when no specific problems exist, the group representative will schedule periodic visits with the employer to discuss such items as the administration of the plan, claim trends, and new federal or state regulations that affect the plan. These visits may lead to suggestions that changes be made in the plan so that it will better meet the desires and needs of the employer.

One of the most important and possibly most difficult aspects of servicing a group insurance case will occur at the time of renewal, particularly if a rate increase is proposed. The shock of a large rate increase may be a catalyst that encourages an employer to seek out another insurance company. For this reason it is important for the group representative to keep the employer informed throughout the year of the group's experience and current trends so that the size of the increase will not be unexpected. It is also at renewal time that the group representative, often accompanied by the agent or broker, should thoroughly review the group insurance case to determine whether it is appropriate to make any changes. If the employer is considering changing insurance companies, the group representative should emphasize any potential limitations of such an action. For example, additional administrative costs will undoubtedly be incurred with the installation of a new plan. In addition, there may be the potential for some employees to lose benefits in the transfer because of differing provisions of the new insurance company's plan or the application of its preexisting-conditions provision.

11

Group Insurance Pricing

One of the least understood aspects of group insurance is the pricing process. In the simplest sense group insurance pricing is no different from pricing in other industries. The insurance company must generate enough revenue to cover its costs (claims and expenses) and to contribute to the net worth of the company. However, this similarity is often overlooked because of the unique terminology that is associated with insurance pricing and because the price of a group insurance product is initially determined on the basis of expected, but uncertain, future events rather than on current tangible cost estimates. In addition, a group insurance plan may be subject to experience rating so that the final price to the consumer can be determined only after the coverage period has ended.

The purpose of this chapter is not to make readers experts in the actuarial intricacies of group insurance pricing, commonly referred to as *rate making,* but rather to provide an understanding of basic principles and concepts. Rate making consists of two distinct steps: (1) the determination of a unit price, referred to as a rate or premium rate, for each unit of benefit (such as each $1,000 of life insurance); and (2) the determination of the total price, or premium, that will be paid by the policyowner for the entire amount of coverage purchased. The mechanics of rate making differ, depending upon whether a particular group is subject to manual rating or experience rating. When *manual rating* is used, the premium rate is determined independently of a particular group's claims; when *experience rating* is used, the past claims experience of a group is considered in determining future premiums for the group and/or in adjusting past premiums after a policy period has ended.

The major objective of rate making for all types of group insurance is to develop premium rates that are both adequate and equitable. Adequate rates must be sufficient to cover both incurred claims and expenses and to generate the desired profit or contribution to the insurance company's surplus. Obviously the success and solvency of any group insurance operation is contingent on the long-run adequacy of premium rates. Therefore several states, concerned about the solvency of insurance companies, have laws and regulations regarding the adequacy of rates. The most significant of these is the New York law that prohibits any insurance company doing business in that state from issuing in any state a group health insurance contract (either medical expense or disability income) that does not appear to be self-supporting on the basis of reasonable assumptions concerning expected claims and expenses. New York also specifies the minimum group term life insurance rates that these companies may charge for any group that has not previously been insured for life insurance.

Equitable rates require each group to pay a premium that reflects the cost of providing coverage to that group. Again, practical considerations and state regulations act to encourage equity. The overpricing of group coverage for some segments of the market will result in lost business; the underpricing for other segments will attract unprofitable business. Most states also have laws and regulations that try to encourage equity by prohibiting unfair discrimination in insurance rates. The objective of equity has resulted in group insurance rates that differ because of such factors as the age, sex, and income distribution of a group's members and the size of a group, its geographic location, its occupational hazards, and its claims experience. As will be discussed later, the factors that are considered vary with the type of group insurance coverage.

MANUAL RATING

In the manual-rating process premium rates are only established for broad classes of group insurance business, and the insurance company does not consider the past claims experience of a particular group when determining that group's rates. However, claims experience is not entirely ignored since the aggregate claims experience for a class of business is used to determine the premium rates for that class.

Manual rating is used with small groups for which no credible individual loss experience is available. This lack of credibility exists because the group's size is such that it is impossible to determine whether other-than-average loss experience is due to random chance or is truly reflective of the group. Manual rating is also frequently used to determine the initial premiums for groups that are subject to experience rating, particularly when a group's past experience is unobtainable or when a group is being written for the first time. In addition, for all but the largest groups, experience rating uses a weighting of manual rates and the actual experience of a group to determine the premium.

Rating Basis

Prior to the actual calculation of manual premium rates it is necessary to develop a basis on which the rates will be determined. This involves a decision regarding (1) what benefit unit to use, (2) the extent to which rates will be refined by factors affecting claims, and (3) the frequency with which premiums will be paid.

Benefit Unit

Subject to certain adjustments, the premium for a group is calculated by multiplying the premium rate by the number of benefit units provided. While variations do occasionally exist, the following are the benefit units predominantly used for the most common types of group insurance:

Type of Group Insurance	Benefit Unit
Term life (including accidental death and dismemberment)	Each $1,000 of death benefit
Short-term disability income	Each $10 of weekly income
Long-term disability income	Each $100 of monthly income
Medical expense (including dental)	Each employee and each category of dependents

Factors Affecting Claims

As previous mentioned, equity requires that rates reflect those factors that result in different claims experience for different groups. Although there are variations among insurance companies, the following table represents the factors that are used by most insurance companies:

Type of Group Insurance	Age	Sex	Geographic Location
Term life	Yes	Yes	No
Short-term disability income	Yes	Yes	No
Long-term disability income	Yes	Yes	No
Medical expense	Yes	Yes	Yes
Dental	No	Yes	Yes

In addition, occupation is virtually always reflected in both group term insurance rates and accidental death and dismemberment rates. It may also be reflected in disability income, medical expense, and dental insurance rates, but the number of groups for which it is of concern is relatively small. Consequently some companies ignore it as a rating factor but may not write such coverages when certain occupations are involved.

At one time the income level of group members was commonly used as a factor in establishing disability income, medical expense, and dental insurance rates. Currently income level is still a factor in determining dental insurance premiums, but it is more likely to only be an underwriting consideration in disability income and medical expense insurance.

The size of a group will also affect rates since the proportion of the premium needed for expenses will decrease as the size of a group increases. All manual premium rates are based on an assumption that the size of a group falls within a certain range. If the size of a group varies from this range, an appropriate adjustment is made to the rate to reflect this differential.

A final factor considered in the calculation of rates is the length of time for which the rates will be used. This is a concern primarily for coverages that involve medical and dental claims, which over time will be expected to increase in severity because of inflation. In inflationary times monthly rates that are guaranteed for three months can be lower than those guaranteed for one year.

Frequency of Premium Payment Period

Because group insurance premiums are usually paid monthly, this is the period for which rates are generally determined. When premiums can be paid less frequently (such as annually), they are usually slightly lower than the sum of the monthly premiums for the same period of coverage.

Calculation of Manual Rates

Manual rating involves the calculation of the *manual premium rates* (also called tabular rates) that are quoted in an insurance company's rate book. These manual rates are applied to a specific group insurance case in order to determine a *final premium rate* (sometimes called an average premium rate) that will then be multiplied by the number of benefit units to obtain a premium for the group. There are three different manual-rating methods. However, if identical assumptions are used, each method should result in approximately the same premium for any given group. The first method determines separate manual rates for groups that possess certain characteristics that an insurance company feels will affect claims experience. A second approach establishes a single "standard manual rate" that is adjusted in the premium-calculation process to compensate for any characteristics that deviate from those of the standard group. A third method merely combines the first two approaches and considers some factors in determining the manual rate and others in determining the final premium rate.

The first step in the calculation of manual premium rates is the determination of the *net premium rate,* which is the amount necessary to support the cost of expected claims. For any given classification the net premium rate is calculated by multiplying the probability (frequency) of a claim's occurring by the expected amount (severity) of the claim. For example, if the probability that an employee aged 50 will die in the next month is .0005, then the net monthly premium for each $1,000 of coverage will be .0005 x $1,000 or $.50. Since premiums are collected before the claims will be paid, the insurance company will adjust this figure downward for anticipated interest earnings on these funds.

In general, insurance companies that write a large volume of any given type of group insurance will rely on their own experience in determining the frequency and severity of future claims. Insurance companies that do not have enough past data for reliable future projections can turn to many sources for useful statistics. Probably the major source is the Society of Actuaries, which regularly collects and publishes aggregate data on the group insurance business that is written by a number of large group insurance companies. Other sources of information include industry trade organizations and various agencies of the federal government.

The second and final step in the calculation of manual premium rates is the adjustment of the net premium rates for expenses, a risk charge, and a contribution to surplus. Expenses include commissions, premium taxes, claims settlement costs, and other costs associated with the acquisition and servicing of group insurance business. The risk charge represents a contribution to the insurance company's contingency reserve as a cushion against unanticipated and catastrophic amounts of claims. The contribution to surplus or net worth represents the profit margin of the insurance company. While mutual companies are legally nonprofit, they, like stock insurance companies, require a contribution to net worth that is a source of financing for future growth.

From the standpoint of equity the adjustment of the net premium rate is complex. Some factors such as premium taxes and commissions vary with the premium charge. However, the premium tax rate is not affected by the size of a group, whereas the commission rate decreases as the size of a group increases. To a large degree the expenses of settling claims vary with the number, and not the size, of claims. It costs just as much administratively to pay a $10,000 claim under a group life insurance plan as it does to pay a $100,000 claim. Certain other costs also tend to be fixed regardless of the size of a group. For simplicity some insurance companies adjust or load their net premium rates by a constant percentage. However, other insurance companies consider the different patterns of expenses by using a percentage plus a constant charge. For example, if the net premium rate is $.60, this might be increased by 20 percent plus $.10 to arrive at a manual premium rate of $.82 (that is, $.60 x 1.2 + $.10). Because neither approach adequately accounts for the difference in expenses as a result of a group's size, another adjustment based on the size of the group will be made in the calculation of the final premium rate.

Calculation of Premiums

Probably the best way to explain the actual calculation of group insurance premiums is to discuss some examples. The following analysis focuses primarily on group term life insurance, with some emphasis on how the structure of manual premium rates and the premium calculation process differ for certain other types of group insurance.

Group Term Life Insurance

The mechanics of calculating a final premium rate and the premium for a particular group will vary among insurance companies because of the differences in methods of preparing manual premium rates and the process by which adjustments are made to these rates. The usual approach taken for all but the smallest groups parallels that used in the 1961 Standard Group Life Insurance Premium Rates. These rates, based on the 1960 Commissioners Standard Group Mortality Table, were jointly promulgated by the insurance commissioners of several states and were required to be used as minimum initial rates for new group insurance business, including groups that had previously been written by other insurance companies. The rationale for setting these minimum rates was to prevent insurance companies from adversely affecting existing policyowners by writing new business at a loss, with the hope of recovering that loss through rate increases in future years. In effect an insurance company could not charge lower rates than these minimum rates during the first year it had a group insurance case on the books. However, the minimum rates did not apply upon renewal. Since New York applied these rates on an extraterritorial basis, any company licensed in New York had to use these rates in any state where it did business. (Note, however, that the majority of life insurers are not licensed in New York.) Companies licensed in New York are still subject to the 1961 minimum rates but only on group insurance cases that have not been previously written; the rates no longer apply to transferred business. A few other states also have minimum rate laws, but their effect is primarily to apply the minimum rates to companies that do business in these states but are not licensed in New York.

The following example is based on the 1961 minimum rates. It should be pointed out, however, that the manual premium rates of most insurance companies (except when the minimum rates apply) probably fall between 25 and 50 percent below these rates.

The 1961 minimum rates consist of a table of manual premium rates for males (with female rates being 60 percent of male rates) for each age from 15 to 95. The following is an abbreviated version of these rates on a monthly basis per $1,000 of coverage at selected ages. As with most rate tables the ages are those at a person's attained age (nearest birthday).

Age at Nearest Birthday	Male Rate	Female Rate
20	$0.23	$0.14
25	0.25	0.15
30	0.27	0.16
35	0.32	0.19
40	0.45	0.27
45	0.68	0.41
50	1.06	0.64
55	1.65	0.99
60	2.51	1.51
65	3.78	2.27
70	5.81	3.49

These rates assume that the coverage contains both a waiver-of-premium provision on disabled lives and a conversion privilege. Consequently they are higher than if neither of these additional benefits was included. When an employee converts coverage to an individual policy, a charge is assessed against the group insurance business of an insurance company to reflect the increased mortality that results from the adverse selection on conversions. The amount of this assessment (commonly $50 to $75 per $1,000 of converted insurance) is transferred to the individual insurance department of the company to compensate it for having to write the converted business at too low a rate.

The premium-calculation process starts with the determination of an "unadjusted cost," based on a census of the covered employees and the manual rates. For example, assume a firm has 230 employees. For the sake of simplicity also assume that each of these employees is provided with $10,000 of life insurance and that the group has the following age distribution:

Age	Males	Females
25	20	30
30	0	30
35	10	30
40	30	10
45	30	10
50	20	10

The unadjusted cost is then calculated as follows:

Age	Sex	Number of Employees		Amount of Coverage (in thousands)		Unadjusted Rate (per thousand)		Unadjusted Cost
25	M	20	x	10	x	$0.25	=	$ 50.00
35	M	10	x	10	x	0.32	=	32.00
40	M	30	x	10	x	0.45	=	135.00
45	M	30	x	10	x	0.68	=	204.00
50	M	20	x	10	x	1.06	=	212.00
25	F	30	x	10	x	0.15	=	45.00
30	F	30	x	10	x	0.16	=	48.00
35	F	30	x	10	x	0.19	=	57.00
40	F	10	x	10	x	0.27	=	27.00
45	F	10	x	10	x	0.41	=	41.00
50	F	10	x	10	x	0.64	=	64.00
				Total unadjusted cost				$915.00

The unadjusted cost is then "adjusted" for expenses in a procedure consisting of two steps. First, an expense charge equal to the lesser of (1) $.20 per $1,000 of insurance provided or (2) $8.00 is added to the unadjusted cost. In this example, the $8.00 is added because $.20 x 2,300 (based on the providing of $2,300,000 of insurance) is $460. For all practical purposes this charge can be treated as an $8.00 expense constant since virtually no groups exist that provide less than the $40,000 of coverage necessary for a lower charge.

The second step is to reduce the sum of the unadjusted cost and the expense charge calculated above by a percentage that is based on the volume of a group insurance case as determined by its monthly premium. The following reductions (adopted in 1971) are used with the 1961 minimum rates.

Monthly Premium before Reduction	Percentage Expense Reduction
Under $200	0
200–224	1
225–249	2
250–299	3
.	.
.	.
800–899	13
900–999	14
1,000–1,199	15
.	.
.	.
45,000–59,999	33
60,000–79,999	34
80,000 and over	35

Thus the initial monthly premium for the group in this example is

Unadjusted cost	$915.00
Plus lesser of $.20 per $1,000 or $8.00	8.00
Monthly premium before expense reduction	$923.00
Less expense reduction (14 percent)	129.22
Adjusted monthly premium	$793.78

The initial monthly premium is also used to calculate the final monthly premium rate per $1,000 of protection for the group:

$$\text{Monthly premium rate per thousand} = \frac{\text{Adjusted monthly premium}}{\text{Total volume (in thousands)}}$$

$$= \frac{\$793.78}{2,300}$$

$$= \$0.345$$

This final monthly premium rate (usually rounded to either the nearest cent or one-tenth of a cent) is used throughout the first policy year and is multiplied each month by the amount of insurance in force to calculate the monthly premium due. Adjustments to the final monthly premium rate as a result of changes in the makeup of employees by age or sex are not made until the beginning of the next policy year, when a new rate per $1,000 of coverage is determined as part of the renewal process. Thus the initial rate is guaranteed for one year, assuming no change in the benefit structure of the plan.

It is possible to make one other adjustment to the 1961 minimum premium rates. Although the rates are designed so that most industries can be written at the manual rates, employers in industries that are considered hazardous can be charged a higher rate. This increased rate is in the form of a surcharge per $1,000 of coverage and is added to the sum of the unadjusted cost and the expense charge before the expense reduction percentage is applied. The industry ratings used with the 1961 rates are expressed as +1, +2, and so forth. For example, an industry with a +1 rating can be expected to have about one death claim per year per 1,000 employees in excess of those assumed in the manual rates. The charge for this excess mortality is $.08 per $1,000 of coverage per month for each unit of extra rating. In the previous example a +1 rating would have resulted in an increased charge of $184 (that is, 2,300 x $.08) before the expense reduction was made. Therefore the adjusted monthly premium would have been calculated as follows:

Unadjusted cost	$ 915.00
Plus lesser of $.20 per $1,000 or $8.00	8.00
Plus industry surcharge	184.00
Total cost before expense reduction	$1,107.00
Less expense reduction (15 percent)	166.05
Adjusted monthly premium	$ 940.95

Similarly a +2 rating reflects the expectation of two extra death claims per year and would have resulted in an added premium of $.16 per $1,000 per month of $368.

Variations for Large Groups. The premium-calculation process discussed above is used by insurance companies for most groups above a certain size, commonly from 10-or-more to 50-or-more lives. However, variations do exist. For example, some insurance companies do not incorporate a charge for a waiver of premium into their manual rates. Rather an extra charge, which usually differs by industry, will be added for this coverage. In addition, a few companies use manual rates that vary by age but not sex. These unisex rate tables are based on assumptions about the ratio of males to females in the group. However, an adjustment will usually be made in the premium-calculation process if the actual ratio for the group differs from this assumption.

Insurance companies may or may not have a constant expense charge similar to the $8.00 previously described. Some companies incorporate a level of expenses into their manual rate so that there is no expense reduction for a certain-size group. In the final premium-calculation process an adjustment will be made, and larger groups will receive an expense reduction while smaller groups will receive an expense surcharge. The following is one such table of adjustments:

Monthly Premium before Adjustment	Percentage Adjustment
Under $200	+ 25
200–249	+ 22
250–299	+ 18
.	.
.	.
.	.
600–699	+ 2
700–799	+ 1
800–999	0
1,000–1,099	− 1
1,100–1,200	− 2
.	.
.	.
.	.
50,000–74,999	−14
75,000 and over	−15

Variations for Small Groups. The manual-rating process for small groups, including those written by multiple-employer trusts, differs from that of large groups in several ways. In general, the manual rates are banded by age, typically in 5-year intervals. The following is an example of one such monthly rate table for each $1,000 of coverage:

Age at Nearest Birthday	Male Rate	Female Rate
Under 30	.25	.19
30–34	.30	.23
35–39	.35	.27
40–44	.50	.38
45–49	.80	.60
50–54	1.20	.90
55–59	1.70	1.25
60–64	2.50	1.90
65–69	3.70	2.75
70–74	5.50	4.00
75 and over	9.00	6.75

An unadjusted cost is developed based on a census of the employees by age and sex. Since the manual rates are loaded for most expenses, and since the groups written tend to be reasonably close in size, no adjustment for size is usually made. However, to compensate for the expenses of periodic billings, most insurance companies apply a flat fee to all groups, commonly between $10 and $20 per billing. Some companies do not levy this charge if the premium is paid annually. To reflect the administrative costs associated with record keeping, some insurance companies also levy a modest one-time expense charge when coverage is added for a new employee.

In contrast to large groups for which the initial monthly premium is used to determine a monthly premium rate that will apply for a specified period of time, the monthly premium rate for small groups will be recalculated each month based not only on the volume of insurance, but also on changes in the makeup of employees by age and sex, just as if the group was being newly written. However, most insurance companies do guarantee that the manual rates that were used when the group was initially written (and any future manual rates applicable to the group) will remain applicable for some period of time. This period may vary from 60 days to one year, but 6 months is most common.

Accidental Death and Dismemberment Insurance

Accidental death and dismemberment insurance is usually not written as a separate coverage, but rather it is added by an endorsement to a group term insurance contract. A single manual rate typically applies to all employees regardless of age or sex, but it will vary depending on whether coverage is written (1) for nonoccupational accidents or (2) on a 24-hour basis for both nonoccupational and occupational accidents. The rate for nonoccupational coverage generally does not vary by industry and ranges from $.04 to $.06 per $1,000 of principal sum per month. However, the rate for coverage on a 24-hour basis does vary by industry, and although it falls within this same range for low-risk industries, it may be several times higher for hazardous industries. Some companies calculate a separate cost for the accidental death and dismemberment coverage and add it to the charge for the group term life insurance. However, since most employers purchase accidental death and dismemberment coverage, many insurance companies incorporate the cost into the manual rates for group term life insurance. When this is done, the principal sum will be equal to the amount of life insurance protection that is purchased, and an additional charge will be levied only if a higher level of accidental death and dismemberment coverage is desired.

Dependent Life Insurance

Dependent life insurance is typically added as additional coverage to a group life insurance contract that provides life insurance protection for employees. Because dependent life insurance coverage is usually a modest fixed amount (such as $2,000 on the spouse and $1,000 on each child) that generates a relatively small additional premium, a very simplified rate structure tends to be used. However, several variations do exist. Some insurance companies have a single flat rate, independent of the type or number of dependents, for each employee who has dependent coverage. Other companies have two separate flat rates: one for the spouse's coverage and the other for children's coverage. The rate for the children's coverage is a family rate regardless of the number of children, and it is based upon an average-sized family.

Flat rates are based on the assumption that the group has an average age mix of employees. If the group of employees is older than average, the flat rate for dependent coverage may be adjusted (particularly when it applies to spouses) to reflect the likelihood that the dependents are also above average in age when compared to the dependents of most other groups. A flat rate is commonly used when the cost of dependent coverage is paid entirely by the employees. The uniform charge is easy to communicate to employees, and it simplifies the payroll-deduction process for the employer.

Some insurance companies also use a rate for dependent coverage that varies with the employee's age, thereby assuming that older employees have older dependents. Basing the rate on the employee's age may seem illogical, but it is administratively simpler and less expensive than having to determine the ages of dependents. A single variable rate may apply to the total family coverage for the spouse and all children, or it may apply only to the spouse. In this latter case a flat rate is generally used if coverage for children is also provided.

Short-term Disability Income Insurance

In addition to varying by age and sex, manual rates for disability income insurance also differ by (1) the maximum benefit period, (2) the length of the waiting period, and (3) the writing of coverage either on a 24-hour basis or only for nonoccupational disabilities.

Some insurance companies (particularly for small groups) have only a single standard short-term disability income plan that they will sell, and therefore they only need a single manual rate table. Other companies allow the employer some flexibility in designing the plan to be purchased, and rather than make adjustments to a single rate table, these companies will usually have several rate tables that vary by such factors as maximum benefit period (such as 13 or 26 weeks) and waiting period (such as 7 days for all disabilities or 7 days for illnesses and no waiting period for injuries). If any other variations are allowed, appropriate adjustments will be made.

An adjustment may be made for the nature of the industry represented by the group. Ignoring the occupational injuries and diseases that are covered under workers' compensation, a few occupations are still characterized by higher-than-average disability income claims. As an alternative to a rate adjustment, some insurance companies have underwriting standards that prohibit the writing of coverage for these groups.

Until the passage of amendments to the Civil Rights Act pertaining to pregnancy, it was common for insurance companies to have one manual rate for plans that did not provide benefits for pregnancy-related disabilities and another for plans that did provide such benefits. Since most employers can no longer exclude pregnancy as a cause of disability, rates for coverage without this benefit are usually not published, except for the employers of small groups that still have an option regarding this benefit.

In contrast to group life insurance for which the rates for females are lower than the rates for males, disability income rates are higher for females. Ignoring pregnancy-related disabilities, the claims of females at younger ages still somewhat exceed those of males. However, because male and female claims are comparable at older ages, the rates for later years seldom vary. The following illustration of one insurance company's monthly manual rates per $10 of weekly benefit shows how this rate differential is even more pronounced at younger ages if maternity coverage is included:

Age	Male	Female
Under 30	$0.27	$0.91
30–34	0.42	0.91
35–39	0.48	0.91
40–44	0.63	0.91
45–49	0.71	1.03
50–54	1.12	1.12
55–59	1.26	1.26
60–64	1.62	1.62
65–69	2.27	2.27

In the past it was common for short-term disability income rates to be expressed on the basis of each $10 of weekly benefit. This is probably still the norm, but many insurance companies are now expressing their rates in terms of a higher weekly benefit, such as $50 or $100.

Long-term Disability Income Insurance

Like short-term disability income rates the manual rates for long-term coverage vary by age, sex, the length of the benefit period, and the length of the waiting period. In addition, the manual rates reflect the fact that benefits will be integrated with social security and certain other disability income benefits for which an employee might be eligible. To the extent that variations are allowed in the integration provision that was assumed in developing the manual rates, an adjustment will be made in the premium-calculation process. As is also the case with short-term rates, an adjustment might be made for certain occupations.

Unlike short-term disability income rates that are commonly expressed on the basis of a weekly benefit, long-term rates are typically expressed on the basis of a monthly benefit, usually per $100. In contrast to the coverages previously discussed, long-term disability claims fluctuate with general economic conditions. Consequently insurance companies review and possibly revise their manual rates (and/or their underwriting standards) as economic conditions change.

Medical Expense Insurance

In many ways the manual rates for medical expense insurance (and also dental insurance) are similar to those for disability income insurance because variations exist by age, sex, and the provisions of the plan, including the size of the deductible, the coinsurance percentage, and the level of benefits. Most insurance companies have manual rates for the few standard plans that will be sold, and only large employers are given the flexibility to deviate from these plans. Any such deviation will then be reflected in adjustments to the manual rates. Adjustments may also be made to the manual rates if the employer is in an industry that is characterized by higher-than-average claims.

One other factor, geographic location, is a variable in the manual rates because of the significant differences in medical costs across the country. Depending on group size, an adjustment for location may be made in one of two ways. For large groups the rating process usually starts with a manual rate that does not consider the location of employees. Each county (or other geographic subdivision) where coverage will be written is then assigned a factor that is based on the cost of health care in that location as compared with the "average" cost that is assumed in the manual rates. For example, if Seattle were 20 percent higher than average, it would have a factor of 1.2. If all a firm's employees were there, the manual rates for that group would be multiplied by a location factor of 1.2 in the process of determining the group's premium. If employees were in several locations, a composite factor would be calculated as shown in the following example:

	Number of Employees		Location Factor		Product
Seattle	100	x	1.2	=	120
Kansas City	70	x	1.0	=	70
Birmingham	30	x	0.7	=	21
	200				211

$$\text{Location Factor} = \frac{\text{Total product}}{\text{Total number of employees}} = \frac{211}{200} = 1.055$$

Consequently the manual rate for this group would be increased by 5.5 percent because of the location of the employees.

A slightly different approach is used for small groups. Because employees are usually in one location, most companies have manual rate tables for between 10 and 15 rating territories, and each county in which employees are located is assigned a specific territorial rating. The following territorial classifications are from the rating manual of one insurance company for counties in three of the states where it writes business:

California
   Los Angeles   10
   Alameda, Contra Costa, Marin, Orange, Riverside, San Bernardino,
      San Francisco, San Mateo, Santa Clara, Solano   9
   Imperial, Kern, San Diego, San Luis Obispo, Santa Barbara,
      Ventura   8
   All other counties   7

Georgia
   Clayton, Cobb, DeKalb, Fulton   6
   Catoosa, Chatham, Gwinnett, Walker   4
   All other counties   3

Maine
   Entire state   2

An excerpt from the manual rate tables of the same company shows how the monthly cost for coverage under a plan written through one of their multiple-employer trusts varies by geographic area:

Age	Class of Coverage	Area 2	Area 4	Area 7	Area 10
Under 30	Male	$ 67.20	$ 78.80	$ 98.80	$ 108.40
Under 30	Female	73.00	86.40	110.50	144.80
Under 30	Male and dependents	196.60	234.70	305.80	401.50
Under 30	Female and dependents	191.20	229.40	298.10	396.10
30–44	Male	100.70	117.10	147.40	188.70
30–44	Female	107.60	127.70	163.00	212.60
30–44	Male and dependents	263.80	314.00	404.80	535.00
30–44	Female and dependents	255.20	305.80	396.10	526.30

The previous example lists manual rates for dependent coverage that are applied regardless of the number of dependents, the relationship of the dependents to the employee, or the ages of the dependents. For any size group this is one of the three common methods for developing a rating basis for dependent coverage. Under all three methods the rate for dependent coverage is usually a function of the employee's age rather than of the dependents' ages. However, the other two methods do take the number of dependents and their relationship to the insured into consideration. One method uses a certain rate for dependent coverage if there is only one dependent and another rate if there are two or more dependents. However, the other approach has three rates: one for coverage that is elected only for a spouse, another for coverage that is elected only for children, and a third for coverage that is elected for both a spouse and children.

Because medical expense claims are continually increasing as a result of inflation, a trend factor must be applied to past claims experience when developing manual rates. This is a complex and often perplexing task for most insurance companies. Not only has the overall cost of medical care increased faster than the general cost of living (as measured by the consumer price index), but the increases have been erratic from year to year and virtually impossible to predict with any degree of accuracy. In addition, because these increases vary significantly for each category of medical expenses, different trend factors must be applied to different categories of claims.

At one time group insurance premium rates were guaranteed by insurance companies for at least 12 months and possibly for as long as 2 or 3 years. However, to protect themselves against unexpected increases in claims as a result of increases in the cost of medical care, many insurance companies will now guarantee medical expense rates for no more than 6 months. In fact, a number of multiple-employer trusts have only 3-month guarantees, or they contain provisions whereby rates can be increased at any time, provided notice of the rate increase is given 30 or 60 days in advance. Some companies allow an employer to select the length of the rate guarantee, such as 6 months or one year. However, the longer the rate guarantee, the higher the rate.

Dental Insurance

In many ways the rating of dental insurance is similar to the rating of medical expense insurance. However, there are some significant differences. Most insurance companies do not vary their manual rates by the ages of group members. Rather, an adjustment is usually made for the income levels of employees since higher-paid persons are much more likely to obtain dental care. This adjustment is usually in the form of a percentage that is based on the extent to which the portion of employees with incomes higher than some figure (such as $30,000) exceeds the proportion of such employees that is assumed in the manual rates. An adjustment is also made for certain occupations (such as salespeople or teachers) that use dental services more frequently than average. Finally, the manual rates will usually be increased when a plan is new (or expands benefits) if the employees have been informed beforehand. Under these circumstances there is a tendency to postpone needed dental care until the plan is installed.

EXPERIENCE RATING

With experience rating an insurance company considers a group's claims experience, either at the issue date or at the end of a policy period, when determining the premium rate for that group. When applied prospectively (that is, to future periods), experience rating is used to determine (1) adjustments in renewal premiums (either upward or downward) for those groups whose claims experience has deviated from what was expected and (2) initial premiums for large groups that change insurance carriers.

In addition to determining the premium rate for the next policy period (usually 12 months), experience rating is also used to compute the refund for those groups that had better claims experience than anticipated. This refund is commonly referred to as a *dividend* by mutual insurance companies and a *retrospective rate credit* or premium refund by stock insurance companies. (Since the majority of group insurance business is written by mutual companies, the term *dividend* will be used here.) Under some experience-rating arrangements the premium at the end of a policy period may also be retroactively adjusted upward if a group's claims experience has been worse than anticipated, and an additional premium will be charged. However, because these arrangements are not very common, they will be discussed as an alternative funding method in chapter 12.

Rationale for Experience Rating

One argument in favor of experience rating is that it achieves the ultimate degree of premium equity among policyowners. Even though manual rating also results in equity because it considers the obvious factors that affect claims, it is impossible to measure and make adjustments in the manual rates for such factors as life-style, working conditions, and morale, all of which contribute to the level of claims experience. Experience rating is also the most cost-effective way to reflect the general health of a group in the premium that is charged.

Probably the major reason for using experience rating is the competition that exists in the group insurance marketplace. If an insurance company were to use identical rates for all groups regardless of their experience, the employers with good experience would soon seek out insurance companies that offered lower rates, or they would turn to self-funding as a way to reduce costs. The insurance company that did not consider claims experience would therefore be left with only the poor risks. This is exactly the situation that led most of the Blues to abandon community rating for group insurance cases above a certain size. Experience rating allows an insurance company to acquire and retain the better cases (from a claims-experience standpoint) and to determine an appropriate premium for the groups that have worse-than-average claims experience.

Dividend Calculation

It is perhaps putting the cart before the horse to explain experience rating for dividend purposes (which occurs at the end of a policy period) before discussing the use of experience rating to determine premiums (which occurs at the beginning of that period). However, the process of calculating dividends tends to be somewhat more complicated and is easier to discuss first. This discussion is followed by an explanation of how the experience-rating process is different for determining premiums on a prospective basis.

At first glance the process of using experience rating to determine dividends appears complex. However, the actual mechanics are relatively simple, and much of the confusion stems from the fact that the process is lengthy. In addition, both the format and the terminology vary somewhat among insurance companies. This discussion will focus on the illustration in table 11-1 and will explain the steps used to calculate the dividend for a group term life insurance case. Although this illustration can be considered a typical example of a dividend calculation, variations could have been (and often are) used in several steps. Therefore the more commonly used and significant variations will be described for group term life insurance as well as for other types of group insurance.

Premiums Paid

Step 1 shows the total amount of premiums that were actually paid by the policyowner during the experience-rating period (usually one year) before any adjustment was made to reflect the actual experience of the group. In most instances this will be the sum of 12 monthly premiums. The premiums paid may have been based on manual rates or on the past experience of the group.

Incurred Claims

Step 2 involves the determination of incurred claims, which are those claims attributable to the recently ended period of coverage that was subject to experience rating (that is, the *experience period*). It may seem as if the incurred claims are those claims that were paid during the experience period. Unfortunately it is not that simple. Some of the claims that were paid during the experience period may actually be attributable to prior periods and must be subtracted from the incurred claims. In addition, other claims that are attributable to the experience period may not have been reported or may be in the course of settlement. However, their value must be estimated. Therefore an appropriate determination of incurred claims is as follows:

incurred claims	=	claims paid during the experience period
	−	claims paid during the experience period, but incurred during prior periods
	+	estimate of claims incurred during the experience period, but to be paid in future periods

In actual practice incurred claims are usually expressed as follows:

incurred claims	=	paid claims
	+	ending claim reserve
	−	beginning claim reserve
		or
incurred claims	=	paid claims
	+	change in claim reserve

Table 11-1 Illustrative Dividend Calculation		
1. Premiums paid		$100,000
2. Incurred claims [a + (c − b) + d + e]		$79,800
a. Paid death claims	$70,000	
b. Beginning reserve for death claims	$14,000	
c. Ending reserve for death claims	$15,000	
d. Charge for approved disability claims	$7,500	
e. Conversion charges	$1,300	
3. Stop-loss limit (120% of premium paid)		$120,000
4. Incurred claims subject to experience rating (lesser of 2 or 3)		$79,800
5. Expected claims		$84,000
6. Credibility factor		0.8
7. Claims charge [(0.8 x 4) + (0.2 x 5)]		$80,640
8. Retention charge (f + g + h + i + j −k)		$9,800
f. Charge for stop-loss coverage	$2,500	
g. Commissions	$2,000	
h. Premium taxes	$2,000	
i. Administration	$1,500	
j. Contingency reserve (risk charge) and surplus contribution	$3,000	
k. Interest on reserves	$1,200	
9. Dividend earned [1 − (7 + 8)]		$9,560
10. Deficit carried forward from prior periods		$3,000

11. Deficit to be carried forward to future periods
    (9 − 10) if less than 0
             OR
    Dividend payable (9 − 10) if greater than 0
		–
		
		$6,560

This *claim reserve,* which is often referred to as the open-and-unreported claim reserve, represents an estimate by the insurance company for (1) claims that have been approved but not yet paid, (2) claims that are in the course of settlement, and (3) claims that have been incurred but not yet reported. In addition, when disability income coverage or medical expense coverage is experience rated, an additional amount must be added to this estimate for any claims that have been incurred, reported, and approved but are not yet payable. Essentially these claims arise from disabilities or current medical claims that will continue beyond the experience period.

Based on past experience, most insurance companies can closely estimate the percentage of claims that will be paid after the close of the experience period for a given type of coverage. While this estimate reflects company-wide experience and may not reflect the experience of a particular policyowner, it is usually applied to each group insurance case rather than determining the claim reserve on a case-by-case basis. In general the claim reserve is based either on a percentage of the annual premium (before experience rating) or on a percentage of claims paid. The first approach is most common for small groups, and the latter approach tends to be used for large groups. This percentage varies considerably by type of coverage, with the claim reserve for group term life insurance usually ranging between 10 to 15 percent of the annual premium (and up to 25 percent if a waiver of premium for disability is included), and the claim reserve for medical expense coverage often ranging from 20 to 65 percent, depending on what benefits are involved.

Two other factors enter into the incurred claims amount for group term life insurance: disability claims and conversion charges. In addition to death claims, there may be disability claims if a group insurance contract contains a waiver-of-premium provision or another type of disability provision. Once a waiver-of-premium claim has been approved, a charge is made for future death claims since no future premiums will be received for the disabled employee. This charge is based on the probability that the disabled employee will die prior to recovery or termination of coverage (for example, at age 65). On the average the charge will be about $750 for each $1,000 of coverage. If the insurance contract continues, an additional $250 per $1,000 of coverage will be charged if a death claim is paid. If the employee recovers or coverage terminates prior to death, the $750 charge will be credited back to the policyowner.

As mentioned earlier in this chapter, a conversion charge is levied against the group insurance department of an insurance company to reflect the increased mortality on converted coverage. In the experience-rating procedure this charge is transferred to the group policyowner as a charge per $1,000 of coverage converted (commonly $50 to $75).

Stop-Loss Limit

In step 3 the stop-loss limit is specified. This is the maximum amount of claims that will be charged to the group in step 4 of the experience-rating calculation. Its purpose is to minimize the effect of any chance fluctuations that might occur from year to year, including catastrophic losses within the group, such as an accident that kills several employees. These chance fluctuations tend to become relatively smaller as the size of a group increases, and a stop-loss limit may not be used for very large groups.

The stop-loss limit is usually expressed as a percentage of the premiums paid, and the actual percentage is subject to negotiation between the policyowner and the insurance company. In this illustration 120 percent is used. Therefore the amount of incurred claims that will enter into the experience-rating calculation is limited to a maximum of $120,000. Since this exceeds the actual amount of incurred claims, the latter amount is used in step 4.

Obviously a charge must be made somewhere for incorporating a stop-loss provision into an experience-rating contract since the insurance company is obligated to pay any excess amount over the stop-loss limit. The charge in this illustration is shown in step 8. In practice this charge will be the same for all similar-sized groups that use the same stop-loss percentage. The charge is a percentage of premiums paid, and it becomes smaller as either the size of the group or the stop-loss percentage increases. In effect this charge for stop-loss coverage can be viewed as a manual rate charge for losses in excess of some limit, with only those losses below the limit subject to experience rating.

Expected Claims

The amount of expected claims in step 5 represents the portion of the premiums paid that the insurance company has anticipated would be necessary to pay claims during the experience period. This amount may have been derived either from average experience as in manual rating or from the past experience of the particular group.

Credibility

The credibility factor (step 6), which can vary from zero to one, is a statistical measure of the reliability of the group's past experience. In other words, it is a measure of the probability that the group's actual experience is a true reflection of the group and is not the result of chance occurrences. The credibility factor varies by the size of the group and the type of coverage. In general, the larger the group is, the greater the reliability of estimates (because of the law of large numbers) will be. In addition, actual experience tends to deviate less from the estimates of expected claims (on a relative basis) as the frequency of claims rises. Therefore a greater degree of credibility can be attributed to a group's medical expense claims than to its life insurance claims.

In actual practice credibility factors are usually based on the size of a group as determined by the number of persons (lives) who are insured. However, some insurance companies base their credibility factors on the annual premium of a group. The factors vary somewhat among insurance companies, but the following excerpt from the rate manual of one insurance company is a typical example of the first approach:

Size of Group (Lives)	Life Insurance and Long-term Disability Income Insurance	Medical Expense Insurance and Short-term Disability Income Insurance
100	0.0	0.2
200	0.2	0.5
400	0.4	0.8
600	0.7	1.0
800	0.9	1.0
1,000 or more	1.0	1.0

Adjustments may be made in these factors to reflect any characteristics of either the group or the insurance contract that are not the norm. For example, an older group of employees might be assigned a higher credibility factor than a younger group whose claims are more likely to be due to random fluctuations. In addition, the level of any stop-loss limit may have an effect. As the stop-loss charge is increased (meaning the stop-loss limit is lowered), the credibility that can be assigned to the remaining claims below the stop-loss limit also increases.

Similarly the size of the credibility factor may be influenced by the amount of the risk charge that is levied on the group for the establishment of a contingency reserve. If an insurance company has an adequate contingency reserve for a group insurance case, it is more likely to allow the use of a higher credibility factor than can be justified from a statistical standpoint. This practice will result in reduced claims charges for years in which the employer has good experience, and increased claims charges for years in which it has bad experience. Although it is desired by employers that have a history of better-than-average claims experience, a higher-than-justified credibility factor will lead to a larger-than-usual deficit for a group whose experience is bad. It will also increase the probability that the employer will terminate the contract before the deficit is eliminated. A larger contingency reserve can balance the financial consequences of this possibility.

Claims Charge

Once the credibility factor is determined, the process of calculating what claims will be charged against the group in the experience period is relatively simple and can be expressed by the following formula:

claims charge = (z) (incurred claims subject to experience rating)
  + (1 − z) (expected claims)
where z is the credibility factor

In effect the claims charge is a weighted average of (1) the incurred claims that are subject to experience rating and (2) the expected claims, with the incurred claims being assigned a weight equal to the credibility factor and the expected claims being assigned a weight equal to one minus the credibility factor. In the illustration (step 7) the claims charge is calculated as follows:

claims charge = .8 ($79,800) + (1 − 0.8) ($84,000)
  = 0.8 ($79,800) + 0.2 ($84,000)
  = $63,840 + $16,800
  = $80,640

If a credibility factor of 1.0 is used, the claims charge will be equal to the incurred claims that are subject to experience rating, and the expected claims will not be taken into consideration.

Large Amounts of Coverage

In many group term life insurance contracts there is considerable disparity in the amounts of coverage, and top executives often have much greater coverage than the lowest-paid employees. Claims that arise from the deaths of employees who have large amounts of coverage can have a significant impact on a group's experience for the years in which they occur. Consequently several methods have been used to exclude these claims (or at least a portion of these claims) from the process of determining the claims charge in experience rating. One of these methods is the stop-loss limit that was previously mentioned. However, its primary purpose is to limit the claims charge because of a higher-than-anticipated frequency of claims, rather than because of a few high-severity claims. Some of the other methods used to handle these large claims include

- excess-amounts pooling. Under this approach the amount of insurance that is subject to experience rating on any one person is limited. Amounts in excess of the limit are not experience rated but are subject to manual rates that are based on the ages of the individuals involved. This results in a "pooling" or an "insurance" charge being added to either the claims charge or the retention charge, depending on the practice of the insurance company. These excess amounts may also be subject to evidence of insurability.
- a lower credibility factor. Under this method the credibility factor normally used for a certain-size group is reduced if there is a significant difference between the smallest and largest amounts of coverage. This results in more weight being placed on the group's expected claims than on their incurred claims.
- an extra contingency reserve. Under this approach the excess of claims above a certain limit is ignored in the experience-rating process for dividend purposes but is charged against a contingency reserve that has been established (with an appropriate annual charge) for this reason.

Retention

The *retention* (step 8) in a group insurance contract is usually defined as the excess of premiums paid over claims payments and dividends. It consists of charges for (1) the stop-loss coverage, (2) expenses (commissions, premium taxes, and administrative expenses), (3) a risk charge, and (4) a contribution to the insurance company's surplus. In this particular illustration the sum of these charges is reduced by the interest that is credited to certain reserves that the insurance company holds in order to pay future claims attributable to this contract. These include the claim reserve and any contingency reserves. However, some insurance companies do not subtract this interest when determining retention, but rather they treat it as an additional premium paid.

For large groups each item in the retention is calculated separately, based on the group's actual experience. For small groups a formula is usually applied that is based on insurance company averages. This formula varies by the size of a group and the type of coverage involved, and most often it is either a percentage of the claims charge or a flat charge plus a percentage of the claims charge.

Dividend Earned

The dividend earned (step 9) is computed by adding the retention to the claims charge and then subtracting this sum from the premiums paid. This is the dividend amount attributable to the group insurance case for the current experience period.

Prior Deficits

Under most experience-rated group insurance plans, any deficits from past periods must be made up before any future dividends will be paid. Whenever the sum of the claims charge and the retention charge for any experience period exceeds the premiums paid and results in a negative dividend earned, there is a deficit. In this illustration (step 10) a $3,000 deficit from prior periods exists. Interestingly the insurance company will have no opportunity to recover this deficit if the insurance contract is not renewed. However, the fact that there is always a chance of nonrenewal is one of the reasons why a risk charge is levied.

As additional protection against the nonrenewal of insurance contracts that have a deficit, some insurance companies require that part of any dividend earned be placed in a *claims fluctuation reserve* when experience is favorable. Monies are drawn from the reserve to indemnify the insurance company for the years in which there is a deficit. Since this reserve lessens the possibility that the insurance company will lose money on a group insurance case, it is usually accomplished by a lower risk charge.

Dividend Payable

The final step in the dividend-calculation process (step 11) is to establish whether a dividend is payable. This is determined by subtracting any deficit that has been carried forward (or placed in a claims fluctuation reserve) from the dividend earned for the experience period. If this figure is positive, it is the amount of the dividend; if the figure is negative, it is the amount of the cumulative deficit that is to be carried forward.

In this illustration only one type of coverage is experience rated. However, when an employer has more than one type of coverage that is experience rated with the same insurance company, a single dividend is usually determined for the combined package. This typically involves the determination of a separate claims charge for each coverage and a single retention charge for the entire package. Because "losses" for one type of coverage will often be offset by "gains" for other types of coverage, the relative fluctuation in the overall experience will tend to be less than the fluctuations in the experience of some or all of the individual coverages. Therefore the overall premium can often be reduced (or the dividend increased) because the insurance company will levy a lower risk charge and/or require a lower contingency reserve.

Renewal Rating

Experience rating is also often used to develop future premiums ror group insurance cases based on the past experience of the group. For the most part the procedure is similar to that for determining dividends, and in fact, the two procedures are usually done at the same time. However, there are some differences. In most cases the experience-rating period will be 3 to 5 years instead of a single year, and thus cumulative premiums and charges for this period will be used. In addition, a more conservative (that is, lower) credibility factor will normally be applied. For example, an insurance company that uses a credibility factor of 0.8 for dividend purposes for a particular case might use a factor of 0.6 for renewal-rating purposes. Furthermore, since a premium is being developed for the future, it is also necessary to adjust past claims and the retention, not only to reflect current cost levels but also to include expected trends for the next year. Adjustments must also be made to account for any changes in the coverage. Once a renewal premium expected to be sufficient to cover claims and retention is calculated, an additional amount is added for future dividends. This amount in effect becomes a safety margin for the insurance company should both claims and retention be higher than anticipated; otherwise it is returned as an experience dividend to the policyowner.

Experience rating may also be used to develop the initial premiums for any transferred business, requiring the insurance company to obtain past data from the policyowner regarding its experience with the previous carrier. A policyowner may be reluctant to provide this information because poor experience (and the resulting rate increase) is often the reason for changing insurance companies. However, the existence of the poor claims experience is exactly the information needed by the insurance company. In fact, some insurance companies actually refuse to write transferred coverage, particularly for large groups, unless verifiable prior claims experience is provided.

If possible the past data are used to determine what the premiums and charges would have been if the new contract had been written by the new carrier in previous years. If this can be accomplished, the procedure is a simplified application of the principles previously described. If it cannot be accomplished, manual rating may be used for small groups, but judgment may play a large role in determining the premiums for large groups.

12

Alternative Funding Methods

In recent years employers have increasingly considered—and often adopted—benefit funding methods that are alternatives to the traditional fully insured group insurance contract. Under the traditional group insurance contract the employer pays premiums in advance to the insurance company, which then has the financial responsibility both for paying claims (if and when they occur) and for assuming the administrative expenses associated with the contract. In addition, the insurance company bears the risk that claims will be larger than anticipated.

REASONS FOR ALTERNATIVE FUNDING

The increasing interest in alternatives to the traditional fully insured group arrangement has focused on two factors: cost savings and improved cash flow. To a large extent this interest has grown in response to the rising cost of medical care that has resulted in an increase in the cost of providing medical expense benefits. Even though alternative funding methods are most commonly used for providing medical expense benefits, many of the methods described here are also appropriate for other types of benefits.

Cost Savings

Savings can result to the extent that either claims or the insurance company's retention can be reduced. Retention is that portion of the insurance company's premium over and above the incurred claims and dividends. It includes such items as commissions, premium taxes, risk charges, and profit. Traditionally alternative funding methods have not focused on reducing claims, since the same benefits will normally be provided (and therefore the same claims will be paid) regardless of which funding method is used. However, this focus has changed as state laws and regulations increasingly mandate the types and levels of benefits that must be contained in medical expense contracts. To the extent that these laws and regulations apply only to benefits that are included in insurance contracts, employers can avoid providing these mandated benefits by using alternative funding methods that do not involve insurance contracts.

Modifications of fully insured contracts are usually designed either to lower or eliminate premium taxes or to reduce the insurance company's risk and consequently the risk charge. Alternative funding methods that involve a degree of self-funding may be designed to also reduce other aspects of retention and to reduce claims by excluding mandated benefits.

Improved Cash Flow

Under a fully insured contract an employer has the ability to improve cash flow because premiums are collected before the funds will actually be needed to pay claims. The employer will generally be credited with interest while these funds are held in reserves. Alternative funding arrangements that are intended to improve cash flow are designed either to postpone the payment of premiums to the insurance company or to keep the funds that would otherwise be held in reserves in the hands of the employer until they are needed by the insurance company. This is particularly advantageous to the employer when these funds can be invested at a higher rate of interest than that credited by the insurance company to reserves. It must be remembered, however, that earnings on funds invested by the employer are generally subject to income taxation, while interest credited to reserves by the insurance company is tax free.

METHODS OF ALTERNATIVE FUNDING

Totally self-funded (or self-insured) employee benefit plans are the opposite of traditional fully insured group insurance plans. Under totally self-funded plans the employer is responsible for paying claims, administering the plan, and bearing the risk that actual claims will exceed those expected. However, very few employee benefit plans that use alternative methods of funding have actually turned to total self-funding. Rather, the methods used typically fall somewhere between the two extremes.

The methods of alternative funding can be divided into two general categories: those that primarily modify traditional fully insured group insurance contracts and those that have some self-funding (either partial or total). The first category includes

- premium-delay arrangements
- reserve-reduction arrangements
- minimum-premium plans
- cost-plus arrangements
- retrospective-rating arrangements

These alternative funding methods are regarded as modifications of traditional fully insured plans because the insurance company has the ultimate responsibility for paying all benefits promised under the contract. Most insurance companies will allow only large employers to use these modifications, and although practices differ among insurance companies, generally a group insurance plan must generate between $150,000 and $250,000 in claims before these funding methods will be available to the employer.

The second category of alternative funding methods includes

- total self-funding from current revenue and self-administration
- self-funding with stop-loss coverage and/or ASO arrangements
- funding through a 501(c)(9) trust

In contrast to the first category of alternative funding methods, some of these alternatives can be used by small employers.

Premium-Delay Arrangements

Premium-delay arrangements allow the employer to defer payment of monthly premiums for some time beyond the usual 30-day grace period. In fact, these arrangements lengthen the grace period, most commonly by 60 or 90 days. The practical effect of premium-delay arrangements is that they enable the employer to have continuous use of the portion of the annual premium that is approximately equal to the claim reserve. For example, a 90-day premium delay allows the employer to use 3 months (or 25 percent) of the annual premium for other purposes. This amount roughly corresponds to what is usually in the claim reserve for medical expense coverage. Generally the larger this reserve is on a percentage basis, the longer the premium payment can be delayed. The insurance company still has a statutory obligation to maintain the claim reserve, and therefore it must use other assets besides the employer's premiums for this purpose. In most cases these assets come from the insurance company's surplus.

A premium-delay arrangement has a financial advantage to the extent that an employer can earn a higher return by investing the delayed premiums than by accruing interest on the claim reserve. In actual practice interest is still credited to the reserve, but this credit is offset by either an interest charge on the delayed premiums or an increase in the insurance company's retention.

Upon termination of an insurance contract with a premium-delay arrangement the employer is responsible for paying any deferred premiums. However, the insurance company is legally responsible for paying all claims incurred prior to termination, even if the employer fails to pay the deferred premiums. Consequently most insurance companies are concerned about the employer's financial position and credit rating. For many insurance companies the final decision of whether to enter into a premium-delay arrangement, or any other alternative funding arrangement that leaves funds in the hands of the employer, is made by the insurer's financial experts after a thorough analysis of the employer. In some cases this may mean that the employer will be required to submit a letter of credit or some other form of security.

Reserve-Reduction Arrangements

A reserve-reduction arrangement is similar to a premium-delay arrangement. Under the usual reserve-reduction arrangement the employer is allowed (at any given time) to retain an amount of the annual premium that is equal to the claim reserve. Generally such an arrangement is allowed only after the contract's first year, when the pattern of claims and the appropriate amount of the reserve can be more accurately estimated. In succeeding years if the contract is renewed, the amount retained will be adjusted according to changes in the size of the reserve. As with a premium-delay arrangement the monies retained by the employer must be paid to the insurance company upon termination of the contract. Again, the advantage of this approach lies in the employer's ability to earn more on these funds than it would earn under the traditional insurance arrangement.

A few insurance companies offer another type of reserve-reduction arrangement for long-term disability income coverage. Under a so-called limited-liability arrangement the employer purchases from the insurance company a one-year contract in which the insurer agrees to pay claims only for that year, even though the employer's "plan" provides benefits to employees for longer periods. Consequently enough reserves are maintained by the insurance company to pay benefits only for the duration of the one-year contract. At renewal the insurance company agrees to continue paying the existing claims as well as any new claims. In effect, the employer pays the insurance company each year for existing claims as the benefits are paid to employees, rather than when disabilities occur. A problem for employees under this type of arrangement is the lack of security for future benefits. For example, if the employer goes bankrupt and the insurance contract is not renewed, the insurance company has no responsibility to continue benefit payments. For this reason several states will not allow this type of arrangement.

The limited-liability arrangement contrasts with the usual group contract in which the insurance company is responsible for paying disability income claims to an employee for the length of the benefit period (as long as the employee remains disabled). On the average each disability claim will result in the establishment of a reserve equal to approximately five times the employee's annual benefit.

Minimum-Premium Plans

Minimum-premium plans were designed primarily to reduce state premium taxes. However, many minimum-premium plans also improve the employer's cash flow.

Under the typical minimum-premium plan the employer assumes the financial responsibility for paying claims up to a specified level, usually from 80 to 95 percent of estimated claims (with 90 percent most common). The specified level may be determined on either a monthly or an annual basis. The funds necessary to pay these claims are deposited into a bank account that belongs to the employer. However, the actual payment of claims is made from this account by the insurance company, which acts as an agent of the employer. When claims exceed the specified level, the balance is paid from the insurance company's own funds. No premium tax is levied by the states on the amounts deposited by the employer into such an account, as it would have been if these deposits had been paid directly to the insurance company. In effect, for premium-tax purposes the insurance company is only considered to be the administrator of these funds and not a provider of insurance. Unfortunately the IRS considers these funds to belong to the employer, and death benefits in excess of $5,000 represent taxable income to beneficiaries. Consequently minimum-premium plans are used to insure disability income and medical expense benefits rather than life insurance benefits.

Under a minimum-premium plan the employer pays a substantially reduced premium, subject to premium taxation, to the insurance company for administering the entire plan and for bearing the cost of claims above the specified level. Because such a plan may be slightly more burdensome for an insurance company to administer than would a traditional group arrangement, the retention charge may also be slightly higher. Under a minimum-premium arrangement the insurance company is ultimately responsible for seeing that all claims are paid, and it must maintain the same reserves that would have been required if the plan had been funded under a traditional group insurance arrangement. Consequently the premium will include a charge for the establishment of these reserves, unless some type of reserve-reduction arrangement has also been negotiated.

Some insurance regulatory officials view the minimum-premium plan primarily as a loophole used by employers to avoid paying premium taxes. In several states there have been attempts to seek court rulings or legislation that would require premium taxes to be paid either on the funds deposited in the bank account or on claims paid from these funds. Most of these attempts have been unsuccessful, but recent court rulings in California require the employer to pay premium taxes on the funds deposited in the bank account. If similar attempts are successful in the future, the main advantage of minimum-premium plans will be lost.

Cost-Plus Arrangements

Cost-plus arrangements (often referred to by other names such as flexible funding) are frequently used by large employers to provide life insurance benefits. Under such an arrangement the employer's monthly premium is based on the claims paid by the insurance company during the preceding month, plus a specified retention charge that is uniform throughout the policy period. To the extent that an employer's loss experience is less than that assumed in a traditional premium arrangement, the employer's cash flow is improved. However, an employer with worse-than-expected experience, either during the early part of the policy period or during the entire policy period, could also have a more unfavorable cash flow than if a traditional insurance arrangement were used. To prevent this from occurring, many insurance companies place a maximum limit on the employer's monthly premium so that the aggregate monthly premiums paid at any time during the policy period do not exceed the aggregate monthly premiums that would have been paid if the cost-plus arrangement had not been used.

Retrospective-Rating Arrangements

Under retrospective-rating arrangements the insurance company charges the employer an initial premium that is less than what would be justified by the expected claims for the year. In general this reduction will be between 5 and 10 percent of the premium for a traditional group insurance arrangement. However, if claims plus the insurance company's retention exceed the initial premium, the employer will be called upon to pay an additional amount at the end of the policy year. Because an employer will usually have to pay this additional premium, one advantage of a retrospective-rating arrangement is the employer's ability to use these funds during the year.

This potential additional premium is subject to a maximum amount that is based on some percentage of expected claims. For example, assume that a retrospective-rating arrangement bases the initial premium on the fact that claims will be 93 percent of those actually expected for the year. If claims in fact are below this level, the employer will receive an experience refund. If they exceed 93 percent, the retrospective-rating arrangement will be "triggered," and the employer will have to reimburse the insurance company for any additional claims paid, up to some percentage of those expected, such as 112 percent. Claims in excess of 112 percent are borne by the insurance company. Therefore some of the risk associated with claims fluctuations is passed on to the employer. This will reduce both the insurance company's risk charge and any reserve for claims fluctuations. The amount of these reductions will depend on the actual percentage specified in the contract, above which the insurance company will be responsible for claims. This percentage and the one that triggers the retrospective-rating arrangement are subject to negotiations between the insurance company and the employer. In general the lower the percentage that triggers the retrospective arrangement is, the higher will be the percentage above which the insurance company is fully responsible for claims. In addition, the better cash-flow advantage the employer has, the greater the risk of claims fluctuations will be.

In all other respects a retrospective-rating arrangement is identical to the traditional group insurance contract.

Total Self-Funding from Current Revenue and Self-Administration

The purest form of a self-funded benefit plan is one in which the employer pays benefits from current revenue (rather than from a trust), administers all aspects of the plan, and bears the risk that benefit payments will exceed those expected. In addition to eliminating state premium taxes and improving cash flow, the employer has the potential to reduce its operating expenses to the extent that the plan can be administered at a lower cost than the insurance company's retention (other than premium taxes). A decision to use this kind of self-funding plan is generally considered most desirable when all the following conditions are present:

- predictable claims. Budgeting is an integral part of the operation of any organization, and it is necessary to budget for benefit payments that will have to be paid in the future. This can best be done when a specific type of benefit plan has a claim pattern that is either stable or shows a steady trend. Such a pattern is most likely to occur in those types of benefit plans that have a relatively high frequency of low-severity claims. Although a self-funded plan may still be appropriate when the level of future benefit payments is difficult to predict, the plan will generally be designed to include stop-loss coverage (discussed later in this chapter).
- a noncontributory plan. Several difficulties arise if a self-funded benefit plan is contributory. Some employees may resent paying "their" money to the employer for benefits that are contingent on the firm's future financial ability to pay claims. If claims are denied, employees under a contributory plan are more likely to be bitter toward the employer than they would be if the benefit plan were noncontributory. Finally, ERISA requires that a trust must be established to hold the employees' contributions until the funds are used by the plan. Both the establishment and maintenance of the trust will result in increased administrative costs to the employer.
- a nonunion situation. Self-funding of benefits for union employees may not be feasible if a firm is subject to collective bargaining. Self-funding (at least by the employer) clearly cannot be used if benefits are provided through a negotiated trusteeship. Even when collective bargaining results in benefits being provided through an individual employer plan, unions often insist that benefits be insured in order to guarantee that union

members will actually receive them.   An employer's decision about whether to use self-funding is most likely motivated by the potential to save money.   When unions approve of self-funding, they also frequently insist that some of these savings be passed on to union members through additional or increased benefits.

- the ability to effectively and efficiently handle claims. One reason that many employers do not use totally self-funded and self-administered benefit plans is the difficulty in handling claims as efficiently and effectively as an insurance company or other benefit-plan administrator would handle them. Unless an employer is extremely large, only one person or a few persons will be needed to handle claims. Who in the organization can properly train and supervise these people? Can they be replaced if they should leave? Will anyone have the expertise to properly handle the unusual or complex claims that might occur? Many employers want some insulation from their employees in the handling of claims. If employees are unhappy with claim payments under a self-administered plan, dissatisfaction (and possibly legal actions) will be directed toward the employer rather than toward the insurance company. The employer's inability to handle claims, or its lack of interest in wanting to handle them, does not completely rule out the use of self-funding. As will be discussed later, employers can have claims handled by another party through an administrative-services-only contract.
- the ability to provide other administrative services. In addition to claims, the employer must determine whether the other administrative services normally included in an insured arrangement can be provided in a cost-effective manner. These services are associated with plan design, actuarial calculations, statistical reports, communication with employees, compliance with government regulations, and the preparation of government reports. Many of these costs are relatively fixed, regardless of the size of the employer, and unless the employer can spread them out over a large number of employees, self-administration will not be economically feasible. As with claims administration, an employer can purchase needed services from other sources.

The extent of total self-funding and self-administration differs significantly among the different types of group benefit plans. Plans that provide life insurance or accidental death and dismemberment benefits do not usually lend themselves to self-funding because of infrequent and large claims that are difficult to predict. Only very large employers can expect stable and predictable claims on an annual basis. In addition, federal income tax laws impede the use of self-funding for death benefits, since any payments to beneficiaries in excess of $5,000 are considered taxable income to the beneficiaries. Such a limitation does not exist if the plan is insured.

The most widespread use of self-funding and self-administration occurs in short-term disability income plans, particularly those in which the maximum duration of benefits is limited to 6 months or less. For employers of most any size the number and average length of short-term absences from work are relatively predictable. In addition, the payment of claims is relatively simple, since benefits can be (and usually are) made through the usual payroll system of the employer.

Long-term disability income benefits are occasionally self-funded by large employers. Like death claims long-term disability income claims are difficult to predict for small employers because of their infrequent occurrence and potentially large size. In addition, because small employers receive only a few claims of this type, such claims are economically unjustifiable to self-administer.

The larger the employer is, the more likely it is that its medical expense plan will be self-funded. The major problem with a self-funded medical expense plan is not the prediction of claims frequency but rather the prediction of the average severity of claims. Although infrequent, claims of $300,000 to $500,000 or more do occasionally occur. Most small and medium-size employers are unwilling to assume the risk that they might have to pay such a large claim. Only employers with several thousand employees are large enough to anticipate that such claims will regularly occur and to have the resources that will be necessary to pay any unexpectedly large claims. This does not mean that smaller employers cannot self-fund medical benefits. To avoid the uncertainty of catastrophic claims, these employers often self-fund basic medical expense benefits and insure major medical expense benefits or self-fund their entire coverage but purchase stop-loss protection.

It is not unusual to use self-funding and self-administration in other types of benefit plans, such as those providing coverage for dental care, vision care, prescription drugs, or legal expenses. Initially it may be difficult to predict the extent to which these plans will be utilized. However, once these plans have "matured," the level of claims tends to be fairly stable. In addition, these plans are commonly subject to maximums so that the employer has little or no risk of catastrophic claims. Although larger employers may be able to economically administer these plans themselves, smaller employers commonly purchase administrative services.

Self-Funding with Stop-Loss Coverage and/or ASO Arrangements

Two of the problems associated with self-funding and self-administration are the risk of catastrophic claims and the inability of the employer to provide administrative services in a cost-effective manner. For each of these problems, however, solutions have evolved that still allow an employer to use elements of self-funding. These are stop-loss coverage and administrative-services-only (ASO) contracts. Although an ASO contract and stop-loss coverage can be provided separately, they are commonly written together. In fact, most insurance companies require an employer with stop-loss coverage to have a self-funded plan administered under an ASO arrangement, either by the insurance company or by a third-party administrator.

Until recently stop-loss coverage and ASO contracts were generally provided by insurance companies and were available only to employers with at least several hundred employees. However, these arrangements are increasingly becoming available to small employers, and in many cases the administrative services are now being purchased from third-party administrators who operate independently from insurance companies.

Stop-Loss Coverage

Aggregate stop-loss coverage is one form of protection for employers against an unexpectedly high level of claims. If total claims exceed some specified dollar limit, the insurance company assumes the financial responsibility for those claims that are over the limit, subject to the maximum reimbursement specified in the contract. The limit is usually applied on an annual basis and is expressed as some percentage of expected claims (typically between 115 percent and 135 percent). This arrangement can be thought of as a form of reinsurance and is treated as such by some regulatory officials. It is interesting to note that the employer is responsible for the paying of all claims to employees, including any payments that are received from the insurance company under the stop-loss coverage. In fact, since the insurance company has no responsibility to the employees, no reserve for claims must be established.

Aggregate stop-loss coverage results in (1) an improved cash flow for the employer and (2) a minimization of premium taxes, since they must be paid only on the stop-loss coverage. However, these advantages will be partially (and perhaps totally) offset by the cost of the coverage. In addition, many insurance companies will insist that the employer purchase other insurance coverages or administrative services in order to obtain aggregate stop-loss coverage.

Stop-loss plans may also be written on a "specific" basis, similar to the way an insured plan with a deductible is written. In fact, this arrangement (most commonly used with medical expense plans) is often referred to as a *big-deductible plan* or as *shared funding*. The deductible amount may vary from $1,000 to $250,000 but is most commonly in the range of $10,000 to $20,000. It is usually applied on an annual basis and pertains to each person insured under the contract. In the past stop-loss coverage was written primarily for large employers. More recently this coverage has been written for employers with as few as 25 employees. These plans have particular appeal for small employers who have had better-than-average claims experience but who are too small to qualify for experience rating and the accompanying premium savings.

The deductible specified in the stop-loss coverage is the amount the employer must assume before the stop-loss carrier is responsible for claims. It is different from the deductible that an employee must satisfy under the medical expense plan. For example, employees may be provided with a medical expense plan that has a $200 annual deductible and an 80 percent coinsurance provision. If stop-loss coverage with a $5,000 stop-loss limit has been purchased, an employee will have to assume the first $200 in annual medical expenses, and the plan will then pay 80 percent of any additional expenses until it has paid a total of $5,000. At that time the stop-loss carrier will reimburse the plan for any additional amounts that the plan must pay to the employee. The stop-loss carrier has no responsibility to pay the employer's share of claims under any circumstances, and most insurance companies require that employees be made aware of this fact.

Misunderstandings often arise over two variations in specific stop-loss contracts. Most contracts settle claims on a *paid* basis, which means that only those claims paid during the stop-loss period under a benefit plan are taken into consideration in determining the liability of the stop-loss carrier. Some stop-loss contracts, however, settle claims on an *incurred* basis. In these cases the stop-loss carrier's liability is determined on the basis of the date a loss took place rather than when the benefit plan actually made payment. For example, assume an employee was hospitalized last December, but the claim was not paid until this year. This is an incurred claim for last year, but a paid claim for this year.

A second variation has an impact on an employer's cash flow. For example, assume an employer has a medical expense plan with a $20,000 stop-loss limit and that an employee has a claim of $38,000. If the stop-loss contract is written on a *reimbursement* basis, the employer's plan must pay the $38,000 claim before the plan's administrator can submit an $18,000 claim to the stop-loss carrier. If the stop-loss contract is written on an *advance-funding* basis, the employer's plan does not actually have to pay the employee before seeking reimbursement.

ASO Contracts

Under an administrative-services-only contract the employer purchases specific administrative services from an insurance company or from an independent third-party administrator. These services will usually include the administration of claims, but they may also include a broad array of other services. In effect, the employer has the option to purchase services for those administrative functions that can be handled more cost effectively by another party. Under ASO contracts the administration of claims is performed in much the same way as it is under a minimum-premium plan; that is, the administrator has the authority to pay claims from a bank account that belongs to the employer or from segregated funds in the hands of the administrator. However, the administrator is not responsible for paying claims from its own assets if the employer's account is insufficient.

In addition to listing the services that will be provided, an ASO contract also stipulates the administrator's authority and responsibility, the length of the contract, the provisions for terminating and amending the contract, and the manner in which disputes between the employer and the administrator will be settled. The charges for the services provided under the contract may be stated in one or some combination of the following ways:

- a percentage of the amount of claims paid
- a flat amount per processed claim
- a flat charge per employee
- a flat charge for the employer

Payments for ASO contracts are regarded as fees for services performed, and they are therefore not subject to state premium taxes. However, two similarities to a traditional insurance arrangement may be present. Sometimes the administrator (if it is an insurance company) will agree to provide a conversion contract to employees whose coverage terminates. In addition, the administrator may agree to continue paying any unsettled claims after the contract's termination but only with funds provided by the employer.

Funding Through a 501(c)(9) Trust

Section 501(c)(9) of the Internal Revenue Code provides for the establishment of *voluntary employees' beneficiary associations* (commonly called either *501(c)(9) trusts* or *VEBAs*), which are funding vehicles for the employee benefits that are offered to members. The trusts have been allowed for many years, but until the passage of the 1969 Tax Reform Act, they were primarily used by negotiated trusteeships and association groups. The liberalized tax treatment of the funds accumulated by these trusts resulted in their increased use by employers as a method of self-funding employee benefit plans. However, the Tax Reform Act of 1984 imposed more restrictive provisions on 501(c)(9) trusts, and their use has diminished somewhat, particularly by smaller employers who previously had overfunded their trusts primarily as a method to shelter income from taxation.

Advantages

The use of a 501(c)(9) trust offers the employer some advantages over a benefit plan that is self-funded from current revenue. Contributions can be made to the trust and can be deducted for federal income tax purposes at that time, just as if the trust were an insurance company. Appreciation in the value of the trust assets or investment income earned on the trust assets is also free of taxation. The trust is best suited for an employer who wishes to establish either a fund for claims that have been incurred but not paid or a fund for possible claims fluctuations. If the employer does not use a 501(c)(9) trust in establishing these funds, contributions cannot be deducted until they are paid in the form of benefits to employees. In addition, earnings on the funds will be subject to taxation.

Although the Internal Revenue Code requires that certain fiduciary standards be maintained regarding the investment of the trust assets, the employer does have some latitude and does have the potential for earning a return on the trust assets that is higher than what is earned on the reserves held by insurance companies. A 501(c)(9) trust also lends itself to use by a contributory self-funded plan, since ERISA requires that under a self-funded benefit plan a trust must be established to hold the contributions of employees until they are used to pay benefits.

There is also flexibility regarding contributions to the trust. Although the Internal Revenue Service will not permit a tax deduction for "overfunding" a trust, there is no requirement that the trust must maintain enough assets to pay claims that have been incurred but not yet paid. Consequently an employer can "underfund" the trust in bad times and make up for this underfunding in good times with larger-than-normal contributions. However, any underfunding must be shown as a contingent liability on the employer's balance sheet.

Disadvantages

The use of a 501(c)(9) trust is not without its drawbacks. The cost of establishing and maintaining the trust may be prohibitive, especially for small employers. In addition, the employer must be concerned about the administrative aspects of the plan and the fact that claims might deplete the trust's assets. However, as long as the trust is properly funded, ASO contracts and stop-loss coverage can be purchased.

Requirements for Establishment

In order to qualify under Section 501(c)(9), a trust must meet certain requirements, some of which may hinder its establishment. These requirements include the following:

- Membership in the trust must be objectively restricted to those persons who share a common employment-related bond. Internal Revenue Service regulations interpret this broadly to include active employees and their dependents, surviving dependents, and employees who are retired, laid off, or disabled. Except for plans maintained pursuant to collective-bargaining agreements, benefits must be provided under a classification of employees that the IRS does not find to be discriminatory in favor of highly compensated individuals. It is permissible for life insurance, disability, severance pay, and supplemental unemployment compensation benefits to be based on a uniform percentage of compensation. In addition, the following persons may be excluded in determining whether the discrimination rule has been satisfied: (1) employees who have not completed 3 years of service, (2) employees under age 21, (3) seasonal or less-than-half-time employees, and (4) employees covered by a collective-bargaining agreement if the class of benefits was subject to good-faith bargaining.
- With two exceptions membership in the trust must be voluntary on the part of employees. Members can be required to participate (1) as a result of collective bargaining or (2) when participation is not detrimental to them. In general, participation is not regarded as detrimental if the employee is not required to make any contributions.
- The trust must provide only eligible benefits. The list of eligible coverages is broad enough so that a trust can provide benefits because of death, medical expenses, disability, and unemployment. Retirement benefits, deferred compensation, and group property and liability insurance cannot be provided.
- The sole purpose of the trust must be to provide benefits to its members or their beneficiaries. Trust assets can be used to pay the administrative expenses of the trust, but they cannot revert to the employer. If the trust is terminated, any assets that remain after all existing liabilities have been satisfied must either be used to provide other benefits or be distributed to members of the trust.
- The trust must be controlled by (1) its membership, (2) independent trustees (such as a bank), or (3) trustees or other fiduciaries, at least some of whom are designated by or on behalf of the members. Most 501(c)(9) trusts are controlled by independent trustees that are selected by the employer.

Limitation on Contributions

The contributions to a 501(c)(9) trust (except collectively bargained plans for which Treasury regulations prescribe separate rules) are limited to the sum of (1) the qualified direct cost of the benefits provided for the taxable year and (2) any permissible additions to a reserve (called a qualified asset account). The qualified direct cost of benefits is the amount that would have been deductible for the year if the employer had paid benefits from current revenue.

The permissible additions may be made only for disability, medical, supplemental unemployment, severance pay, and life insurance benefits. In general the amount of the permissible additions includes (1) any sums that are reasonably and actuarially necessary to pay claims that have been incurred but remain unpaid at the close of the tax year and (2) any administration costs with respect to these claims. If medical or life insurance benefits are provided to retirees, deductions are also allowed for funding these benefits on a level basis over the working lives of the covered employees. However, for retirees' medical benefits, current medical costs must be used rather than costs based on projected inflation. In addition, a separate account must be established for postretirement benefits provided to key employees. Contributions to these accounts are treated as annual additions for purposes of applying the limitations that exist for contributions and benefits under qualified retirement plans.

The amount of certain benefits for which deductions will be allowed is limited. Life insurance benefits for retired employees cannot exceed amounts that are tax free under Section 79. Annual disability benefits cannot exceed the lesser of (1) 75 percent of a disabled person's average compensation for the highest 3 years or (2) $90,000. Supplemental unemployment compensation benefits and severance benefits cannot exceed 75 percent of average benefits paid plus administrative costs during any 2 of the immediately preceding 7 years. In determining this limit annual benefits in excess of $45,000 cannot be taken into account.

In general it is required that the amount of any permissible additions be actuarially certified. However, deductible contributions can be made to reserves without such certification as long as certain safe-harbor limits with respect to the size of the reserve are not exceeded. The safe-harbor limits for supplemental unemployment compensation benefits and severance benefits are the same as the amounts previously mentioned. For short-term disability benefits the limit is equal to 17.5 percent of benefit costs (other than insurance premiums for the current year), plus administrative costs for the prior year. For medical benefits the percentage is 35. The Internal Revenue Code provides that the limits for life insurance benefits and long-term disability income benefits will be those prescribed by regulations. However, no regulations have been issued.

Employer deductions cannot exceed the limits as previously described. However, any excess contributions may be deducted in future years to the extent that contributions for those years are below the permissible limits.

There are several potential adverse tax consequences if a 501(c)(9) trust does not meet prescribed standards. If reserves are above permitted levels, additional contributions to the reserves are not deductible and earnings on the excess reserves are subject to tax as unrelated business income. (This effectively negates any possible advantage of using a 501(c)(9) trust to prefund postretirement medical benefits.) In addition, an excise tax is imposed on employers maintaining a trust that provides disqualified benefits. The tax is equal to 100 percent of the disqualified benefits, which include (1) medical and life insurance benefits provided to key employees outside the separate accounts that must be established, (2) discriminatory medical or life insurance benefits for retirees, and (3) any portion of the trust's assets that revert to the employer.

13

Other Group Benefits

In the first chapter employee benefits were divided into five categories:

- legally required social insurance payments
- payments for private insurance and retirement plans
- payments for time not worked
- extra payments to employees
- services to employees

Variations exist among employers, but typically about one-third of the sum spent on employee benefits is devoted to payments for legally required social insurance programs. Another one-third spent on employee benefits is devoted to payments for retirement plans and group insurance. Often overlooked is the significance of all the remaining types of benefits that may be provided to employees, which as a group account for the final one-third of the employee benefit dollars spent by employers. Since the list is extensive, not every possible benefit will be described. Rather, the discussion will be devoted to the following list of more commonly provided "other" benefits:

- vacations
- holidays
- personal time off with pay
- personal time off without pay (family leave)
- supplemental unemployment benefit plans
- educational assistance
- moving-expense reimbursement
- suggestion awards
- service awards
- productivity and safety achievement awards
- holiday bonuses and gifts
- no-additional-cost services
- employee discounts
- dependent-care assistance
- wellness programs
- employee-assistance programs
- financial planning programs for executives
- preretirement-counseling programs
- transportation/free parking
- company cars
- subsidized eating facilities

Some of these benefits, such as holidays and vacations, are provided by most employers; other benefits, such as financial planning, are provided by relatively few employers. Some employers provide many such benefits; others provide few. The reasons one employer may provide a certain array of benefits are many: to satisfy specific needs of its employees, for competitive reasons, or because of traditions within its locality or industry. Collective bargaining, the personal whims of the employer, and state laws may also play a role.

With rare exceptions the costs of providing these benefits are tax deductible to the employer. However, the tax treatment of employees receiving benefits varies and will be described separately for each benefit.

MEANING OF HIGHLY COMPENSATED EMPLOYEE

Several of the benefits discussed in this chapter are subject to nondiscrimination rules. Specifically these benefits are educational assistance, service awards, safety achievement and productivity awards, no-additional-cost services, employee discounts, dependent-care assistance, and employee-assistance programs. In each case there are rules designed to prevent or discourage the benefit plan from discriminating in favor of highly compensated employees.

The consequences of a plan's being discriminatory vary. In some cases no employees can receive benefits on a tax-favored basis; in other cases this penalty applies to highly compensated employees only.

As used in this chapter, a highly compensated employee is one who meets the definition in Sec. 414(q) of the Internal Revenue Code. This definition is also used for the nondiscrimination rules that apply to qualified retirement plans. A highly compensated employee is an employee who at any time during the current year or the preceding year was one the of the following:

- a 5 percent owner of the firm
- an employee who earned more than $96,368 in annual compensation in 1993 from the employer
- an employee who earned more than $64,245 in annual compensation in 1993 from the employer and was in the top 20 percent of the firm's employees in terms of compensation
- an officer of the firm who earned more than $52,820.50. In firms with fewer than 500 employees, no more than the greater of 3 employees or 10 percent of all employees are treated as officers. In firms with 500 or more employees, no more than 50 employees are treated as officers.

All the above dollar figures are subject to annual indexing.

It is interesting to note that this definition of highly compensated employee is not the same as the one used with the nondiscrimination rules for self-insured medical reimbursement plans (chapter 8) or the one used for cafeteria plans (chapter 15).

PAYMENTS FOR TIME NOT WORKED

Vacations

In terms of employer cost the most significant benefit mentioned in this chapter is paid vacations. In 1991 the U.S. Chamber of Commerce estimated that the cost to employers of providing vacations to employees was equal to 5.5 percent of base pay.[1] The number of vacation days provided to employees increased steadily from World War II until the adverse economic times of the late 1970s. During the last few years this trend has leveled off, and few companies have increased the number of vacation days provided.

While the specifics of vacation plans vary widely, most plans are based on length of service, and the number of vacation days given to any particular employee normally increases over time. There is usually a short waiting period (3 to 6 months) during which employees are ineligible for vacations, but for competitive reasons there is often no waiting period for management employees. The following is one employer's benefit schedule for its vacation plan:

Length of Service	Vacation Days
First 6 months	0
After 6 months	1 for each month in the remaining calendar year (max., 10)
1–5 years	10
6–15 years	15
16 years or more	20

Some firms have different schedules for different classes of employees, with higher-paid employees tending to have more vacation time, particularly in the earlier years of service. In contrast to many types of benefits vacation benefits are often given to part-time employees.

In recent years many employers have adopted cafeteria plans in which employees have some choice in designing their own benefit plans. Most companies with cafeteria plans have a basic vacation schedule that is outside the cafeteria plan. However, employees may be given the option of using their benefit dollars to purchase extra vacation days, often subject to approval of their supervisor and usually subject to a maximum additional number of days.

Several major issues must be addressed in properly designing a vacation plan. One is the treatment of unused vacation days. Some employers require that any unused vacation days be forfeited; others allow them to be carried over to the next year, subject to certain limitations. A few businesses compensate employees for unused vacation days. Another issue is the question of when employees can take their vacations. In general, supervisory approval is necessary, and vacations may not be allowed during busy work times. Junior employees may also have to schedule their vacations around those of senior employees so that the number of people away from work at the same time is minimized. Other issues that must be addressed are those of how unused vacation days will be treated upon termination of employment and whether sicknesses and holidays occurring during vacation periods will be treated as vacation days.

The compensation received by employees during periods of vacation is treated the same as compensation for time worked and is taxed accordingly.

Holidays

Employers normally pay employees for certain holidays. At a minimum employees usually receive pay for

- New Year's Day
- Memorial Day
- the Fourth of July
- Labor Day
- Thanksgiving
- Christmas

In addition, most employees receive at least 3 and sometimes as many as 9 or 10 additional holidays. These may include

- Martin Luther King's Birthday
- Washington's Birthday
- Lincoln's Birthday
- Presidents' Day
- Good Friday
- Columbus Day
- the Friday after Thanksgiving
- Veterans Day
- Christmas Eve
- New Year's Eve
- the employee's birthday
- various state holidays

For some institutions, such as banks, holidays are prescribed by law. However, for the vast majority of companies management decides which holidays to give, subject to collective bargaining if applicable.

When a scheduled holiday falls on a Saturday, employees who normally do not work on that day are given the preceding Friday off. When a holiday falls on Sunday, it is normally observed on Monday. Restaurants and retail establishments are increasingly open for business on holidays. When this occurs, employees who work are usually paid at least time and a half and sometimes as much as triple time.

Some companies, realizing that not all employees want to take the same holidays, try to satisfy these needs by adopting holiday plans that include a minimum number of *scheduled holidays* coupled with a specific number of *floating holidays* to be taken at an employee's option. Usually there is no requirement that the days taken actually be holidays, so in effect they become additional vacation days in lieu of holidays.

Like vacation pay, holiday pay is taxed as regular income.

Personal Time Off with Pay

Personal situations that require an employee to be away from work often arise. Consequently many employers allow employees to take time off with pay for certain reasons, the more common of which include the following:

- reserve/National Guard duty. Laws sometimes require that employees be given time off for reserve or National Guard duty, but there is no stipulation that pay continue during this period. However, the majority of employers compensate their employees for the difference between their regular pay and any compensation received for the reserve or National Guard duty.
- voting time. Many states require that employees be given time off to vote, but most of these laws do not require the employee to be compensated for this time. However, the time period is short, usually no more than two hours, and most employers who grant such time off continue regular pay. Since polls are typically open 12 hours or more, it is questionable whether this benefit is necessary in the absence of state law.
- jury duty. Most employers grant (and may be required to grant) time off for jury duty. Since employees are usually compensated for jury duty, some employers pay only the difference between this amount and an employee's regular pay. However, the amount paid for jury duty is small and often just barely covers an employee's extra expenses. Therefore many employers continue regular compensation with no deduction.
- a death in the family. Employers often allow up to 5 days off with pay because of the death of family members. At a minimum this usually includes the death of a parent, child, spouse, or other relative residing in the household. Some employers allow a shorter period of time, such as a day or a half day, to attend funerals of other relatives and sometimes even persons other than relatives.
- sabbatical leaves. Sabbatical leaves are well established as employee benefits at educational institutions. Typically faculty members are permitted an extended leave of a semester or a year after a specified period of service, such as 7 years. During the sabbatical leave the faculty member receives full or partial pay while performing no services for the employer. However, the faculty member is often required to complete a research project or some similar activity as a condition of the sabbatical. Noneducational employers, particularly those having employees with professional degrees, sometimes provide similar benefits to professional employees in order to afford them an opportunity to engage in research or study that is not directly job related.

Some less common reasons that employers may allow time off with pay include the employee's marriage and serving as a witness in a court proceeding. Since other personal reasons for needing time off may occasionally arise, employers may grant two or three days of personal leave that can be taken at an employee's discretion.

Personal Time Off without Pay (Family Leave)

For many years most industrialized countries have had legislation that enables employees to be away from work for extended periods without jeopardizing their jobs. The reasons for such leave vary among countries, as does the extent to which the employer must continue to provide pay and benefits to an employee on leave.

Over the last two decades an increasing number of American employers have voluntarily begun to allow employees to take time off without pay. Reasons for such leave may include active military duty, extended vacations, honeymoons, education, the birth or adoption of a child, and the illness of a family member. Usually such time off has been subject to the approval of the employer. The practice is becoming more and more common as many states and the federal government adopt family-leave legislation.

State Laws

In recent years the legislatures of almost every state have considered family-leave legislation. By early 1993, 28 states had enacted such legislation. As a general rule these laws allow an employee to take an unpaid leave of absence for reasons such as the birth or adoption of a child and the illness of a family member. The length of leave allowed varies considerably among states, but most often it ranges from 3 to 6 months. When the family leave is completed, the employer is required to allow the employee to return to the same or a comparable job.

Almost all family-leave laws apply to public employers, and about half of the laws apply to private employers with more than a minimum number of employees, which is usually in the range of 25 to 100. In all states employers are allowed to limit family leave to employees who have met certain eligibility requirements. While these requirements vary, the most common requirement is at least one year of full-time employment. At a minimum most family-leave laws allow an employee to continue medical expense coverage at his or her own cost. Some laws require all employee benefits to be made available.

Federal Law

In February 1993, President Clinton signed into law the first federal family-leave legislation. The provisions of this legislation, which became effective in August 1993, cover only about 5 percent of the nation's employers but about 50 percent of all employees.

The legislation applies only to employers who have more than 50 employees within a 75-mile radius. Unlike some federal legislation it applies not only to private employers but also to nonprofit organizations and government entities, including Congress.

With some exceptions a worker must be allowed to take up to 12 weeks of unpaid leave in any 12-month period for the birth or adoption of a child; to care for a child, spouse, or parent with a serious health condition; or for the worker's own serious health condition that makes it impossible to perform a job. An employer is allowed to substitute an employee's accrued paid leave for any part of the 12-week period of family leave. Leave can be denied to anyone who has not worked for the employer for at least one year and worked at least 1,250 hours during that period. In addition, an employer can deny leave to a salaried employee within the highest-paid 10 percent of its work force if the leave would create a substantial and grievous injury to the organization's operations.

An employee is required to provide 30 days' notice for foreseeable leaves for birth, adoption, or planned medical treatment. The employer can require an employee to provide a doctor's certification of a serious illness, which is defined as the employee's needing ongoing care and being unable to perform the job or the employee's being needed to care for an ill family member. An employer can also require a second opinion.

The legislation requires that an employee must be given his or her old job or an equivalent job upon returning to work. During the period of leave an employer has no obligation to continue an employee's pay, and the employee is ineligible for unemployment compensation. However, an employer must continue to provide health care benefits during the leave as if the worker was still employed. The employer is allowed to recover the cost of the health care benefits paid during the leave if the employee does not return to work.

Supplemental Unemployment Benefit Plans

Collective-bargaining agreements may require employers to contribute to a supplemental unemployment benefit (SUB) plan that is designed to supplement state unemployment insurance benefits for workers who are unemployed. These plans rarely exist for nonunion employees. Benefits are often payable for at least a year and with regular unemployment benefits may be as high as 95 percent of what the worker was earning while employed.

SUB plans typically require employers to contribute to a SUB fund on the basis of the compensation of currently active employees. Employee contributions may also be required. The fund is usually maintained by trustees selected by the collective bargaining agent, and it is frequently a common fund maintained for several employers. Employer contributions to the fund are income tax deductible, and if the fund is properly designed, earnings on fund assets may also be exempt from income taxation. Benefit payments to employees are fully taxable.

EXTRA PAYMENTS TO EMPLOYEES

Educational Assistance

For several years the Internal Revenue Code has provided favorable tax treatment to the employees who receive benefits from their employers for educational assistance. At the time this book was being revised, Sec. 127 of the Code allows employees to receive annually the first $5,250 of these benefits on a tax-free basis, but this Code section is scheduled to expire for taxable years beginning after June 30, 1992. (However, the date has been extended several times before and will probably be extended again, or the Code section may be made permanent.) In order for benefits to be tax free, the employer's plan cannot discriminate in favor of officers, shareholders, highly compensated employees, or their dependents. In addition, no more than 5 percent of the benefits may be paid out to shareholders or owners (or their dependents) who are more-than-5-percent owners of the firm.

Eligible benefits include tuition, fees, and books. The costs of supplies and equipment are also included as long as they are not retained after completion of the course. Meals, lodging, and transportation associated with educational expenses cannot be received tax free. Courses involving sports, games, or hobbies are also ineligible for favorable tax treatment. Although an employer's plan *could* pay for any of these types of courses, an employee would be taxed on the value of the employer's contribution to their cost.

If Congress fails to extend the favorable tax treatment for a broadly defined educational assistance program, employees will still be allowed to deduct any educational expenses that are incurred (1) to maintain or improve a skill required in employment or (2) to meet the express requirements of the employer as a condition for retaining employment. To the extent that these benefits are paid for by the employer, they will be treated as taxable compensation. However, the corresponding deduction effectively makes them a tax-free benefit. Other types of educational expenses, such as costs incurred to qualify the employee for a new trade or business, are not deductible.

Moving-Expense Reimbursement

In order to attract new employees and to encourage current employees to move to suit the needs of the employer, many businesses provide reimbursement for moving expenses. Such reimbursement is includible in the income of an employee, but the employee is allowed certain offsetting income tax deductions if specified rules are satisfied. To receive the deductions the employee must have moved because of a change in job location. In addition, the employee must satisfy both a distance test and a time test. The distance test requires that the employee's new workplace be at least 35 miles farther from the employee's old residence than the employee's old workplace (or old residence if the employee was previously unemployed). The time test requires the employee to work full time in the general location of the new residence for at least 39 weeks during the 12 months following the move. An employee may take the applicable deductions in anticipation of satisfying the time test, but additional taxes will be payable if the time test is not ultimately met.

If all the preceding rules are satisfied, an employee may deduct the following expenses:

- transportation expenses in moving household goods and personal effects
- travel, meals, and lodging expenses in moving to the new residence
- premove travel, meals, and lodging expenses in looking for a new residence
- temporary living expenses in the new location or area during any consecutive 30 days after getting the new job
- certain costs of selling or exchanging the old residence and buying the new residence or, if renting, certain costs of settling an unexpired lease and obtaining a new lease

The first two items may be deducted in full. The third and fourth items are subject to a maximum deduction of $1,500 in the aggregate, and the last item is subject to a maximum deduction of $3,000 that is reduced by any amount deducted under the previously mentioned $1,500 deduction for travel, meals, and lodging. If any employer reimbursement exceeds these amounts, no offsetting deduction is allowed. It should also be pointed out that an employee is entitled to all applicable deductions even if there is no employer reimbursement. If reimbursement is less than actual deductible expenses, the unreimbursed amount is deductible, but the total of the reimbursement and the deduction cannot exceed the limits discussed above.

Moving expenses are classified as a miscellaneous deductible expense but are not subject to the 2-percent-of-adjusted-gross-income limitation. Employees who already itemize their deductions will get an additional deduction. However, employees who would otherwise take the standard deduction cannot take the standard deduction and also deduct their full moving expenses. Therefore employers will need to provide some employees with additional compensation to fully cover their moving costs.

Suggestion Awards

Some employers, particularly those in manufacturing industries, give awards to employees who make suggestions that, if implemented, will improve the operating efficiency of the firm. The awards are often a percentage of the firm's estimated savings over some specified future period of time but may be subject to a maximum dollar amount. If a suggestion plan is properly administered, the benefits of the plan may far exceed its costs while at the same time increasing the motivation and involvement of employees.

Suggestion awards are included in an employee's gross income for tax purposes.

Service Awards

Many employers provide awards to employees for length of service. These awards are often nominal for short periods of service (5 or 10 years) and may consist of such items as key chains, flowers, or pens. Awards typically increase in value for longer periods of service, and employees may actually be given some choice in the award received.

If the value of a service award is *de minimis,* it is not included in an employee's income. To be *de minimis* the value of the benefit must be so minimal that accounting for the cost of the benefit would be unreasonable or administratively impractical. Service awards of higher value may also be excludible from an employee's income if they are considered *qualified plan awards.* However, the total amount excludible from an employee's income for qualified plan awards (which also include awards for safety) cannot exceed $1,600 per year. Qualified plan awards must be provided under a permanent written program that does not discriminate in favor of officers, shareholders, or highly compensated employees. In addition, the average annual cost of all awards under the plan cannot exceed $400.

Productivity and Safety Achievement Awards

Some employers provide awards for productivity and safety achievement. Productivity awards are fully treated as compensation. However, while awards for safety achievement given to professional, administrative, managerial, or clerical employees are fully taxable, such awards are treated as qualified plan awards for other employees and are included in the $1,600 figure mentioned previously under service awards.

Holiday Bonuses and Gifts

Many employers give gifts or bonuses to employees, particularly at Christmastime. Since the value of such gifts is typically small, some employees tend to resent gifts of money. Therefore gifts such as liquor or a ham are often given.

As with service awards, a holiday gift does not result in taxation for an employer as long as the market value of the gift is small.

SERVICES TO EMPLOYEES

No-Additional-Cost Services

Employers in many service industries provide their employees with free or discounted services. Examples include telephone service to employees of phone companies and airline tickets to employees of airlines. As long as the following rules are satisfied, the cost of these services is not includible in an employee's gross income for tax purposes:

- The services cannot be provided on a basis that discriminates in favor of highly compensated employees.
- The employer must not incur any significant additional cost or lost revenue in providing the services. For example, giving a standby ticket to an airline employee if there were unsold seats on a flight would satisfy this requirement, but giving an airline ticket to an employee when potential paying customers were denied seats would not.
- The services must be those that are provided in the employer's line of business in which the employee actually works. Therefore if a business owns both an airline and a chain of hotels, an employee of the hotels can be given a room as a tax-free benefit but not an airline ticket. However, unrelated employers in the same line of business, such as airlines, may enter into reciprocal arrangements under which employees of any party to the arrangement may obtain services from the other parties.

Employee Discounts

Just as no-additional-cost services are an important employee benefit in certain service industries, discounts on the merchandise sold by manufacturers and retailers are an important benefit to employees in these industries. Discounts may also be provided on services sold by other types of business, such as the commission charged by a brokerage house or insurance company.

Rules similar to those discussed for no-additional-cost services apply to discounts. Employees have no taxable income as long as the discounts are made available on a nondiscriminatory basis and are provided on goods or services ordinarily sold to nonemployees in the employer's line of business in which the employee works. However, there are also some additional rules. Discounts received on real estate or on personal property normally held as an investment (for example, gold coins or securities) are not received tax free. In addition, there is a limit on the size of a discount that can be received tax free. For merchandise the discount cannot exceed the gross profit percentage of the price at which the merchandise is offered for sale to customers. For example, if an employer had a gross profit margin of 40 percent on a particular product and an employee purchased the merchandise at a 50 percent discount, the extra 10 percent would be taxable income to the employee. In the case of services, including insurance policies, the tax-free discount cannot exceed 20 percent of the price at which the service is offered to nonemployee customers in the normal course of the employer's business. The type of service that cannot be received tax free involves loans given to employees by financial institutions at a discounted rate of interest.

Dependent-Care Assistance

As the number of families headed by two wage earners or by a single parent has increased, so has the need for child-care facilities. As a result child-care assistance has become a popular benefit offered by a growing number of employers, particularly those in the service industries. Some firms also provide benefits for the care of other dependents, such as parents. The assistance may be in the form of employer-provided day-care centers or payments to employees.

Under the Internal Revenue Code dependent care is a tax-free benefit to employees up to statutory limits as long as certain requirements are met. The amount of benefits that can be received tax free is limited to $5,000 for single parents and married persons who file jointly and to $2,500 for married persons who file separately. The benefits must be for care to a qualifying individual—a child under age 13 for whom the employee is allowed a dependency deduction on his or her income tax return and a taxpayer's spouse or other dependent who is mentally or physically incapable of caring for himself or herself. Although benefits must generally be for dependent care only, educational expenses at the kindergarten or preschool level can also be paid.

Dependent-care benefits are subject to a series of rules. If the rules are not met, highly compensated employees are taxed on the amount of benefits received. However, the benefits for other employees still retain their tax-free status. The rules are as follow:

- Eligibility, contributions, and benefits under the plan cannot discriminate in favor of highly compensated employees or their dependents.
- No more than 25 percent of the benefits may be provided to the class composed of persons who own more than a 5 percent interest in the firm.
- Reasonable notification of the availability of benefits and the terms of the plan must be provided to eligible employees.

- By January 31 of the following year each employee must receive an annual statement that indicates the amounts paid or expenses incurred by the employer to provide benefits.
- The average benefit provided to nonhighly compensated employees must be at least 55 percent of the average benefit provided to highly compensated employees.

In meeting the 55 percent benefit test, an employer can exclude employees earning under $25,000 if benefits are provided through a salary reduction agreement. For both the 55 percent benefit test and nondiscrimination rule for eligibility, an employer can exclude employees who (1) are under age 21, (2) have not completed 1 year of service, or (3) are covered under a collective bargaining unit that has bargained over dependent-care benefits.

Even if an employer does not provide assistance for dependent care, other tax-saving options may be available to employees. Under the Code a tax credit is available so that employees can deduct a portion of unreimbursed expenses. In addition, the employer may have the opportunity to make before-tax contributions to a cafeteria plan that includes dependent care as an option.

Wellness Programs

Traditional benefit programs have been designed to provide benefits (1) to employees for their medical expenses and disabilities or (2) to their dependents if the employee should die prematurely. In the last few years there has been an increasing trend among employers, particularly large corporations, to initiate programs that are designed to promote the well-being of employees (and possibly their dependents). Some of these programs have been aimed at the discovery and treatment of medical conditions before they become severe and result in large medical expenses, disabilities, or death. Other programs have focused on changing the life-styles of employees in order to eliminate the possible causes of future medical problems. Recent studies have shown that the costs of establishing and maintaining many of these programs are more than offset by the lower amounts paid for medical expense, disability, and death benefits. In addition, if long-term disabilities and premature deaths can be eliminated, the expenses associated with training new employees can be minimized. Many firms also feel these programs increase productivity by improving the employees' sense of well-being, their work attitudes, and their family relationships.

Medical Screening Programs

The use of a medical screening program to discover existing medical conditions is not new, but it has often covered the costs (frequently up to some dollar limit) of routine physical examinations only for selected groups of management employees. Although this benefit may be highly valued by these employees, and its use as an executive benefit has been increasing somewhat, there are doubts—even among the medical profession—as to its cost effectiveness, particularly when it is provided on an annual basis. Certain medical conditions will undoubtedly be discovered during a complete physical, but most of them could also be diagnosed by less-frequent and less-costly forms of medical examinations.

In recent years there has been a significant increase in the number of employers that sponsor periodic medical screening programs. These screenings detect specific medical problems, such as hypertension (high blood pressure), high cholesterol levels, breast cancer, and colon-rectal cancer. Generally they are conducted at the employment site during the regular working hours of the employees. Sometimes a screening will be conducted by a physician, but it is usually performed by lower-paid medical professionals. In addition, screenings can sometimes be obtained at little or no cost through such organizations as the American Red Cross, the American Heart Association, or the American Cancer Association.

Life-style Management Programs

Life-style management programs are primarily designed to encourage employees and often their dependents to modify their behavior so that they will lead healthier lives. Most of these programs strive to discover and eliminate conditions that increase the likelihood of cardiovascular problems (the source of a significant percentage of medical expenses and premature deaths). Some of these conditions (such as obesity and smoking) are obvious, but medical screening can also detect less obvious conditions like hypertension, high cholesterol levels, and the degree of an employee's physical fitness. The types of programs often instituted to promote cardiovascular health include

- smoking-cessation programs
- fitness programs. These may consist of formal exercise programs or only exercise facilities (such as swimming pools, exercise rooms, or jogging tracks). Some employee benefit consultants question whether facilities for competitive sports (such as racquetball courts) can be cost justified because their availability is limited, and they are often a source of injuries.
- weight-reduction programs
- nutrition programs. These are often established in conjunction with weight-reduction programs, but they can also teach methods of cholesterol reduction even if there is no weight problem.
- stress-management programs

These programs may be available to any employees who express an interest in them, or they may be limited only to those employees who have been evaluated and found to be in a high-risk category for cardiovascular disease. This evaluation may consist of questionnaires regarding health history, blood pressure reading, blood chemistry analyses, and fitness tests. Generally these evaluations and meetings to describe the programs and their value are conducted during regular working hours. However, the programs themselves are usually conducted during nonworking hours, possibly at lunchtime or just after work.

Many wellness programs are designed to include employees, their spouses, and sometimes other family members. In many instances it will not be possible to change an employee's life-style unless the life-style of his or her entire family also changes. For example, it is not very probable that an employee will stop smoking if his or her spouse also smokes and is making no attempt to stop. Similarly a weight-reduction or nutrition program will probably be more effective if all family members alter their eating habits.

The employer may either conduct these wellness activities on the premises or use the resources of other organizations. For example, overweight employees might be sent to Weight Watchers, employees with alcohol problems might be encouraged to attend Alcoholics Anonymous, and employees with back problems might be enrolled in programs at a local YMCA.

Some employers have also instituted programs that seek to minimize back problems—the reason for a large percentage of employee absenteeism and disability claims. These programs are generally intended for employees who have a history of back trouble, and they consist of exercises as well as education in how to modify or avoid activities that can aggravate existing back conditions.

More recently many employers have become concerned with the spread of AIDS and its effect on the cost of benefit plans. As a result they have instituted educational programs aimed at encouraging employees to avoid those activities that may result in the transmission of AIDS.

Employers in increasing numbers are subscribing to wellness newsletters and distributing these to employees. To encourage wellness for the entire family, these newsletters are often mailed to employees' homes.

Taxation of Benefits

Medical screening programs are treated as medical expenses for tax purposes. Therefore employees have no taxable income as a result of participating in these programs. Unless the cost of providing life-style management programs is *de minimis,* participation will probably result in taxation to employees. The costs of programs that promote general health, such as smoking cessation or weight control, are not considered medical expenses. While the cost of providing these programs to employees is deductible by the employer, an employee will incur taxable income unless the purpose of the program is to alleviate a specific medical problem. However, there is one exception to this general rule. Employees incur no taxable income as a result of being provided with or using athletic facilities that are located on the employer's premises.

Employee-Assistance Programs

As the trend toward fostering wellness in the workplace continues, an increasing number of employers are establishing employee-assistance programs. These programs are designed to help employees with certain personal problems through a plan that provides

- treatment for alcohol or drug abuse
- counseling for mental problems and stress
- counseling for family and marital problems
- financial, legal, and tax advice
- referrals for child care or elder care
- crisis intervention

Numerous studies have shown that proper treatment of these problems is very cost effective and leads to reduced sick days, hospital costs, disability, and absenteeism. It is also argued that employee morale and productivity are increased as a result of the concern shown for employees' personal problems.

Traditionally employee-assistance programs have used job performance as the basis for employer concern. Essentially an employee is told that his or her work is substandard and asked if a problem exists that he or she would like to discuss with someone. If the employee says yes, referral is made to an appropriate counselor or agency. No attempt is made by the employee's supervisor to diagnose the specific problem. Newer employee-assistance programs go beyond this approach by allowing employees who have problems to go directly to the program and seek help. Dependents can usually use the employee-assistance program and often can seek help without the employee's knowledge.

Another recent trend in employee-assistance programs is to coordinate them more closely with the employer's medical expense plan. For example, several employee-assistance programs act as the gatekeeper for mental health and substance abuse services. An employee must go through the employee-assistance program before benefits can be received under his or her medical expense coverage. The objective of this approach is to establish a course of treatment that will have maximum effectiveness for the costs incurred.

Access to an employee-assistance program is through a counselor who may be a company employee, but most often an employer establishes the plan through a professional organization that specializes in such programs. Information provided to the counselor by the employee is kept confidential. Many problems can be solved by discussion between the counselor and the employee, and most plans have 24-hour counseling available, through either a telephone hotline or on-duty personnel. If the counselor cannot solve an employee's problem, it is the counselor's responsibility to make a preliminary determination about the type of professional help the employee should receive. In many cases this treatment can be provided under existing medical expense or legal expense plans or through community agencies. The costs of other types of treatment are usually paid totally or in part by the employer. As long as the treatment is for the purpose of alleviating medical conditions, including mental illness, an employee has no taxable income. If the treatment is for a nonmedical condition, the employee will have taxable income as the result of employer payments.

Financial Planning Programs for Executives

Employers are increasingly providing financial planning as a benefit to employees. Traditionally this benefit was limited to a small number of top executives. However, many firms are now expanding their programs to also include members of middle management. In addition, financial planning education and advice are now offered to many employees as part of a broader preretirement-counseling program. Any program in overall financial planning must take into consideration the benefits that are provided or that are potentially available under group insurance plans, under social insurance programs, and through the individual efforts of employees.

The concept of providing financial planning for a limited number of top executives has been widely practiced for many years, particularly in large corporations.   However, within the last few years a significant number of corporations have expanded these programs to include middle management employees in the $50,000 to $100,000 annual salary range.   Businesses have deemed this financial planning benefit as necessary for top executives, who have limited time for their own financial affairs, so that they can be free to devote their full talents to important business decisions. A company may also find it easier to attract and retain executives who look upon the financial planning program as a way to make existing compensation more valuable (for example, by providing a larger spendable income through tax planning or a greater accumulation of wealth through investment planning).

Although group meetings are sometimes used (for example, to explain certain types of investments or changes in the tax laws), most financial planning programs provide for individual counseling of employees to suit their own particular circumstances and needs.

Types of Planning

Financial planning is composed of many separate but interrelated segments:

- compensation planning, including the explanation of employee benefits and an analysis of any available compensation options
- preparation of tax returns
- estate planning, including the preparation of wills and planning to both minimize estate taxes and maintain proper estate liquidity
- investment planning, including both investment advice and investment management
- insurance planning, including information on how to meet life insurance, medical expense, disability, and property and liability needs

A financial planning program may be designed to provide either selected services from the list above or a comprehensive array of services. Comprehensive financial planning can be thought of as a series of interrelated and continuing activities that begin with the collection and analysis of personal and financial information, including the risk attitudes of an employee. This information is used (1) to establish the priorities and time horizons for attaining personal objectives and (2) to develop the financial plan that will meet these objectives. Once the plan is formulated, the next critical step is the actual implementation of the plan. A proper financial planning program should also include a process for measuring the performance of any plan so that, if unacceptable, either the plan can be changed or the objectives of the employee revised.

Sources of Financial Planning

A few firms provide financial planning services using the organization's own employees. Most firms purchase the services either from outside specialists (such as lawyers, accountants, insurance agents, or stockbrokers) or from companies that do comprehensive financial planning.

Significant differences exist among financial planning firms. Some operate solely on a fee basis and give only advice and counseling, in which case it is the employee's responsibility to have his or her own attorney, insurance agent, or other financial professional implement any decisions. These financial planning firms often work closely with the other professionals in handling the employee's affairs. The cost of using a fee-only financial planning firm varies, depending upon what services it provides, but initial fees of $5,000 per employee and annual charges of $1,000 to $2,000 are not uncommon.

Other financial planning firms operate on a product-oriented basis and sell products (usually insurance or investments) in addition to other financial planning services. The fact that these firms receive commissions from the products they sell may eliminate or reduce any fees paid by the employer. Unfortunately the insurance or investment advice of these firms may be slanted in favor of the products they sell. Therefore employers must make sure that the advice of outside specialists will be unbiased and will be presented in a professional manner.

Taxation

Fees paid for financial planning are tax deductible by the employer as long as the total compensation paid to an employee is reasonable. The amount of any fees paid to a financial planning firm or other professional in behalf of an individual employee becomes taxable income to the employee. However, an employee may be allowed an offsetting income tax deduction for certain services relating to tax matters and investment advice. Services provided to executives on an individual basis by the employer also result in taxable income.

Preretirement-Counseling Programs

Businesses, aware of the pitfalls that can await unprepared retired employees, have increasingly begun to offer preretirement counseling. It has been estimated that this benefit is offered by approximately 75 percent of companies with 20,000 or more employees. For companies with under 1,000 employees, the figure is closer to 15 or 20 percent. Most of these companies have made this benefit available to all employees over a specific age (such as 50 or 55), but an increasing number of organizations allow employees of any age to participate. Preretirement-counseling programs differ from financial planning programs for executives in that there is very little individual counseling. Rather, employees meet in groups to listen to media presentations and speakers, and they are given the opportunity to ask questions and discuss their concerns. This counseling may take place during nonwork hours, but there is an increasing trend to have it provided during work hours, often in a concentrated one- or two-day period. Most companies encourage spouses to participate. Often one program is developed for all employees, although some organizations vary their programs for different classifications of employees (such as management employees and blue-collar workers).

When these programs are successful, the fears that many employees have about retirement can be alleviated. They will learn that with proper planning retirement can be not only financially possible but also a meaningful period in their lives.

Financial Planning

Some preretirement-counseling programs devote at least half their time to the financial aspects of retirement. Because proper financial planning for retirement must begin many years prior to actual retirement, the amount of time devoted to this subject will be greatest in those programs that encourage employees to begin participation at younger ages.

Some financial planning meetings help employees identify and determine what their financial needs will be after retirement and what resources will be available to meet those needs from the company's benefit plans and from social security. If retirement needs will not be met by these sources, employees are informed about how their individual efforts can supplement retirement income through savings or investments. They are also told about the specific advantages and risks associated with each method of saving or investment. Such preretirement financial planning is conducted on a group basis, the programs are unlikely to provide investment advice on an individual basis or through an investment management service, as described in the previous section on financial planning programs for executives. However, some employers do provide employees with financial planning reports that are prepared through a computerized financial planning system. These reports, which may vary in length from 20 to 60 pages, are generated from the data on a questionnaire completed by the employee. They may offer advice on such topics as the additional amount of money that should be saved for retirement or compare the cost of working with the cost of retiring.

Many employers now make computer software available to employees so that an employee can enter basic personal and financial data for varying scenarios related to retirement, education funding, and the like. The major advantage of these computer programs is that an employee can quickly evaluate alternative assumptions about factors such as retirement dates and savings rates. One potential drawback to the use of computer programs is the lack of employee understanding about the assumptions and reasoning that lie behind the input into the program and about the output that results. Therefore it is important that computer programs be accompanied by proper training in their purpose, use, and interpretation.

Other Aspects of Preretirement Counseling

Preretirement counseling focuses on other aspects of retirement besides financial needs. The following are some of the questions that must also be faced by most retired workers and that are often addressed in preretirement-counseling programs:

- living arrangements. What are the pros and cons of selling a house and moving into an apartment or condominium? Is relocation in the Sunbelt away from family members and friends advisable?
- health. Can changes in life-style lead to healthier retirement years?
- free time. How can the time that was previously devoted to work be used? What opportunities are available for volunteer work or part-time employment? What leisure activities or community activities can be adopted that will continue into retirement? (Studies have shown that

alcoholism, divorce, and suicide tend to increase among the retired. Much of this increase has been attributed to the lack of activities to fill free time and to the problems encountered by husbands and wives who are constantly together for the first time in their lives.)

Sources of Preretirement Counseling

An organization may establish and maintain its own program of preretirement counseling. However, many organizations (such as benefit-counseling firms and the American Association of Retired Persons) have developed packaged programs that are sold to other organizations. These programs typically consist of media presentations and information regarding the types of speakers that should be used in counseling sessions. Generally these packaged programs are flexible enough to be used with almost any type of employee group. Most firms actually conduct preretirement-counseling programs with a combination of their own employees and outside speakers or organizations. It is becoming common to see the use of an organization's own retirees in the counseling process.

Taxation

As long as no specific services are provided to employees on an individual basis, the employees do not have taxable income to report as a result of participating in preretirement counseling programs.

Transportation/Free Parking

Some employers have long provided transportation benefits to employees as a fringe benefit. These benefits have been in the form of various types of reimbursement for commuting expenses, the use of company-owned vehicles for vanpooling, and free parking. However, except for free parking, employees have usually had taxable income as a result of these benefits. In order to increase the use of public transportation and decrease the reliance on the use of private passenger automobiles, the Comprehensive National Energy Policy Act of 1992 changed the tax rules governing transportation benefits. As a result of the act, beginning in 1993 the Internal Revenue Code provides favorable taxation to transportation benefits that meet the definition of a *qualified transportation fringe,* which includes the following:

- transportation in a commuter highway vehicle if such transportation is in connection with travel between the employee's residence and place of employment. The commuter vehicle must have a capacity of at least six adults other than the driver. In addition, at least 80 percent of the mileage use of the vehicle must reasonably be expected to be for transporting employees to and from work and occur when at least one-half of the seating capacity of the vehicle is filled. Traditional vanpools, in which one employee usually has possession of an employer-provided vehicle to drive other employees to work, come under this definition as long as these criteria are satisfied.

- transit passes. These include any pass, token, fare card, voucher, or similar item entitling a person to transportation as long as such transportation is on a mass transit facility or in a commuter highway vehicle as previously described.
- qualified parking. This includes parking provided on or near the business premises of the employer or near a location from which the employee commutes to work by using a mass transit facility or a commuter highway vehicle. Qualified parking does not include any parking on or near a premises used by the employee for residential purposes.

As long as a qualified transportation fringe is provided in addition to (and not in lieu of) any compensation otherwise payable to an employee, the value of the benefit is excluded from gross compensation up to the following amounts, which are subject to cost-of-living adjustments after 1993:

- $60 per month in the aggregate for any transit passes and transportation in a commuter highway vehicle
- $155 per month for qualified parking

Amounts in excess of the above and the value of employer transportation benefits that do not meet the definition of a qualified transportation fringe are fully taxable to employees.

Two additional points should be made about qualified benefits. First, they can be provided on a discriminatory basis. Second, the employer can either provide the benefits directly or give a cash reimbursement to the employee with one exception: cash reimbursement for a transit pass is not acceptable if such a pass is available for direct distribution by the employer to the employee.

Company Cars

Employers often provide employees with company cars (or other types of vehicles). In addition to using a vehicle for business purposes, an employee may also be allowed to use the car for commuting to and from work and for other personal purposes. However, an employee who drives a company car for personal use must include the value of this use in his or her taxable income.

The method for valuing the use of a car is determined by the employer, and several choices are available. The most common method for valuing the car is for the employer to report an annual cost that is a percentage of the car's annual lease value. The annual lease value is determined by a table prepared by the IRS and is based on a car's fair market value unless an employer can clearly justify a lower value. Under this table a car with a fair market value of $20,000 to $20,999 has an annual lease value of $5,600. This figure is then multiplied by the ratio of personal-use miles to total miles. For example, if 20 percent of the miles driven are personal miles, the employer must report $1,120 of income for the employee. Additional income must also be reported if the employer pays for gas.

A second alternative is for the employer to annually report the entire lease value of the car as taxable income. If the employer uses this alternative, the employee can claim an income tax deduction for any business use of the vehicle if the employee itemizes his or her deduction. However, this deduction is subject to the 2 percent floor requirement for miscellaneous deductions. This alternative is less favorable to the employee but administratively less burdensome to the employer.

A third alternative is to report a value that is based solely on the employee's use of the vehicle. Under IRS regulations a flat mileage rate may be used for each personal mile driven. This rate, which is adjusted annually, was $0.28 in 1992 if gas was paid for by the employer and $0.225 if gas was provided by the employee. This alternative is available only if a car's fair market value does not exceed a specified value ($13,400 for 1992) and one of the following criteria is satisfied: (1) more than 50 percent of the car's use is for business, (2) the car is used each day in an employer-sponsored commuting pool, or (3) the car is driven at least 10,000 miles per year and is used primarily by employees.

The final alternative is available if the employer has a written policy that the employee must commute in the vehicle and cannot use the vehicle for other than minimal personal use. In this case the value of the car's use is $1.50 times the number of one-way commutes or $3.00 times the number of round-trip commutes.

Subsidized Eating Facilities

Employers often provide fully or partially subsidized eating facilities for employees. While lunch is the most commonly served meal, breakfast and dinner may also be provided. Such facilities provide a place for employees to discuss common issues and may minimize the chance that employees will take prolonged lunch periods at off-site restaurants. The popularity of these facilities will tend to vary with the price of meals, the convenience of alternative places to eat, and the quality of the food served.

The value of meals served to employees may or may not result in taxable income. If the meals are provided without charge, they are tax free as long as they are (1) provided on the business premises and (2) furnished for the convenience of the employer. In general, meals are considered to be furnished for the employer's convenience if there are inadequate facilities in the area for employees to obtain meals within a reasonable period of time.

The situation is different when a charge is made for meals. If the employees have the option of purchasing the meals, employees who do purchase them will have taxable income to the extent of any subsidy in excess of the employer's cost. However, if a periodic deduction for meals is made from an employee's paycheck regardless of whether the employee eats the meals, the amount of this deduction will be excludible from income only if the meals are furnished for the convenience of the employer.

NOTE

1. United States Chamber of Commerce, *Employee Benefits 1991.* (Washington: Chamber of Commerce, 1991), 6.

14

Group Benefit Plan Design

If either a single type of group insurance plan or an overall employee benefit plan is to be properly designed and managed, many questions must be asked. For example, should the plan reflect the wants of employees or the needs of employees as perceived by the employer? Should it have a probationary period for eligibility? Under what circumstances should the plan be self-insured? These questions are only subparts of five much broader issues:

- What are the employer's objectives?
- What types of benefits should be provided in the plan?
- What provisions for controlling costs should be contained in the plan?
- How should the plan be communicated to employees?
- How should the plan be funded?

The last question was discussed in chapter 12 and will not be discussed further. The remaining questions have been touched upon throughout this book, but a more detailed discussion will follow.

Unfortunately for those who like precise answers, plan design and management is an art rather than a science. However, decisions must be made. In some cases the advantages and disadvantages of the various answers to these five questions must be weighed; in other cases compromises must be made when the answers to two or more questions conflict.

Too often the proper design of a group benefit plan is viewed as a one-time decision rather than as an evolving process. However, benefit plans that were appropriate for yesterday's work force may not meet the needs of tomorrow's work force. As times and organizations change, employers' answers to the questions raised in this chapter may also have to change. For this reason these issues must frequently be restudied to determine whether a group benefit plan is continuing to meet its desired purpose.

WHAT ARE THE EMPLOYER'S OBJECTIVES?

No benefit plan is properly designed unless it meets the employer's objectives. Unfortunately these objectives may be unclear or nonexistent, particularly in small firms. However, most large corporations have (and all firms should have) specific written objectives that have been approved by the board of directors (or by the owners of the firm). These objectives will vary for each individual organization, depending on such factors as size, location, industry, the results of collective bargaining, and the philosophy of the employer. Without such objectives it is difficult for the agent, broker, benefit consultant, or third-party administrator to make recommendations or for the benefit specialist within a firm to make decisions.

Objectives for benefit plans can be general and part of a firm's overall compensation objective (that is, cash and fringe benefits in the aggregate). This may be done to achieve a compensation package that is competitive within the firm's geographic area or industry. Such an "average" objective usually means that the firm wants both its wages and salaries and its fringe benefits to be similar to what the competition is offering its employees. There is usually some, but not much, room for creativity in the design of a group benefit plan, unless the plans of the competition are quite diverse.

Some firms have separate objectives for cash compensation and employee benefits. For example, a growing firm may want its cash compensation to be competitive, but it may want its overall employee benefit plan to be above average in order to attract new employees. A difficulty with this type of objective for the plan designer is determining whether the firm wants all aspects of the employee benefit plan to be better than average, or whether it would be willing to accept, for example, an average program of group insurance benefits but a better-than-average pension plan and more vacation time for its employees. It should be noted that most objectives, even when they are much more detailed, tend to apply to employee benefits in the aggregate rather than to specific types of benefits.

It has become increasingly common for firms, particularly large ones, to maintain a lengthy and often detailed list of objectives for their employee benefit programs. The following are the objectives of one such firm:

- to establish and maintain an employee benefit program that is based primarily on the employees' needs for leisure time and protection against the risks of old age, loss of health, and loss of life
- to establish and maintain an employee benefit program that complements the efforts of employees in their own behalf
- to evaluate the employee benefit plan annually for its effect on employee morale and productivity, giving consideration to turnover, unfilled positions, attendance, employee complaints, and employee opinions
- to compare the employee benefit plan annually with that of other leading companies in the same field and to maintain a benefit plan with an overall level of benefits (based on cost per employee) that falls within the second quintile of these companies
- to maintain a level of benefits for nonunion employees that represents the same level of expenditures per employee as for union employees
- to determine annually the cost of new, changed, and existing programs as a percentage of salaries and wages; and to maintain this percentage as much as possible
- to self-fund benefits to the extent that long-run cost savings can be expected for the firm and catastrophic losses can be avoided
- to coordinate all benefits with social insurance programs to which the company makes payments
- to provide benefits on a noncontributory basis, except benefits for dependent coverage, for which employees should pay a portion of the cost
- to maintain continual communications with all employees concerning benefit programs

Most lists of objectives contain few, if any, specific details regarding what provisions or what types of benefits should be contained in an employee benefit plan. Rather, they establish guidelines—instead of specific performance goals—within which management must operate. For example, the objectives listed above indicate that this firm wants a plan that is understood and appreciated by employees and that is designed with employee opinion in mind. No mention, however, is made of how this is to be done. As will be seen later in this chapter, there may be alternative ways for this firm to achieve its objectives. Similarly the objectives establish guidelines for the cost of providing benefits. Although the firm wants to have a better-than-average plan, it does not want to be a leader. There is a very specific objective about what the relationship between the cost of benefits for union and nonunion employees should be. However, nothing is mentioned to indicate that the benefits for the two groups must also be identical. If the two groups have different needs, different types and levels of benefits may be desirable.

One additional point about employer objectives should be made. Often the primary (and possibly the only) objective of a firm is to establish an overall employee benefit plan that channels as large a portion of the benefits as possible to the owner or owners. Although this is a poor objective for an overall plan, it is a reality that must be recognized, most commonly in small firms or in firms that have few owners. Large, publicly held corporations sometimes wish to provide better benefits for their executives than for other employees. However, these extra benefits are likely to be provided under separate executive compensation plans, rather than under the benefit plan that applies to all employees.

WHAT TYPES OF BENEFITS SHOULD BE PROVIDED IN THE PLAN?

A major decision for any employer is what types and levels of benefits to include in an overall employee benefit plan. For those few firms that do not have an employee benefit program, this decision involves choosing which benefits to offer initially. However, in most cases the decision is ongoing and involves either the offering of new or improved benefits or the redesigning of all or a major portion of the benefit plan. An objective of most employee benefit plans is to meet the "needs" of employees. But what are these needs? If they vary for different groups of employees, should different benefit plans be established? Or should a single plan be designed in which employees are allowed to choose from alternative benefits?

Determining Needs

Every employer wants its employees to appreciate the benefits that are provided. However, employers are becoming increasingly aware that employee benefit programs are failing to achieve this desired level of appreciation. To some extent this is due to the fact that as employee benefit plans have grown more comprehensive, employees have begun to take the benefits for granted. In addition, the growing consensus seems to be that the traditional methods of determining what types and levels of benefits to offer have lost much of their effectiveness. These include basing benefits on the following factors:

- the employer's perception of the employees' needs. This perception is largely based on the opinions of a firm's top management employees, whose compensation is much higher than that of the average employee. Therefore it is not surprising that many recent studies have shown that management's perception of employees' needs often differs from what the employees themselves feel they need.
- what competitors are doing. Too often the emphasis is placed on having an employee benefit package that is virtually identical to that of the competition, even though the makeup of the work force may be different and the employees may have different needs.
- collectively bargained benefits. Many employers pattern their benefit plans for salaried employees after their negotiated plans for union employees. Again, the needs of salaried employees may be substantially different and may call for a totally different plan.
- tax laws and regulations. Benefit plans are often designed to include those benefits that are best suited to the high tax brackets of top executives. The average employee who is in a modest tax bracket may actually have a preference for certain benefits even though they will result in currently taxable income.

In the last few years employers have increasingly taken a marketing-research approach to employee benefit planning. The employees' preferences for benefits are determined similarly to the way that consumers' demands for products are determined. For the most part this approach has been used only for nonunion employees, since benefits for union employees are decided by collective bargaining. However, some employers and some unions use this procedure as a guide in their negotiations over benefits for union employees.

A marketing-research approach can be used for different purposes. Most often it is selected as a way to determine (1) how funds should be allocated to new types of benefits or (2) how funds should be used to improve current benefits. This can be for a one-time change in a firm's benefit plan or for changes that are implemented over time. In addition, a marketing-research approach can also help an employer to determine what alternative provisions employees would prefer regarding a specific type of benefit. For example, a firm that allocates additional funds to a long-term disability plan could determine whether employees would prefer a shorter waiting period or an increase in the size of the monthly benefit.

Marketing-research techniques must be used with caution. They can have a negative effect on employee morale unless the employer is committed to using their results in benefit decision making. Therefore this approach should not be undertaken unless the employer intends to base expenditures for benefits on satisfying what employees perceive as their needs. In addition, employees must be made aware that changes in an overall benefit program will be subject to financial constraints and possibly trade-offs among benefits.

Although a variety of marketing-research techniques can be used in benefit planning, those most commonly chosen fall into three major categories: personal interviews, simplified questionnaires, and sophisticated research methods.

Personal Interviews

Personal interviews with employees (either alone or in small groups) are probably the most effective marketing-research technique for a small firm or for a benefit program that is limited to a small number of employees. On this scale it is also usually the least expensive technique. An advantage of personal interviewing is that it can be used to collect the same type of information as both simplified questionnaires and sophisticated research techniques. It is important in personal interviewing that the employees feel they can speak candidly. For this reason it may be desirable to have the interviews conducted by someone outside the firm and to hold group interviews without the supervisor's presence.

Simplified Questionnaires

A simplified questionnaire often has two major parts: one determines benefit preferences, the other determines demographic data (such as age, sex, marital status, years of service, and salary range). The questionnaire is called "simplified" because employees are basically asked only to indicate and/or rank their preferences. However, the actual analysis of the data that are gathered may be a complex task, and unless a firm is small, it will probably require the use of a computer. It is important to use a clear, brief questionnaire that is not annoying to employees. Consequently it is best that the questionnaire be initially given to a few employees in order to determine their reactions.

Figure 14-1 contains a sample of a portion of a simplified questionnaire on benefit preferences. The example is typical of most questionnaires because it applies to a broad range of benefits, and not just to group insurance. It should be noted that the questionnaire is essentially a structured one and is not open-ended. Employees are requested only to rank their preferences, and they are not given the opportunity to state whether each benefit is important or whether it should be improved. They are also required to make their preferences known regarding possible trade-offs between benefits and pay. Even though the questionnaire is structured, employees are still given the opportunity to make general comments. Such a feature should be incorporated into any questionnaire as a way of letting employees know that their opinions will be heard. It may also result in useful and sometimes surprising information for the employer.

Sophisticated Research Methods

One difficulty with simplified questionnaires, and to some extent personal interviews, is that they fail to measure the intensity of employees' preferences. Consequently some firms have used more sophisticated marketing-research techniques in an attempt to measure the degree of importance that employees place on various benefit alternatives. These more sophisticated research techniques are typically used only when specific alternatives have been formulated by the employer. Therefore they are often used as a follow-up to personal interviews and simplified questionnaires, and they frequently involve additional interviews and/or questionnaires.

Figure 14-2 illustrates one example of how preferences might be measured with a questionnaire.

FIGURE 14-1

Employee Benefit Questionnaire

1. In the right-hand column below rank the benefits from 1 to 7 in their importance to you and your family. Use 1 for the most important, 2 for the next important, etc.

Benefit	*Importance*
Pension Plan	_____
Life Insurance	_____
Sick Pay	_____
Long-term Disability Income	_____
Medical Insurance	_____
Holidays	_____
Vacations	_____

2. To the list of benefits below add the two benefits you would most like to see added by this company. In the right-hand column rank the benefits listed according to their need for improvement or adoption. Use 1 for the benefit you feel should have the highest priority for improvement or adoption, 2 for the next highest, etc.

Benefit	*Need for Improvement or Adoption*
Pension Plan	_____
Life Insurance	_____
Sick Pay	_____
Long-term Disability Income	_____
Medical Expense Insurance	_____
Holidays	_____
Vacations	_____
_____	_____
_____	_____

3. How would you prefer that additional funds for benefits be used? (check one)

    _____ improve or add benefit programs
    _____ reduce currently required employee contributions

4. Which of the following statements reflects your opinion? (check one)

    _____ More emphasis should be placed on improving wages and salaries and less on improving benefits.
    _____ More emphasis should be placed on improving benefits and less on improving wages and salaries.
    _____ The same emphasis as in the past should be placed on improving both benefits and wages and salaries.

5. Please use the back of this form to make any additional comments you feel will be of use to the company in its desire to improve the employee benefit programs.

FIGURE 14-2

Employee Benefit Questionnaire

The following benefit changes are being considered for adoption by this company in the next fiscal year. Although the company is committed to making improvements in its benefit package, financial considerations dictate that only some of these proposed changes can be adopted at that time. The first item on the list has been given a "value" of 100. Please rank the other items in their relative importance to you. For example, if item 2 is 3 times as important, it should be given a value of 300. If it is only half as important, it should be given a value of 50.

Proposed Change	*Value*
1. Increase lifetime major medical maximum from $500,000 to $1 million	100
2. Eliminate employee contributions to long-term disability coverage	_____
3. Increase life insurance coverage from 1 1/2 to 2 times base earnings	_____
4. Add Columbus Day to list of holidays	_____
5. Increase the annual number of sick days from 10 to 12	_____

Once the information is gathered, the firm must decide which benefits to adopt, based on employees' preferences and other cost and administrative considerations. For example, assume that the firm using the questionnaire is willing to spend up to $400 annually per employee to improve its benefit package. Also assume that the following figures represent the average importance of each proposed benefit to employees, as well as the expected annual cost per employee of providing each benefit:

Change	Average Value	Annual Cost per Employee
1	100	$100
2	310	200
3	140	100
4	240	200
5	190	250

It is clear that the employees feel the second proposed change (which has an annual cost of $200 per employee) is most important by a substantial margin. Therefore it will most likely be adopted. However, it is difficult to determine what other benefit or benefits will be offered. The last proposed change will definitely not be made because only $200 per employee remains for additional benefit changes. The firm is therefore faced with two alternatives—either add Columbus Day as a holiday or increase both the life insurance coverage and the major medical lifetime maximum. Because the average importance of each alternative to employees is 240, and only one can be made within the cost constraint, the deciding factor will hinge on other considerations. The firm may look at the administrative aspects of each change or the effect of inflation on long-range costs. The firm may also analyze the data in terms of the demographic characteristics of employees. For example, long-time employees may have a slight preference for the insurance benefits, while younger employees would like the extra holiday. If the firm wishes to favor the older employees, it will change the insurance benefits; if morale is low among younger employees, it might decide to add the holiday instead.

It should be pointed out that these other considerations may also be the deciding factor for employers even when employee preferences are clear. However, if employees are led to believe that their preferences will be the primary consideration, other considerations should be weighed only when there are modest differences in employee preferences.

Different Plans

From an administrative standpoint it is easiest for a firm to have a single employee benefit plan that applies to all employees. Nevertheless, some firms have different plans for different groups of employees. This most commonly occurs when the benefits for union employees are determined by collective bargaining. If the benefits for the union employees are provided through a negotiated trusteeship, a separate plan must be designed for the nonunion employees. The employer must then decide whether to play "follow the leader" and provide identical benefits to the nonunion employees or to design a plan that reflects their different needs. When benefits are provided through a negotiated trusteeship, the employer is more likely to develop a "different" plan for nonunion employees than when the employer is required to provide benefits to union employees through group insurance contracts that are purchased by the employer. Under these circumstances employers often find it simpler administratively to purchase a single contract that covers all employees.

Even when unions are not involved, an employer may still decide to have different plans for different groups of employees. Usually one plan will be limited to hourly employees, another to salaried employees. In addition, a plan that offers supplemental benefits to top management may also be provided (but it will often be publicized only to those employees who are eligible for these benefits). Some firms that have employees located in different parts of the country have also found it desirable to provide somewhat different benefits at some or all locations in order to remain locally competitive.

Having different plans for different groups of employees is not without its disadvantages. Administrative costs are usually increased, communications with employees become more difficult, and resentment can occur if one group of employees feels its benefit plan is inferior to that of another group. To minimize this latter possibility, some firms have designed their plans so that an overall comparison is difficult. Each plan will have its own positive and negative features when examined next to the plans for other groups of employees.

A trend in recent years has been the growth of cafeteria plans. Because of their popularity and complexity, a separate chapter (chapter 15) is devoted to them.

WHAT PROVISIONS FOR CONTROLLING COSTS SHOULD BE CONTAINED IN THE PLAN?

Employers have always been concerned about the costs of providing employee benefits. Traditionally this concern has led to plan provisions that transfer these costs to employees rather than reduce them. These provisions include probationary periods, benefit limitations, and contributory financing. More recent attempts to control costs have been directed primarily toward the rapidly increasing costs of medical care, and for the most part these cost-containment provisions have been designed to reduce administrative and claim costs without transferring them to employees. Since methods for controlling the costs of medical expenses were discussed throughout chapters 7 and 8, they will not be discussed here. Rather, the focus will be on provisions and activities that can be used with other types of benefit plans.

Probationary Periods

Probationary periods reduce costs to employers because any claims that employees incur during this time must be borne by the employees themselves. In addition, probationary periods reduce the adverse selection that would most likely exist without their use. Administrative costs are also minimized for employees who terminate employment shortly after being hired. However, probationary periods do impose hardship on newer employees who incur claims but find themselves without benefits. Primarily for competitive reasons in attracting employees, the use and length of probationary periods, particularly in medical expense plans, have been decreasing except in high turnover situations.

Benefit Limitations

Benefit limitations in the form of deductibles, coinsurance, maximum benefits, and exclusions for certain types of expenses are common in medical expense insurance. However, some of these techniques can also be used in other types of insurance. The following are some examples:

- the limiting of benefits to a maximum percentage of income in disability income plans. In addition to reducing the amount of the benefits paid by the employer, a maximum percentage also minimizes the possibility of feigned and unnecessarily prolonged disabilities.
- the setting of maximum benefits under dental plans for expenses such as orthodontics. There is little doubt that the availability of benefits will encourage treatment of orthodontic conditions, particularly when the

treatment is primarily sought for cosmetic reasons. There is also the feeling that dentists will encourage the treatment of relatively minor conditions if a patient has coverage for orthodontics.

Contributory Financing

Many benefit plans require each employee to pay a portion of the premium costs for his or her own coverage. This may lower the employer's costs and/or may enable the employer to use these saved dollars to provide additional or improved benefits. There are several arguments both for and against contributory financing, but in many instances it is a moot point, since the decision is determined by collective bargaining or competition.

When contributory financing is used for benefits other than pension plans, employees are generally able to voluntarily elect or decline coverage. To the extent that some employees decline coverage, the costs to the employer will be further lowered. However, this savings may be offset by the adverse selection that can result because of those who did elect coverage. Furthermore, having the option to decline coverage could mean that employees or their dependents will be without coverage should a loss occur. Finally, there tend to be greater administrative costs associated with a contributory plan than with a noncontributory plan.

Advocates of contributory plans feel that sharing in the cost will increase the employees' awareness and appreciation of both the plan and the contribution the employer is making. However, this can be countered by the argument that payroll deductions for benefits are a source of employee dissatisfaction since they may view the employer as "cheap" for not paying the entire cost of the plan.

Although there are no empirical studies to support the contention, it has been argued that employees are less likely to misuse medical and dental benefits under a contributory plan, because they realize that such misuse will probably lead to an increase in their future contributions.

Cost Containment

Recent attempts to control benefit costs have concentrated on either reducing the size of claims or minimizing the administrative costs associated with benefit plans. Rather than transfer the costs to employees, these techniques try to lower costs, or to at least lower the rate at which costs are increasing. Although employers are concerned primarily with their own costs, some of the advantages of this cost containment will affect the employees in the form of increased benefits or a lower rate of increase for the employees' own out-of-pocket expenses.

Other than provisions or practices associated solely with medical expense plans, the following is a list of some of the more common cost-containment techniques that are currently being used by employers:

- alternative funding methods that lower administrative costs and improve cash flow
- competitive bidding among insurance companies and third-party administrators that lowers administrative costs

- wellness programs and employee assistance plans that reduce future claims

HOW SHOULD THE PLAN BE COMMUNICATED TO EMPLOYEES?

Traditionally employers placed a low priority on the communication of their benefit plans to employees. They took the attitude that employees appreciated any benefits given to them. The little information that was made available tended to be only the literature that had been prepared by the insurance companies providing the coverage. Over the last few years this situation has changed dramatically. Employers are required by federal law to disclose a substantial amount of information to employees about their benefit plans. In addition, employers have come to realize that many employees take their benefits for granted, that they fail to realize the value of these benefits to themselves and their families, and that they are unaware of the employer's dollar outlay. Not only will effective communication solve this problem, it may also minimize the dissatisfaction that arises from misunderstandings about the benefit program, and it may reduce turnover to the extent that employees realize the true value of their benefits. Employers have also learned that effective communication is necessary to obtain employee support if cost-containment efforts are to be successful.

Most benefit consultants feel that an effective communication program should have three primary objectives. These are

- to create an awareness and appreciation of the way current benefits improve the financial security of employees
- to provide a high level of understanding about available benefits
- to encourage the wise use of benefits

The communication of benefit plans to employees is now regarded as a highly sophisticated task. No single method of communication is likely to accomplish all the desired objectives, so several methods must be combined. To meet these objectives, many employers hire communications experts who generally report to the person responsible for employee benefits. Other employers use the services of benefit-consulting firms, many of which have developed specialized units for advising their clients in this particular area. Benefit plans can be communicated to employees in audiovisual presentations, in face-to-face meetings, through printed materials, and more recently with computers.

Audiovisual Presentations

Audiovisual presentations are a very effective way to communicate benefit plans to new employees or to explain significant changes in existing benefit plans to current employees. It is much easier to require employees to view audiovisual presentations than to read printed materials. In addition, if properly done, audiovisual presentations can convey the employer's concern for the well-being of its employees, and they can explain proper benefit use more effectively than printed materials. In the past many audiovisual presentations have been dull and sometimes uninformative. Recently, however, many employers have adopted more sophisticated communications methods, and they view these presentations, if not their entire communication program, as a way of "advertising" their employee benefit plans. In fact, some employers have actually hired advertising firms to design not only their audiovisual programs but other aspects of their communication program as well.

Meetings with Employees

Face-to-face meetings with employees can also be an effective way to explain employee benefit plans and to answer employee questions. For small employers this technique is generally used to present benefit plans to new employees or to explain the changes in existing plans. Large employers often combine meetings with audiovisual presentations. It is obvious that whoever conducts these meetings (be it the employer, agent, broker, consultant, or group representative) must be truly knowledgeable about the plan. In addition, it is just as important that he or she be able to effectively communicate this knowledge to the employees.

The number of employees who attend a meeting may determine its effectiveness. A large meeting may be satisfactory if its purpose is primarily to present information. However, a series of small meetings may be more manageable and appropriate if employee opinions or questions are being solicited. These smaller-sized meetings can be used in lieu of a large meeting or as follow-up meetings to a large group presentation. When employees must make decisions regarding their benefit plans, meetings with individual employees may also be necessary.

Group meetings can be used for other purposes besides explaining new or changed benefit plans. They can be held periodically to reexplain benefits, to answer employee questions, or to listen to employee concerns and suggestions. However, every employer should also have a procedure by which employees can have ready access to a "knowledgeable" person when they have any problems to discuss or questions to ask. Although this can often be accomplished by telephone, face-to-face meetings should be used when necessary.

The employer's attitude toward a group meeting can influence its effectiveness. Employers should not regard these meetings as necessary formalities, but rather they should view them as a way to communicate their concern about the security of their employees and the benefits with which they are provided. The success of face-to-face meetings may also depend to some degree on the time and location of the meeting. To achieve maximum employee interest and attention, the facilities should be comfortable and not overcrowded. In addition, meetings should be held during normal working hours, but not at the end of the working day, when many employees may be concerned with whether the meeting will end on time.

Printed Materials

Virtually every employer provides employees with some printed materials about their employee benefit plans. At a minimum this material consists of group insurance certificates and the information that is required to be distributed under the disclosure provisions of ERISA. The next most commonly provided source of information is the benefit handbook. If there is a typical benefit handbook, it can best be described as a reference book that summarizes the benefit plans that are available to all employees. In addition to describing group insurance benefits, it will include information about an organization's retirement plan, vacation policy, and possibly other benefits (such as educational assistance). Each plan will be described in terms of eligibility, benefits, and what employee contributions are required. Traditionally these benefit handbooks merely described each benefit plan separately; they did not discuss the relationship between the various benefit plans or the availability of certain social insurance benefits. Newer benefit handbooks are more likely to focus on the potential causes of lost income to an employee or his or her family. For example, rather than discuss short-term and long-term disability income plans separately, they will include a single section on disability income that describes how a short-term disability plan will initially pay benefits and at what point it will be replaced by the long-term disability plan and social security.

Because of the general nature of benefit handbooks, many employers also give each employee a *personalized benefit statement,* usually on an annual basis. Some employers feel that employees will better appreciate the value of their benefits if they are aware of the magnitude of the cost to the employer. Figure 14-3 is an example of one form that is used for reporting this information. However, the most common form of personalized benefit statement specifies the plans for which the employee is eligible and what benefits are available to that particular employee (or his or her family) under each of these plans. Figure 14-4 shows a portion of one such statement.

Other types of printed information (such as company newsletters, personal letters to employees at home, or notices in pay envelopes) may also be of value. This may be the simplest and least expensive way of announcing benefit changes that need little explanation (such as an increase in the daily hospital room-and-board benefit). In addition, they are an effective way to advertise or remind employees about the wellness programs that are available or what cost-containment provisions are included in their medical expense coverage. Experience has shown that without occasional reminders, the use of these programs and provisions by employees will decrease.

Computers

An increasing number of employers are turning to computers to help communicate various provisions of their benefit plans to employees. A few employers actually provide diskettes to employees who have access to personal computers, but the most common approach is to have computer terminals located in central locations. The monitors of these terminals can be accessed through a keyboard. By pressing the appropriate key an employee can get a general description of the company's various plans. By inputting appropriate data (including an identification number) an employee may also be able to obtain information about his or her own particular situation. For example, an employee could determine potential disability income or retirement benefit. An employee may also be able to obtain the answers to "what if" questions. For example, if I contribute $100 per month to a 401(k) plan that is expected to earn 7 percent annually, how much will I have at age 65? Or if I elect these options under a cafeteria plan, will any additional employer dollars remain for other benefits, or will I have to make an additional contribution through a payroll deduction?

FIGURE 14-3

BENEFIT STATEMENT REVIEW FOR

_____

Many of us forget that there is more to our paycheck than the amount we take home. The following are the "extras" that were provided in 19___ and their value as determined by the cost to your employer.

	Annual Value	Value per Hour
(1) Social Security (employer's contribution)	$_____	$_____
(2) Worker's Compensation Insurance Premium	_____	_____
(3) State Unemployment Insurance Premium	_____	_____
(4) Paid Holidays	_____	_____
(5) Vacation Days	_____	_____
(6) Pension	_____	_____
(7) Salary Continuation	_____	_____
(8) Long-term Disability Income Insurance	_____	_____
(9) Life Insurance	_____	_____
(10) Medical Expense Insurance (employer's contribution)	_____	_____
(11) Others	_____	_____
_____	_____	_____
_____	_____	_____

The $_____ value of those sometimes forgotten benefits is equal to _____% of the $_____ you received as salary or wages in 19___. These benefits are provided to protect you and your family from certain financial risks and to help provide for your future retirement.

As the last question indicates, the use of computers can facilitate the administration of a cafeteria plan. In fact, some employers are actually using the computer to make benefit selections. To have some verification in writing, a form is either printed on the spot for an employee to sign and return or generated in the personnel office, reviewed, and sent to the employee for signing.

There seems to be little doubt that as the role of the computer expands in the business world, its uses for communicating with employees will also increase.

FIGURE 14-4

PERSONAL STATEMENT OF BENEFITS

This Personal Statement of Benefits lists the benefits that both protect you and your family now and provide security for your future. We know you will find this statement informative, and we hope it will be useful in your personal planning.

Health-Care Benefits

You have elected coverage for
☐ yourself   ☐ your family   ☐ You have not elected coverage.

The highlights of your Comprehensive Medical Plan are summarized in the following table. See your employee handbook for further details.

In-Hospital Benefits	Out-of-Hospital Benefits	Special Benefits
$100 deductible per person each calendar year (3-deductible maximum per family)		100% of outpatient emergency treatment of accidental injury (no deductible)
100% of covered expenses, including maternity care, after the deductible is met	80% of first $3,000 of covered expenses, then 100% of remaining covered expenses	
	50% of psychiatric treatment up to $1,000 a year ($20-a-visit maximum benefit)	80% of diagnostic X-ray and laboratory tests (deductible applies)

Overall Plan Maximum: $1,000,000 per person

Disability Income Benefits

Salary Continuation Plan

- Your full salary continues for _____ weeks, then 3/4 of your salary continues for _____ weeks.

Long-term Disability Income Plan

- If disabled over 26 weeks, you will receive _____ a month. This is 60 percent of your base pay and includes benefits under the corporation's plan and any social security benefits, other than family benefits, for which you are eligible.

- If you have eligible dependents you can receive additional family benefits under social security up to _____ a month.

- If total long-term disability income from the above sources exceeds 80 percent of your base pay, disability benefits under the corporation's plan will be reduced to bring the total to the 70 percent level.

15

Cafeteria Plans

For several years some organizations have had benefit plans that give a limited number of key executives some choice in the selection of types and levels of employee benefits that will be provided with employer contributions. Although many organizations have benefit programs in which optional or supplemental benefits may be elected by all (or many) employees, the cost of these benefits must normally be borne by the employees on an aftertax, payroll-deduction basis. With the possible exception of an HMO option, employees have no choice about how employer dollars will be spent.

In the past few years many organizations have established benefit programs in which all (or almost all) the employees can design their own benefit packages by purchasing benefits with a prespecified amount of employer dollars from a number of available options. Generally these *cafeteria plans* (often referred to as flexible benefit plans or cafeteria compensation plans) also allow additional benefits to be purchased on a payroll-deduction basis. Today it is estimated that at least 25 percent of employers with more than 1,000 employees have a full-fledged cafeteria plan. Even more of these employers and many smaller employers offer premium-conversion plans and/or flexible spending accounts.

THE RATIONALE FOR CAFETERIA PLANS

The growth in employee benefits has caused two problems. First, some employers feel that many employees do not recognize and appreciate the magnitude of their employee benefits because as benefits increase, employee appreciation often seems to decrease. Advocates of cafeteria plans argue that by giving employees a stated dollar amount with which they must select their own benefits (from a list of options), employees will become more aware of the actual cost of these benefits and will be more likely to appreciate the benefits they choose.

A second problem is that the inflexible benefit structure of conventional employee benefit plans does not adequately meet the various benefit needs of all employees, often leading to employee dissatisfaction. For example, single employees often resent the medical coverage that married employees receive for their families, since the single employees receive no benefit of corresponding value. Similarly employees who have no dependents often see little value in life insurance and would prefer other benefits. Those who favor the concept of cafeteria plans feel that such dissatisfaction can be minimized if employees have the option to select their own benefits. Advocates of cafeteria plans hope that this increased employee satisfaction will result in a better employee-retention record and in greater ability to attract new employees.

Some employers see the cafeteria approach to benefit planning as an opportunity to control the escalating benefit costs associated with inflation and with the new requirements of recently enacted federal and state legislation. Since a cafeteria plan is essentially a defined-contribution plan rather than a defined-benefit plan, it provides a number of opportunities for controlling increases in costs. For example, it may encourage employees to choose medical expense options that have larger deductibles so they can more efficiently use the fixed number of dollars allotted to them under the plan. A cafeteria plan may also enable the employer to pass on to the employees any increased benefit costs that result from having to comply with legislation that mandates additional benefits. In addition, since increases in employer contributions for optional benefits are not directly related to increases in benefit costs, the employer can grant percentage increases in the amounts available for benefits that are less than the actual overall increase in employee benefit costs.

It should be noted that early cafeteria plans were designed primarily to meet the varying needs of employees. In contrast, newer plans are much more likely to be instituted as a cost-saving technique.

THE NATURE OF CAFETERIA PLANS

In its purest sense a cafeteria plan can be defined as any employee benefit plan that allows an employee to have some choice in designing his or her own benefit package by selecting different types or levels of benefits that are funded with employer dollars. At this extreme a benefit plan that allows an employee to select an HMO as an option to an insured medical expense plan can be classified as a cafeteria plan. However, the more common use of the term *cafeteria plan* denotes something much broader—a plan in which choices can be made among several different types of benefits and possibly cash.

Prior to the addition of Sec. 125 to the Internal Revenue Code by the Revenue Act of 1978, the use of cafeteria plans had potentially adverse tax consequences for an employee. If an employee had a choice among benefits that were normally nontaxable (such as medical expense insurance or disability income insurance) and benefits that were normally taxable (such as life insurance in excess of $50,000 or cash), then the doctrine of constructive receipt would result in an employee's being taxed as if he or she had elected the maximum taxable benefits that could have been obtained under the plan. Therefore if an employee could elect cash in lieu of being covered under the employer's medical expense plan, an employee who elected to remain in the medical expense plan would have taxable income merely because cash could have been elected. Obviously this tax environment was not conducive to the use of cafeteria plans unless the only benefits contained in them were normally of a nontaxable nature.

Permissible Benefits

Currently Sec. 125 of the Code defines a cafeteria plan as a written plan under which all participants are employees and under which all participants may choose between two or more benefits consisting of (1) *qualified benefits* and (2) cash. Qualified benefits essentially include any welfare benefits excluded from taxation under the Internal Revenue Code except scholarships and fellowships, transportation benefits, educational assistance, no-additional-cost services, employee discounts, and dependent group term life insurance. Thus medical expense benefits, disability benefits, accidental death and dismemberment benefits, vacations, coverage under a qualified legal expense plan, and dependent-care assistance (such as day-care centers) can be included in a cafeteria plan. The Code also allows group term life insurance to be included even in amounts exceeding $50,000. In general a cafeteria plan cannot include benefits that defer compensation except for a qualified Sec. 401(k) or similar plan.

The prohibition of benefits that defer compensation has an important impact on vacation benefits. If an employee elects vacation benefits for the plan year of a cafeteria plan, the vacation days cannot be carried over into the following plan year because this would be a deferral of compensation. (Note: Regular vacation days are considered to have been taken before the additional days elected under the cafeteria plan.) However, an employee can elect to exchange these days for cash as long as the election is made and the cash is actually received prior to the end of the plan year. If this is not done, the days are forfeited and their value is lost.

Because of recent IRS regulations, the term *cash* is actually broader than it would otherwise appear. In addition to the actual receipt of dollars, a benefit is treated as cash as long as (1) it is not a benefit specifically prohibited by Sec. 125 (that is, one that defers compensation or is among the list of previously mentioned exceptions, such as scholarships and educational assistance) and (2) it is provided on a taxable basis. This latter provision means that either (1) the cost of the benefit is paid by the employee with aftertax dollars on a payroll-deduction basis or (2) employer dollars are used to obtain the benefit, but the employer reports the cost of the benefit as taxable income for the employee. This recent change, for example, would allow the inclusion of group automobile insurance in a cafeteria plan. It also allows long-term disability coverage to be provided on an aftertax basis, so that disability income benefits can be received tax free.

As long as a benefit plan offering choice meets the definition of a cafeteria plan, the issue of constructive receipt does not apply. Employees will have taxable income only to the extent that normally taxable benefits are elected. These include group term life insurance in excess of $50,000 and cash. An employer can have a benefit plan that offers choice but does not meet the statutory definition of a cafeteria plan. In such a case the issue of constructive receipt will come into play if the plan contains any benefits that normally result in taxable income.

Benefit Election

Sec. 125 requires that benefit elections under a cafeteria plan be made prior to the beginning of a plan year. These elections cannot be changed during the plan year except under certain specified circumstances if the plan allows such changes. While there is no requirement that these changes be included in a plan, some or all of them are included in most plans.

Changes in benefit elections are permissible under the following circumstances:

- changes in family status. IRS regulations do not specifically define what is meant by changes in family status. However, the regulations include examples of the following:

- an employee's marriage or divorce
- the death of an employee's spouse or a dependent
- the birth or adoption of a child
- the commencement or termination of employment by the employee's spouse
- a change from part-time to full-time employment status or vice versa by the employee or the employee's spouse
- an unpaid leave of absence taken by either the employee or the employee's spouse
- a significant change in an employee's or spouse's health coverage that is attributable to the spouse's employment

- separation from service. An employee who separates from service during a period of coverage may revoke existing benefit elections and terminate the receipt of benefits. However, the plan must prohibit the employee from making new benefit elections for the remainder of the plan year if he or she returns to service for the employer. It should be noted that an employee must be allowed to continue health insurance coverage under COBRA upon separation from service.
- cessation of required contributions. A cafeteria plan can terminate coverage if an employee fails to make the required premium payments for the benefits elected. The employee is then prohibited from making new elections for the remainder of the plan year.
- plan cost changes. A cafeteria plan can allow for an automatic adjustment of employee contributions if the cost of a health plan is increased or decreased by an insurance company or other independent third-party provider of benefits. Such an adjustment is not allowed because of changes in self-insured health plans. Regulations also allow the revocation of previous elections and the selection of another health plan with *similar* coverage if costs are increased *significantly*. IRS regulations do not define either of the italicized terms.
- plan coverage changes. An employee may also change to a *similar* health plan if a third-party provider of health benefits *significantly* curtails or ceases to provide health coverage during a plan year. This provision is particularly helpful in situations involving the insolvency of a provider of health benefits.

Payroll Deductions and Salary Reductions

Under some cafeteria plans employees are only allowed to allocate a predetermined employer contribution for benefits. Other cafeteria plans are designed so that employees can obtain additional benefits with optional payroll deductions or salary reductions.

Many cafeteria plans that provide a wide array of benefits allow an employee to elect an aftertax payroll deduction to obtain additional benefits. For example, under a cafeteria plan an employee might be given $200 per month with which to select varying types and levels of benefits. If the benefits the employee chooses cost $240, the employee has two options—either to decrease the benefits selected or to authorize a $40 payroll deduction. Even though the payroll deduction is on an aftertax basis, the employee will gain to the extent that the additional benefits can be selected at a lower cost through a group arrangement than in the individual marketplace.

Sec. 125 also allows employees to purchase certain benefits on a before-tax basis through the use of a premium-conversion plan or a flexible spending account (FSA). Premium-conversion plans or FSAs, which are technically cafeteria plans, can be used by themselves or incorporated into a more comprehensive cafeteria plan. They are most commonly used alone by small employers who are unwilling to establish a broader plan, primarily for cost reasons. The cafeteria plans of most large employers contain one or both of these arrangements as an integral part of the plan.

Premium-Conversion Plans

A premium-conversion plan allows an employee to elect a before-tax salary reduction to pay his or her premium contribution to any employer-sponsored health or other welfare benefit plan. For example, an employer might provide medical expense coverage to employees at no cost but make a monthly charge for dependent coverage. Under a premium-conversion plan the employer can pay for the dependent coverage with a before-tax salary reduction.

As a rule premium-conversion plans are established for medical and dental expenses only. If such plans are used for group term life insurance, the cost of coverage in excess of $50,000 must be reported as income, which defeats the purpose of the salary reduction. If these plans are used for disability income coverage, benefits will be taxable as noncontributory employer-provided coverage because the amount of any salary reduction is considered to be the employer's money.

Flexible Spending Accounts

An FSA allows an employee to fund certain benefits on a before-tax basis by electing to take a salary reduction, which can then be used to fund the cost of any qualified benefits included in the plan. However, FSAs are used almost exclusively for medical and dental expenses not covered by the employer's plan and for dependent-care expenses.

The amount of any salary reduction is, in effect, credited to an employee's reimbursement account, and benefits are paid from this account when an employee properly files for such reimbursement. Reimbursements are typically made on a monthly or quarterly basis. The amount of the salary reduction must be determined prior to the beginning of the plan year. Once the amount is set, changes are allowed only under the specified circumstances previously mentioned for benefit elections. A separate election must be made for each benefit, and the funds are accounted for separately. Monies from a salary reduction for one type of expense cannot be used as reimbursement for another type of expense.

If the monies in the FSA are not used during the plan year, they are forfeited and belong to the employer. Although some employers kept the forfeited money and use it to offset the cost of administering the FSA program, almost anything can be done with the money, except for giving it back only to the persons who have forfeited it. Some employers give the money to charity; others credit it on a pro rata basis to the amounts of all participants in the FSA program for the following year or use it to reduce future benefit costs (such as contributions to a medical expense plan) for all employees.

An election to participate in an FSA program not only reduces salary for federal income tax purposes but also lowers the wages on which social security taxes are levied. Therefore those employees who are below the wage-base limit after the reduction will pay less in social security taxes, and their future income benefits under social security will also be smaller. However, the reduction in benefits will be small in most cases unless the salary reduction is large. It should be noted that the employer's share of social security tax payments will also decrease. In some cases the employer's savings may actually be large enough to fully offset the cost of administering the FSA program.

One issue employers have faced over the years has been whether to limit benefit payments to the amount of an account balance or to allow an employee at any time during the year to receive benefits equal to his or her annual salary reduction. For example, an employee might contribute $100 per month to an FSA to provide benefits for the cost of unreimbursed medical expenses. During the first month of the plan the employee makes only $100 of the $1,200 annual contribution. If the employee incurs $300 of unreimbursed medical expenses during the month, should he or she be allowed to withdraw $100 or the full $300? The objection to allowing a $300 withdrawal is that the employer will lose $200 if the employee terminates employment before making any further contribution. IRS regulations no longer give the employer any choice with respect to health benefits (that is, medical and dental expenses). FSAs must allow an amount equal to the full annual contribution to be taken as benefits any time during the year. Therefore the employee will be entitled to a benefit of $300 after the first month. However, the IRS regulations do allow a choice in reimbursement policies for other types of benefits, such as dependent-care expenses. For these benefits most plans limit aggregate benefits to the total contributions made until the time the benefits are received.

TYPES OF PLANS

Core-Plus Plans

Probably the most common type of full-fledged cafeteria plan is one that offers a basic core of benefits to all employees, plus a second layer of optional benefits that permits an employee to choose which benefits he or she will add to the basic benefits. These optional benefits can be "purchased" with dollars, or credits, that are given to the employee as part of the benefit package. If these credits are inadequate to purchase the desired benefits, an employee can make additional purchases with aftertax contributions or with before-tax reductions under a premium-conversion plan and/or a flexible spending account.

Perhaps the best way to demonstrate how cafeteria plans operate is to include a brief description of some existing plans.

EXAMPLE 1: The first example is the core-plus plan of an education organization with 3,000 employees. While this type of plan is common, it should be noted that the list of optional benefits in this example is more extensive than what is found in most cafeteria plans.

All employees receive a minimum level of benefits, called *basic benefits.* These include

- term life insurance equal to one-half of salary
- travel accident insurance (when on the employer's business)
- disability income insurance
- 2 to 4 weeks' vacation

Employees are also given *flexible credits,* equal to between 3 and 6 percent of salary (depending on length of service, with the maximum reached after 10 years), which can be used to purchase additional or "optional" benefits. There is a new election of benefits each year, and no carryover of any unused credits is allowed. The optional benefits include

- an array of medical expense options. Although there is no charge for HMO coverage, a charge is made for coverage under an indemnity plan, and additional flexible credits are given if a person elects no medical expense coverage.
- additional life insurance up to 4 1/2 times salary
- accidental death insurance when the basic travel accident insurance does not apply
- dental insurance for the employee and dependents
- up to 2 weeks' additional vacation time
- cash

If an employee does not have enough flexible credits to purchase the desired optional benefits, additional amounts may be contributed on a payroll-deduction basis for all but more vacation time. In addition, a salary reduction may be elected for contributions to a flexible spending account that provides dependent-care-assistance benefits.

A variation of the core-plus approach is to have the core plan be an "average" plan for which the employee makes no contribution. If certain benefits are reduced, the employee may then receive credits that can be used either to increase other benefits or, if the plan allows, to increase cash compensation. Additional benefits can also be typically obtained through employee payroll deductions.

EXAMPLE 2: This plan covers 15,000 nonunion employees in one division of a major industrial conglomerate. Employees may elect to reduce certain benefits and receive credits that can be used to purchase additional benefits, can be taken in cash, or can be contributed to the company's 401(k) plan. Additional benefits may be purchased on a payroll-deduction basis.

The plan applies to four types of benefits:

- medical expense insurance
- employee life insurance

- accidental death and dismemberment insurance
- dependent life insurance

Several medical expense insurance options are available. The standard coverage, for which there is neither a charge nor a credit, provides basic hospitalization coverage for 120 days, surgical coverage based on a predetermined schedule, and major medical coverage for 80 percent of expenses after a yearly deductible ($100 for an individual and $200 for a family) has been met. Lifetime benefits are limited to a maximum of $100,000. Employees may elect a more comprehensive option that offers 365 days of hospital coverage, a higher surgical schedule, and major medical coverage with a large maximum and more favorable coinsurance and deductible provisions, but this option results in an additional charge to the employee. On the other hand, employees may elect a less comprehensive option that results in a credit. In addition, several HMO options are available, all of which result in credits.

There are several employee life insurance options that range from 1/2 to 5 times salary. The standard coverage for which there is no credit or charge is 1 1/2 times salary.

Although several supplemental accidental death and dismemberment options and a single dependent life insurance option are available, they result in a charge to the employee. So in effect there is no basic benefit in these areas.

Modular Plans

Another type of cafeteria plan is one in which an employee has a choice among several predesigned benefit packages. Typically at least one of the packages can be selected without any employee cost. If an employee selects a more expensive package, the employee will be required to contribute to the cost of the package. Some employers may also include a bare-bones benefit package, which results in cash being paid to an employee who selects it.

Under some cafeteria plans using this approach (often referred to as a modular approach), the predesigned packages may have significant differences. A comparison of two packages may show one to be better than others in certain cases but inferior in other cases. Other employers using this approach have virtually identical packages, with the major difference being in the option selected for the medical expense coverage. For example, the plan of one large bank offers three traditional insured plans, two HMOs, and a preferred-provider organization.

Modular plans are growing in popularity for two reasons. First, adverse selection can be more easily controlled under modular plans than under core-plus plans. Second, modular plans are easier to administer and communicate. For both these reasons small employers who have full-fledged cafeteria plans are most likely to take a modular approach.

EXAMPLE 3: The third example is a large financial institution's cafeteria plan that covers almost 20,000 employees. There are seven predesigned benefit packages that can be chosen, with each package designed for a specific segment of the employee population. Each package contains one of three medical expense plans and varying amounts of group term life insurance. The packages contain differing combinations of dental insurance, vision coverage, and dependent care benefits. All packages contain the same level of disability income coverage.

A "cost" is associated with each package. Some packages cost an employee nothing, other packages require an employee contribution, and at least one option has a negative cost, meaning that an employee who selects it gets additional cash compensation. The cost of each package can vary for two reasons. First, an employee can elect whether to have medical expense coverage for dependents. Second, HMO and PPO choices are available in many of the employee locations.

Salary Reduction Only Plans

The final example is a cafeteria plan that consists solely of the two types of salary reductions that can be used in a cafeteria plan—a premium-conversion option and a flexible spending account.

EXAMPLE 4: Employees are allowed to elect salary reductions for each of the following:

- the employee's share of the cost of medical and dental insurance premiums for dependents. (Under this plan the employer pays the full cost of the employee's coverage.)
- qualifying medical care expenses. These are any medical expenses normally deductible on Schedule A of an employee's federal income tax return (without regard to any gross income limitations). Note that these deductible expenses must not have been reimbursed by insurance.
- eligible dependent-care expenses. These are expenses for the types of benefits that could be provided in a qualified dependent-care-assistance program as described in chapter 13. The maximum annual salary reduction for this category of benefits is limited to $5,000 to prevent the plan from being discriminatory because too large a portion of the benefits would be provided to key employees.

Employees can request reimbursements at the end of each month and must file an appropriate form accompanied by documentation (bills and receipts) to support their request. For administrative purposes reimbursement requests must be for at least $50 except in the last quarter of the year.

The maximum reimbursement at any time for dependent-care expenses is the accumulated amount in an employee's account. Unused amounts in reimbursement accounts at the end of the year are donated to the United Way.

OBSTACLES TO CAFETERIA PLANS

Certain obstacles must be overcome before a cafeteria plan can be successfully implemented. Recent changes in federal tax laws and proper plan design would seem sufficient to overcome many of these obstacles. However, it must be realized that any organization that adopts a cafeteria plan other than a simple flexible spending account will face a complex, costly, and time-consuming project.

The Legislative Environment

Undoubtedly the largest obstacle to cafeteria plans for several years was the unsettled federal income tax picture. This picture was finally clarified in 1984 by the passage of the Tax Reform Act and the IRS issuance of regulations governing cafeteria plans. Since then the number of cafeteria plans has grown significantly, particularly among large firms. However, almost every year either a federal tax bill alters Sec. 125 in some way or new IRS regulations are issued. The benefits that can be included in a cafeteria plan are changed, the nondiscrimination rules are altered, or the rules for flexible spending accounts are "clarified." This continuing uncertainty has caused many employers to take a wait-and-see attitude toward cafeteria plans.

Meeting Nondiscrimination Rules

Sec. 125 imposes complex nondiscrimination tests on cafeteria plans, causing many employees to view the establishment of a cafeteria plan unfavorably. If these tests are not met, adverse tax consequences for key employees and/or highly compensated employees may actually result in higher taxable income for these employees than if no cafeteria plan existed. From a practical standpoint the test will usually be met if an employer has a full-fledged cafeteria plan that applies to all employees. However, care must be exercised in designing a plan that either covers only a segment of the employees or has only a small percentage of employees participating. The latter situation often occurs with flexible spending accounts.

As is often the case, the nondiscrimination tests are not applicable if a plan is maintained under provisions of a collective bargaining agreement.

The Concentration Test

Under the concentration test no more than 25 percent of the tax-favored benefits provided under the plan can be provided to *key employees* (as defined in chapter 4 for the Sec. 79 nondiscrimination rules). This test is a particular problem if an employer has a large percentage of key employees and if key employees, being higher paid, contribute large amounts to a flexible spending account.

If a plan fails the concentration test, key employees must include in gross income the maximum taxable benefits that could have been elected under the plan. In effect these employees are subject to the doctrine of constructive receipt.

The Eligibility Test

Cafeteria plans are subject to a two-part eligibility test, both parts of which must be satisfied. The first part of the test stipulates that no employee be required to complete more than 3 years of employment as a condition for participation and that the employment requirement for each employee be the same. In addition, any employee who satisfies the employment requirement and is otherwise entitled to participate must do so no later than the first day of the plan year following completion of the employment requirement unless the employee has separated from service in the interim.

The second part of the test requires that eligibility for participation must not be discriminatory in favor of highly compensated employees, who are defined as any of the following:

- officers
- shareholders who own more than 5 percent of the voting power or value of all classes of the firm's stock
- employees who are highly compensated based on all facts and circumstances
- spouses or dependents of any of the above

The eligibility test uses table 15-1, which is contained in IRS regulations and can best be explained with an example:

An employer has 1,000 employees, 800 nonhighly compensated and 200 highly compensated. The percentage of nonhighly compensated employees is 80 percent (800/1000), for which the table shows a safe harbor percentage of 35. This means that if the percentage of nonhighly compensated employees eligible for the plan is equal to at least 35 percent of the percentage of highly compensated employees eligible, the plan satisfies the eligibility test. Assume that 160 people, or 80 percent of the highly compensated employees, are eligible. Then at least 28 percent, or 224, of the nonhighly compensated employees must be eligible for the plan (calculations: .80 x .35 = .28 and .28 x 800 = 224).

The table also shows an unsafe harbor percentage of 25 percent. Using this figure instead of 35 percent yields 160 employees. If fewer than this number of nonhighly compensated employees are eligible, the eligibility test is failed.

If the number of eligible nonhighly compensated employees falls between the numbers determined by the two percentages (from 160 to 223 employees in this example), IRS regulations impose a facts-and-circumstances test to determine whether the eligibility test is passed or failed. According to the regulations, the following factors will be considered: (1) the underlying business reason for the eligibility classification, (2) the percentage of employees eligible, (3) the percentage of eligible employees in each salary range, and (4) the extent to which the eligibility classification is close to satisfying the safe harbor rule. However, the regulations also state that none of these factors alone is determinative, and other facts and circumstances may be relevant.

If a plan fails the eligibility test, highly compensated employees must include in gross income the maximum taxable benefits that could have been elected under the plan.

Nondiscriminatory Contributions and Benefits

Cafeteria plans cannot discriminate in favor of highly compensated participants with respect to contributions or benefits. Sec. 125 states that a cafeteria

Table 15-1

Nonhighly Compensated Employee Concentration Percentage	Safe Harbor Percentage	Unsafe Harbor Percentage
0–60	50	40
61	49.25	39.25
62	48.50	38.50
63	47.75	37.75
64	47	37
65	46.25	36.25
66	45.50	35.50
67	44.75	34.75
68	44	34
69	43.25	33.25
70	42.50	32.50
71	41.75	31.75
72	41	31
73	40.25	30.25
74	39.50	29.50
75	38.75	28.75
76	38	28
77	37.25	27.25
78	36.50	26.50
79	35.75	25.75
80	35	25
81	34.25	24.25
82	33.50	23.50
83	32.75	22.75
84	32	22
85	31.25	21.25
86	30.50	20.50
87	29.75	20
88	29	20
89	28.25	20
90	27.50	20
91	26.75	20
92	26	20
93	25.25	20
94	24.50	20
95	23.75	20
96	23	20
97	22.25	20
98	21.50	20
99	20.75	20

plan is not discriminatory if the plan's nontaxable benefits and total benefits (or the employer contributions allocable to each) do not discriminate in favor of highly compensated employees. In addition, a cafeteria plan providing health benefits is not discriminatory if contributions under the plan for each participant include an amount equal to one of the following:

- 100 percent of the health benefit cost for the majority of similarly situated (that is, family or single coverage) highly compensated employees
- at least 75 percent of the health benefit cost for the similarly situated participant with the best health benefit coverage

Contributions exceeding either of these amounts are nondiscriminatory if they bear a uniform relationship to an employee's compensation.

The Obligation of the Employer

Under the most liberal cafeteria plan each employee has an unrestricted choice of the benefits provided by his or her employer. Some critics of this concept argue that both the motivational and security aspects of a cafeteria plan may be damaged by unwise employee selection because many employees may not have the expertise to select the proper benefits. In addition, there is concern about the organization's moral and perhaps legal obligation to prevent employees from financial injury through faulty decisions. These concerns have been incorporated into the design of most plans presently in existence. Employees are given both certain basic benefits that provide a minimum level of security and a series of optional benefits on top of the basic ones.

Negative Attitudes

Some negative attitudes toward cafeteria plans have been expressed by employees, insurers, and unions. No cafeteria plan can be truly successful without the support of the employees involved. In order to win the employees' initial support and to overcome any potential negative attitudes, companies that contemplate the development of such programs must spend a considerable amount of time and resources in making sure that employees are adequately informed about (1) the reasons for the proposed program, (2) its advantages and disadvantages, and (3) its future implications. For best results the opinions of employees should be solicited and weighed, and employees should be involved in various aspects of the decision-making process.

Some insurers have been reluctant to participate in cafeteria plans. A few seem unwilling to try anything new; others are concerned about the problem of adverse selection as a result of employee choice. However, as explained below, the problem of adverse selection can be minimized.

The attitude of unions has also generally been negative. Union management often feels that bargaining for a cafeteria plan is contrary to the practice of bargaining for the best benefit program for all employees. There is also a concern that a cafeteria plan will be used primarily as a cost-containment technique to pass on the cost of future benefit increases to union members. Consequently the programs in existence often apply only to nonunion employees.

Adverse Selection

When employees are allowed a choice in selecting benefits, the problem of adverse selection arises. This means that those employees who are likely to have claims will tend to pick the benefits that will minimize their out-of-pocket costs. For example, an employee who previously selected a medical expense option with a high deductible might switch to a plan with a lower deductible if medical expenses are ongoing. An employee who previously rejected dental insurance or legal expense benefits is likely to elect these benefits if dental care or legal advice is anticipated in the near future.

It should be noted that adverse selection is a problem whether a plan is insured or self-funded. The problem even exists outside of cafeteria plans if choice is allowed. However, the degree of choice within a cafeteria plan tends to make the potential costs more severe unless actions are taken to combat the problem.

Several techniques are used to control adverse selection in cafeteria plans. Benefit limitations and restrictions on coverage can be included if a person wishes to add or change coverage at a date later than initial eligibility. This technique has been common in contributory benefit plans for many years. Another technique is to price the options accordingly. If an option is likely to encourage adverse selection, the cost to the employee for that option should be higher than what would have been charged if the option had been the only one available. Such pricing has been difficult in the past, but it is becoming easier and more accurate as more experience with cafeteria plans develops. The control of adverse selection is also one reason for the use of predesigned package plans. If, for example, the medical expense plan in one option is likely to encourage adverse selection, the option may not include other benefits for which adverse selection is also a concern (such as dental or legal expense benefits). To further counter increased costs from the medical expense plan, the option may also offer minimal coverage for other types of benefits.

Cost

It is an accepted fact that an organization that adopts a cafeteria plan will incur initial development and administrative costs that are over and above those of a more traditional benefit program. Some of this extra cost is the value of the employee hours that must be spent in preparing the program for implementation. Another sizable portion must be paid for the reprogramming of the organization's computer system to include necessary information and to accept the employees' benefit elections.

Until recently the cost of a cafeteria plan was beyond the means of all but large employers. However, package plans developed by many insurers now make this approach financially available to employers with only a few hundred employees.

Continuing costs will depend on such factors as the benefits included in the plan, the number of options available with each benefit, the frequency with which employees may change benefit elections, and the number of employees covered by the plan. The firms with cafeteria plans have incurred increased costs because of the need for additional employees to administer the program and additional computer time to process employee choices. However, the costs have been regarded as small in relation to the total cost of providing employee benefits. In addition, as cafeteria plans have grown in popularity, many vendors have developed software packages that can be used to provide administrative functions more cost effectively.

ISSUES IN PLAN DESIGN

Before committing itself to the establishment of a cafeteria program, an employer must be sure a valid reason exists for converting the company's traditional benefit program to a cafeteria approach. For example, if there is strong employee dissatisfaction with the current benefit program, the solution may lie in clearly identifying the sources of dissatisfaction and making appropriate adjustments in the existing benefit program, rather than making a shift to a cafeteria plan. However, if employee dissatisfaction arises from their widely differing benefit needs, conversion to a cafeteria plan may be quite appropriate. Beyond having a clearly defined purpose for converting from a traditional benefit program to a cafeteria program and being willing to bear the additional administrative costs associated with a cafeteria approach, the employer must face a number of considerations in designing the plan.

The Type and Amount of Benefits to Include

Probably the most fundamental decision that must be made in designing a cafeteria plan is determining what benefits should be included. An employer who wants the plan to be viewed as meeting the differing needs of employees must receive employee inputs concerning the types of benefits perceived as being most desirable. An open dialogue with employees will undoubtedly lead to suggestions that every possible employee benefit be made available. The enthusiasm of many employees for a cafeteria plan will then be dampened when the employer rejects some—and possibly many—of these suggestions for cost, administrative, or psychological reasons. Consequently it is important that certain ground rules be established regarding the benefits that are acceptable to the employer.

The employer must decide whether the plan should be limited to the types of benefits provided through traditional group insurance arrangements or be expanded to include other welfare benefits, retirement benefits, and possibly cash. At a minimum it is important to ensure that an overall employee benefit program provide employees with protection against all major areas of personal risks. This suggests a benefit program with at least *some* provision for life insurance, disability income protection, medical expense protection, and retirement benefits, but it is not necessary that *all* these benefits be included in a cafeteria plan. For example, most employers have a retirement plan separate from their cafeteria plan because of Sec. 125 requirements. Other employers make a 401(k) plan one of the available cafeteria options.

In some respects a cafeteria plan may be an ideal vehicle for providing less traditional types of benefits. Two examples are extra vacation time and child care. Some plans allow an employee to use flexible credits to purchase additional days of vacation. When available, this option has proven a popular benefit, particularly among single employees. A problem may arise, however, if the work of vacationing employees must be assumed by nonvacationing employees in addition to their own regularly assigned work. Those not electing extra vacation time may resent doing the work of someone else who is away longer than the normal vacation period.

In recent years there has been increasing pressure on employers to provide care for employees' children, which represents an additional cost if added to a traditional existing benefit program. Employees who include child-care benefits in a cafeteria plan can pay for the cost of such benefits, possibly with dollars from an FSA. However, lower-paid employees may be better off financially by paying for child care with out-of-pocket dollars and electing the income tax credit available for dependent-care expenses.

Cost is an important consideration in a cafeteria plan. The greater the number of benefits, particularly optional benefits, the greater the administrative costs. A wide array of options may also be confusing to many employees and require extra personnel to counsel employees or to answer their questions.

Level of Employer Contributions

An employer has considerable latitude in determining the amount of dollars that will be available to employees to purchase benefits under a cafeteria plan. These dollars may be a function of one or more of the following factors: salary, age, family status, and length of service.

The major difficulty arises in situations in which the installation of a cafeteria plan is not accompanied by an overall increase in the amount of the employer's contributions to the employee benefit plan. It is generally felt that each employee should be provided with enough dollars so that he or she can purchase optional benefits, that, together with basic benefits, are at least equivalent to the benefits provided by the older plan.

Including a Premium-Conversion or FSA Option

A premium-conversion or FSA option under a cafeteria plan enables employees to lower their taxes and therefore increase their spendable income. Ignoring any administrative costs, there is probably no reason not to offer this option to employees for benefits such as dependent care or for health insurance premiums. However, salary reductions for unreimbursed medical expenses pose a dilemma. While such deductions save taxes for an employee, they may also result in his or her obtaining nearly 100 percent reimbursement for medical expenses, which may negate many of the cost-containment features in the employer's medical expense plan.

Change of Benefits

Because employees' needs change over time, a provision regarding their ability to change their benefit options must be incorporated into a cafeteria plan. As a rule, changes are allowed prior to the beginning of the plan year. Additional changes may be allowed as long as they are permissible under Sec. 125 regulations.

Two situations may complicate the issue of the frequency with which benefits may be changed. First, the charges to employees for optional benefits must be adjusted periodically to reflect experience under the plan. If the charges for benefits rise between dates on which employees may change benefit selections, the employer must either absorb these charges or pass them on to the employees, probably through increased payroll deductions. Consequently most cafeteria plans allow benefit changes on annual dates that are the same as the dates when charges for benefits are recalculated as well as the date on which any insurance contracts providing benefits under the plan are renewed.

The second situation arises when the amount of the employer's contribution is based on compensation. If an employee receives a pay increase between selection periods, should he or she be granted more dollars to purchase additional benefits at that time? Under most cafeteria plans the dollars available to all employees are calculated only once a year, usually before the date by which any annual benefit changes must be made. Any changes in the employee's status during the year will have no effect on the employer's contribution until the following year on the date on which a recalculation is made.

Appendix

FEDERAL TAX LAWS AFFECTING GROUP BENEFIT PLANS

The following citations are for students who wish to research further the tax laws pertaining to group benefits that are provided by employer contributions. Federal tax laws treat employee contributions for group insurance like payments for individual insurance, and therefore they are not deductible to employees, except for certain medical and dental costs if an employee itemizes deductions. In addition, benefits attributable to employee contributions are treated like benefits from individual insurance and are generally free of income taxation. All references are to sections (§) of the Internal Revenue Code or to regulations (Reg.) under the Code.

GROUP TERM LIFE INSURANCE

Deductibility of Employer Contributions

- deductibles as ordinary-and-necessary business expense   §162
- exception if employer is beneficiary   §264

Income Tax Liability to Employees

- first $50,000 generally tax free   §79
- determination of cost on amounts in excess of $50,000   Reg. 1.79-3(d)
- special rules for groups of fewer than 10   Reg. 1.79-1(d)

Taxation of Proceeds

- free of income tax   §101
- subject to estate tax unless incidents of ownership assigned   §2042

GROUP LIFE INSURANCE WITH PERMANENT BENEFITS

Deductibility of Employer Contributions

- deductible as business expense   §162

Income Tax Liability to Employees

- allocation of premiums and benefits   §79
- favorable tax treatment of term insurance portion   §79
- premiums for permanent portion subject to taxation   §61

Taxation of Proceeds

- free of income tax   §101
- subject to estate tax unless incidents of ownership assigned   §2042

RETIRED LIVES RESERVE

Deductibility of Employer Contributions

- deductible as business expense   §162

Income Tax Liability to Employees

- no taxation from contribution to reserve   §83

GROUP DISABILITY INCOME INSURANCE

Deductibility of Employer Contributions

- deductible as business expense   §162

Income Tax Liability to Employees

- no taxation from employer contributions   §106

Taxation of Benefits

- generally taxable, possibly subject to tax credit   §22

GROUP MEDICAL AND DENTAL INSURANCE

Deductibility of Employer Contributions

- deductible as business expense   §162

Income Tax Liability to Employees

- no taxation from employer contributions   §106

Taxation of Benefits

- tax free in general   §105
- exception for discriminatory self-insured medical reimbursement plans §105

GROUP LEGAL EXPENSE PLANS

Deductibility of Employer Contributions

- deductible as business expense   §162

Income Tax Liability to Employees

- no taxation from employer contributions   §120

Taxation of Benefits

- none if "prepaid"   §120
- taxable if not "prepaid"   §61

GROUP PROPERTY AND LIABILITY INSURANCE

Deductibility of Employer Contributions

- deductible as business expense   §162

Income Tax Liability to Employees

- employer contributions represent taxable income   §61

Taxation of Benefits

- free of taxation   §165

CAFETERIA PLANS

Avoidance of Constructive Receipt

- constructive receipt avoided if plan properly designed   §125

Before-Tax Contributions

- before-tax contributions allowed   §125

OTHER GROUP BENEFITS

Vacations

- taxed as compensation   §61

Holidays

- taxed as compensation   §61

Supplemental Unemployment Benefits

- benefits taxed as compensation   §85
- tax-free growth of earnings on fund to provide benefits   §501

Educational Assistance

- tax-free receipt of first $5,200 of benefits under nondiscriminatory plan §127

Moving Expenses

- reportable as income §61
- allowal of offsetting deductions for certain expenses §217

Awards

- suggestion awards included in income §74
- qualified plan awards tax free within limits §§74, 274
- any awards tax free if *de minimis* §132

Holiday Bonuses and Gifts

- tax free only if *de minimis* §132

No-Additional-Cost Services

- tax free with satisfaction of certain rules §132

Employee Discounts

- tax free with satisfaction of certain rules §132

Dependent-Care Assistance

- tax free up to $5,000 ($2,500 for marrieds filing separately) with satisfaction of certain rules §129

Wellness Programs

- tax free to extent considered medical expenses §105
- most other benefits result in taxable income unless *de minimis* §132

Employee Assistance Plans

- benefits tax free if purpose is to alleviate medical conditions §105

Financial Planning Programs

- fees to outside professionals represent taxable income §61
- offsetting deductions allowed for certain expenses §212

Transportation/Free Parking

- tax free within limits if provided as a qualified transportation fringe §132

Subsidized Eating Facilities

- tax free if furnished for employer's convenience   §119

Index

Accelerated benefits, 55–56, 205
Accidental death and dismemberment
 insurance, 57–59
 beneficiary designation, 58
 benefits, 57–58
 continuation of coverage, 58
 conversion, 58
 eligibility, 57
 exclusions, 58–59
 in group universal life insurance, 80
 rate making, 233–34, 241–42
 self-funding, 262
 taxation, federal, 70
 voluntary plans, 57–59
Actively-at-work provision, 47
ADA. *See* Americans with Disabilities
 Act
AD and D. *See* Accidental death and
 dismemberment insurance
ADEA. *See* Age Discrimination in
 Employment Act
Adult day care, 207
Adverse selection, 8, 10, 19, 22, 44, 57,
 61, 161, 199, 237, 318
Age Discrimination in Employment Act,
 28–31
 effect on group disability income
  benefits, 30–31, 116–17
 effect on group medical expense
  benefits, 31, 185
 effect on group term life insurance
  benefits, 30, 46
 effect on salary continuation plans,
  30
 general provisions, 28–29
Agents, 220–22, 224–31
AIDS
 education, 282
 effect of Americans with Disabilities
  Act, 40
 reason for increasing medical costs,
  118
 use of accelerated benefits, 55

All-causes deductible, 163
Alternative funding methods. *See*
 Funding methods
Ambulatory care expense benefits, 151
Americans with Disabilities Act, 39–42
 effect on employee benefits, 41–42
 effect on employment practices,
  40–41
 general provisions, 39–40
Annual return/report, ERISA, 38
ASO contracts, 263, 265
Assignment
 dependent life insurance, 62
 group disability income insurance, 112
 group medical expense benefits, 192
 group term life insurance, 51, 69
Awards, 277–78
 productivity, 278
 safety achievement, 278
 service, 277
 suggestion, 277
 taxation, 277–78, 325

Basic medical expense insurance. *See*
 Group medical expense
 insurance
Beneficiary designation
 accidental death and dismemberment
  insurance, 58
 dependent life insurance, 61
 group term life insurance, 48–49
Benefit plan design, 5–6, 290–304
Benefit schedules
 accidental death and dismemberment
  insurance, 57–58
 dependent life insurance, 61–62
 group dental insurance, 199–200
 group legal expense insurance, 211
 group long-term disability income
  insurance, 106–7

group short-term disability income
insurance, 106–7
group term life insurance, 43–46
supplemental life insurance, 56–57
survivor income benefit insurance,
60–61
vision care plans, 154–55
Benefit statements, 301–4
Benefit unit, 233–34
Big-deductible plans, 14, 264
Birthing centers, 151
Blue Cross and Blue Shield Association,
124
Blue Cross–Blue Shield plans, 123–28
coinsurance, 126
community rating, 127–28
comparison with insurance
companies, 124–28
deductibles, 126
dental coverage, 197
growth and significance, 15, 122
hospital expense benefits, 146
marketing, 128, 223
maternity benefits, 143
organization, 123–24
prescription drugs, 154
rate making, 127–28
regulation, 124–25
reimbursement of providers, 126–27,
144, 146
service benefits, 125–26
sponsorship of HMOs, 130
sponsorship of multiple-option plans,
137
sponsorship of PPOs, 136
with supplemental major medical,
158
surgical expense benefits, 144, 146
taxation
federal, 125, 192–93
state, 124
types of benefits, 126
vision care benefits, 154
Bonuses, 278, 325
Bonus plans, for group term carve-outs,
82–83
Brokers, 222–23, 224–51

Cafeteria plans, 305–21
benefit election, 307–8
design issues, 319–21

examples, 310–13
flexible spending accounts, 309–10,
320
nondiscrimination rules, 314–17
obstacles, 313–19
premium-conversion plans, 309
qualified benefits, 306–7
rationale, 305–6
taxation of benefits, 306–7, 324
Cafeterias, subsidized, 289
Calendar-year deductible, 164–65
Carryover provision, 165
Carve-outs. *See* Group term carve-outs
Certificate of insurance, 7
Chamber of Commerce, U.S., 2–3
Child care. *See* Dependent-care
assistance
Civil Rights Act, pregnancy provisions,
31–32
effect on disability income benefits,
32, 105, 243
effect on medical expense benefits, 32,
142–43
Claim provisions
group disability income insurance, 112
group medical expense insurance, 192
group term life insurance, 50–51
Claim reserve
definition, 249
effect on alternative funding methods,
257, 258–59
Claims charge, in experience rating, 252
Claims fluctuation reserve
definition, 254
effect on alternative funding methods,
260–61
Claims review, 119–20
Closed-panel plans
group legal expense insurance, 210
health maintenance organizations, 131
COBRA, 186–88
effect on dental plans, 186, 202
effect on prescription drug plans, 186
effect on vision care plans, 186
general provisions, 186–88
relationship with conversion privilege,
191
Coinsurance
basic hospital expense insurance, 143
Blue Cross–Blue Shield plans, 126
as a cost-containment measure, 119
group dental expense insurance, 200

group major medical insurance,
166–69
HMO plans, 171
preservation under coordination of
benefits, 182–83
stop-loss limit, 168
Collective bargaining
for determining benefits, 270, 293
effect on cafeteria compensation
plans, 317
effect on employer's objectives, 290
effect on 501(c)(9) trusts, 267
effect on HMO dual-choice
provision, 134
effect on prescription drug plans, 153
effect on supplemental
unemployment benefits, 275
formation of negotiated trusteeships,
18
reason for growth of employee
benefits, 3
Commissioners Standard Group
Mortality Table (1960), 236
Commission scales
of agents, 221–22
mass-marketed individual insurance,
213–14
Common accident provision
accidental death and dismemberment
coverage, 59
medical expense insurance, 164
Communication, benefit plan, 7,
300–304
audiovisual presentations, 300–301
computers, 302–3
meetings with employees, 301
need for, 6, 307
printed materials, 301–2
employee benefit handbook,
301–2
personalized benefit statement,
302
Community rating, 127–28
Company cars, 288–89
taxation, 288–89
Competitive bidding, 228
as a cost-containment measure, 299
Comprehensive major medical
insurance, 156–59
Computers, in benefit communication,
302–3
Consolidated Omnibus Budget
Reconciliation Act of 1985

effect of exclusion for care in VA
and military hospitals, 142
effect on continuation of medical
expense coverage. *See* COBRA
Constructive receipt, 306
Consultants. *See* Employee benefit
consultants
Continuation of coverage
accidental death and dismemberment
insurance, 58
group disability income insurance,
113
group medical expense insurance,
186–91
group ordinary life insurance, 86
group paid-up life insurance, 85
group term life insurance, 53–54,
72–73
mass-marketed individual insurance,
212
Contribution to surplus, 235
Contributory plans, 10–11
adverse selection, 10
as a cost-containment measure,
299
disability income taxation, 115–16
eligibility under, 11
evidence of insurability, 11
open enrollment, 11
required employer contributions,
11, 50
Conversion
accidental death and dismemberment
insurance, 58
dependent life insurance, 62
group disability income insurance, 113
group medical expense insurance,
191–92
group ordinary life insurance, 86
group paid-up life insurance, 85
group term life insurance, 54–55
survivor income benefit insurance, 61
Conversion charge, 237, 250
Coordination of benefits
as a cost-containment measure, 119
group disability income insurance,
95–96, 109–11
group medical expense benefits,
179–84
salary continuation plans, 102
Copayments. *See* Coinsurance
Corridor deductible, 162–63
Cost containment, 117–22, 298–300

alternative funding methods, 119,
    256, 299
alternative providers, 119
ambulatory care centers, 119, 151
benefit exclusions and limitations,
    119, 298–99
benefit plan design, 118–19
birthing centers, 119, 151
claims review, 119–20
coinsurance, 119
competitive bidding, 228, 299
contributory financing, 299
coordination of benefits, 119
deductibles, 119
external cost-control systems, 120
health education and preventive care,
    120
HMOs, 119, 128
home health care, 119, 150–51
hospice benefits, 119, 151
managed care, 120–22
outpatient surgery, 144
preadmission certification, 141
preadmission testing, 119, 141
preapproval of specialists, 179
preferred provider organizations,
    119, 136–37
probationary periods, 298
reasons for, 117–18
second surgical opinions, 119, 146
skilled nursing facilities, 119, 149
use of group universal life insurance,
    73
utilization management, 178–79
utilization review, 119–20
wellness programs, 120, 280–82, 300
Cost-of-living adjustments
    group long-term care insurance, 207
    group long-term disability income
        insurance, 113
Cost-plus arrangements, 260
Credibility, 251–52, 254
Creditor-debtor groups, 20–21

Death-benefit-only plans, 83
Deductibles
    basic hospital expense plans, 143
    Blue Cross–Blue Shield plans, 126
    carryover provision, 165
    as a cost-containment measure, 119
    group dental insurance plans, 200

group major medical insurance plans,
    162–66
prescription drug plans, 153
preservation under coordination of
    benefits, 182–83
types
    all-causes, 163
    calendar-year, 164–65
    corridor, 162–63
    family, 163
    initial, 162
    integrated, 163
    per-cause, 163
Delta Plans, 197
Dental insurance. *See* Group dental
    insurance
Dental maintenance organizations
    (DMOs), 197
Dental PPOs, 197
Dependent-care assistance, 279–80
    nondiscrimination rules, 279–80
    taxation, 279–80, 325
    use of flexible spending account, 309
Dependent life insurance, 61–62
    assignment, 62
    beneficiary designation, 61
    benefits, 61–62
    conversion, 62
    eligibility, 61
    under group universal plans, 80
    rate making, 242
    taxation, federal, 71
    waiver-of-premium provision, 62
Design of benefit plans. *See* Benefit plan
    design
Diagnostic X-ray and laboratory expense
    benefits, 152
Disability, definitions
    Americans with Disabilities Act, 40
    disability income insurance, 103–4
    group term life insurance waiver of
        premium, 53–54
    social security, 96
    temporary disability laws, 100
    workers' compensation insurance,
        98–99
Disability income coverage. *See specific
    types of coverage:* Group long-
    term disability income insurance;
    Group short-term disability
    income insurance; Salary
    continuation plans; Social
    security; Temporary disability

laws; Workers' compensation
insurance
Disability income insurance. *See* Group
long-term disability income
insurance; Group short-term
disability income insurance
Disability insured, social security, 96
Discounts, employee. *See* Employee
discounts
Discrimination
age. *See* Age Discrimination in
Employment Act
nondiscrimination rules. *See*
Nondiscrimination rules
unfair, in rating, 232–33
Dividends
from experience rating, 247–54
tax treatment, 87
use in group term life insurance, 50
Doctrine of comity, 27
Domestic partners, eligibility for
benefits, 177

Educational assistance, 275–76
nondiscrimination rules, 275–76
taxation, 275–76, 325
EEOC. *See* Equal Employment
Opportunity Commission
Eligibility
accidental death and dismemberment
insurance, 57
dependent life insurance, 61
for domestic partners, 177
group disability income insurance,
103
group long-term care insurance, 206
group medical expense insurance,
171, 177–78
group term life insurance, 46–48
salary continuation plans, 101
social security disability benefits,
96–97
survivor income benefit insurance, 60
temporary disability laws, 100
as an underwriting consideration,
9–10
workers' compensation disability
benefits, 98–99
Eligible groups, 17–25
minimum size, 18
types, 18–25

Elimination period. *See* Waiting period
Employee-assistance programs, 282–83
taxation, 283, 325
Employee benefit consultants, 222–23,
224–31
Employee benefit handbook, 301–2
Employee benefits. *See also specific*
types of plans
definitions, 1–2
factors influencing growth, 3–5
funding methods, 256–68
plan design, 290–304
significance, 2–3, 14–16
Employee discounts, 278–79
nondiscrimination rules, 279
taxation, 279, 325
Employee needs. *See* Needs of
employees
Employee Retirement Income Security
Act. *See* ERISA
Employee welfare benefit plan, ERISA
definition, 33–34
Enrollment, 229–30
Entire contract provision, 51–52, 111
Equal Employment Opportunity
Commission, 28, 32, 40
Equity, in rate making, 232–3
ERISA, 24, 26, 32–39, 74, 301
administration, 33
definition of employee welfare
benefit plans, 33–34
effect on group universal life
insurance, 74
fiduciary requirements, 35–37
general requirements, 34–39
preemption of state laws, 26
relationship to multiple-employer
welfare arrangements, 24
reporting and disclosure, 37–39, 301
requirements for small groups, 39
Evidence of insurability
in contributory plans, 11
group dental insurance, 198
in group insurance generally, 8
group term life insurance, 48
group universal life insurance, 76
in multiple-employer welfare
arrangements, 23
supplemental life insurance, 57
Excess-amounts pooling, 253
Exclusions and limitations
accidental death and dismemberment
insurance, 58–59

basic hospital expense benefits, 142−43
basic physicians' visits expense benefits, 149
basic surgical expense benefits, 147
as cost-containment provisions, 119, 298−99
effect of Americans with Disabilities Act, 41
group dental insurance, 201
group disability income insurance, 104−5
group legal expense insurance, 211−12
group major medical expense benefits, 160−62
in multiple-employer welfare arrangements, 22−23
state limitations, 26
Experience period, 248
Experience rating. *See* Rate making
Extended care facility benefits, 149−50
Extended death benefit, 54
Extension of benefits, 191

Facility-of-payment provision
group disability income insurance, 112
group term life insurance, 48
Family deductible, 163
Family leave, 274−75
federal law, 274−75
state laws, 274
FASB. *See* Financial Accounting Standards Board
Fee schedules
group dental insurance, 200
surgical expense benefits insurance, 144−45, 162
Fictitious group insurance statutes, 216
Fiduciary, under ERISA, 35
Final premium rate, definition, 235
Financial Accounting Standards Board, 188−89
Financial counseling. *See* Financial planning programs
Financial planning programs, 283−87
preretirement counseling, 285−87
programs for executives, 283−85
taxation of benefits, 285, 287, 325
Financing. *See* Funding methods

First-dollar coverage, 158−59
501(c)(9) trust, 265−68
advantages and disadvantages, 266
limitations on contributions, 267−68
requirements for, 266−67
for retired lives reserves, 90
Flexible benefits. *See* Cafeteria compensation plans
Flexible spending accounts, 309−10, 320
Franchise health insurance. *See* Mass-marketed individual insurance
Free parking, 287−88
taxation, 288, 326
FSAs. *See* Flexible spending accounts
Funding methods, 14, 256−68
ASO contracts, 263, 265
big-deductible plans, 14, 288
as a cost-containment measure, 119, 256−57, 299
cost-plus arrangements, 260
501(c)(9) trust, 90, 265−68
limited-liability arrangements, 258−59
minimum-premium plans, 14, 259−60
in multiple-employer welfare arrangements, 21−24
postretirement life insurance, 72−93
premium-delay arrangement, 14, 258
rationale for alternative methods, 256−57
reserve-reduction arrangements, 14, 258−59
retired lives reserves, 87−93
retrospective-rating arrangements, 260−61
shared funding, 264
stop-loss coverage, 14, 263−65
total self-funding, 14, 261−63

Gifts to employees, 278
taxation, 278, 325
Grace period, 51, 111
Group dental insurance, 196−203
benefits, 199−200
coinsurance, 200
combination plans, 201
deductibles, 200
effect of COBRA, 186, 202
eligibility, 198−99

exclusions, 201
growth and significance, 196
integrated plans, 212
limitations, 201–2
managed care, 197
nonscheduled plans, 201–2
predetermination of benefits, 202
probationary periods, 198
providers of coverage, 196–97
rate making, 233–34, 246
scheduled plans, 200
self-funding, 263
taxation, federal, 192–95, 323
termination of coverage, 202–3
underwriting, 13
Group insurance. *See also specific types of plans*
eligible groups, 17–25
factors encouraging growth, 3–4
general characteristics, 7–14
plan design, 6, 290–304
significance, 14–16
Group legal expense insurance, 208–12
benefit schedules, 211
exclusions, 211–12
growth and significance, 208–9
requirements for prepaid status, 209–10
self-funding, 263
taxation, federal, 209–10, 323–24
types of plans, 210–11
Group life insurance. *See specific type of life insurance:* Group ordinary life insurance; Group paid-up life insurance; Group term life insurance; Group universal life insurance
Group Life Insurance Standard Provisions Model Bill, 25, 43
Group long-term care insurance, 203–8
benefits, 207
cost, 206
cost-of-living adjustments, 207
eligibility, 206
growth and significance, 203
need for coverage, 203–5
portability, 208
preexisting conditions, 208
renewability, 208
taxation, federal 203
types of care covered, 206–7

Group long-term disability income insurance, 102–16
benefit schedules, 106–7
claims provisions, 112
continuation of coverage, 113
conversion, 113
coordination with other benefits, 95–96, 109–11
definition of disability, 104
duration of benefits, 108–9
effect of Age Discrimination in Employment Act, 30–31, 108–9
effect of Civil Rights Act, 32, 105
eligibility, 103
exclusions, 104–5
growth and significance, 15, 102–3
pension supplement, 113–14
preexisting conditions, 105
probationary periods, 103
rate making, 233–34, 243–44
rehabilitation provisions, 112–13
self-funding, 263
survivor's benefit, 114
taxation
federal, 114–16, 323
state, 116
termination of coverage, 113
underwriting, 13, 95–96
waiting period, 108–9
Group medical expense insurance, 117–95
assignment of benefits, 192
basic coverages, 138–55
ambulatory care benefits, 151
birthing centers, 151
coinsurance, 143
deductibles, 143
diagnostic X-ray and laboratory expense benefits, 152
extended care facility benefits, 149–50
home health-care benefits, 150–51
hospice benefits, 151
hospital expense benefits, 139–43
physicians' visits expense benefits, 147–49
prescription drug expense benefits, 153–54
radiation therapy expense benefits, 152–53
supplemental accident expense benefits, 155

surgical expense benefits, 143–47
vision care expense benefits, 154–55
Blue Cross–Blue Shield plans, 123–28, 143, 144, 146, 154, 158
claim provisions, 192
claims review, 119–20
COBRA, 186–88
coinsurance
    basic coverages, 143
    major medical, 166–69
continuation of coverage, 186–91
    under family leave legislation, 275
conversion, 191–92
coordination of benefits, 179–84
cost containment, 117–22
coordination with medicare, 184–85
deductibles
    basic coverage, 143
    major medical, 162–66
effect of Age Discrimination in Employment Act, 31, 185
effect of Civil Rights Act, 32
eligibility, 171, 177–78
exclusions
    basic hospital expense coverages, 142–43
    basic physicians' visits expense benefits, 149
    basic surgical expense coverages, 147
    major medical coverage, 160–62
extension of benefits, 191
flexible spending accounts, 309–10
growth and significance, 15–16, 122–23
HMO coverage, 128–35, 171–76
major medical, 156–92
    benefit maximums, 169–70
    coinsurance, 166–69
    comprehensive plans, 156–59
    covered expenses, 159–60
    deductibles, 162–66
    exclusions, 160–61
    limitations, 161–62
    supplemental plans, 156–59
managed care, 120–22
nondiscrimination rules, 193–94
postretirement benefits, 188–90
preadmission certification, 141
preadmission testing, 141
preexisting conditions, 161

premium-conversion plans, 309
rate making, 233–34, 244–46, 249
second surgical opinions, 146
self-funding, 263
self-insurance medical reimbursement plans, 193
stop-loss limit, 168
taxation, federal, 192–95, 323
termination of coverage, 185–86
underwriting, 13
utilization review, 119–20
Group ordinary life insurance, 85–86
    benefits, 85
    continuation of coverage, 86
    conversion, 86
    structure of products, 85
    taxation, federal, 86–87, 322–23
Group paid-up life insurance, 84–85
    benefits, 84
    continuation of coverage, 85
    conversion, 85
    taxation, federal, 86–87, 322–23
Group property and liability insurance, 215–18
    growth and significance, 215–17
    mass-marketed plans, 217
    taxation, federal, 215, 324
    true group plans, 217–18
Group proposals. *See* Proposals, group insurance
Group representative, 223
Group short-term disability income insurance, 102–16
    assignment, 112
    benefit schedules, 106–7
    claim provisions, 112
    continuation of coverage, 113
    conversion, 113
    coordination with other benefits, 95–96, 109–10
    definition of disability, 103–4
    duration of benefits, 107–8
    effect of Age Discrimination in Employment Act, 30–31, 116–17
    effect of Civil Rights Act, 32, 105
    eligibility, 103
    exclusions, 104–5
    growth and significance, 15, 102–3
    probationary periods, 103
    rate making, 233–34, 242–43
    self-funding, 262–63

taxation
  federal, 114–16, 323
  state, 116
termination of coverage, 113
underwriting, 13, 95–96
waiting period, 107–8
Group term carve-outs, 82–83
  bonus plans, 82–83
  death-benefit-only plans, 83
  split-dollar life insurance, 83
  taxation, federal, 82–83
Group term life insurance, 45–71
  accelerated benefits, 55–56, 70
  assignment, 51, 69
  beneficiary designation, 48–49
  benefit schedules, 43–46
  claim provisions, 50–51
  continuation of coverage, 53–54
  conversion, 54–55
  effect of Age Discrimination in
      Employment Act, 30, 46
  eligibility, 46–48
  grace period, 51
  growth and significance, 14–15
  incontestability provision, 52
  misstatement-of-age provision, 52
  nondiscrimination rules, 66–67
  postretirement coverage, 72–93
  premiums, 50
  probationary periods, 47
  rate making, 233–34, 236–41,
      247–54
  self-funding, 262
  settlement options, 49–50
  supplemental coverage, 56–57
  taxation
      federal, 63–71, 322
      state, 71
  termination of coverage, 52–53
  underwriting, 47–48, 57
  waiver-of-premium provision, 53–54
Group universal life insurance, 73–82
  advantages, 73–74
  characteristics, 77–81
  as a cost-containment technique, 73
  dependent coverage, 80
  effect of ERISA, 74
  enrollment and administration, 81
  general nature, 74–75
  options at retirement and
      termination, 80–81
  reasons for use, 73
  taxation, 81

types of products, 75
underwriting, 76

Health Maintenance Organization Act
    of 1973, 133–35
  dual-choice provision, 134–35
  requirements for federal
      qualification, 133–34
Health maintenance organizations
    (HMOs), 128–35, 137
  benefits, 133–34, 171–76
  comparison with PPOs, 136
  copayments, 171
  emphasis on cost containment, 119,
      129
  experience rating, 134
  general characteristics, 128–29
  group practice plans, 130–31
  growth and significance, 15,
      132–33
  individual practice association plans,
      131
  marketing, 223
  point-of-service plans, 137
  sponsorship, 130
Health system agencies (HSAs), 120
Highly compensated employee,
      definitions
  cafeteria plans, 315
  dependent-care plans, 270
  educational assistance plans, 270
  employee-assistance programs,
      270
  employee discounts, 270
  no-additional-cost services, 270
  productivity awards, 270
  safety awards, 270
  self-funded medical reimbursement
      plan, 193
  service awards, 270
HMOs. *See* Health maintenance
      organizations
Holiday bonuses, 278
Holidays, 272
  taxation, 272, 324
Home health-care benefits, 150–51
Hospice benefits, 151
Hospital, definition, 139
Hospital expense benefits, 139–43
  exclusions, 142–43
  inpatient benefits, 139–41

outpatient benefits, 141–42

Incontestability provision, 52, 111
Incurred claims, 248–50
Individual employer groups, 18
Initial deductible, 162
Insurance companies
    comparison with Blue Cross and
        Blue Shield, 124–28
    premium taxes, 26
    as providers of dental insurance,
        196–97
    as providers of medical expense
        coverage, 122, 158
    role in prescription drug plans, 154
    role in vision care plans, 154
    sponsorship of HMOs, 130
    sponsorship of multiple-option
        plans, 137
    sponsorship of PPOs, 136
Integrated deductible, 163
Integrated dental plan, 196
Integration with social security. *See*
        Coordination of benefits
Internal Revenue Code. *See* Taxation,
        federal

Joinder agreement, 21
Jury duty, 273

Key employee, definition
    cafeteria plans, 314
    Sec. 79, 66–71, 88

Labor union groups, 21
Legal expense insurance. *See* Group
        legal expense insurance
Level commission schedule, 221–22
Life insurance. *See* Group ordinary life
        insurance; Group paid-up life
        insurance; Group term life
        insurance
Life-style management programs,
        281–82

Limitations. *See* Exclusions and
        limitations
Limited-liability arrangements,
        258–59
Living benefits. *See* Accelerated benefits
Long-term care insurance. *See* Group
        long-term care insurance
Long-term disability income insurance.
        See Group long-term disability
        income insurance

Major medical expense insurance. *See*
        Group medical expense
        insurance
Managed care
    as a cost-containment technique,
        120–22
    in dental plans, 197
    significance, 122
Mandated benefits
    effect on growth of employee
        benefits, 4, 25–26
    for maternity, 178
    for mental health and substance
        abuse, 162
    reason for use of alternative funding,
        256
Manual premium rate, definition, 235
Manual rating. *See* Rate making
Marketing, 219–31
    process of, 224–31
        enrollment, 229–30
        installation, 230
        proposal development, 225–29
        proposal presentation, 229
        prospecting, 224–25
        servicing, 230–31
    types of buyers, 219–20
    types of sellers, 220–24
        agents, 220–22
        Blue Cross–Blue Shield, 223
        brokers, 222–23
        employee benefit consultants,
            222–23
        group representatives, 223
        HMOs, 223
        third-party administrators, 223–24
Mass-marketed individual insurance,
        212–14
    money-purchase plans, 213–14

salary allotment (reduction) plans,
212–13
for universal life insurance, 214
Master contract, 7
Maternity benefits, 142–43. *See also*
Civil Rights Act, pregnancy
provisions
Maternity management, 178–79
Maturity-value benefit, 54
McCarran-Ferguson Act, 17
Meals. *See* Subsidized eating facilities
Medical expense insurance. *See* Group
medical expense insurance
Medical screening programs, 280–81
Medicare
medicare carve-out, 184–85
medicare supplement, 184–85
secondary to group health insurance,
31, 184
MET. *See* Multiple-employer welfare
arrangements
MEWA. *See* Multiple-employer welfare
arrangements
Minimum-premium plans, 14, 259–60
Misstatement-of-age provision, 52
Model Group Coordination of Benefits
Regulation, 180
Model Regulation on Group Coverage
Discontinuance and
Replacement, 171
Money-purchase plans, 213–14
Morbidity, 9
Mortality, 9
Moving-expense reimbursement,
276–77
taxation, 276–77, 325
Multiple-employer trusts, 22–23. *See
also* multiple-employer welfare
arrangements
Multiple-employer welfare
arrangements, 21–25
definition, 21
effect of ERISA, 24
fully insured multiple-employer
trusts, 22–23
insured, third-party administered,
23–24
self-funded, 24–25
Multiple-option plans, 137

NAIC. *See* National Association of

Insurance Commissioners
National Association of Insurance
Commissioners, 17
Group Life Insurance Standard
Provisions Model Bill, 25, 43
Model Group Coordination of
Benefits Regulation, 180
Model Regulation on Group
Coverage Discontinuance and
Replacement, 171
National Council on Health Planning and
Development, 120
National Health Planning and Resources
Development Act of 1974, 120
Needs of employees, 292–98
determination of, 292–98
use of cafeteria compensation plans,
305–6
use of different plans, 297–98
Negotiated trusteeships, 18–19, 217
Net premium rate, definition, 235
No-additional-cost services, 278
nondiscrimination rules, 278
taxation, 278, 325
No-loss no-gain legislation, 12
Noncontributory plans, 10
advantage in self-funded plans, 261
disability income taxation, 115
Nondiscrimination rules
cafeteria plans, 314–17
dependent-care assistance, 279–80
educational assistance, 275–76
employee discounts, 279
501(c)(9) trusts, 267–68
in general, 42
group medical expense insurance,
193–94
group term life insurance, 66–67
no-additional-cost services, 278
retired lives reserves, 89
Nonoccupational disability insurance, as
an employee benefit, 1. *See also*
Temporary disability laws

Objectives, benefit plan, 6, 290–92
Open-ended HMO. *See* Point-of-service
plans
Open enrollment period
in contributory plans, 11
under Health Maintenance
Organization Act, 135

Open-panel plans
  group legal expense insurance,
    210
  health maintenance organizations,
    131

Paid-up life insurance. *See* Group
    paid-up life insurance
Party-in-interest, under ERISA, 36
Payroll deductions
  for flexible spending accounts,
    308–10
  for mass-marketed individual
    insurance, 212
Pension supplement, 113–14
Per-cause deductible, 163
Personalized benefit statement, 302
Personal time off, 273–75
Physicians' visits expense benefits,
    147–49
  exclusions, 149
  hospital coverage, 148
  outpatient coverage, 148–49
Point-of-service plans, 137
Postretirement medical expense
    benefits, 188–190
PPOs. *See* Preferred provider
    organizations
Preadmission certification, 141
Preadmission testing, 141
Predetermination-of-benefits provision,
    202
Preexisting conditions
  disability income coverage, 105
  effect of Americans with Disabilities
    Act, 41
  long-term care coverage, 206
  major medical coverage, 161
  multiple-employer trusts, 23
Preferred provider organizations,
    136–37
  comparison with HMOs, 136
  as a cost-containment measure,
    119, 136
  dental, 197
Pregnancy Discrimination Act. *See* Civil
    Rights Act, pregnancy
    provisions
Premium, definition, 232
Premium-conversion plans, 309
Premium-delay arrangements, 14, 258

Premium taxes, 26–27
Prepaid legal expense plans. *See* Group
    legal expense insurance
Preretirement counseling programs,
    285–87
  financial planning, 286
  nonfinancial planning, 286–87
  sources, 287
  taxation, federal, 287
Prescription drug expense benefits,
    153–54
  effect of COBRA, 186
Pricing. *See* Rate making
Probationary periods
  as a cost-containment measure, 298
  definition, 9
  group dental insurance, 198
  group disability income insurance,
    103
  group term life insurance, 47
  multiple-employer trusts, 23
  salary continuation plans, 101
  use in underwriting, 9
Productivity awards, 274
Prohibited transactions, under ERISA,
    36–37
Property and liability insurance. *See*
    Group property and liability
    insurance
Proposals, group insurance, 225–29
  development, 225–29
  presentation, 229
Prospecting, 224-25

Qualified benefits, cafeteria plans, 306–7
Qualified transportation fringe, 287
Questionnaires, for determining
    employee needs, 294

Radiation therapy expense benefits,
    152–53
Rate, definition, 232
Rate making, 127–28
  Blue Cross–Blue Shield plans,
    127–28
  experience rating, 9, 247–54
    calculation of dividends, 249
    group medical expense insurance,
    249

group term life insurance, 247–54
  by HMOs, 134
  rationale for, 247
  renewal rating, 254–55
manual rating, 233–46
  accidental death and
    dismemberment insurance,
    233–34, 241–42
  benefit unit, 233–34
  calculation of manual premium
    rates, 235–46
  dependent life insurance, 242
  factors affecting claims, 234
  frequency of premium payments,
    234
  group dental insurance, 233–34,
    246
  group long-term disability income
    insurance, 233–34, 243–44
  group medical expense insurance,
    233–34, 244–46
  group short-term disability income
    insurance, 233–34, 242–43
  group term life insurance,
    233–34, 236–41
Reasonable-and-customary charges,
  145–46, 172
Regulatory jurisdiction, 27–28
Rehabilitation benefits
  group long-term care insurance, 112
  workers' compensation insurance, 99
Relative value schedules, 145
Reserve-reduction arrangements, 14,
  258–59
Retention, 253, 256
Retired lives reserves, 87–93
  methods of funding, 87–93
  requirements for favorable tax
    treatment, 88, 323
Retirement planning. *See* Preretirement
    counseling programs
Retrospective rate credit, 247
Retrospective-rating arrangements,
  260–61
Revenue Act of 1978
  effect on cafeteria compensation
    plans, 306
Risk charge
  effect on alternative funding
    methods, 256, 260–61
  nature of, 235, 253
Room-and-board benefits

basic hospital expense coverage,
  139–40
group major medical expense
  coverage, 160

Sabbatical leaves, 273
Safety achievement awards, 274
Salary allotment (reduction) plans,
  212–13
Salary continuation plans, 100–102
  benefits, 101–2
  effect of Age Discrimination in
    Employment Act, 31
  eligibility, 101
  probationary period, 101
  taxation, federal, 114–16
Salary reductions, cafeteria plans,
  308–10
Second surgical opinions, 146
Sec. 79, 63–71, 322
  general requirements, 63–65
  general tax rules, 65–66
  key employee, 66–67, 88
  nondiscrimination rules, 66–67
  treatment of dependent life insurance,
    71
  treatment of group ordinary life
    insurance, 86–87, 322
  treatment of group paid-up life
    insurance, 86–87, 322
  treatment of group term life
    insurance, 63–68, 322
  treatment of supplemental life
    insurance, 70
  treatment of survivor income benefit
    insurance, 71
  under-10 requirements, 67–68, 322
  Uniform Premium Table I, 65–66,
    70–71
Self-funding, 138, 261–68. *See also*
    Funding methods
  accidental death and dismemberment
    benefits, 262
  dental benefits, 263
  disability benefits, 262–63
  effect of Americans with Disabilities
    Act, 41
  growth and significance, 15
  legal expense benefits, 263
  life insurance benefits, 262
  medical expense benefits, 263

in multiple-employer welfare
    arrangements, 24–25
in negotiated trusteeships, 18
prescription drugs, 263
vision care benefits, 263
Self-insurance. *See* Funding methods
Self-insured medical reimbursement
    plans, 193–95
Service awards, 277
Service benefits
    Blue Cross–Blue Shield plans,
        125–26
    group legal expense plans, 211
    prescription drug plans, 154
Settlement options, group term life
        insurance, 49–50
Shared funding, 264
Short-term disability income insurance.
        See Group short-term disability
        income insurance
SIBI. *See* Survivor income benefit
        insurance
Sick-leave plans. *See* Salary
        continuation plans
Social insurance. *See specific types of
        programs*
Social security
    disability benefits, 96–97
        definition of disability, 96
        eligibility, 96–97
        size of, 97
        taxation, federal, 114
        waiting period, 96–97
    effect of flexible spending accounts,
        310
    as an employee benefit, 1
    medicare secondary to group health
        insurance, 31, 184
Split-dollar life insurance, in carve-out
        plans, 83
Standard commission schedule, 221–22
Standard Group Life Insurance
        Premium Rates (1961),
        236–37
Stop-loss coverage, 14, 264–65
Stop-loss limit
    in experience rating, 250
    in major medical plans, 168
Subsidized eating facilities, 289
    taxation, 289, 326
Successive beneficiary provision, 48
Suggestion awards, 277
Summary annual report, 38–39

Summary of material modification, 38
Summary plan description, 37–39
Supplemental accident expense benefits,
        155
Supplemental life insurance, 56–57
    determination of benefits, 55–57
    taxation, federal, 71
    underwriting, 57
Supplemental major medical insurance,
        156–59
Supplemental unemployment benefit
        plans, 275
    taxation, 275, 324
Surgical expense benefits, 143–47
    benefit amounts, 144–46
    exclusions, 147
    second surgical opinions, 146
    types of benefits, 143–44
Surgical fee schedule, 144–45, 162
Survivor income benefit insurance,
        59–61
    benefits, 60–61
    conversion, 61
    eligible survivors, 60
    general characteristics, 59
    taxation, federal, 71

Taft-Hartley Act, 18, 209
Taft-Hartley trusts. *See* Negotiated
        trusteeships
Taxation, federal
    accelerated benefits, 70
    accidental death and dismemberment
        insurance, 70
    awards, 277–78, 325
    Blue Cross–Blue Shield benefits,
        75, 192–93
    bonuses, 278, 325
    cafeteria plans, 306–7, 324
    company cars, 288–90
    dependent-care assistance, 279–80,
        325
    dependent life insurance, 71
    educational assistance, 275–76, 325
    effect on growth of employee benefits,
        4
    employee-assistance programs, 283,
        325
    employee discounts, 279, 325
    favorable tax treatment of employee
        benefits, 4

financial planning programs, 285, 287, 325
free parking, 288, 326
gifts to employees, 278, 325
group dental insurance, 192–95, 323
group disability income insurance, 114–16, 323
   deductibility of premiums, 114, 323
   income tax liability of employees, 114–16, 323
   social security taxation, 116
   withholding, 116
group legal expense insurance, 209–10, 323–24
group long-term care insurance, 203
group medical expense insurance, 192–95, 323
   deductibility of contributions, 192–93, 323
   income tax liability of employees, 192–95, 323
   self-insured medical reimbursement plans, 193–95, 323
group ordinary life insurance, 86–87, 322–23
group paid-up life insurance, 86–87, 322–23
group property and liability insurance, 215, 324
group term carve-outs, 82–83
group term life insurance, 63–71, 322
   deductibility of premiums, 63, 322
   income tax liability of employees, 63–68, 322
   taxation of proceeds, 69–70, 322
group universal life insurance, 81
holidays, 272, 324
moving-expense reimbursement, 276–77, 325
no-additional-cost services, 278, 325
preretirement counseling programs, 287
retired lives reserve, 88, 323
salary continuation plans, 114–16
social security disability benefits, 114
subsidized eating facilities, 289, 326
supplemental life insurance, 71

supplemental unemployment benefit plans, 275, 324
survivor income benefit insurance, 71
temporary disability benefits, 114
transportation benefits, 288, 326
vacations, 272, 324
wellness programs, 282, 325
workers' compensation benefits, 114
Taxation, state
   Blue Cross–Blue Shield, 124
   group disability income insurance, 116
   group term life insurance, 71
   income taxation of premiums and benefits, 26–27
   premium taxes, 26
Tax Reform Act of 1976
   effect on group legal expense insurance, 209
Tax Reform Act of 1984
   effect on 501(c)(9) trusts, 266
   effect on retired employees, 89
Tax Reform Act of 1986
   effect on Blue Cross–Blue Shield, 125
   effect on deductibility of medical expense premiums, 193
   effect on Sec. 79, 67
   imposition of uniform nondiscrimination rules, 42
Temporary disability laws, 99–100
   benefits, 100
   definition of disability, 100
   eligibility, 100
   taxation, federal, 114
   waiting period, 100
Terminal report, 39
Termination of coverage
   group dental insurance, 202–3
   group disability income insurance, 113
   group medical expense insurance, 185–86
   group term life insurance, 52–53
   group universal life insurance, 80–81
Term life insurance. *See* Group term life insurance
Third-party administrators
   marketing activities, 223–24
   role in group universal life insurance, 81
   role in multiple-employer welfare arrangements, 23–24

role in prescription drug plans, 154
role in self-funding, 263
role in vision care plans, 154
Trade association groups, 19
Transportation benefits, 287–88
  taxation, 288, 326

Under-10 requirements. *See* Sec. 79
Underwriting, 8–16
  general consideration, 8–16
    administration, 11–12
    age, 13
    determination of benefits, 9–10
    eligibility, 10
    geographic location, 14
    income, 13
    industry, 13
    persistency, 9
    premium payments, 10–11
    prior experience, 12
    reason for existence, 9
    sex, 13
    size of group, 12–13
    stability, 9
  type of plan, 8–16
    group dental expense, 13
    group disability income, 13, 95–96
    group medical expense, 13
    group term life insurance, 47–48,
      57
    group universal life insurance,
      76
    mass-marketed individual
      insurance, 212–14
    for multiple-employer trusts,
      22–23
    supplemental life insurance, 57
Unemployment compensation. *See*
  Supplemental unemployment
  benefit plans
Uniform Premium Table I, 65–66,
  70–71
Universal life insurance. *See also*
  Group universal life insurance
  individual policies in mass-marketed
    plans, 214
Utilization management, 178–79
Utilization review, 119–20, 136

Vacations, 271–72
  taxation, 272, 324
Vision care expense benefits, 154–55
  effect of COBRA, 186
  self-funding, 263
Voluntary accidental death and
    dismemberment insurance,
    57–59

Waiting periods
  group long-term disability income
    insurance, 108–9
  group short-term disability income
    insurance, 107–8
  social security disability benefits,
    96–97
  temporary disability laws, 114
  workers' compensation disability
    benefits, 99
Waiver-of-premium provision
  dependent life insurance, 62
  group term life insurance, 53–54
  group universal life insurance, 80
Welfare benefits, meaning, 2, 33–34
Wellness programs, 280–82
  as a cost-containment measure, 120,
    280–82, 300
  life-style management, 281–82
  medical screening, 280–81
  rationale for, 280
  taxation, 282
Wholesale life insurance. *See* Mass-
    marketed individual insurance
Workers' compensation insurance
  disability coverage, 97–99
    definition of disability, 98–99
    eligibility, 98–99
    size of benefits, 99
    taxation, federal, 114
    waiting period, 99
  as an employee benefit, 1
  federal laws, 98

X-ray benefits. *See* Diagnostic X-ray and
    laboratory expense benefits